Arts Management
(second edition)

The second edition of *Arts Management* has been thoroughly revised to provide an updated, comprehensive overview of this fast-changing subject. Arts managers and students alike are offered a lively, sophisticated insight into the artistic, managerial and social responsibilities necessary for those working in the field.

With new case studies and several new chapters, Derrick Chong takes an inter-disciplinary approach in examining some of the main impulses informing discussions on the management of arts and cultural organizations. These are highly charged debates, since arts managers are expected to reconcile managerial, economic and aesthetic objectives. Topics include:

- arts and the State, with reference to the instrumentalism of the arts and culture
- business and the arts
- ownership and control of arts organizations
- arts consumption and consumers, including audience development and arts marketing
- managing for excellence and artistic integrity
- financial investing in the arts, namely fine art funds and theatre angels
- philosophies of philanthropy.

Incorporating a deliberately diverse range of sources, *Arts Management* is essential reading for students on arts management courses and provides valuable insights for managers already facing the management challenges of this field.

Derrick Chong is Senior Lecturer in Management at Royal Holloway, University of London, UK. He is the author of *Arts Management* (Routledge, 2002) and co-author of *The Art Business* with Iain Robertson (Routledge, 2008).

Arts Management

(second edition)

Derrick Chong

First published 2010
by Routledge
2 Park Square, Milton Park, Abingdon, Oxon OX14 4RN

Simultaneously published in the USA and Canada
by Routledge
270 Madison Avenue, New York, NY 10016

Routledge is an imprint of the Taylor & Francis Group, an informa business

© 2010 Derrick Chong

Typeset in AmasisMT-Light by
RefineCatch Limited, Bungay, Suffolk
Printed and bound in Great Britain by
CPI Antony Rowe, Chippenham, Wiltshire

British Library Cataloguing in Publication Data
A catalogue record for this book is available from the British Library

Library of Congress Cataloging in Publication Data
Chong, Derrick
Arts management / Derrick Chong. – 2nd ed.
p. cm.
Includes bibliographical references and index.
1. Arts – Management.   I. Title.
NX760.C48 2009
706.8 – dc22
2009021772

ISBN10: 0-415-42390-2 (hbk)
ISBN10: 0-415-42391-0 (pbk)
ISBN10: 0-203-86534-0 (ebk)
ISBN13: 978-0-415-42390-8 (hbk)
ISBN13: 978-0-415-42391-5 (pbk)
ISBN13: 978-0-203-86534-7 (ebk)

CONTENTS

PREFACE

Arts Management is designed to help stimulate interest and advance developments in the field of arts management by setting something of its basic character in an engaging form. The Association of Arts Administration Educators (AAAE) recognizes that 'arts administration as a profession is a recent development' and that 'higher education remains the appropriate response to these demands [arts institutions are demanding higher levels of sophistication from their administrators] and to the present and future management needs of the arts'. The European Network of Cultural Administration Training Centres (encatc) seeks 'to stimulate and encourage the development of cultural management and policy within the context of great changes in the fields of culture, arts and media'. The basic educational aims of the book for postgraduate (MA and MBA) and undergraduate readers include the following: to educate existing and future arts managers to assess their artistic, managerial, and social responsibilities; to judge the context and conditions faced by arts organizations in contemporary society and associated management issues; and to understand the role of interdisciplinary approaches to management solutions facing arts organizations.

Substantial citations are used to illustrate the engagement of commentators including arts managers and artists: what they say is as important as how they say it. This is to suggest that interpreting rhetorical strategies is part of any genuine arts management education. Moreover, works of art communicate: they sharpen our thinking by offering new perspectives. This is to suggest that the text does not serve as a so-called how-to guide to management and the arts, yet it would be idealistic, nay irresponsible, to argue that art as a domain ought to be free from the constraints which now characterize much social activity in advanced western economies. To what extent should arts management be considered an academic (or research-led) pursuit? To what extent is arts management vocational in orientation, that is to say grounded in current application? In order to avoid excluding an entire set of concerns in what can become competing interests, a concerted effort is made in each chapter to strike a balance between theories (including those advanced by cultural critics), which support a fuller understanding of arts organizations as socio-political institutions, and pressing managerial imperatives as economic organizations; at the same time, problems arise if aesthetic objectives start to fade from view. The literature on arts management has become large and increasingly diverse: one task of the book is to highlight some of the more prominent writers and to suggest sources for more engaged readers.

What is the relevance of art and aesthetics in the practice and study of organizations and their management? How can we better understand the management of creativity and innovation in complex knowledge flows between cultural production and consumption? The points of contact between the arts and management are many and complex. We are particularly interested in 'arts management' as an emerging (i.e. post-1960s) sub-discipline worthy of critical investigation. An interdisciplinary approach is required, given the diverse range of theoretical texts from disciplines that continue to be important to the writing about arts management. As opposed to writing a manual on so-called best practice – there are numerous books on arts marketing, fundraising, and sponsorship, for example – our aim is to examine some of the main impulses informing discussions in the management of arts and cultural organizations. The desire is to offer assistance to students and researchers in identifying various signposts.

Since the publication of the first edition of *Arts Management* in 2002, my own engagement with arts and culture has focused on art business organizations, including a fruitful relationship with Sotheby's Institute of Art. *The Art Business* (with Iain Robertson as co-editor), a companion text published by Routledge, is one outcome. I benefited from serving for five years as an inaugural external examiner of the MA in Cultural and Creative Industries at King's College London and examining several PhD theses from British and Australian universities. Feedback to the first edition has been instructive. Gregory Sholette, then at the School of the Art Institute of Chicago, was particularly generous in sharing with me how he used the text. Comments by anonymous reviewers received via Routledge have also shaped the revised second edition.

Consistent with the first edition, synthesis has been crucial. Theoretical texts from a diverse range of disciplines – sociology of art, cultural economics, museology, cultural policy, art history, economic sociology, and management (including marketing, strategy, organization studies, corporate governance, and critical accounting) – continue to have a profound impact on arts management writing. Artists and works of art have been invaluable with imprints dotted throughout.

The organization of the text has been restructured. Three sections – Institutional Partners (I), Relationships with Stakeholders (II), and Wealth and the Economy (III) – are used to organize the core chapters. Section I on Institutional Partners examines two key arrangements, namely 'Arts and the State' (Chapter 2) and 'Business and the Arts' (Chapter 3). Section II on Relationships with Stakeholders focuses on the 'Ownership and Control of Arts Organizations' (Chapter 4), which includes an appendix on 'Philosophies of philanthropy', 'Arts Consumption and Consumers' (Chapter 5), which includes an appendix on 'Marketing and the arts', and 'Managing for Excellence and Artistic Integrity' (Chapter 6), which includes an appendix on 'Personal development in arts management'. Section III on Wealth and the Economy addresses two contemporary issues: 'Financial Investing in the Arts' (Chapter 7), which includes an appendix on 'Alternative passion investments'; and 'Globalization and the Art World' (Chapter 8).

1

INTRODUCTION

Arts management, since its emergence in the 1960s, is a more complex term than one first imagines. The original attention on supporting prominent not-for-profit arts organizations, often in receipt of public subsidy, now includes complementary commercial organizations operating in the creative industries. Thus an art market system includes public art museums and intermediaries such as art dealers and auction houses. Opera houses, which rely on public subsides, and commercial music companies represent different business models. This introductory chapter is organized into six sections with attention devoted to how conventional boundaries defining arts organizations – public/private and not-for-profit/for-profit – are being challenged. Charged debates as arts managers need to reconcile managerial, economic, and aesthetic objectives are raised.

What is the proper role of arts management? In the first instance, our task is drawn to several disciplines including management (e.g. Henry Mintzberg and the Harvard Business School), sociology (e.g. Pierre Bourdieu and Paul DiMaggio), and critical theory (e.g. the Frankfurt School). Engaged contemporary artists such as Hans Haacke, Andrea Fraser, the Guerrilla Girls, and Carey Young – offering institutional critiques in advance of new institutionalism – have been astute in drawing attention to the closer links between business and the arts.

The foundations of arts management as a sub-discipline with reference to developments in the USA and the UK are broached in the first section. Various definitions of arts management, essentially attempts at defining its parameters, are considered in the second section. This is developed in the third section, with reference to Raymond Williams's keywords project, by looking at the constituent parts of arts management, namely art and culture, management, creativity, culture industry, and consumerism, which need to be disentangled and investigated. The fourth section considers how all sorts of organizations in non-commercial sectors of the economy have had to address the encroachment of managerialism. Performing and visual arts and cultural institutions have not been exempt, though there are signs of resistance in some quarters of arts management. Given the complexities faced by arts organizations and those charged with governing and managing them, several arts management systems are presented in the fifth section. First, the classical three-stage industrial model of production, distribution, and consumption highlights the importance of process and the interconnectedness of players – both cooperation and competition – at distinct stages of artistic development. Moreover, it helps to demythologize romantic notions of lone creative genius as normal. Second, challenging commitments applicable to different types of arts organizations – to excellence and artistic integrity; to accessibility and audience development; and to accountability and cost effectiveness – highlight the complexity associated with their management. Third, management with key stakeholders – owners, customers, employees, suppliers, and society – has taken on greater relevance during the first decade of the twenty-first century. As indicative of the approach to arts management adopted in this text, the sixth and final section of the introductory chapter presents Gareth Morgan's work on organizational metaphors by drawing on narratives of arts organizations presented by artists, historians, and curators.

FOUNDATIONS OF ARTS MANAGEMENT

There is some attraction in the thesis that arts management, as formalized within higher education, is an outgrowth of the experiences of arts organizations in the United States during the 1960s. The assumption of a monolithic and universal arts management is based on American hegemony in commercial spheres near the end of the so-called American Century. The logic of industrialization assumes that the goals of arts organizations converge like those of business corporations, with deviations from the one best way eliminated by a process of social Darwinism. But do the facts bear out this Americanization thesis? Once arts management had developed in the USA, was it inevitable that other countries would go through the same process? Do various environmental and institutional factors suggest otherwise? What are the international repercussions of the American model of arts management? Has an American ethos altered the terms of reference by which issues are defined, relationships maintained, and contentions resolved?

Though the USA of the 1960s has been pegged as a starting point for arts management, it is instructive to move the historical marker to developments around 1945, namely the creation of the Arts Council of Great Britain (ACGB).[1] The ACGB was incorporated in 1946 as an outgrowth of the Committee for the Encouragement of Music and the Arts, which formed in 1939 as a wartime programme to bolster morale. Prominent features of the ACGB, including an arm's length relationship with government and peer review as a method of adjudication for awarding funds, served as a model for arts councils that emerged in other industrialized Commonwealth countries (Canada, Australia, and New Zealand) and the USA. Moreover, the ACGB played a leading role in initiating arts management courses and encouraging greater business involvement in the arts. The health of arts councils and the debates in which they are involved serve as barometers of wider cultural concerns.[2]

Two other institutional players in the USA, along with the National Endowment for the Arts (NEA), showed an interest in the arts during the 1960s: prominent foundations including Ford, Rockefeller, and Carnegie funded arts research; and the largest business corporations such as IBM, Exxon, Chase Manhattan, and Mobil helped to establish the Business Committee for the Arts (BCA). One impetus was a desire to address an imbalance: the USA's arts and culture record did not match the country's leading geopolitical and economic position. Social unrest forced business corporations to think about the communities in which they operated and how they might contribute to society; likewise, arts and cultural institutions started to examine programming objectives and decision-making processes to encourage wider participation. The USA has helped to advance a nexus between business and the arts, including business sponsorship and the art and culture as subjects of economic inquiry, which other countries have adopted.

There was an attempt in the USA to learn from the European experiences of arts patronage. This is illustrated in Frederick Dorian's *Commitment to Culture* (1964), which sought to find out what Americans could learn from European patterns of arts patronage. It was recognized that 'private patronage has already been established in our country', but that it 'alone cannot carry the burden' (Dorian 1964: 457, 459). The case for government allocations (or subsidies) to the arts at all levels (federal, state, and local) to complement private sponsorship never established a strong following in the USA. The NEA, which did not exist at the time of Dorian's study, has been subjected to criticisms concerning liberty under government patronage; the notable absence of a so-called secretary of state for culture in the USA is a direct consequence of a distrust of a closer relationship between art and politics (except when seeking to promote American cultural interests abroad).

A dominant motif since the 1960s has been the rise of managerial imperatives. For example, Thomas Raymond and Stephen Greyser, both at the Harvard Business School, and Douglas Schwalbe, an arts administrator at Harvard, founded the Arts Administration Research Institute in 1966; and, in 1970, the trio established the Harvard Summer School Institute in Arts Administration. Yet the emergence of a new breed of arts manager has been depicted as pernicious and regressive, according to visual artist Hans Haacke (in Wallis 1986: 60–61):

> Trained by prestigious business schools, they are convinced that art can and should be sold like the production and marketing of other goods. They make no apologies and have few romantic hang-ups.
>
> It is expected that the lack of delusions and aspirations among new arts administrators will have a noticeable impact on the state of the industry. Being trained primarily as technocrats, they are less likely to have an emotional attachment to the peculiar nature of the product they are promoting. And this attitude, in turn, will have an effect on the type of products we will soon begin to see.

Haacke was concerned that the commercial language of management would become naturalized in the discourse and practice of managing arts and cultural organizations (see Chong 1997). He was not alone: John Pick (1986: 7), for example, criticized the adoption by British organizations of 'half-baked Americanised notions of "management" ' as 'a new breed of arts managers . . . make[s] it clear that one should not look for pleasure from the Arts, but market returns'.

More specifically, Haacke (in Wallis 1986: 61) criticized 'arts administration courses taught according to the Harvard Business School case method . . . by professors with little or no direct knowledge of the peculiarities of the art world'. Haacke was taking aim at the inclusion of his celebrated 1971 dispute with the Solomon R. Guggenheim Museum, which was represented in *Cases for Arts Administration*, edited by Raymond, Greyser, and Schwalbe (1975: 217–22): 'Director of a major museum weighs whether or not to cancel a show by controversial artist'. It goes without saying that the Haacke/Guggenheim controversy was much more complex; it raised questions concerning the idealist concept of the autonomy of art, and the belief that the art museum is a neutral, nonsocial, apolitical institution (for an excellent account of the case, see Burnham 1971). As the case study method has been criticized for fostering cursory debates and rewarding quick and detached decision-making with limited information. It encourages 'an approach to the practice of management that is "thin" and "superficial" ', according to Henry Mintzberg (1989: 90). In *Managers Not MBAs*, Mintzberg (2004: 39) criticizes traditional MBAs, which 'push theories, concepts, models, tools, techniques in a disconnected class-room' whereas 'management practice is about pull – what is needed is a particular situation'.

Arts management has taken root at leading business schools: the Judge Institute (University of Cambridge) includes an elective MBA module, Arts and Cultural Management; the Schulich Business School (York University in Canada) offers an MBA with a specialization in Arts and Media Administration; and Southern Methodist University offers a joint graduate degree (MA/MBA) in Business and Arts Administration, which 'is based upon the philosophy that a successful career in arts management requires a through knowledge of contemporary business practices coupled with a deep appreciation for the arts'.

Specialist, private universities in the commercial worlds of arts and culture have thrived. Full Sail University, based in Florida, was established in the late 1970s, with a focus on media arts and entertainment (e.g. music, film, video games, design, and animation). Both leading auction houses are associated with educational arms operating in the core art markets of London and New York: Sotheby's Institute of Art ('advanced object-based art education whose graduates combine a passion for the visual arts with scholarship and market sophistication') and Christie's Education ('investigation of works of art in order to train through direct exposure to art-world practice').

There have been prominent examples of training in cultural and management and leadership. Finding the right person for senior posts is increasingly difficult given the combination of skills desired by arts and cultural organizations. For example, it is a rare prize to find a major dancer with professional management training. In the museum world, the Museum Management Institute (MMI) was established in 1978, by the American Association of Museums and the University of California, Berkeley, to offer an intensive summer residential course designed for mid- to senior-level museum professionals to develop and apply their managerial capabilities and leadership skills more effectively. Admission requirements – including at least five years of full-time museum experience and currently in a position involving direct responsibility for planning, decision-making, and supervising staff and sponsorship by the candidate's museum as evidence of its commitment – are consistent with 'criterion for entry to management education' namely 'proven success in managerial work'

gained by 'intensive experience within at least one industry, preferably one organization, so that the knowledge base is deep' (Mintzberg 1989: 83). The MMI is now
the Museum Leadership Institute (MLI). The Getty Foundation operates the Getty
Leadership Institute, 'a leading source of continuing professional development for
current and future museum leaders . . . created to respond to the growing complexities faced by leaders of museums and other nonprofit institutions'; the MLI serves as
the 'primary executive development opportunity of the Getty Leadership Institute'
with an 'in-depth residential leadership program [that] is designed both to enhance
the leadership of experienced museum executives and strengthen their institutions'
capabilities'. The original MMI served as the model for the Museum Leadership
Programme, a two-week summer residency, at the University of East Anglia, which
'emphasises such things as recognising and applying different leadership styles; ana-
lysing and developing interpersonal skills; leading teams and organisations through
projects and organisational change and dealing with funding and governing bodies
and with the media'. The John F. Kennedy Center for the Performing Arts 'strives to
impart hands-on arts management experience to participants in its fellowship and
internship programs. Through practical application of management skills, fellows and
interns gain in-depth knowledge and expertise used by successful managers in
today's complex world of performing arts'.[3] The UK's Clore Leadership Programme,
an initiative of the Clore Duffield Foundation, 'aims to strengthen leadership across a
wide range of cultural institutions' through fellowships, board development training,
and residential short courses.

DEFINING ARTS MANAGEMENT

The opening paragraph on 'arts administration (arts management)' in the *International
Encyclopedia of Public Policy and Administration*, by Dan Martin (in Shafritz 1998:
128), is instructive:

> The application of the five traditional management functions – planning, organ-
> izing, staffing, supervising, and controlling – to the facilitation of the production
> of the performing or visual arts and the presentation of the artists' work to
> audiences. The administration and facilitation of the creative process and its
> communication to an audience is common to both public, nonprofit arts organiza-
> tions (e.g. nonprofit theaters, symphony orchestras, opera companies, dance
> companies, museums, public broadcasting, and performing arts centers) and pri-
> vate, commercial, for-profit artistic entities (e.g. commercial theater, 'popular'
> music, private galleries, film, television, and video).

Megan Matthews (2006: Module 1), of the University of Wisconsin at Whitewater,
seeks to articulate an understanding of arts management to her students:

> Arts management is an exciting field that allows people to combine business,
> artistic and organizational skills with activities that make a difference in the lives
> of individuals and communities.

Arts management [is] the facilitation and organization of arts and cultural activity. The arts manager is a person working in the field of arts management; a person who, on some level, enables art to happen. Simply put, arts managers bring art and audiences together.

A fuller articulation of 'management of the arts' is provided by François Colbert (in Towse 2003: 287–92), founder editor of the *International Journal of Arts Management*, in *A Handbook of Cultural Economics*. Colbert begins with reference to the two constituent elements of arts management:

> Management is a relatively new discipline [e.g. Frederick Taylor] and the management of arts and culture an even more recent offshoot [reference to the early 1960s]. The non-profit status of many arts and cultural organizations not only means that they must be managed in a particular way, it also imposes a specific set of professional requirements on the manager and the board of trustees.

He then suggests that 'arts and cultural management is hampered by a twofold legitimacy problem . . . it is viewed with suspicion by the arts world . . . [yet] . . . it is often taken less than seriously by management scholars'.

Colbert proffers specific characteristics of the arts sector: discontinuous mode of production with an emphasis on project-based creation, which also affects the management of human resources (including charismatic leaders with highly personal motivational styles); dual management with artistic and administrative direction sharing tasks (e.g. both having equal status with conflicts resolved by the board of directors); the immateriality of the product whose value depends on the evolution of public taste. Colbert also distinguishes between three major sectors, 'the arts, cultural industries, and the media':

> While most companies in the arts sector are product- rather than market-oriented, the reverse is true for cultural industries and the media. In fact, one of the defining characteristics of the arts sector is that artistic vision takes precedence over market conditions. Rather than selling a product that satisfies the needs and desires of consumers, these organizations offer an artistic vision likely to be of interest to a certain audience. In practice, the job of the marketing staff is to identify a market segment interested in the product being offered, not to provide consumers with what they want to see.

Finally, sociologists Volker Kirchberg and Tasos Zembylas have suggested what might be an oppositional definition of arts management at the European Sociological Association conference in 2009:

> Traditionally, arts management encompasses tasks of leading, financing, planning as well as organizing, distributing and marketing cultural services and goods. Mostly, arts management has been a topic of business administration and management studies. However, for several reasons sociological frames of reference enlarge the analysis. This research stream aims to introduce arts management as a

topic for theoretical and empirical sociological inquiry, within the realms of arts sociology, sociology of culture, organizational sociology, sociology of economy and professions, and other sub-disciplines. Papers could deal with arts management as social acting at the interface of production, distribution and consumption of arts and culture.

These four entries invite comment. Martin, like Byrnes (2008) in his undergraduate book on arts management, stresses an adherence to the contribution of Henri Fayol (1841–1925), arguably the first modern management writer, who remains important for proffering what has become the classical notion of management, namely leading (or commanding), planning, organizing, coordinating, and controlling. Likewise, Kirchberg and Zembylas imply Fayol plus marketing as helping to define arts management from a conventional sense. But how relevant is Fayol's notion of management, which focuses on the process of management as reflective and systematic, in the twenty-first century? This is a question Henry Mintzberg has considered: first, in *The Nature of Managerial Work* (1973) and, more recently, in *Managers Not MBAs* (2004), which builds on the earlier conclusions while advancing his views of the management process and implications for the development of managers. Colbert suggests, as with the thesis in this book, that arts management started to take root in the 1960s.

Martin proffers two distinct but related spheres of activity: public, non-profit alongside private, for-profit.[4] Such boundaries may be useful for including commercial firms involved in the arts, which widens the conventional perspective. It also encourages one to think about the historical role of cultural entrepreneurs and arts impresarios in formation of what have become public, non-profit arts organizations and the legacy of private/public collaborations. Paul DiMaggio (in DiMaggio 1986: 41–42) reminds us that such divisions are constructed: 'Not until two distinct organizational forms – the private or semiprivate, non-profit cultural institution and the commercial popular culture industry – took shape did the high/low-culture dichotomy emerge in its modern form'. Furthermore, 'if we look at our high-culture industries today, we soon see that non-profit organization is not the only form. Indeed, in art, classical music, and even theatre, our museums, symphonies, and resident stages are only the non-profit jewels in a for-profit crown' (DiMaggio in DiMaggio 1986: 87) Yet, it is important, as suggestive of Colbert, to accentuate the significance of the non-profit arts organizations – as distinct from cultural industries and the media which are often profit-seeking – as this sets conditions for arts managers and trustees.

Three sectors of the economy can be identified. First, the private sector, often called the market economy, emphasizes profit maximization for the long-term interests of its owners. These owners – called shareholders or stockholders in the case of publicly listed corporations in the arts like many record companies – are removed from direct control of the business, now in the hands of salaried managers. There is interest in financial return on investment such as measured by share price movement. In contrast to this form of managerial capitalism, smaller commercial businesses in the arts such as art dealers are owner-operated (or what can be termed personal capitalism). From the perspective of the arts consumer there is often a direct buyer–seller relationship. Second, that wealth distribution takes place via taxes to provide public services for citizens is central to understanding the public sector, where the relationship is one between the state and citizens. The state has competing demands for tax expenditures with the arts often trailing behind health, education, and social wealth. The notion that the *citizen* as taxpayer is a *consumer* of government services has started to take hold outside of the USA. In such a context – where taxes are no longer viewed as the price to pay to live in a civilized country – there is a real challenge for government to prevent a desire to opt-out of services (i.e. pay lower taxes). Third, the not-for-profit – also termed the non-profit, voluntary, or third sector – has been described as offering so-called humanistic service – by filling a gap between the private and public sectors. Certain services could not survive on purely commercial grounds, yet there may not be the desire to have taxpayers foot the bill. Of course, there is a political (or ideological) basis – from one nation to the next – for what should be included as part of the third sector. In the case of not-for-profits, which is arguably the most complex sector, it is necessary to manage relationships with two sets of stakeholders: donors and recipients. In many cases in the arts, there is some overlap between those who donate and those who are recipients of the arts organization's programming. Moreover, there are links between the sectors, according to Tyler Cowen (2006: 40):

> We should not think of the non-profit and for-profit sectors as fully separate. Too frequently commentators paint a picture of the one subsidized sector and another capitalist sector. But in reality popular culture often draws on government-subsidized high culture for 'research and development' efforts. Indirect subsidies to the arts have made American popular culture much stronger.

'When most people in the arts industry talk of arts management, they are referring primarily to the purely administrative functions of an arts organization, not the management practices involved in producing the artistic work', according to Martin (1998: 129), who identifies five management departments – strategic planning, finance management, fundraising, marketing, and facility or physical plant management – in support of the art for which the organization has been established. This can be interpreted as a positivistic perspective whereby managerialism is applied to arts organizations. Audiences, visitors, or spectators are reconceptualized along mainstream corporate marketing management lines as consumers. As a prominent example, critics of the Solomon R. Guggenheim Foundation under the direction of Thomas Krens (1988–2008) contend that the cultural organization adopted brand strategies associated with fast-food outlets to engage in global cultural franchising (New York, Venice, Bilbao, Berlin, and Las Vegas (between 2001 and 2008), with Abu Dhabi in the works to open in 2012) by recognizing that the asset value of its permanent collection can be leveraged as a financial instrument.

The line of demarcation between 'purely administrative functions' and 'producing the artistic work', with arts management focusing on the former, means that the insights of artists and cultural critics on the relationship between the arts and management may be sidelined. So it is encouraging that Matthews views the arts manager as someone who 'enables art to happen'; in a complementary manner Colbert emphasizes the importance of 'artistic vision'. This resonates with Mintzberg

(2004: 10), who considers 'management as a practice': 'There is no "one best way" to manage; it depends on the situation'. In doing so, Mintzberg (2004: 11) is advancing an 'experience-based style labelled engaging – quiet and connected, involving and inspiring'. More management writers are starting to agree with Matthews, who includes to 'make a difference in the lives of individuals and communities' as part of the wider social mandates all organizations need to consider.

Colbert acknowledges that there remains a legitimacy problem when it comes to arts and cultural management research within management studies. This may be due to the focus of arts and cultural management research on application within conventional management functions. As such the interest in arts management by sociologists, such as Kirchberg and Zembylas, is one way to remind students of the pioneering work of Bourdieu, DiMaggio, and Howard Becker (1982), and developments in economic sociology by the likes of Mark Granovetter (1973; 1985) that are applicable to arts and cultural organizations.

KEYWORDS IN ARTS MANAGEMENT

A critical perspective on arts management is an apposite starting point – even for those interested in the more utilitarian purpose of identifying legitimate areas of managerial intervention. An inquiry into arts management, which disentangles constituent terms and related ones, complements Martin, Matthews, Colbert, and Kirchberg and Zembylas, moreover, it introduces some of the decisions which have informed thinking on arts management. First, what is art? What are the arts? Second, what is management? Who are managers? What do managers do? Third, what is the role of consumption and consumers?

Arts and culture

In examining the treatment of 'art' it is instructive to include the complementary term 'culture', which Raymond Williams (1983: 76–82) described as 'one of the two or three most complicated words in the English language' owing to its four diverse states: a general state or habit of the mind; the general state of intellectual development in society as a whole; the general body of arts; and, a whole way of life, material, intellectual, and spiritual. Williams drew attention to culture in its current and most widespread use, namely the third state: 'an independent noun which describes works and practices of intellectual and especially artistic activity'. Thus performing and visual arts in the traditional sense – namely art music, ballet, opera, theatre, and painting and sculpture – are included. By extension, there is a concern with the institutions – often not-for-profit in orientation and in receipt of public subsidy – that allow the arts and culture to be put on display.

Related debates of earlier generations remain unresolved. That 'there is no document of civilization which is not at the same time a document of barbarism', a well-known dictum from the 1930s by Walter Benjamin (1969: 256), is diametrically opposed to what Kenneth (later Lord) Clark (1969) refers to as 'Civilisation' in his acclaimed BBC television series. However, the current focus may be on other concerns: certain mass cultural forms and practices – such as the rise of reality television and online content – may comprise the most significant culture of our time, precisely because of its popular character. An example is provided by UK pop singer Lily Allen, who has commented on the manufacture of celebrity in 'The Fear' (2009): 'I want to be rich and I want lots of money / I don't care about clever I don't care about funny' and 'I'll take my clothes off and it will be shameless / 'Cuz everyone knows that's how you get famous'. A generation earlier, Barbara Kruger framed culture with a politically charged yet whimsical slogan: 'When I hear the word culture, I reach for my cheque book'.

Management

Williams (1983: 189–92) also included 'management' in his vocabulary of culture and society: 'The word "manage" seems to have come into English directly from *maneggiare*, Italian – to handle or train horses'; he differentiated three groups, civil servants (or bureaucrats), administrators, and managers, as corresponding to public, semipublic, and private concerns respectively. Whereas the 'actual activities were identical', according to Williams, distinctions in tenor were 'received and ideological'. However, the distinctive traditions associated with civil service were giving way to 'management' as a generic function suitable to each and every organization. Indeed a case has even been made that the so-called manager – particularly chief executive officers (CEOs) of publicly listed companies, as represented by popular management writers such as Peter Drucker and Charles Handy and in journals like the *Harvard Business Review* – was promoted as the cultural hero of the twentieth century.

The continuing relevance of the classical notion of management associated with Fayol has been raised by Mintzberg (1973; 2004), a particularly virulent critic, who has depicted managers working at an unrelenting pace, such that their activities are marked by brevity, variety, and discontinuity. In addition to handling exceptions, managerial work involves performing a number of regular duties, including ritual and ceremony, negotiations, and processing soft information that links the organization to its environment, according to Mintzberg (1973: 38):

> The pressure of the managerial environment does not encourage the development of reflective planners, the classical literature notwithstanding. The job breeds adaptive information-manipulators who prefer the live, concrete situation. The manager works in an environment of stimulus-response, and he develops in his work a clear preference for live action.

A leading arts manager characterized the contemporary balance of skills and competencies as scholar, aesthete, and connoisseur on the one hand; fundraiser, publicist, and diplomat on the other (Hoving 1992).[5] Greater attention is being accorded by arts organizations to individuals who can clarify achievable overall missions and goals and practical targets, resolve conflicts and priorities that are always going to exist, and manage business information flows as they get more complex. This is largely consistent with the accepted roles of corporate CEOs, as identified by the Harvard Business School: an *organizational leader* is responsible for planned results, which include integrating specialist functions; beyond formal structure and policy, the skills of persuasion and articulation are required to be a *personal leader*, and, finally, an *architect of organizational change* has the intellectual and creative capacity to conceptualize the organization's purpose and the dramatic skill to invest it with some degree of magnetism (Bower *et al.* 1995: 13–23). For Mintzberg this represents *heroic* management, which is a dysfunctional style of management. In its place Mintzberg (2004: from Table 9.4) advances *engaging* management: 'managers are important to the extent that they help other people who develop products and deliver services to be important'; 'an organization is an interacting network, not a vertical hierarchy' such that 'effective leaders work throughout; they do not sit on top'; 'out of the network emerge strategies, as engaged people solve little problems that grow into big initiatives'; 'implementation is the problem because it cannot be separated from formulation' which is 'why committed insiders are necessary to resist ill-considered change imposed from above and without'; 'to manage is to bring out the positive energy that exists naturally within people'; 'rewards for making the organ-ization a better place go to everyone' which is to say 'human values matter, few of which can be measured'; and 'leadership is a sacred trust earned from the respect of others'.

Creativity

City life remains one of the great cultural legacies of modernity. It goes without saying that each modern city has its own unique loci: one needs to explore the cultural depths extending beyond buildings and streets. A wide range of services 'once regarded as unserious and even effete' may be harnessed to serve as 'diverse sources of innovation', according to Peter Hall, in his preface to *The Creative City* (Landry and Bianchini 1995). The argument linking creativity, cities, and clustering appears to be quite straightforward. The current definition of creative industries in the UK lists 13 sectors: advertising, architecture, the art and antiques market, craft, design, design of fashion, film, interactive leisure software, music, the performing arts, publishing, software and computer services, and television and radio.[6] Thus arts in the traditional sense, not least of all in receipt of public subsidy, sit alongside more commercially-oriented, knowledge-intensive sectors of the economy based in cities, such that the creative city 'emphasizes the new, progress and continual change' (Landry and Bianchini 1995: 11). Clusters are represented by 'critical masses – in one place – of unusual competitive success in particular fields' (Porter 1998: 78).

There has been a general shift in mood about the arts starting in the USA, accord-ing to DiMaggio (in DiMaggio 1986: 6):

And it might seem odd to speak of 'the arts' as an economic sector, the notion that they constitute an 'industry' would have positively repelled most cultural leaders before the 1960s. With the advent of public funding, however, advocates of government aid lost no time in gathering industry statistics useful for constructing reports on the 'economic impact of the arts' and other instruments of political persuasion . . . The concept of arts as 'industry' now seems increasingly natural and suggestive of an almost corporate gravity of purpose.

Whether policy makers will emphasize creative industries, which draw tourists and contribute to export earnings at the expense of performing and visual arts organizations requiring public subsidy, is an ongoing concern. 'The Warhol Economy' is used by sociologist Elizabeth Currid (2007) to make a case that New York's cultural industries – which includes fashion, art, music, and night clubs – serve as a significant economic hub (alongside financial services). In particular, she draws attention to developing social networks – made through face-to-face contact – as crucial to succeeding in the worlds of fashion and art. This is consistent with the rise of creative class, a term with key associations to Richard Florida (2002; 2005; 2008), who makes a compelling case for quality of life and economic benefits from so-called creative cities.[7]

However, some disentanglement is needed. What does it mean to be so-called creative? Williams (1983: 84) included 'creative' as an original keyword having both 'serious and trivial senses':

> The difficulty arises when a word once intended, and often still intended, to embody a high and serious claim, becomes so conventional, as a description of certain kinds of activity, that it is applied to practices for which, in the absence of the convention, nobody would think of making such claims.

Works of artistic activity, as a dominant reading of culture, include art music, literature, painting and sculpture, theatre, and film.[8] At the same time, Williams (1983: 84) cites, for example, that advertising copywriters officially describe themselves as creatives; however, this widening of the keyword is not unproblematic as 'a description of everything of this kind as creative can be confusing and at times seriously misleading'. This is a theme of advertising examined in a dictionary of modern thought (Bullock and Trombley 1999: 11):

> The creativity used by advertisers must be instant attention-getting, resulting in a glibness or lateral cleverness . . . [and] is exposed as a new form of post-war sloganeering; [moreover, the advertising industry has established] a plethora of self-aggrandizing award festivals, locally and internationally, at which 'creatives' award each other glittering prizes to celebrate the quality of their creative thinking.

Of course, commercial firms may be creative. Alessi views itself as one of the 'factories of Italian design' (Alessi 1998: 7). The blending of manufacturing and art at a high level of accomplishment means that Alessi is considered a leader in applied arts and industrial design. With particular reference to household articles, Alessi has had celebrated collaborations including Michael Graves, *Kettle with Bird* (1985); Philippe Starck, *Juicy Salif* (lemon squeezer, 1990); and Alessandra Mendini, *Anna G* (corkscrew, 1994). More recently, design has been billed as art, with the sale at auction in October 2007 by Christie's of Marc Newson's *Lockheed Lounge*, an aluminium chaise lounge, for £748,500, a world record for a living designer, cited as a lead example. Newson is represented by the Gagosian Gallery, which emphasizes the designer's status, and design fairs now coincide with leading contemporary art fairs such as Art Basel Miami Beach and Frieze in London. Detractors view so-called designart as a method for greater commercial value through the marketing of elite design, according to Helen Kirwan-Taylor (*WSJE*, 7–9 March 2008).

Culture industry

The National Endowment for Science, Technology and the Arts (NESTA) in the UK has the strapline 'making innovation flourish', and includes 'arts and innovation' as a core area of interest:

> A society with a healthy and vibrant creative sector is more likely to be a healthy, vibrant and innovative society. Creativity (and creative people in particular) is the engine room of innovation.
>
> For businesses and organizations in the UK to survive and succeed over time, they need to generate, or have access to, new ideas. And new and imaginative thinking is needed to solve the issues we face today in health, the environment and our wider society. Put simply, we need more creativity in the UK, and more ways to nurture, develop and reward it.

A special report on the UK's creative industries in *Spectator Business* (March 2009) highlights areas of competitive advantage: fashion, television, film, drama schools, computer games, and popular music. Thus the entrepreneurship of *Big Brother*, *Wife Swap*, and *Supernanny* as helping to boost the national balance of payments, *Slumdog Millionaire*, funded by Celador Films, an arm of the television company that owns the rights to *Who Wants to be a Millionaire*, and an ex-Sony BMG executive who founded two music companies. Included within the financial performance indicators of success, it was instructive to note references to the important role of UK universities – including Central St. Martins, the Central School of Speech and Drama, RADA, the Guildhall School of Music and Drama, LAMDA, and the Dundee Institute of Technology (now Abertay) – in fostering talent.

Is the term culture industry regressive? Writing in the *Times Literary Supplement* (26 September 1997) during the heyday of Cool Britannia, former UK politician George Walden opined that 'arts industry' represents a solecism:

> [It] is also frequently invoked by ministers as a major tourist attraction and export earner. Appeals for more investment in the arts are now made on the same premise as for investment in the infrastructure. Seen as a commitment to the arts themselves, such calls are attractive to politicians suspected of congenital philistinism. The philistinism implicit in the notion that more cash produces more and better goes unnoticed.

Such sentiments reference ideas advanced decades earlier by Adorno and Horkheimer, who coined 'culture industry', in 1947, as a derogatory term. In a subsequent work (from 1975), 'Culture industry re-considered', Adorno (1991: 85) refined his position:

> The culture industry fuses the old and familiar into a new quality. In all its

branches, products which are tailored for consumption by masses, and which to a great extent determine the nature of that consumption, are manufactured more or less according to plan.

Central to his critique is the application of capitalist industrialism, namely the profit motive, to creative activity: 'the total effect of the culture industry is one of anti-enlightenment. . . . It impedes the development of autonomous independent individuals who judge and decide consciously for themselves', according to Adorno (1991: 921). Mass culture is identical and the lines of its artificial framework begin to show through: 'The customer is not king, as the culture industry would have us believe, not its subject but its object' (Adorno 1991: 85). Marxist historian Eric Hobsbawn expanded on this theme, in *Age of Extremes* (1994), by examining the decline of the avant-garde and the arts after 1950. Moreover, the marketing of artists and works of art post-Warhol forces us to look at the mechanics of presentation within the culture industry, and to assess the role of the merchandiser. One recognizes that all arts organizations are engaged in expressions of self-promotion, trying to cultivate the right image and identity. Business dealings with the arts have expanded beyond corporate sponsorship to include more complex collaborations involving the enhancement of creativity and innovation skills. Any examination of the interdependence between the arts and business raises issues concerning aesthetic integrity and the role of artists and arts organizations in contemporary society. As entrepreneurial norms of performance have become social norms of behaviour, a new layer of non-artistic managers (say in marketing, fundraising, and project management) has emerged.

Adorno's criticism of the manufacture of mass culture – as kitsch versus the genuine art of the avant-garde – is part of a political Left critique (see, for example, the early writings of art critic Clement Greenberg); at the other end of the political spectrum, popular culture is a bugbear of conservative journals of criticism like *The New Criterion* and *Salisbury Review*. That the market economy corrupts culture is an argument Tyler Cowen (1998: 1) seeks to counter by 'encouraging a more favorable attitude towards the commercialization of culture that we associate with modernity'. Contemporary art is a good place to start.

The Art Dealers Association of America (2000: 5), in making a case that its members 'are a pivotal link between artists and their public, between sellers of art and collectors', secures an endorsement from Philippe de Montebello, the then director of the Metropolitan Museum of Art: 'Here in the City of New York, the greatest museum of contemporary art is the aggregate of hundreds of commercial galleries. That's the great museum of contemporary art galleries'. The legacy of contemporary art dealer Leo Castelli is a prime example. A well-known twenty-fifth anniversary luncheon photograph by Hans Namuth – dated February 1982 – appears on the current website of the Leo Castelli Gallery. The art dealer is the centre of attention: standing behind him, left to right, are Ellsworth Kelly, Dan Flavin, Joseph Kosuth, Richard Serra, Lawrence Weiner, Nassos Daphnis, Jasper Johns, Claes Oldenburg, Salvatore Scarpitta, Richard Artschwager, Mia Westerland Rosen, Cletus Johnson, Keith Sonnier; Castelli is seated between Andy Warhol and Robert Rauschenberg, to the left, and Ed Ruscha, James Rosenquist, and Robert Barry, to the right. Castelli, who died in 1999, has a secure place in any survey of art collecting, let alone art dealing, in the twentieth century. Art critic Clement Greenberg, as the dominant voice of Modernism, played a seminal role in promoting Jackson Pollock and the New York School of painting, yet it was Castelli who promoted Pop (e.g. Johns, Rauschenberg, Warhol, Lichtenstein), Minimalism (e.g. Flavin and Judd), and Conceptualism (e.g. Weiner and Kosuth). This service to art history was not immediately apparent, according to Calvin Tomkins in his 1980 profile for *The New Yorker*, as art dealing is considered 'an often dubious profession' and Castelli was originally 'portrayed as an immensely shrewd manipulator of prices and reputations, a suave super-salesman who could sell anything, and who, in fact, by a combination of questionable business tactics and slick relations, managed to kill off Abstract Expressionism' to promote his own artists.[9]

Consumerism

Consumerism, according to the conservative philosopher Roger Scruton (1982), is a label that is beginning to be applied to political outlooks that see acquisition and consumption as the principle ends of existence. 'I shop therefore I am', goes the slogan adopted by Barbara Kruger. Under such circumstances it is more or less standard to view consumerism as a term of abuse. Williams's bone of contention was that the term consumer, during the latter half of the twentieth century, gained widespread and overwhelming extension into traditionally noncommercial fields including politics, health, education, and the arts. The realignment of relationships with consumer as the preferred term to describe virtually all human exchange served to negate distinctions in relationships; moreover, social human needs 'are not covered by the consumer ideal: they may even be denied because consumption tends always to be materialist as an individual activity', according to Williams (1980: 188). This fits the view of Adorno (1991: 85–86, 92) that the spectator is offered only the illusion of choice by the culture industry:

> The customer is not king, as the culture industry would have us believe, not its subject but its object.
> The entire practice of the culture industry transfers the profit motive naked onto cultural forms.
> The total effect of the culture industry is one of anti-enlightenment ... It impedes the development of autonomous, independent individuals who judge and decide consciously for themselves.

Andrew Clark, writing in the *FT Magazine* (22/23 March 2008), might counter with the case of *West Side Story* (1957): when 'classical and modern cross-fertilised in a way that was accessible and genuinely popular'. This corresponds with DiMaggio (1986: 88–89): 'Where markets for an art form are highly segmented, pluralism and often innovation thrive'. *West Side Story* is considered as a 'defining moment': 'a quasi-operatic musical that incorporated dance sequences as separate, dramatically eventful numbers rather than appendages to songs'. The mass audiences of Broadway were introduced 'to a form of large-scale musical theatre that drew inspiration from grand opera and 20th century dance while remaining worlds away in style'.

RISE OF MANAGERIALISM IN ARTS MANAGEMENT

What is the proper role of arts management (see Chong 2000)? This question has been posed for at least several decades. In a special section, 'Administering for the Arts' in *California Management Review* (Winter 1972), the editor Ichak Adizes, an assistant professor of managerial studies at UCLA, sought to identify a new area of study: 'Art as an area of human activity – in its organizational aspects and managerial functions – has been relatively unexplored. Training for the administrative side of artistic organization has been neglected'. Almost a generation later, in 1988, Joan Jeffri acknowledged that her discipline 'is still decried . . . for being soft, undisciplined, not rigorous enough', in her capacity as an editor of the *Journal of Arts Management and Law*, which is part of the legitimacy problem mooted by Colbert. More recently, Andrew Brighton edited two volumes of *Critical Quarterly* (Autumn and Winter 2002), 'The rise and rise of managerial discourse', with a tendentious thesis, according to Colin McCabe's 'Editorial':

> The long-term poison of management is that it pretends all questions of politics have already been answered. Much management discourse, groaning under its ugly and rebarbative platitudes, is little more than a restatement of basic ethics which, from Aristotle to Bloomsbury, have been held crucial to a civilised society. But this discourse avoids all questions of power.

Gary Day (2002: 42–43), in concluding 'how culture and commerce were really made for each other', notes:

> As management has become ever more generalised, culture, in the form of criticism, has become ever more specialised. It has shrunk from being a normative discourse applied to the whole of society to a technique applied to texts, and the abstract character of some aspect of theory mirrors the abstract nature of the exchange itself. . . . In short, what seems to have happened is that the discourse of culture now functions in a more cultural one. Managers, not critics, are deemed to know what's best for a successful society. Ironically, part of the reason for this lies within criticism itself. Its very existence as a discipline depends on its ability to *manage* the experience to art, to process the raw material and align it with society's governing values. Consequently, there was no real opposition between culture and commerce, just a merger waiting to happen (emphasis in the original).[10]

At least two divergent views can be interpreted: arts management as a sub-discipline within MBA studies, say following Adizes's route, with attention to application; or arts management as a zone of contact for various intellectual lines of analysis to be pursued, as intimated by Brighton and pursued by those interested in so-called critical management studies (see, for example, Alvesson and Willmott 1992; Parker 2002).

Is what appears to be a growing divide inevitable? Certain applications of concepts from the business world have been disappointing, but does that discredit the notion of application? There are benefits to be gained by broadening the base of discussion and investigating the possibilities available from different perspectives; however, so-called interdisciplinary approaches can become a prop to compensate for academic deficiencies. For example, if the use of theory is overwhelming, disciplined observation gives way to irrelevance and tedium.

It is beneficial to consider the interventions of artists and cultural critics when examining the relationship between the arts and management, even if one is conducting an exercise to identify legitimate areas of managerial intervention in the name of effectiveness and efficiency. Not unlike the marketing-savvy tactics adopted by the Guerrilla Girls to expose imbalances in the art world or Komar and Melamid, who have highlighted the partial truths gained from marketing research, there can be virtue in pragmatism, according to Bourdieu and Haacke (1995: 107):

> One can learn a lot from advertising. Among the mercenaries of the advertising world are very smart people, real experts in communications. It makes practical sense to learn techniques and strategies of communications. Without knowing them, it is impossible to subvert them.

Even for those who are not interested in subversion, there is the added value of sharpened awareness. It helps to expose how language serves different interests. John Tusa (1997: 38) – the then director of the Barbican Centre (1995–2007) in London and now Sir John and chair of the Clore Leadership Programme – asked for a balance to be struck regarding the use of the language of management by arts organizations:

> It is not that any of us want to buck the currently predominant managerial culture – we do not. It is not that difficult to learn – it isn't. We in the arts above all have a pressing need and obligation to use the little money we have as well as we can. But managerialism should be a tool rather than an end; a method rather than an absolute; a rule of thumb rather than a tablet of stone; a system of analysis rather than a panacea for every problem. If applied without discrimination, it threatens to swamp the very activity that it is, overtly, intended to support. It is the servant not the master. It is a necessary part of our lives but it is not sufficient in itself to make a good arts centre or to allow great art to be created. Even once that assumption is accepted, once managerialism and consultants, the high priests of the doctrine, are put in their rightful place, the questions we as organisers of the arts centres must answer [in the twenty-first century] are legion.

ARTS MANAGEMENT SYSTEMS

Martin (in Shafritz 1998) distinguishes between 'public, nonprofit arts organizations' and 'private, commercial, for-profit artistic entities'. The not-for-profit, charitable-status arts organization can either be in receipt of significant public subsidy, or rely on generating its own revenue for survival. One thinks of the former as the model for the most established art museums and performing arts organizations (apart from the USA); this is to suggest that many would find it more challenging to continue in the absence of government funding. However, there are pockets of artistic achievement (again, excluding the case of the USA) – county house opera in England is an example – in the absence of public funding. For our purposes, two forms of 'private, commercial, for-profit artistic entities' are cited: publicly listed firms such as Sony and Sotheby's, which represent a form of managerial capitalism; and personal capitalism associated with owner-operated enterprises such as art dealers and independent record labels.

Various sets of complementary relations that help to elucidate systems to better appreciate the complexity of arts management can be cited. First, the classical industrial economy, as represented as a three-stage process from production to distribution to consumption, is relevant to arts organizations. Artistic creation (production) is linked to artistic reception (consumption) through the intermediation role of arts organizations (such as art museums for exhibitions or theatres for plays). Second, arts organizations need to address three mutually supporting commitments: to excellence and artistic integrity; to accessibility and audience development; and to public accountability and cost effectiveness. A primary challenge is mission conflict – with excellence versus access a longstanding one – given resource constraints. Third, key stakeholders – owners (or share/stockholders in the case of publicly listed firms), customers, employees, suppliers, and society (encompassing the community and environment) – are even more important for arts organizations not motivated by profit maximization.

Production – distribution – consumption

The classical industrial economy is represented as a three-stage process from *production* to *distribution (or intermediation)* to *consumption*. This is analogous to how some perceive the basic elements of a performance or exhibition: the creative raw material and a person or persons to interpret the material to create the performance or work of art (production or creation); a place to present the performance or work of art (distribution/intermediation); and an audience to witness the performance or view the work of art (consumption or reception). Indeed, consumption has taken on greater importance due to current attention devoted to identity; individuals as consumers may look to the products they consume to affirm their overall identity.[11] Likewise, technological changes have allowed greater access to more diverse channels of distribution.

Consider the art world through the classical industrial economy. Production leads to the creation of works of art. Some producers – that is to say artists – are living; most are dead. In the case of dead artists, reputations are established, though market taste can shift individual artists up or down a pecking order over time. The work of living artists, which is a temporal marker, can be more challenging as there is an unlimited supply of varying quality. In the current environment, (MA or MFA) degree qualification from a leading art school is one indicator of an artist's potential. The distribution of art is conducted by interdependent intermediaries – public dealers (or gallerists), private dealers, and auction houses – who all thrive in a booming art market, even though there can be tensions regarding how the spoils are shared.

Dealers and auction houses do not engage in traditional sales associated with intermediaries in other market sectors. Connoisseurship still matters, which has much to do with art's status as an aesthetic object in the absence of utilitarian function. Art critics, art historians, and art museum curators help to shape and refine market taste, which in turn can have an impact on market value. This is about the cross-valuation and certification – subscription and endorsement are other terms used – of artists and works of art. Collectors of art are of two main categories: institutions – such as public art museums adding to the permanent collection or business corporations building corporate art collections – and private collectors, who represent a particular form of high-level and engaged consumption.

The goal of art is to find a home, with provenance being the ownership history of the work since it was created. The idealized repository of art is the museum, as this often serves as a precursor to entering the primers of art history. With this in mind, the significance of museum quality is better appreciated: it is part of the sales flattery used by dealers and auctioneers to signal works of the highest aesthetic value – that is to say, worthy to be on display in a public art museum. In some cases, a dealer or auctioneer will reference a comparable work in a public collection for the purposes of indicating comparative worth. Marcel Duchamp, in an address to the American Federation of Arts in 1957 (in Battcock 1973: 47), no doubt with his own case in mind, recognized that the artist (producer) and the spectator (consumer) represented the two poles in the creation of art:

> In the final analysis, the artist may shout from all the rooftops that he is a genius; he will have to wait for the verdict of the spectator in order that his declarations take a social value and that, finally, posterity includes him in the primers of art history.

The making of a work of art is often restricted to the figure of the individual artist, yet as Duchamp has argued, the spectator completes the art work through an aggregation of interpretations. The case of Vincent Van Gogh, who never sold a painting in his lifetime, is one of artistic reception being absent.

Three commitments of arts organizations

Arts organizations need to consider three mutually supporting commitments: to excellence and artistic integrity; to accessibility and audience development; and to public accountability and cost effectiveness.[12]

First and foremost, an arts organization needs to make a commitment to *excellence* (international, national, or local) and *artistic integrity*. A distinctive style must be protected and nurtured. Attempts to communicate its identity and image to a wide range of audiences, specialist and non-specialist, is deemed crucial. Artistic integrity needs to be maintained to avoid so-called plastic apples, namely falsifying the arts. This is to suggest that merely offering the public what it wants is an abdication of responsibility. Arts organizations should be in the business of helping to shape taste, which suggests leading rather than merely reacting. This is how Nicholas Serota (in Grant 2003: 52), Tate director, responds when asked, 'Is it the role of Tate specifically, and the national collections broadly, to reflect or to establish taste?':

I think that the collections, if they are doing their job, will establish taste. There are plenty of examples going back to the nineteenth century that demonstrate how the National Gallery established taste, particularly in terms of collecting early quattrocento painting. You could say the same is true of Tate at certain moments, for example when it collected minimal art in the 1970s. This was regarded as an affront by some parts of the popular press at the time, but I don't think there is any doubt that it was the right thing for Tate to bring that work into this collection.

The public may not be able to articulate what it wants. However, those charged with the stewardship of arts organizations cannot divorce programming decisions from broader ethical concerns and social responsibilities. For example, what is the proper role of Wagner given his links to Adolph Hitler? Father M. Owen Lee (1999: 3, 20) believes that it is possible for 'a terrible man to produce art that is good, true, and beautiful'; and that Wagner's works 'are about the healing of the hurt in, the drawing off of the evil in, the integration of the conflicting forces in, the human psyche'. Using music as a means to heal wounds helps to explain Daniel Barenboim's decision, in 2001 (London *Guardian*, 4 August 2001), to breach the taboo of playing Wagner in Israel:

> I don't think that Hitler and his people should prevent us from playing and hearing Wagner's music simply because they saw in it something that made them what they were. Not playing Wagner has harmed the Israel Philharmonic artistically. There is a vacuum in their music because there are few composers as important as Wagner. I don't see how you can really understand Mahler and Schoenberg if you don't know your Wagner.

Wagner's *Die Meistersinger* has a special resonance, according to Edward Said (1991: 61): 'Few operas in my opinion have done so relentlessly detailed a job of literally enacting the way in which music, if it is looked at not simply as a private, esoteric possession but as a social activity, is interwoven with, and is important to social reality'. Barenboim's decision needs to be viewed in the context of the East West Divan Orchestra, a project conceived with Said, to close the chasm between Arabs and Israelis (Barenboim and Said 2004). *Gramophone* (31 March 2009) recognized it as one of the world's most inspiring orchestras: young musicians across the Middle East divide are brought together to build personal and cultural bridges; improving one's level of technical ability through hours of rehearsal and performance is followed by discussion.[13]

Second, a commitment to make the arts organization more accessible (particularly as measured by socio-demographic variables) strikes at the heart of genuine *audience development*. There can be an uneasy relationship between artistic programming and audiences. For too long, audience development has been constrained within the confines of a marketing discourse. Arts marketing has been useful in areas like attendance stimulation, membership development, fundraising, crisis management, merchandising, awareness building, and business sponsorship. Popular exhibitions, which treat culture as an event and art as entertainment, provide benefits to visitors, host institutions, and corporate sponsors. But is it all so-called win-win?

What about sustainability and the longer term impact on audience development? According to the NEA (Larson 1997: 163):

> The challenge is to reach out to the majority of Americans who currently have no direct involvement with the professional, nonprofit arts, to expand the nation's cultural palette to include a full range of participatory activities, without losing sight of the standards of professional excellence that still have a role in providing benchmarks of achievement. The opportunity is to build a much larger, more inclusive base of support for the arts, one that gives all Americans a stake in the preservation and transmission of our cultural legacy.

Barriers to first-time visitors are actual and perceived. Education, touring, and electronic media represent ways audiences can be grown. The political mantras of education, education, education and arts for all are used to justify increased public funding. A wider geographic scope is offered by touring activities of bringing art to audiences. Traditional broadcasting (television and radio) continues to offer opportunities; even more dramatic changes to reach wider audiences involve digital technology and the internet. New York's Metropolitan Opera has been a leader in making some of its live productions available in cinemas in the USA and worldwide with great success, according to its general manager, Peter Gelb. Some criticisms have emerged, though: more conservative programming may be needed to attract new audiences; listeners will be trained to hear electronic music and lose an appreciation for live performance, not least of its visceral power; vocal training may change, deemphasizing the ability to project; and audiences from local opera houses will be diverted to the Met's performances at a mall cinema (*NYT*, 13 February 2009).

Third, in order to maximize the benefit from available funds – which is not the same as minimizing costs – an arts organization needs to make a commitment to *public accountability* and *cost effectiveness*. Efficient management structures, not least at the level of the board of trustees, can help to secure financial stability. Revenue enhancement, which often means diversifying the revenue stream (or plural funding), is necessary, yet to be successful, an arts organization cannot be guided by money. This is not to suggest that quality and profitability are mutually exclusive – indeed such a tandem should not be viewed with hostility. Securing financial stability is a necessary starting point to allow the aesthetic programming to take place. In many respects, the adoption of a managerial orientation is about presentation: the smart and savvy arts organization is concerned with safeguarding core aesthetic values, but recognizes and appreciates that prudent financial stewardship and corporate governance are viewed by existing and potential funding sources (both public and private) as a signal of institutional sustainability. For example, in his report on *The Future of Lyric Theatre in London*, Richard Eyre (1998: foreword) recognized that the problems of a high-profile arts organization, in receipt of significant state subsidy, may have wider repercussions:

> As a barometer of the health of the performing arts [the Royal Opera House] has inspired righteous indignation, invited mockery, invoked accusations of

irresponsibility, overspending, mismanagement and elitism, and begged questions about the validity of the principle on which all organisations receive taxpayers money.

Managing relationships with stakeholders

Managing relations with stakeholders addresses the purposes and values of organizations. In the early 1990s Robert Kaplan and David Norton (Kaplan and Norton 1992) coined the term balanced scorecard to suggest that financial performance was not the only benchmark of a successful firm, even in the case of multinational enterprises. The first decade of the twenty-first century has been witness to corporate scandals, namely Enron, WorldCom, and Tyco, and a credit crisis, including the collapse of financial titans such as Lehman Brothers and Bernard Madoff's Ponzi scheme. Issues of corporate governance and stewardship have become more important. This speaks to a role in society. Several key stakeholders, as proffered by the Institute of Business Ethics, can be identified for all types of organizations: *owners* (or share/stockholders in the case of publicly listed firms), *customers, employees, suppliers*, and *society* (encompassing community and environment).

An arts organization with not-for-profit, charitable status cannot distribute any surplus to shareholders; any surplus must be retained to support the organization. One impact of public funding is a requirement to meet certain performance targets or metrics. In the case of publicly listed companies, the separation of financial ownership (by individual and institutional shareholders) from management control – with the rise of a professional managerial class – has been characterized as managerial capitalism. Owner-operated businesses represent a form of personal capitalism where ownership and control is vested in the owner-operator or is tightly held; such entrepreneurial initiatives may face succession obstacles when the founder exits (through retirement or death).

Audiences and spectators – or customers to use the increasingly common language of marketing – matter in both generating revenue and because artistic production requires artistic reception for the work to be complete. Commercial companies focus on financial measures such as profitability and market share, which result from satisfying customers and some businesses such as the leading auction houses may decide to focus on particular market segments: from the mass affluent – a term from retail banking to denote a growing consumer class earning in excess of $100,000 per annum – at the bottom level, to ultra high net worth individuals (UHNWIs) – a term from private wealth management to indicate an individual or family group with investible assets in excess of $30 million. Publicly funded arts organizations have a more challenging mandate when it comes to customers. Non-attenders can be an important target market in order to satisfy public funding bodies, and as part of ethical mandates that the arts matter to all.

More and more organizations, in the light of a focus on knowledge industry and creativity and innovation as forms of competitive advantage, have reconceptualized the employee as an important intangible asset. The arts, as advanced by Arts & Business (A&B), have become part of management development programmes in companies such as Unilever. In large publicly funded arts organizations, those vested with artistic mission mandates may feel that resources are shifting to bases considered as support roles.

Suppliers have appeared most recently as the key stakeholder group. The conventional reference has been to the supply chain, including outsourcing and offshoring, thus issues associated with managing principal-agent relationships. However, there is a desire to promote terms like partners, alliances, collaborations (with benefits accruing from establishing and maintaining interdependent relationships). External collaborations and partnering are important, but difficult to implement. The World Collections Programme (WCP), with the British Museum, the British Library, the Natural History Museum, the Royal Botanical Gardens (Kew), Tate, and the Victorian & Albert Museum as UK institutions, aims to establish two-way cultural exchange partnerships – in the priority regions of Africa, the Middle East, India, and China – to increase access to UK collections and expertise. At a sectoral level, auction houses and dealers can be viewed as a two legs of the same stool to borrow a metaphor often used in the art world. Informal networks are crucial for contemporary art dealers to succeed given the need to develop relationships with both artists (the importance of aesthetic taste) and collectors (the necessity of social networks).

Society and the wider community can be viewed as an elastic stakeholder category, yet one that has gained greater significance. Exclusive emphasis on the financial interests of stock/shareholder, as promoted by Milton Friedman – who argued that 'the social responsibility for business is to increase its profits' (*NYT*, 13 September 1970) – is fading even amongst the chief executives of S&P 500 and FTSE 100 firms. Corporate social responsibility policy can include donations to charitable organizations, though the arts face challengers from sectors – like education and health – with higher visibility and impact. Within higher education, the Principles for Responsible Management Education (PRME) initiative of the United Nations seek to promote and embed 'corporate responsibility and sustainability' as part of 'the mainstream of business-related education' as a way to shape mindsets of the new generation of business leaders.[14]

ORGANIZATIONAL METAPHORS

'The European Iceberg: creativity in Germany and Italy today' (1985) was a large-scale, interdisciplinary exhibition of German Neo-Expressionism and the Italian Transavantgarde, mounted at the Art Gallery of Ontario (AGO) by guest curator Germano Celant (1985: 12):

> The image of a 'European Iceberg' has several functions. It serves to indicate the enormous complexity of European culture, which cannot be shown in totality. And the metaphor also emphasizes that the visible part here – Italy and Germany – leaves all other countries hidden underwater. Furthermore, the portion of Canada is the one now emerging in the territory of the arts, and it must always bear this in mind because of its profound influences on the visible situation.

The exhibition was a defining moment for the AGO. It provided the impetus for the then chief curator, Roald Nasgaard, to develop an impressive collection of international (i.e. non-Canadian) art. Lothar Baumgarten's contribution was *Monument aux nations indiennes de l'Ontario/Monument to the Native Peoples of Ontario* (1984–85), a site-specific installation that set out to interact with the place of its display, as both architecturally and geographically defined. In particular, the German artist was responding to a society in which Native culture was absent, thus he named some tribes (Huron, Algonkin, Ojibwa, Iroquois, Petun, Ottawa, Neutral, and Nippissing) in a manner of European heros of arts and sciences sometimes found carved in classical architecture. Following the 1994 reopening of the AGO, Baumgarten's installation was revisited by Robert Houle, an artist from Canada's First Peoples community, in a three-part installation, *Anishnake Walker Court* (1994), which represented a wry commentary on the manufacture of so-called Indianness in which ethnic identity masks a critical intersection between ambivalence and intentionality. The most recent reopening of the AGO, at the end of 2008, with a Frank Gehry addition, makes reference to the significance of 'The European Iceberg' exhibition in highlighting the AGO's early promotion of Gerhard Richter in Canada. However, Baumgarten's installation has been expunged from institutional memory: the work has been removed from a specific and prominent site with no visible note indicating why.

'Organizations are many things at once!', according to Gareth Morgan (1986: 339; emphasis in the original). In *Images of Organization*, Morgan (1986) poses a series of 'what if' questions based on eight metaphors: what if we think of organizations as *machines*? as *organisms*? as *brains*? as *cultures*? as *political systems*? as *psychic prisons*? as *flux and transformation*? as *instruments of domination*? This is part of Morgan's creative approach to exploring organizations. His belief in the role played by images and metaphors in the social construction of reality makes him prominent and somewhat unconventional amongst management writers (for another example, see Czarniawska 1999).

Complementary and competing insights are created via the metaphorical frameworks, each with strengths and limitations. For example, the *machine* view, which remains a dominant metaphor, approaches the organization as outlined by classical management theorists like Fayol and Urwick, and along the scientific management principles of Taylor: 'set goals and objectives and go for them'; 'organize rationally, efficiently, and clearly'; and 'plan, organize, and control, control, control' (Morgan 1993: 33). The *political systems* metaphor emphasizes issues of interest, conflict, and power; this 'helps to explode the myth of organizational rationality' explicit in the machine view (Morgan 1993: 195). The *psychic prisons* metaphor examines 'how people in organizations can become trapped by favoured ways of thinking . . . [and] how organizations can become trapped by unconscious processes that lend organizations a hidden significance' (Morgan 1993: 200). Organizations as *instruments of domination* is a metaphor that focuses on the (sometimes unintended) negative activities of organizations on their employees or their environment (e.g. patterns of inequality in global economic development), and is often viewed as articulating 'an extreme form of left-wing ideology, serving to fan the flames of the radical frame of reference and thus adding to the difficulties of managers in an already turbulent world' (Morgan 1993: 319).

Particular reference to the Louvre as a model is often used in a history of the modern, public art museum (Bazin 1967; Carrier 2006). A full account of the development of the Louvre requires a very complex bureaucratic history which begins with the French Revolution, as one of transformation from private (namely royal) collection to public institution. This is to say that the Louvre was born out of a contestation: it is an 'institution which embodied a form of publicity that functioned to challenge the "representative" publicity of royal collections (in order to realize a conception of publicness opposed to the secret politics of absolutism)' (Ward 1995: 76). Morgan's instrument of domination metaphor is evident in the critique of New York's Museum of Modern Art by Duncan and Wallach (1978: 28–51), who viewed MoMA as a 'masculine museum space'. A similar theme was articulated in the 1940s by the then director of the Detroit Institute of Arts (William Valentiner in Zuker 1944: 658): 'The building of the National Gallery [of Art] in Washington is not only a triumph of capitalism but is in accordance with the buildings in its neighbourhood, an expansion of the growing world power of the USA'.

Interventions by artists, like Brian O'Doherty (aka the artist Patrick Ireland), Marcel Broodthaers (d. 1976), and Andrea Fraser, have contributed to our understanding of organizational metaphors and museum fictions (McShine 1999; Newhouse 2005; O'Doherty 1986; Fraser 1991). O'Doherty (1986: 15) has examined the ideology of the gallery space by arguing against the perceived neutrality afforded by the so-called white cube (particularly popular for the display of contemporary art):

A gallery is constructed among laws as rigorous as those for building a medieval church. The outside world must not come in, so windows are usually sealed off. Walls are painted white. The ceiling becomes the source of light. The wooden floor is polished so that you click along clinically, or so carpeted so that you tread soundlessly. . . . Unshadowed, white, clean, artificial – the space is devoted to the technology of aesthetics. . . . Art exists in a kind of eternity of display . . . there is no time. This eternity gives the gallery a limbolike status.

Morgan's organization as psychic prison, which results in a severely restricted physical, conceptual, and cultural arena, corresponds with O'Doherty's characterization.

Broodthaers's fictive or invented museum, *Musée d'art Moderne, Department des Aigles, Section XIXeme*, was opened, in 1968, in the artist's studio, in Brussels; it closed in 1972 at Documenta V. *Musée d'art Moderne* served as an adversary art practice: the artist raised pointed questions concerning the 'double stranglehold of the museum and the marketplace' while attempting 'to become engaged in the political struggles of its time'. Through a close reading of Broodthaers's press releases for his fictive museum, a leading critic was confident in concluding that the artist's 'suggestion that the museum might wish to seduce "customers and the curious" by employing the mock-Kantian formula "disinterestedness plus admiration" is perhaps the most elliptical yet precise critique of institutionalized modernism ever offered' (Crimp 1993: 212).

Adopting the persona of docent (or education guide) Jane Castelton, Andrea Fraser created a performance piece using the Philadelphia Museum of Art as a site of investigation. The artist documented the tour, 'Museum Highlights', in an essay first prepared for publication in *October*. In part, Fraser (1991: 107) offered an examination of the volunteer docent, who is invariably female and smartly attired:

[S]he is the museum's representative. Unlike members of the museum's nonprofessional maintenance, security, and gift shop staff that visitors come into contact with, the docent is a figure of identification for a primarily white, middle-class audience. And unlike the museum's professional staff, the docent is the representation of the museum's volunteer sector.

While docents are usually trained by the professional staff, I would say that they aspire less to professional competence than to what Pierre Bourdieu [in *Distinction*] calls the 'precious', 'status-induced familiarity' with legitimate culture that marks those to whom the objects within the museum belong(ed); an 'imperceptible learning' that can only be 'acquired' with time and applied by those who can take their time.

Fraser (1991: 107–8) continued by describing how she perceived the fictional docent Jane, in the language of women's work:

Jane is determined above all by the status of the docent as a nonexpert volunteer. As a volunteer, she expresses the possession of a quantity of the leisure and the economic and cultural capital that defines the museum's patron class. It is only a small quantity – indicating rather than bridging the class gap that compels her to volunteer her services in the absence to capital; to give, perhaps, her body in the absence of art objects. Yet it is enough to position her in identification with the museum's board of trustees, and to make her the museum's exemplary viewer.

As the preceding art museum examples illustrate, the use of metaphor to engage in problems associated with reading (or interpreting) organizations has benefits. By going against conventional orthodoxy with subtle analysis, visual artists remind us that 'all images are man-made' and 'every image embodies a way of seeing' (Berger 1972: 9–10). Morgan (1993: 281) is at pains to stress that 'any particular way of seeing is limited . . . the challenge is to become skilled in the art of seeing, in the art of understanding, and in the art of interpretation and reading situations we face'.

STRUCTURE OF THE TEXT

The text for the revised second edition of *Arts Management* has been restructured. Three sections – 'Institutional Partners' (I), 'Relationships with Stakeholders' (II), and 'Wealth and the Economy' (III) – are used to organize the core chapters. Several complementary appendices to the core chapters are also included in order to offer fuller coverage and analysis.

Chapter 1 as an introduction asks one to consider the role of arts management. Taking action and conceptual thinking appear to be two sides of the same coin when addressing the interaction between managerial, economic, and aesthetic objectives. Any definition of arts management confronts various classifications: high/low, public/private, and not-for-profit/commercial. Examining constituent and related terms like arts, management, and culture industry is a way also to highlight the various and sometimes conflicting positions adopted by prominent commentators including Henry Mintzberg, Raymond Williams, Paul DiMaggio, the Frankfurt School, Pierre Bourdieu, Hans Haacke, John Pick, Gareth Morgan, Andrea Fraser, and the Harvard Business School. Several complementary approaches to arts management are presented. The industrial economy flow of production to distribution to consumption is an explicit acknowledgement that arts and cultural organizations have structural features similar to other sectors of the economy. Three commitments – to aesthetic excellence and integrity; to accessibility and audience development; and to cost effectiveness and transparency – serve as an introduction to the challenges facing different types of arts and cultural organizations. The need to manage relationships with key stakeholders, namely owners, customers, employees, suppliers, and society, can take on enhanced significance in the absence of a profit-motive. Morgan's exploration of images and metaphors in the social construction of reality is instructive in what it suggests of our understanding of arts and cultural organizations.

Section I on 'Institutional Partners' examines the role of two primary institutions, the state and business, in arts and cultural organizations. 'Arts and the State' (Chapter 2) adopts a cross-national perspective to examine arts and cultural policy which includes the role of direct and indirect public subsidies. Cultural economics, namely the cost disease associated with William Baumol and William Bowen and economic impact studies, has shaped contemporary discussions in arts and cultural management. Likewise, the instrumentalism of the arts and culture responds to extra-aesthetic concerns as part of broader social welfare agendas of creating a civil society. 'Business and the Arts' (Chapter 3) begins in the 1960s, in the USA, including the pioneering initiative of the Business Committee for the Arts, which influenced like organizations around the world such as the UK's A&B. That corporate sponsorship is now taken for granted, as a necessary component for virtually any performing and visual arts programme, is a considerable consequence. It has been challenged by cultural critics as the privatization of public space. That the arts can enhance business relationships is discussed with reference to corporate art collections and collaborations between contemporary artists and commercial brands (often in the so-called luxury and fashion retailing sectors of the economy). More recently, A&B has taken a lead in promoting what business can learn from the arts as part of wider initiatives on management development and the reconceptualization of the employee as an investment in human capital.

Section II on 'Relationships with Stakeholders' is grouped around owners, customers, and employees, as three key stakeholders, although each chapter adopts a particular orientation to allow a sharper focus to emerge; moreover, each chapter also has a complementary appendix. 'Ownership and Control of Arts Organizations' (see Chapter 4) begins by considering the relationship between financial ownership and management control via different types of commercial arts enterprises (e.g. owner-operated, publicly listed company, and large private equity). Attention is drawn to art market intermediaries (art dealers and the auction house Sotheby's) and a record company (EMI under private equity firm Terra Firma). The role of trustees and elite arts patronage, as representing issues core to not-for-profit arts and cultural organizations, is discussed to indicate the complex relations in the absence of financial metrics. DiMaggio and Powell's term institutional isomorphism, from a sociological perspective, is instructive to help explain the institutional pressures that make organizations within the same field (e.g. art museums) resemble one another. An appendix on 'Philosophies of philanthropy' spans conventional notions of philanthropy associated with fundraising to venture philanthropy, which adopts a sharper commercial focus. 'Arts Consumption and Consumers' (Chapter 5) starts with arts appreciation and taste formation – namely what helps to predict who consumes arts and cultural products and why – by drawing on research from cultural economics and sociology of the arts, with particular reference to the influence of Bourdieu. This is followed by the challenges facing genuine audience development, namely how to widen the socio-demographic profile of arts and cultural consumers in the face of structural impediments. Owning art and being a collector can be viewed as an engaged form of consumption beyond appreciation, which requires access to discretionary income to purchase what is a non-utilitarian product. The consumer is linked to the management function of marketing, hence an appendix on 'Marketing and the arts'. Two strands of development are pursued: 'arts marketing' outlines the conventional approach of marketing in arts management, namely the application of marketing principle and practice to performing and visual arts organizations; and 'the arts for marketing', as part of interpretive approaches to marketing, considers how contemporary artists might shed new perspectives on marketing and the role of consumers in society. 'Managing for Excellence and Artistic Integrity' (Chapter 6), which addresses the employee as stakeholder, places a key commitment – as expressed in the chapter title – for arts and cultural organizations at the fore. The organization as social system, core to industrial sociology, is relevant to current discussions regarding enhancing human capital and the importance of creativity within organizations. Cultural leaders from the Walt Disney Company, Tate, and the English Chamber Orchestra sit alongside some of the challenges to romanticized notions of leadership, with a contribution from Mintzberg on management development. Mintzberg's 'parallel administrative hierarchies' suggests the possibilities of dual executive management structures (of aesthetic and business responsibilities) within arts and cultural organizations. The appendix on 'Personal development in arts management' considers how the notion of a career has changed, not least of all for arts and cultural workers, with some suggestions on managing several forms of capital.

Section III on 'Wealth and the Economy' assumes an increasingly globalized marketplace to address the impact of money on arts and cultural production and consumption, which creates opportunities for intermediaries. 'Financial Investing in the Arts' (Chapter 7) makes reference to two particular financial instruments: fine art investment funds, which emerged as a response to speculation during the art boom of the early 2000s, and angel investors, who have been important in funding theatrical productions (in London and New York). An appendix on 'Alternative passion investments', a term promoted by Capgemini and Merrill Lynch, examines wine, automobiles, and racehorses in order to offer a wider comparative perspective of financial investing. 'Globalization and the Art World' (Chapter 8) begins with the role of global brands, narrative storytelling associated with branding, and the marketing experiences. Two art world discussions are pursued. First, the role of dealers as market markers for contemporary art, with reference to an elite group based in New York, London, and continental Europe, reflects the attention that the recent art boom devoted to the contemporary art sector. Second, leveraging art museums for audience and identity addresses the rise of so-called superstar art museums, with particular reference devoted to the prominent example of the Guggenheim Foundation.

SECTION I

Institutional Partners

ARTS AND THE STATE

The state has a major stake in the arts and culture. In some cases, such as Europe before democratic governments took root, this may have meant royal patronage or church commissions, what has been described as 'public sector aristocracy' (Cowen 2006: 93). More recently, attention has turned to art's role in improving student learning, in building a strong workforce, and in developing creative industries. Investment in the arts helps to strengthen the economy by promoting tourism, revitalizing the core commercial district, and attracting business to expand local job opportunities.[1]

Three main areas are addressed in this chapter. First, state (public) subsidy for the arts, either direct or indirect, remains a major preoccupation regarding public policy and the arts. This is keenly noted in looking at several examples of national arts and cultural policy. Cross-national comparative analysis is attempted, though direct comparisons are not easy to make as arts researchers and policy makers use various forms of data as the basis for analysis. Second, cultural economics is viewed through two key terms: Baumol's cost disease, which proffered structural deficiencies in labour-intensive (service-based) sectors that are difficult to exploit productivity gains through advances in technology such as the performing arts; and economic impact studies, which presuppose that the arts and culure can be viewed – and measured – as any other industrial sector. Third, the instrumentalization of arts policy addresses the encroachment of extra-artistic concerns by governments, including the rise of performance management techniques associated with auditing for both economic and social inclusion agendas.

ARTS AND CULTURAL POLICY

State (public) subsidy for the arts, either direct or indirect, remains a major preoccupation regarding public policy and the arts. Direct subsidies are transfer of money via government departments or agencies (like arts councils) to arts organizations or artists. Tyler Cowen (2006: 30) describes indirect subsidies – government policy that influences relative prices, or relative returns, to encourage the production of art – as 'the genius of the American system'. In particular, the tax system (for private donors, foundations, and business corporations) provides the most significant arts subsidy in the USA.

Some of the traditional arguments proffered in support of subsidies can be identified. First, the arts can be considered a so-called merit good: the arts are considered to have merit beyond private benefits; at the same time, the arts would be under-consumed, or under-produced, in a free market economy. Second, the arts produce positive externalities in the form of public benefits – such as civilizing society, enhancing national pride, and engendering a collective identity – that outweigh private benefits. Third, economic externalities from the arts, in helping to promote tourism and to attract businesses to expand local job opportunities, are considered spillover effects (that economists attempt to measure as a multiple of arts spending). Fourth, the equity argument holds that the arts should be made available to all, not least of all citizens with low socio-demographic profiles. Thus the arts have a social impact role in helping to address inequalities.

Detractors of subsidies cite the following reasons. First, a high degree of state paternalism – nannyism in British English – is behind the merit good assumption that the state knows best. Some people – such as an Arts Establishment, according to critics – wish to use the state's resources for their own purposes. Second, there is a regressive nature of supporting high income groups who are more likely than others to consume publicly funded arts.[2] Writing from an American perspective, Cowen (2006: 100) suggests that direct subsidies work best when the arts agency or institution is free to experiment or otherwise be idiosyncratic; and the focus is on producing a few artistic winners, rather than imposing accountability for each and every grant. Cowen (2006: 148) concludes:

> We must resist the temptation to find too much of our aesthetic satisfaction in the state as a source of direct subsidies. Instead the role of the state is to support a legal and institutional framework – emphasizing a market economy and indirect subsidies – in which broad and diverse notions of the aesthetic can flourish.

The interest in comparative analysis among social scientists is an intellectual repercussion of the Second World War and its aftermath. An essential feature of comparative analysis is highlighting and explaining commonalities and differences in the content, formulation, and implementation of policies. One wants to develop concepts and generalizations at the level of the nation: What is true in all nations? What is true in one nation at a particular point in time? Comparative research contributes to the development of a relevant knowledge base which can fill gaps in our understanding of how countries deal with similar situations. Identifying the differences among various national approaches to management and policy problems can highlight different kinds of constraints: structural, institutional, and cultural.

Cross-national comparisons help one to answer certain types of questions. Is the logic of a particular process the same across nations? Are the effects of policy interventions homogeneous across (or even within) nations? A sophisticated research methodology is required when making comparisons across different political and social systems: comparative studies run the risk of passing too lightly over the particularities of national cultures, surely one of the most significant factors, both ideologically and contextually, in the establishment of arts organizations. Note that the selection of countries for comparative arts research remains highly concentrated on G-7 members (i.e. USA, Canada, UK, Germany, France, Italy, and Japan), other advanced western European economies (like Austria, The Netherlands, Belgium, Denmark, Finland, Sweden, and Switzerland), and Australia and New Zealand. Though acknowledging that 'the arts are everywhere subsidized', economist Mark Blaug (1976: 13–24) noted that 'the level of subsidies varies enormously between countries and between different types of artistic activities within countries' and 'the ratio of private charity to public subsidy likewise varies enormously from country to country'; he continued by questioning whether 'it is conceivable that neither subsidies themselves nor their variations between countries can be explained on economic grounds: they may simply reflect custom and historical tradition'.

Francine Ostrower (2002) has examined elite patronage of arts and culture, such as art museums and opera companies in the USA. Private support and governance has been crucial at the local level of metropolitan cities. Of course, such cultural entrepreneurship operates within a particular context. Cultural policy is linked to wider political agendas. This is clear in the USA, according to Stanley Katz (in Lowry 1984: 36), now director of Princeton's Center for Arts and Cultural Policy Studies:

> To have no policy is to have a policy. That [Americans] do not have a national cultural policy, in other words, means that we have made a decision (this goes back to our history) to leave to *private* and *local* institutions the determination of the decisions most overtly affecting the creation and conduct of cultural institutions (my emphasis).

The capitalist spirit of the political economy in the USA has influenced the formation of its leading arts and cultural institutions. A system, based on optimism and faith in the individual – as expressed in essays by Ralph Waldo Emerson (1803–82) – has taken root in the USA and is complemented by a taxation system, according to Kingman Brewster (in Appignanesi 1984: 7), former USA ambassador to the UK and former president of Yale University:

> As befits a heterogeneous, sprawling, nouveau-riche nation, conceived in the self-evident truth that nobody is better than anybody else, we in the United States have devoted public bounty to the arts by agreeing not to collect the full taxes on income or testamentary estates devoted to civic or educational purposes.
>
> This remarkable delegation to private citizens of the power to spend funds which would otherwise have gone to the government certainly did not assure taste or even responsibility. But in a huge country with hundreds of thousands of new fortunes arising, and tens of hundreds of private foundations coming into existence, it did assure the richness of calculated cultural anarchy.

There has been no large-scale and continuous tradition of direct subsidy by the government to support the arts and humanities in the USA. Yet the arts have flourished in the USA following the end of the Civil War due to private support for local institutions. Growing prosperity was the norm in the USA between the Gilded Age

(1865–1901) and the Great Crash of 1929. During this period, following the end of the Civil War, great private fortunes were made, marked by the rise of the so-called robber barons, and the making of America's aristocratic families such as Rothschild, Vanderbilt, Astor, Rockefeller, and Cabot. Some of the money that was amassed was spent on buying art from Europe: 'Shipload after shipload of works of art arrived in New York, Philadelphia and Boston and were sold to the more prosperous propertied gentry' (Taylor 1945: 20). More importantly, the vast accumulation of private capital was used to create what are now considered leading museums, such as the Metropolitan Museum of Art, the Museum of Fine Arts, Boston, the Philadelphia Museum of Art, the Art Institute of Chicago, the Detroit Institute of Art, and the Cleveland Museum of Art, and universities including Harvard, Yale, and Princeton. These art museums were directly and self-consciously informed by European precedents, but with commitments to education encoded in their charters.[3] Likewise, one can point to a first-mover effect in the formation of what is referred to as the 'Big 5' symphony orchestras in the USA: the New York Philharmonic, the Boston Symphony Orchestra, the Chicago Symphony Orchestra, the Philadelphia Orchestra, and the Cleveland Orchestra.[4] These private initiatives by leading citizens – primarily men – of metropolitan cities meant that the development of museums and symphony orchestras served as an extension of authority as part of a network of male, social, philanthropic, and business venture for the emerging American Establishment (see Baltzell 1964; DiMaggio in DiMaggio 1986).

Arthur Schlesinger (in Pankrantz and Morris 1990: 4) has summarized the case against the public role of art in the USA: public subsidy lacks constitutional authority; public subsidy endangers the autonomy of the arts by making artists and arts organizations dependent on government and thereby vulnerable to government control; public subsidy represents a net transfer of income from the poor to the high-income and educated classes; and public subsidy represents a paternalistic effort to dictate popular taste, which is to say that if a cultural institution cannot please consumers and earn its way in a free market, then it has no economic justification, and if no economic justification, no social justification. Roosevelt's New Deal (1933–43) included government patronage to contemporary artists through the WPA (Work Projects Administration). Yet the social aesthetics associated with some artists, such as Arthur Durston's *Industry* (1934), outraged politicians who read communist influences and embarrassing anti-poverty messages. This inculcated distaste for an active role of government in arts and culture. Cultural dynamism in the USA – the philosophy that it is good to be risk-taking and innovative and with access to capital – extends to the arts such that new arts organizations have a chance to form and prosper (Cowen 2004). Prominent examples that have risen to the first rank within a decade of formation include the Dia Art Foundation (est. 1974) and the New Museum of Contemporary Art (est. 1977).

This national identity of cultural capitalism underpins a muscular American theme of the globalization of culture. As suggested by the likes of Guilbaut (1983) and Duncan and Wallach (1978), any narrative account of New York's Museum of Modern Art (MoMA) cannot avoid its role in a wider ideological battle with communism. During the Cold War, MoMA was viewed as helping to articulate cherished values, defended by liberal democracies, in the face of perceived attacks by the Soviet

Union. In a revisionist interpretation, Guilbaut (1983) examined the convergence of modernist painting – Abstract Expressionism, as the dominant style of the American avant-garde – and the propagandist requirements of a post-1945 American hegemony. Guilbaut's work was informed by the Marxist-inspired critique of Duncan and Wallach (1978) that MoMA may be viewed as a masculine museum space, given the focus on the artist as hero and that stylistic progression means that new artistic intentions require new methods. MoMA's story of modernism accentuates an eventual triumphalism: Cezanne is posited as the father of a properly internationalist, modernist painting; progress in painting is represented by the work of Picasso and Matisse; and Jackson Pollock 'accomplished an extraordinary alchemy whereby drawing, pushed to an extreme of density and elaboration, crossed over (just) into painting', according to Thomas Crow (*Artforum*, October 1999). MoMA's point is to emphasize Abstract Expressionism, an American product, as a heroic movement supplanting Europe.

Superbly illustrative of the American ideals of the arts in support of freedom and democracy was the address by President Eisenhower in praise of MoMA (1954: 3):

To me, in this [twenty-fifth] anniversary, there is a reminder to all of us an important principle that we should ever keep in mind. This principle is that freedom of the arts is a basic freedom, one of the pillars of liberty in our land. For our Republic to stay free, those among us with the rare gift of artistry must be able freely to use their talent. Likewise, our people must have an unimpaired opportunity to see, to understand, to profit from our artists' work. As long as artists are at liberty to feel with high personal intensity, as long as our artists are free to create with sincerity and conviction, there will be a healthy controversy and progress in art. Only thus can there be an opportunity for a genius to conceive and to produce a masterpiece for all mankind.

But, my friends, how different it is in tyranny. When artists are made the slaves and tools of the state; when artists become chief propagandists of a cause, progress is arrested and creation and genius are destroyed.

Eisenhower's words, an example of Cold War propaganda, were grounded in a fundamental aversion to central authority and the belief that state intervention should be limited. As the country where capitalism is most ideologically secure, the model of a free enterprise exchange economy extends to the arts. MoMA reciprocated with the 1955 exhibition, 'The Family of Man', a statement of the universality of the American-style family (Staniszewski 1998). Indeed, Pop artists like Andy Warhol, representing post-Pollock artistic production, were able to elaborate a faith in the openness of the American life in terms supplied by consumer culture. Of course, it is ironic that the American distrust of a closer relationship between the arts and politics has not excluded a direct and active part of the role of government in promoting American art abroad; indeed throughout the Cold War, the arts were considered a valuable tool in foreign policy.

Canada's proximity to the United States – a country that is ten times larger by population – includes a shared border (with an overwhelming majority of Canadians living within 200 miles of the southern behemoth). The USA is an obvious point of reference: Canada (as nation brand) seeks points of parity with the USA, but also points of difference. This is to say that Canada, as a nation state founded in 1867, has been shaped by several forces that also help to understand cultural policy. First, the BNA Act creating Canada did not assign arts and culture specifically to any jurisdiction. Arts funding – including the formation of arts councils – thus operates at three levels of government (federal, provincial, and municipal). Second, English–French duality – the country is officially bilingual – is a response to the country's colonial past. Third, geographic expanse – from the Atlantic Ocean to the Pacific Ocean to the Artic Circle – means that the country is made up of regions: the Atlantic (Newfoundland, including Labrador, New Brunswick, Prince Edward Island, and Nova Scotia), Quebec, Ontario, the Prairies (Manitoba, Saskatchewan, and Alberta) and the North (Nunavut, the Yukon, and the Northwest Territories), and the West Coast (British Columbia). Political and economic power has focused on the triangle of Ottawa-Toronto-Montreal, with pockets of affluence having emerged in Vancouver and Calgary. Fourth, multiculturalism has accelerated in the largest Canadian cities such that there has been a radical change in the ethnic and racial composition since the 1960s. Related to this has been greater self-determination by Indigenous (or Aboriginal) people (i.e. First Nations, Inuit, and Métis). Indeed John Ralston Saul (2008) has characterized Canada as a Métis country, which adds an important dimension to the conventional English–French duality. There is a case that the arts and culture provision in Canada is via network of coordinated activities in response to the forces shaping the country. To see the extent to which localized activity can have an impact outside of Canada, consider the opinion of the eponymous founder of the Ydessa Hendeles Art Foundation: '[Canadian] history is becoming known internationally, as more and more people from here are interacting with there and sharing what has and is happening here' (Hendeles 2004).

The USA is often held in contrast to the more generous and supportive public funding found in Europe, as Cowen (2006: 45) demonstrates:

> European nations are more likely to have a common core of high culture that defines their national background. The German do not quibble over subsidizing performances of Bach, given his centrality to their history and culture. The American citizenry, more ethnically diverse in nature, and less connected to historical high culture, cannot direct subsidies with equal facility.

Yet the main European countries, the UK, France, Germany, and Italy, have adopted differing attitudes to culture and the state (see, for example, O'Hagan 1998).

The UK is highly centralized with an inordinate focus on London for politics, finance, media, and the arts (see Minihan 1977). This has created a core-periphery mentality. For example, a national news agenda is shaped in the morning by BBC Radio 4's *Today* programme; the national circulation of newspapers also leads to similar issues being covered. Private giving to the arts in the UK suffers as measured against the USA. There are initiatives to encourage private giving: A&B is a catalyst, such as launching the Prince of Wales Medal for Arts Philanthropy in 2008. The Culture Minister is cited by A&B: 'The arts in this country greatly depend upon the generous support of philanthropists. They deserve our profound thanks. . . . I congratulate [those being honoured] and thank the Prince of Wales for his support for the arts and encouragement of philanthropy through this new medal'. Encouraging private giving requires a change of mindset following the establishment of the welfare state by Sir William Beveridge, who (in 1942) identified tackling the five giant problems of 'Want, Disease, Ignorance, Squalor, and Idleness'. There is an assumption that arts and culture – like health and education – are funded through taxation, thus one has already paid. Moreover, tax benefits to encourage private giving may be insufficient to encourage more private giving. The pride Americans have in displaying philanthropic prowess is less evident in the UK; rather, much greater social status is attached to the UK honours system of public and highly visible recognition of merit and service to the nation (i.e. peerage or knighthood).

With the formation of France's Fifth Republic, in 1958 under Charles de Gaulle, Andre Malraux was appointed as the first Secretary of State for Cultural Affairs. Malraux promoted decentralization, namely the development of maisons de culture in regional capitals. At the same time, during the 1960s, the French Government was aware that Paris was losing its lustre and pre-eminence as the world's artistic capital. That there is much visible evidence to suggest that Paris matters most when it comes to arts and culture owes much to the presidency of Georges Pompidou, who went against the general principle of decentralization, and immortalized himself by commissioning a museum of modern art. Giscard d'Estaing pushed for the Musée d'Orsay; François Mitterrand is remembered as the president responsible for the *grands projets/travaux*, including La Défence, Bibliothèque Nationale, L'Opéra, and the Grand Louvre, which have been recognized as part of the architectural patronage of the state. Paris is considered the museum capital of the world. Souren Melikian, in his *IHT* (7/8 March 2009) column, describes Paris as 'the best preserved capital of the Western world with the finest urban layout from past centuries [that] acts like a magnet on art lovers'. This is a prime example of prestige arguments for state subsidy. (On the other hand, the central role of Paris in the contemporary art market, as a site for artistic production and distribution, has been declining since the end of the Second World War.)

The redrafting of the (then West) German constitution following the end of the Second World War made education and culture strictly state (*lander*) and local matters. This highly decentralized system was established as a means to deter the worst aspects of fervent nationalism. (Exporting German culture abroad is severely limited to organizations such as the Goethe Institute.) Post-unification Germany has 16 *landers*. Municipalities compete for civic stature via the arts: each claims to be the most *cultural*. One result of this competition is a widespread distribution of museums, orchestras, theatres, and all kinds of arts activities throughout the nation. There is a much clearer case that the great composers of the Western art music tradition – Bach (1685–1750), Mozart (1756–91), and Beethoven (1813–82) – deserve to be subsidized at home. Berlin, with its affordable rents, has emerged at the outset of the twenty-first century as a centre for artists; however, there appears less interest in developing the city as a site for the trade in contemporary art, with business in dealing still vested in New York and London.

Many consider Italy to be one giant museum. It has been noted by an informed commentator that Italy has to address unique cultural issues, according to Sergio

Romano (in Appignanesi 1984: 12), former head of cultural relations at the Italian Ministry of Foreign Affairs:

> This first Italian particularity is that of having the largest 'open-air' heritage in the Western world. Other countries, of course, have important museums, famous collections, libraries and archives of great historical importance. No other country, however, is forced to administer so important an archaeological and architectural heritage that is unguarded and unguardable. Almost all our cities have a historical centre with notable traces of Roman and pre-Roman civilization. Some have preserved, in whole or in part, a circumference of medieval walls often, especially in Italy, embodying Etruscan and Roman elements. All regions have archaeological sites of great historical interest.
>
> In other countries the number of works of art preserved in churches represents a small percentage of what is kept in museums and private collections. In Italy, thanks to the historical role of the Catholic Church, a conspicuous part of the heritage has a double function: it is an object of aesthetic appreciation by visitors and tourists and also an object of worship by millions of the faithful; and as an object of worship it is in practice as far as administration and security are concerned, an 'open-air' object.

Italy's cultural heritage exists *in situ* and forms part of one's daily experience. The buildings housing art are works of art; for example, the first time visitor to the Uffizi is instructed to appreciate it as a work of art in its own right and to look at the works of art on display during another visit. The lack of a mercantile revolution and the secularization in the three centuries between the sacking of Rome in 1527 – which marked the end of the High Renaissance (associated with the works of Leonardo de Vinci, Michelangelo, and Raphael) – and the Napoleonic despoliation, meant that Italy was able to flourish as a gigantic cultural warehouse. But if this is so, the weight of history can become unbearable. At present, conservation, restoration, and protection are paramount issues, with drastic measures being adopted to combat rampant theft. This means that Italy has adopted very strict cultural property export regulations.

Will so-called sovereign wealth fund (SWF) countries become the next cultural hubs? A SWF is a state-owned investment fund composed of financial assets such as stocks, bonds, real estate, or other financial instruments – often based in foreign countries – that is funded by foreign currency reserves but managed separately from official currency reserves.[5] It is a way to manage government wealth in order to generate a profit (though some have raised concerns that political power is what is being bought when investing in foreign companies). Commodities are a source of sovereign wealth; current account surpluses are another source. As such, certain countries are prominent, namely the Gulf states (such as Kuwait, Qatar, Saudi Arabia, the United Arab Emirates), China, and Singapore. The Abu Dhabi Investment Authority (ADIA) is the biggest; the Dubai Investment Corporation (DIC) was touted as a possible suitor for a football club in the English Premiership; Singapore has the Government of Singapore Investment Corporation (GIC) and Temasek. The success of Switzerland – 'as hub for money and a hub for art as the two aspects complement and reinforce one another' (Guex Walliser-Schwarzbart 2003: 42) – is a model for

Singapore and the United Arab Emirates (UAE). Switzerland's success factors include neutrality (determined non-involvement in both World Wars and absence from supranational organizations such as the European Union), extraordinary political stability (including a lack of major strikes and moderate political parties), banking secrecy, and a secured niche in the capital markets by becoming the prime manager of mobile assets for high net worth individuals (Guex in Walliser-Schwarzbart 2003).[6]

Since the 1990s Singapore has promoted the city-state as a centre for arts and culture. The timing is significant: since becoming an independent republic in 1965, Singapore has pursued a market-based economy, under extremely stable political leadership, with great success. Singapore had become a popular transit point for long-haul air travellers with selling points being shopping and eating. Arts and culture lagged behind, including within the country. The National Arts Council (NAC) Singapore was established in 1991 with 'five strategic thrusts' – nurture and develop the arts, develop capabilities and resources, stimulate broader and more sophisticated demand for the arts, facilitate internationalization and enhance global connectivity, and advocate the importance of the arts – with the following 'vision': 'To develop Singapore as a distinctive global city for the arts' (nac.gov.sg). Additionally, 'four core values' are articulated: passionate ('we believe in what we do and will give our best'); creative ('we are imaginative, resourceful, and innovative'); professional ('we achieve excellence through best practice'); and bold ('we are decisive and dare to change'). Singapore's Ministry of Information, Communications and the Arts has the following 'mission': 'To Develop Singapore as a Global City for Information, Communications and the Arts, so as to Build a Creative Economy, Gracious Community and Connected Society with a Singaporean Identity rooted in our Multicultural Heritage' (app.mica.gov.sg). Some fruits include the Singapore Art Museum, which opened in 1996, and two art fairs, ARTSingapore, established in 2000 as regional affair for southeast Asia, and Showcase Singapore, which opened in 2008 with the participation of international dealers.

The UAE is a federation of seven states (emirates) – Abu Dhabi, Ajman, Dubai, Fujairah, Ras-al-Khaimah, Sharjah, and Umm al-Quwain – that was created in 1971. Located in the southeast of the Arabian Peninsula, a volatile region, it is considered relatively liberal and stable. UAE's GDP/capita is third after Qatar and Kuwait. There has been a desire to diversify its economic platforms, which has included self-promotion as an attractive tourist destination. Abu Dhabi and Dubai have been the most aggressive of the emirates in attracting arts and cultural projects. If Abu Dhabi is positioning itself as cultural hub for museums – Guggenheim Abu Dhabi and Louvre Abu Dhabi are set to open in 2013 on Saadiyat Island, which will also include a performing arts centre – Dubai has cultivated strong links with the international art market, including auction salesrooms for Christie's and Bonhams and the Art Dubai art fair.

Cross-national arts research has distinct political motives. In the absence of a theory on the right (or correct) level of public subsidy (or government support) for the arts, the level of arts funding in other countries continues to be used as a yardstick against which one's own country should be compared. As an example, advocates for greater state support in the USA look across the Atlantic, according to Schuster (1987: 5):

The European numbers have to be high enough to be worth working toward, but not too high so as to be completely out of reach. The American figure has to be low enough to indicate that something is going on, but not very much. The ensemble has to coincide with the popular mythology of relative government generosity vis-à-vis the arts.

As a young nation, the American ideals of freedom and individual initiative, built on a strong suspicion of central authority, underlie the formation of arts organizations in the USA following the Civil War, as private organisms managed like business corporations. On the other hand, in Europe 'a cultural continuity has provided unchanging unity in the individual histories – support for things which endure in spite of crucial changes' (Dorian 1964: 433–34); the principle of government patronage is an outgrowth of royal patronage in maintaining a commitment to culture.

What can be done? This is a related issue. Though commendable, at its worst, according to Schuster (1987: 6), 'this type of research is the search for the extraordinary and makes little attempt to learn from the ordinary' such as

the awkward juxtaposition of arm's length arts councils on top of highly centralized government structures, the implementation of matching grants in situations much more constrained than those where matching grants have been most successful, and the adoption of tax incentives in systems where there is little tradition of private support and little reason to believe that these incentives will have much impact.

Defining conceptual boundaries of the field one is proposing to study is a critical decision in cross-national analysis. Some of the perceived variation in arts support can be explained by differences in the structure of arts support. At the same time, part of the variation in funding reflects real, fundamental differences in arts policies. It needs to be added that the consideration of arts policy via a single funding structure (e.g. comparison of funding levels of the central, government funding agency in each country) is not uncommon and problematic.

The per capita comparison has become the sine qua non of comparative arts policy research. One can readily understand why per capita comparisons are made: large numbers (such as total expenditure) are made comprehensible (by dividing by the population of a country); and the calculation is the first step to comparative analysis because it scales the result of expenditure calculations to control for the relative size of the country. The political process also demands a number, which provides a focal point – possibly an attractive headline figure. In short, 'a per capita calculation is certainly a powerful summary: a simple, easy-to-understand, portable distillation of a multidimensional problem into a single measure' (Schuster 1987: 24). However, care needs to be taken in making and interpreting per capita comparisons. First, how are the numerators and denominators defined? It may be possible to alter what is included in order to obtain a more favourable result. For example, GDP/capita is a recognized figure used in cross-national analysis. As a headline number it is used to indicate the level of wealth and economic prosperity the citizens of a nation share. Other league tables – the United Nations Human Development Index is possibly the most visible – have emerged to incorporate so-called quality of life benchmarks of a nation not captured by GDP/capita, such as forms of unpaid labour, the level of disparity between the richest and poorest sectors of society, and level of democratic participation available to citizens; moreover, the United Nations' index views universal health care and the absence of capital punishment as positive. Second, per capita measurements, as *indices*, are often better at measuring change *within* a country over a period of time; this is distinct from the static snapshot of measuring differences across countries at one particular point in time.

No research agenda is neutral. Skilled arts managers are better equipped to make decisions if they have an understanding of how data is collected and interpreted for lobbying purposes. Quantitative approaches (e.g. surveys) are not more objective than qualitative methods (e.g. long interviews).[7]

CULTURAL ECONOMICS: BAUMOL'S COST DISEASE AND ECONOMIC IMPACT STUDIES

We are aware of John Maynard Keynes's interest in the arts, yet John Kenneth Galbraith (1987: 145) astutely recognized that the most prominent economist of the twentieth century 'was not especially concerned to build bridges between economics and the arts. [Keynes] lived in two worlds; he didn't try to merge them'. The situation has changed as some economists now attempt to apply the tools and concepts of what strives to be the most mathematically precise of the social sciences to the arts. Such endeavours are not without controversy. In a stinging rebuke, political scientist F. F. Ridley (1983: 1) argued that 'the values reflected in the literature do not encourage one to recruit many cultural economists as spokesmen in the interest of culture'.

Alvin Toffler (1967: 142) recognized, at the birth of cultural economics in the 1960s, that 'the very idea of measuring the arts is abhorrent to many'; yet he believed that the arts as an important determinant of the quality of life in post-industrial societies made measurement incumbent. In the early 1970s, Kenneth Boulding (1972: 272) remarked: 'It is clear that there is something, which now exists perhaps only in its embryo, which deserves the name of cultural economics. Because it has not yet taken an unambiguous form, it is obviously hard to describe'; and by the mid-1970s, enough worthy essays had been published to justify an anthology of readings, *The Economics of the Arts* (1976), edited by Mark Blaug. The discussion, in the main, focused on two concerns: the rationale for public subsidies to the arts; and evaluating public expenditure on the arts. The former was advanced in four ways: 'efficiency' analysis of the causes of 'market failure'; 'equity' arguments; positive arguments involving the actual mechanisms by which tastes and preferences are formed; and the 'merit goods' argument that the arts possess intrinsic value (Blaug 1976: 13–24). The political climate in Anglo-American countries starting in the 1980s has meant greater scrutiny of public expenditure.

'Finding a rationale and guiding principles for government support of the arts was one of the major areas of concern of the earliest post-war writings in cultural economics and these issues have continued to recur in the literature ever since'

(Throsby 1994: 20). Two prominent examples are discussed. First, the so-called cost disease associated with William Baumol has been used to account for labour costs outpacing revenue in many arts organizations in receipt of public subsidy. Second, economic impact studies became a major preoccupation – namely the so-called spillover effects of the arts on the economy – and have become an entrenched part of the arts management firmament.

Baumol's cost disease

The study by American economists William Baumol and William Bowen, *Performing Arts, the economic dilemma* (1966), which was disseminated in the influential *American Economic Review* (1965) represents 'a point of origin' (Throsby 1994: 2):

> For the first time a major branch of the arts was subject to systematic theoretical and empirical scrutiny. To those economists who cared to read it at the time, it showed the extent to which their discipline could illuminate a new and challenging area of interest, using familiar tools of economic inquiry.

The study, which focused on 'problems common to theater, opera, music, and dance', was recognized as ground-breaking. As the performing arts had already garnered the attention of foundations, the Baumol and Bowen study was well-timed.

Baumol and Bowen put across a compelling 'cost disease' thesis regarding macro-level aspects of unbalanced growth in the not-for-profit performing arts industry and the impact on the individual performing arts organization. In addition to the constraints facing all not-for-profit arts organizations, namely 'the desire to provide a product of as high a quality as possible and to distribute the product in a manner other than that which maximizes revenue' (Baumol and Bowen 1965: 498), performing arts organizations have severe difficulties in achieving productivity advantages from technological advances and exploiting economies of scale as achieved by other industrial sectors for example. Are performing arts organizations – part of what Baumol (1995) has termed 'handicraft services' – able to generate progressive increases in revenue to outpace relative cost increases, not least of all wage rises of labour? In most cases, the answer is no. Individuals, as performers, are key to the productive process, which is to say that the production is the product itself. Hence limitations and difficulties associated with enhancing productivity. Baumol and Bowen (1965: 500) are explicit in their pessimistic forecast:

> In order to join the ranks of the rising productivity industries, the arts would somehow have to learn not only to increase output per man-hour but to continue to do so into the definite future. Otherwise, they must at some juncture fall behind the technologically progressive industries and experience increases in costs which stem not from their own decisions but from the inexorable march of technological change in other parts of the economy.

The labour-intensive nature of the performing arts and the lack of factor substitution results in productivity lags which, in turn, leads to a so-called income gap. The income gap represents the ensuing shortfall between earned revenues and total expenditures; moreover, it was attributed to structural deficiencies rather than being immediately equated to inadequate management practices (though the latter would obviously aggravate an already bad condition). In the absence of a desire by performing arts organizations to 'reduce the rate of increase in their unit costs by permitting some deterioration in the quality of their product' (Baumol and Bowen 1965: 500), either unearned incomes – public subsidies in the main, but also donations from private benefactors – would make up the difference, or deficits would be incurred (i.e. the arts organization as a patient is not to be cured of its 'cost disease').

The factor price adjustments at the core of the cost disease hypothesis have not occurred to the full extent suggested: the realities of labour markets in the arts mean a gradual erosion in the relative earnings position of workers in the performing arts; rising consumer incomes have gone some way to offsetting the negative effects of ticket price rises forced through cost pressures; moreover, many arts organizations have become more sophisticated in marketing, resulting in higher attendance figures and income. As such, according to Throsby (1994: 15), refinements to Baumol and Bowen's original cost disease thesis have taken place:

> Essentially it can now be said that, while the basic logic of the cost disease is, in its own terms, inarguable, the causal chain linking certain characteristics of production of the live arts to a widening income gap is by no means as inexorable as many have supposed.

'The evidence is conflicting', according to Peacock (1998: 293), 'but the disease seems containable if not remediable through the offsetting rise in value productivity', which is about inculcating taste for improved quality in the overall experience. It has been suggested that Baumol and Bowen's research has been adopted by arts campaigners – there is a crisis, the source of the problem is a cost disease, and the solution is government support – even though, according to Besharov (2005: 426), 'The anomaly is that in a welfare analysis, the cost disease itself does not justify a government response'.

There are complementary ways for performing arts companies to address the cost disease. Broadcasting and recording technology can extend consumption of a single performance. Sharing administrations – as has been suggested by having the London Philharmonic Orchestra and the Royal Philharmonic Orchestra appoint the same managing director – is one way to lower costs; however, it is viewed by critics as a first step to a complete merger and job losses. During the redevelopment period of the Royal Opera House at Covent Garden, there was talk that the English National Opera could share the space with existing tenants, the Royal Opera and the Royal Ballet. Opportunities exist for adjustment in factor use such as performing plays with simpler sets or smaller casts. Of course, there is the risk of so-called artistic deficits resulting from initiatives like synthetic (or so-called canned) music. Another sort of artistic deficit – the use of cheaper labour from central and eastern Europe in staging opera in the UK – has been raised by music critic Rupert Christiansen (London *Daily Telegraph*, 27 February 2001):

Taxpayers contribute about £50 million a year towards subsidising a network of opera and ballet companies, as well as considerable amounts towards the training of singers, dancers and musicians. It makes no sense then to deny these performers opportunities to perform by importing third-rate equivalents who contribute nothing of significance to our cultural life. And the eastern Europeans could well do better to look to Asia, where capital cities such as Singapore and Taipei have been busily building superbly equipped new opera houses without establishing the indigenous companies to house them.

Ellen Kent's Opera and Ballet International and the Russian-based Artsworld appear to be central to these touring shows in the UK, as commercial enterprises without corporate sponsors. Christiansen questions the contractual arrangements of the impresarios (e.g. the current basic rates of agreement negotiated between the Theatrical Management Association and Equity and the Musicians' Union), and asks whether 'eastern-European companies have drained audiences away from our subsidised companies'? These opera productions are performed in (the less expensive) concert format, ticket prices are comparable to musicals, and there is an emphasis on first-time visitors living in mid-sized towns. Notwithstanding his earlier comment, Christiansen (London *Daily Telegraph*, 14 April 2009) noted regret, following Ellen Kent's announcement that she was ceasing tour operations to concentrate on presenting her own productions:

> Kent's activities have long rankled in certain quarters, with 'protectionist' complaints being made to the Arts Council and the Home Office about cheap deregulated foreign labour undercutting performers trained in Britain. I can sympathise with that view. But Kent's tours showed a resourcefulness, flexibility and sheer dogged energy that our comfortably unionised singers and dancers may not feel inclined to emulate.

Opera, as the union of poetry, music, and theatre into an art form, was first developed in Italy around 1600. Opera represents the clearest example of an expensive and labour-intensive form of art with limited capability to exploit technological advances and economies of scale. Andrew Clark, the *Financial Times*'s music critic (8/9 and 22/23 September 2001), puts forward the case that 'opera is an art form that was fully developed in the nineteenth century. It's not just hung up on the past, it's also tied to the economic equations of the past, which render it unacceptably expensive today'. He continues:

> The high noon of opera was the late nineteenth century – the high noon of the European bourgeoisie. Aristocracy was still the leading patron: without King Ludwig of Bavaria, Wagner would have been lost. But without an educated middle class there would have been no audience to fill the large, elaborate opera houses that had been built to replace intimate court theatres.

Today, according to Clark, 'opera has become the opium of a rich and educated minority'. One has to learn the core 'repertoire' (say from *Kobbé's Complete Opera*

Book, an authoritative reference work which includes just over 200 works); it is assumed that one arrives well-versed with plot summaries. Indeed many opera aficionados consider the interval quiz an integral part of the Metropolitan Opera's radio broadcasts. A seasoned opera-goer, who focuses on beautiful voices and elaborate stage decor, should be able to make aesthetic comparisons with previous productions. 'Opera may no longer be a living, pulsating entity but its well-preserved corpse will be worthy of inspection for decades to come', according to Clark.

A high cost per patron is a defining characteristic of the performing arts. How to cover this cost is a key concern. Two alternative solutions – apart from the use of cheaper artistic labour – can be cited: English country house opera and blockbuster musicals. Country house opera represents an art form peculiar to England, with Glyndebourne and Garsington as predominant examples. Both are examples of private initiative (in the absence of direct public subsidy): John Christie built a small opera house as an attachment to the manor house of Glyndebourne, with the first performances taking place in 1934; and in the late 1980s, Leonard Ingrams, a successful banker, decided that his manor house at Garsington could be a second Glyndebourne. Both may be viewed as bastions of privilege, with social exclusivity part of a shrewd commercial equation. For example, there are 7,500 names on the waiting list to join the coveted Glyndeboume Festival Society, and that list is now closed. Members of the Festival Society are offered first crack at tickets, with the corporate market limited to 30 per cent of capacity; the season is generally sold out by opening night, with standing place among the hottest tickets for the general public. Picnicking in the grounds is a key part of the country house opera experience – the interval at Glyndebourne is 85 minutes   and for many, the intermission picnic is more important than the opera. The popping of champagne corks suggests a certain style of dress, which is made explicit for the uninitiated on Glyndebourne's website: 'During the Festival season, evening dress (black tie/long or short dress) is customary'. With under 500 seats, Garsington is attempting to recreate an atmosphere reminiscent of Glyndebourne before the new theatre was built: this means that Garsington is an expensive affair, it represents impeccable style, remains aloof from issues of public arts subsidy, and there is an absence of the corporate season.

Innovation is central to understanding the rise of high cost blockbuster musicals aimed at the mass market (see Caves 2000: 260–61). There is the potential for enormous audiences through touring opportunities and merchandising. Productions associated with Cameron Macintosh and Andrew Lloyd Webber, such as *The Phantom of the Opera* and *Cats*, resemble blockbuster films: the emphasis is on grand sets and dazzling special effects; a high concept (i.e. a storyline that can be encapsulated in one sentence and which can be 'translated' outside Anglo-American marketplaces) ensures less focus on character development or individual actors. The revival of touring companies and modern technology makes the special effects of these shows portable. Heavy promotion is used to gain cross-national reach; moreover, the associated media attention when a flashy new musical arrives in town (whether it is Toronto or Helsinki) helps to generate the buzz necessary for the production to develop wide appeal with economic growth potential (or so-called legs).

An amusing and assuming reference to Baumol's thesis is offered by the artistic director of the Barbican Centre (Graham Sutherland in the London *Guardian*, 1 November 2008):

> The tawdry and demeaning spectacle currently masquerading as cricket in the Caribbean prompted me to consider whether there are any much-loved cultural epic rituals which might 'benefit' from the Stanford treatment. Stephen Moss rightly laments the loss of the game's soul and the potential resulting demise, or at least devaluing, of the five-day Test match form of the game.
>
> Wagner's Ring cycle, or indeed any of his operas, would be ideal candidates for the Twenty20 format. Attract younger and new audiences with shorter forms of his tediously long repertoire, pay your opera stars multimillion-dollar purses for a couple of arias, and allow the resulting box office and sponsorship income to filter down into the grassroots infrastructure of classical music and opera to the benefit of all.

Of course, he is right to end his letter with a wry observation: 'I wouldn't be surprised if someone isn't out there already working on it'.

Economic impact studies

Economic impact studies are highly utilitarian. Such studies seek to quantify the total economic benefits of arts expenditure on a community (local, regional, or national). Major quantifiable benefits may be summarized as direct, indirect, and induced. Direct benefits, or the first round of spending initiatives, result from the expenditures by an arts organization to host the event (e.g. salary bill and cost of supplies). Indirect benefits result from the multiplier effect of spending by an arts organization – from direct benefits – as they ripple through the economy. Induced benefits result from spending incidental to an arts activity (e.g. exhibition, concert, or festival), other than the entrance charge. Much of the impact produced by the arts is associated with these extra-artistic activities (e.g. purchases in the gift shop, food and drink, transport, and accommodation). All these activities, which are said to have been stimulated by the decision to attend – that is to consume – an arts event, generate economic wealth.

Quantification in monetary terms has been used to show that the arts are not 'deficit-ridden spongers'. For example, it is increasingly common to discuss the relative economic impact of the arts in revenue, numbers of persons employed, and wages and salaries *vis-à-vis* other industrial sectors. That discussions of the arts quickly turn to the tourism benefits are now taken for granted.

But to what extent is genuine benefit to urban regeneration outpaced by such rhetoric of event planners and developers? There are general limitations to economic impact studies, according to the director of the Centre for Cultural Policy Studies at Warwick University (Bennett 1995: 24–25):

> The economic impact studies of the 1980s, which attempted to measure the economic importance of the arts, have now been largely discredited. The data on employment was highly misleading. The relationship between the arts and tourism was never proven. And the contribution of the arts to inner city regeneration was

exaggerated. . . . Indeed, it is arguable that the economic impact studies have in fact done a great disservice to those seeking greater public expenditure on the arts. Firstly, these studies have had the effect of trivialising and commercialising significant aesthetic and valuation issues. Secondly, the economic judgment of the arts against economic criteria . . . the advocates of economic impact studies, by failing to see the intrinsic weakness of their own position, will have scored a spectacular own goal.

Cowen (2006: 15) believes that 'we should be sceptical of "economic impact" studies that show the importance of the arts to a community'. Moreover, 'to compound the inaccuracies', according to Cowen, 'economic impact studies assume a "multiplier effect" '. Specific weaknesses have also been identified by Mulcahy (1986: 33–48): the multiplier effects are often overstated; the reliance on the multiplier limits the discussion and invites other industries, which may possess more robust multipliers, to be promoted; it cannot be inferred that the economic effects identified would not have occurred had the arts institutions involved not existed; it is often difficult to identify a single event or attraction as the only reason for a visit to a metropolis; and the long-term induced impacts, arguably of greatest significance, need to include a qualitative dimension.

Yet political imperatives require that extra-artistic aims, such as those addressed by economic impact studies, are considered when applying for large arts grants such as to support capital projects. Economic benefits are being supplemented by qualitative (or non-quantifiable) ones. As a basis for innovation in an economy, arts programming is viewed as making a contribution to wealth creation and improving the overall quality of life of the community. According to Raymond Williams (in Appignanesi 1984: 5):

> It is in fact the great cities of Europe which have been the most successful pro-moters of cultural policy. This again is a contemporary fight to preserve the necessary powers of cities, but it is one in which there is the possibility of relating cultural policy to an actual community rather than to a relatively abstract and centralised state.

This sort of sentiment has served as an organizing motif for prosaic studies produced throughout the 1990s on the importance of cities (e.g. Bianchi 1993; Landry and Bianchini 1995; Worpole and Greenhaigh 1996; Rogers 1997; Hall 1998; Worpole 2000) with examples culled from around the world, stressing the role of architecture and aesthetics as part of a revived interest in urban renewal (e.g. Barcelona is a prime example, with the 1992 Olympics serving as an impetus for infrastructure development including the creation of a large number of small, interlinked public spaces; and the cultural diplomacy agenda associated with the 2008 Beijing Olympics cannot be underestimated). Yet the spirit of Williams is most evident in Pier Giorgio Di Cicco (2007), Toronto's Poet Laureate (2004–10), who proffers 'civic aesthetic' as an antidote to the dominant notion of culture as engine of urban prosperity, as in his 2006 'Address to the Creative Cities Network Conference' (toronto.ca/culture/pdf/poet):

My work has not been typical to the task of a Poet Laureate, but useful to the creative cities agenda. When I came on board as Laureate I was expected to be advocate of the arts. But it was clear to me from the start that the arts would be forever handicapped until they were companioned by the notion of 'civic aesthetic'. Until the citizen saw himself/herself as author of the city, the arts were doomed to remain a destination point and not a way of life. Indeed, this is the vision of creative cities – to generate an ethic of creativity that permeates business, recreation, politics, citizenship. All sectors must be creative, and all citizens aware of their imaginative capacity. Governance must know that creativity opens the door to civic trust, and that civic trust is the foundation of good city building. Trust enables co-habitation, racial concord, mercantile prosperity, safer streets, exciting boulevards and, ultimately, sustainability.

'Proximity – the collocation of companies, customers, and suppliers – amplifies all of the pressures to innovate and upgrade', according to Porter (1998: 90). Why do some regions have more enterprise clusters than others? Clustering may develop naturally because of intrinsic advantages found in a region. Some regions may provide more fertile ground for enterprise development because of the presence of an enterprise culture or a more favourable institutional framework. The size of clusters is limited by the size of the national market if there are barriers to international trade.

Clusters affect competition in three broad ways (Porter 1998). First, being part of a cluster increases the *productivity* of firms based in the area. Firms are offered better access to employees and suppliers. Second, clusters can help to drive the direction and pace of *innovation*, which underpins future productivity growth. The constant comparison with peers (other firms and individuals) is a source of competitive pressure. Third, stimulating the *formation of new businesses* expands and strengthens the cluster itself (e.g. individuals working within a cluster may more easily perceive gaps in products around which they build businesses). Contemporary art fairs are examples of temporary economic clusters bringing together main collectors and dealers and other taste makers: the art scene is performative; it is crucial to generate sales and to build and sustain relationships. It is marked by inter-gallery rivalry: entry selection criteria (peer review of quality and mix of countries for a global orientation), exposure to the public, and art that needs to take on the competition. Art Basel (est. 1970), which is held in June, is described as 'a label, marketplace, and service'; indeed it is 'a brand name that constitutes what would seem an almost unique success story' (Muller in Walliser-Schwarzbart 2003: 36). The immediate success of two recent art fairs – Art Basel Miami Beach (est. 2002), held in December, and the Frieze Art Fair (est. 2003) in London, which runs in October – has helped to create an annual calendar. Satellite (or parallel) art fairs are an indicator of success and buoyant market conditions. Key ones include Liste and Volta at Art Basel, Zoo at Frieze, and NADA (New Art Dealers Alliance) at Art Basel Miami Beach. There is competition to graduate from *emerging* to *established*.

Success breeds success, according to informed opinion: 'The benefits of clusters may be cumulative in that once a cluster has developed, its advantage increases with the size of the cluster', according to an OECD (1997: 157) report on entrepreneurship as a source of competitive advantage in the USA: 'A cluster allows each member to benefit as if it had greater scale or as if it had joined with others formally – without requiring it to sacrifice its flexibility' (Porter 1998: 80). However, clusters can and do lose their competitive edge due to both external and internal forces. There is an 'interesting instability in art agglomeration' (Caves 2000: 31). Artists seeking afford-able studio and living spaces are often the first to consider the potential of industrial warehouse spaces in marginal areas of a city. Loft conversions for members of the professional middle classes and the opening of upscale eateries pose so-called crowding out problems. This is encapsulated by the graffiti slogan: 'Artists are the shock troops of gentrification'. As too many artists get pushed out, they will have to move all over again. Artists living and working in close proximity – the creation of an artistic community – can help to raise the overall quality of work as artists criticize each other's work. Within key markets like New York and London, property, often referenced as the process of gentrification, is never far from art market concerns. For example, SoHo, as the hub of the New York art world since the 1960s, started to give way to Chelsea in the 1990s (following the relocation of the Dia Art Foundation in 1987). The decision of Paula Cooper, one of the first SoHo dealers, to move to Chelsea in 1996 was highly symbolic. Lehmann Maupin opened in SoHo in 1996, moved to Chelsea in 2002, and opened a second space, in 2007, in the Bowery, home to the New Museum of Contemporary Art, which is being touted as a new cultural hub. The YBA scene, led by Damien Hirst and associated with 'Cool Britannia' London of the 1990s, saw the emergence of the East End as a site for contemporary art (production and distribution). White Cube's decision to leave its original site at Duke Street, in Mayfair's West End, for Hoxton Square in 2000 excited much atten-tion.[8] Most significant as a cultural boost was the decision of the then Tate Gallery to locate its museum of modern art south of the River Thames, in the depressed London borough of Southwark. The opening of Tate Modern, in May 2000, was an opportunity to showcase London's thriving contemporary art scene. Moreover, it has helped to redirect pedestrian traffic away from a crowded Covent Garden to the south side of the Thames: Tate Modern, the Shakespeare Globe Theatre, and a redeveloped South Bank Centre (by Waterloo Station) have served as a catalyst to revive the Thames, which has been described by architect Will Alsop as 'one of the biggest holes in London'.

'The mere collocation of companies, suppliers, and institutions creates the *poten-tial* for economic value; it does not necessarily ensure its realization' (Porter 1998: 88; emphasis in the original). A cluster of South Kensington's cultural and academic institutions – the Royal Albert Hall, the Royal College of Art, the Royal Geographic Society, the Royal College of Music, Imperial College, the Natural History Museum, the Science Museum, and the Victoria & Albert Museum – put a bid to the Millennium Fund and the National Lottery for approximately £100 million. Albertopolis, the project name adopted by these eight institutions, was a proposal to create a sense of community, linking the arts and sciences, approaching what Prince Albert had in mind in the euphoric aftermath of the 1851 Great Exhibition. According to the V&A's head of public affairs (National Art Collection Fund's *Art Quarterly*, Summer 1994):

> Albertopolis will not only celebrate 150 years of the site, not only underscore the
> sense of confidence with which we can approach a new age, but will re-equip

national and international institutions of the Albertopolis to consolidate and expand their position as a centre of knowledge, inspiration, object-centred study and creativity into the next century.

The bid was rejected. Critics questioned the conceptual basis of such a Victorian-inspired project as a means to enter the twenty-first century (see Chong 1998). Would a different project name have made the main thrust – to create one of the great cultural quarters of Europe – more appealing?

INSTRUMENTALISM OF THE ARTS AND CULTURE

Arts organizations are subject to external pressures to change by activist and marginalized groups opposed to what they perceive to be bastions of the liberal humanist tradition (e.g. Matthew Arnold's 'sweetness and light'), which critics view as far from being classless and politically neutral. Associations with a wealthy, patron class – arts organizations as elitist playgrounds – can clash with demands for social relevance. The USA, more than any other nation, is marked by advanced social politics where issues of race and sex are vocal and often divisive; however, in many arts organizations, there exists a system of corporate governance marked by a self-perpetuating board of trustees. A distinctively American response, as expressed by consumer advocacy groups (e.g. Nader's Raiders and Adbusters), is to pressure organizations to change. Artists can help to articulate pressing social issues. For example, the Guerrilla Girls, a collective of artists who are women, 'use a rapier wit to fire volley after volley of carefully researched statistics at artworld audiences, exposing individuals and institutions that under-represent or exclude women and artists of color from exhibitions, collecting and funding' (Chadwick 1995: 7). Using the tactics of urban warfare, the Guerrilla Girls' first posters materialized in 1985 in lower Manhattan, signed as 'the conscious of the art world'. 'Do women have to be naked to get into the Met. Museum?' demanded one well-known poster, which depicted a reclining nude Venus wearing a gorilla mask. The answer: 'Less than 5 per cent of the artists in the Modern Art Sections are women, but 85 per cent of the nudes are female'. At the time of the 1993 merger between Arnold Glimcher's Pace Gallery and Wildenstein & Co to create PaceWildenstein, which remains one of the largest art dealers, the *New York Times Magazine* (30 October 1993) featured 'Arnold Glimcher and His Art World All-Stars', with the dealer surrounded by his artists including Chuck Close, Jim Dine, Donald Judd, Robert Ryman, and Saul Steinberg. This portrait of the core contemporary art world, as 'all middle-aged white males', prompted the Guerrilla Girls, in 1995, to comment 'Hormone Imbalance. Melanin Deficiency'. One of the signboards installed by Group Material on the West Wing of Boston's Museum of Fine Arts, in the early 1990s, highlighted the belief that the institution, a public art museum, remains private – that is restricted access – and removed from the experiences of those living nearby in subsidized housing:

It's close to Roxbury and yet aesthetically, culturally, and politically it's the furthest point away. The building looks like a rich white person's house. The museum is irrelevant to Roxbury because Roxbury is a community that has been denied anything that is Boston. I think the museum as a concept is obsolete. So I don't go.

The American approach to apply pressure at a local level with individual initiatives can be viewed alongside the situation in the UK, where one has witnessed an impetus to regulate national arts organizations – namely those in receipt of direct subsidy from central government – such that they address public policy issues, like social deprivation, as a condition of funding. Accountability thus enters the arts manager's lexicon in the UK – and elsewhere – and performance management becomes naturalized. Resistance has been detected. Concern has been voiced that the arts are being diluted – in a patronizing manner – to benefit the socially excluded (Mirza 2006; Fox 2007). The UK-based Manifesto Club (manifestoclub.com) includes an Artistic Autonomy Hub, which seeks to counter social impact measures as key criteria for the arts:

> We are a network of artists, arts administrators, researchers and students who want to defend artistic autonomy in all its forms. A vibrant artistic culture is founded upon artistic freedom. The only limits for artists should be the limits of the discipline and limits that they choose for themselves.
>
> We criticize and oppose pressure on artists to work towards the targets of politicians. We also oppose restrictions on freedom of expression, which ultimately affect all artists who seek to address the experience of contemporary life. We seek to encourage an experimental artistic culture, which is not afraid to make mistakes in the search for truthful forms of expression.

Performance management has become an integral part of measuring any organization. This means shareholder value and profitability in the case of commercial organizations along with customer satisfaction, employee morale, supplier relations, and social responsibility obligations. For arts organizations operating in the absence of profit motivation, performance management includes issues associated with quality, governance, and accountability. How well we are doing in fulfilling our core mission, should be at the heart of performance management. Performance indicators, namely 'statistics, ratios, costs and other forms of information which illuminate or measure progress in achieving aims and objectives of an organization as set out in its corporate plan' (Jackson 1991: 51) should be collected. Of course, such numbers may not offer a complete or accurate representation of genuine mission fulfillment.

It is instructive to understand the context which enables auditing and performance management to be identified with securing institutional legitimacy. Implications associated with the extension of auditing into different institutional settings have been articulated by Michael Power in *The Audit Explosion* (1994). Power (1994: 5) challenges the conventional view of auditing, in terms of its technical and operational qualities, as a value-free exercise: 'Auditing has become central to ways of talking about administrative control . . . It has much to do with articulating problems, with rationalising and reinforcing public images of control'. In addition, there is the view that audits thrive 'when accountability can no longer be sustained by informal relations of trust alone but must be formalised, made visible and subject to independent validation' (Power 1994: 11).

Public accountability has been reframed in relation to concepts such as vision and mission statements, aims and objectives, customer satisfaction, and market competition. This stimulated the significance of performance measurement during the 1990s, not least of all in the UK (with an initial focus on health and education). The 3Es of 'economy, efficiency, and effectiveness' are fundamental to the so-called value for money (VFM) framework which serves to evaluate performance. Two areas are key: the relationship between resource inputs and service outputs; and establishing whether or not the service outputs being provided are those valued by the institution's stakeholders.

The VFM framework 'prioritises that which can be measured and audited in economic terms – efficiency and economy – over that which is more ambiguous and local – effectiveness' (Power 1994: 34). 'Efficiency' as it 'is inevitably put into operation' raises the hackles of Henry Mintzberg (1989: 331, 333–34):

It is not a neutral concept but one associated with a particular system of values – economic values. In fact an obsession with efficiency can force the trading off of social benefits for economic ones that drive an organization beyond an economic morality to a social immorality.

Furthermore, according to Power (1994: 34):

For all its proclaimed sensitivity toward context, VFM demands that effectiveness be quantifiable. It does this by standardising measures of effectiveness (on the one hand) and/or by reducing effectiveness to standardisable measures of economy and efficiency. Either way there is a necessary drift towards 'management by numbers' which enables a drift towards centralised forms of control and displacement of concern about good management.

What actually occurs is a displacement from first-order experts to second-order verifactory activities monitored by overseers. At the same time, there 'is now almost no way reservations about audit can be articulated without appearing to defend privileges and secrecy' (Power 1994: 40).

Performance indicators (PIs) are said to offer numerous benefits to arts organizations. First, more objective benchmarks against which to measure progress are established in order to meet aims and objectives identified in the corporate plan. It goes without saying that PIs are of little value or interest until they are compared with something. The best comparisons are with the institution's past performance (i.e. trend or longitudinal analysis) and targets established for planning purposes (i.e. budget versus actual). However, 'the question of benchmarks or other externally derived standards (rules-of-thumb)' remains problematic; and there is the warning that 'too formal a system of performance management invites working towards good PIs results to the exclusion of pursuing those less tangible goals that were not so easily susceptible to measurement or quantification' (Weil 1994: 347). For example, if performance management is equated with ratio analysis, the backbone of financial analysis, the institution runs into the problem of what Hamel and Prahalad (1994: 8) characterize as 'denominator management . . . an accountant's short cut to productivity'. Second, areas of relative strength and weakness are identified in order to aid the decision-making in allocating resources. The 'real utility of performance indicators', it has been contended, derives from their diagnostic value, as opposed to measures of evaluation and assessment (Jackson in Pearce 1991: 43). This requires monitoring key indicators which serve as early warnings of impending problems. Third, indicators encourage and motivate staff: performance management may support organizational learning such as finding out what visitors find appealing about the organization. On the other hand, there is a worrying perspective: 'The audit explosion is characterised less by an opening up of organisations and more by reinvestment of trust in new bodies of audit expertise and its legitimation through such things as accreditation and monitoring systems' (Power 1994: 26).

'A great deal of care needs to be taken in constructing performance measurement systems. The first imperative is to ensure that the purposes for measuring performance are clear and accepted by everyone' (Flynn 1993: 123). Is it possible to recommend a range of performance indicators for any arts sector which could be used, *inter alia*, to make meaningful comparisons between institutions? There is the opinion that effectiveness indicators 'must always be specific to a particular institution and should never be based on some hypothetical benchmark or standard applicable to all museums or even to museums of a specific discipline, scale, or type of governance' (Weil 1994: 345). Even with efficiency indicators, 'more broad-based comparisons – except, perhaps, for something so generic as staff turnover rates or the total return on endowment – could only be misleading' (Weil 1994: 346). It seems that at best such a form of regulation establishes minimum and often crude standards of acceptable behaviour. To mitigate against the promotion of a rigid set of problematic indicators, there is a need to reframe the boundaries of reference so that greater emphasis is placed on linking PIs more clearly to the corporate planning process.

Two conventional management models (or diagrams) have been proffered as typical of an attempt to communicate how performance assessment fits in with other management practices and processes. Model I is based on a four-level hierarchical relationship between *mission*, *objectives*, *do-wells* (or critical success factors), and *performance measures* (for each do-well) at the corporate level – with an emphasis that PIs 'should be an integral part of the setting and monitoring of strategic direction' (KPMG for the DNH 1994: 14). Linked to the first model, Model II seeks to develop a common framework for performance assessment by attempting 'to link the identification and use of performance indicators into the overall organizational mission and objectives' (KPMG for the DNH 1994: 19). Model II is 'both flexible enough to be customized and robust enough to satisfy government requirements' (KPMG for the DNH 1994: 19); it is made up of five concentric rings with the mission at the centre surrounded by *primary objectives*, *change objectives*, *resources* (e.g. people and space), and *financial resources*. Of course, it is recognized that conventional management diagrams often emphasize the manipulation of numbers at the expense of creating visions. More attention needs to be devoted to considering whether relying on management consultants represents an effective use of an organization's funds. It might be argued that developing management talent within the organization offers better results in the longer term.

The current state of performance management, with its strong auditing alignment, raises philosophical problems about the orientation of neophyte arts managers regarding their training and socialization: 'Audits ensure accountability to individuals as "clients" rather than citizens and it is no accident that the audit explosion has accompanied the displacement of old languages with that of markets, missions, and management' (Power 1994: 54). From a management consultancy perspective, McKinsey & Co (Lowell *et al.* 2001: 153) identify the absence of clear performance measures: 'Rather than capturing the right data to track performance, there is often an emphasis on an "ad hoc assortment of metrics" such as money raised, membership growth, the percentage of repeat visitors, or the ratio of such measures to the cost of a programme'. Moreover, weaknesses are recognized: lack of inter-organizational comparisons; focus on process (e.g. administrative efficiency) and outputs (e.g. number of people served) rather than outcomes (e.g. impact measures focus on progress toward mission and long-term objectives that drive organizational focus); and emphasis on the percentage of donations and revenues spent on overheads, which is a crude measure of fiscal responsibility. A president of the Venice Biennale (Paolo Baratta in *WSJE*, 16/17 February 2001) sums up the problem when attention to detail obfuscates a view of what is important: 'More fundamental than public versus private is the divide between bureaucratic mentality and enterprise. And I mean enterprise not efficiency. Efficiency is a cost-benefit calculation. Enterprise aims at quality'.

Is UK arts policy damaging the arts? This was a question posed by Policy Exchange in *Culture Vultures* (Mirza 2006: 14–15):

> Up and down the country, arts organisations – large and small – are being asked to think about how their work can support Government targets for health, social inclusion, crime, education, and community cohesion. Galleries, museums, and theatres are busy measuring their impacts in different policy areas to prove they are worth their subsidy.
>
> This book is an attempt to break the stifling consensus about arts policy today, and challenge the increasing instrumentalism of policy makers.

The Policy Exchange document, which appeared in 2006, had examples such the DCMS/V&A Funding Agreement 2003–6 in mind. The DCMS/V&A Funding Agreement 2003–6 is a sample contract between a funding agency – the Department of Culture, Media and Sport which was created in 1997 by the newly elected Labour Government to replace the Department of National Heritage – and its client, the V&A Museum, a non-departmental public body in receipt of direct funding from central government, and one of the designated national museums in the UK. The DCMS has four key strategic priorities:

> Enhance access to a fuller cultural and sporting life for children and young people, giving them the opportunity to develop their talents to the full;
>
> Opening our institutions to the wider community, to promote lifelong learning and social cohesion;
>
> Maximizing the contribution which the leisure and creative industries can make to the economy; and

Modernizing delivery, by ensuring our sponsored bodies are set, and meet targets which put customers first.

Six quantitative targets are established by the DCMS:

Total number of visitors;

Number of visits by children;

Number of venues in England to which objects from the collection are loaned;

Number of C2DEs [representing the lower half of the six conventional social class groupings – A, B, C1, C2, D, E – used in the UK] required to achieve an 8 per cent increase by 2005–6 on the 2002–3 baseline;

Number of website hits (unique users); and

Number of children in organized educational programmes both on-site and outreach.

As another example of the new language of impact measures, the Transforming Tate Modern project emphasizes successful factors, which may have helped Southwark Council to grant planning permission:

Tate Modern is one of the UK's top three tourist attractions;

Two million people have taken part in Tate Modern's education programmes;

Tate Modern generates £100 million in economic benefits to London annually;

Tate Modern has generated 4,000 new jobs, mostly in the Southwark area;

Time Out readers nominated Tate Modern as their favourite London building; and

60 per cent of visitors to Tate Modern are under 35.

Grayson Perry, 2003 Turner Prize winner, has challenged politicians and policy makers who seek social policy objects from the arts (London *Times*, 8 March 2006):

New Labour has been pouring money into the arts not just because this is a good thing but because of the belief that the arts will help communities, reduce crime and raise the aspirations of those not educated enough to know whether they like Bartók or Birtwistle. ... While I appreciate that artistic activities may have a beneficial effect on some groups, I do not believe that thrusting mediocre culture targets will improve health, enliven run-down cities or bring C2DEs into the political 'we'. ... The evidence that art has this power is sketchy and based mainly on research commissioned by arts institutions with the aim of advocacy in mind.

Perry might support the MA in Arts Politics at the Tisch School of the Arts (New York University):

Arts politics considers art as both a way of knowing and a kind of action, as an invitation to claim artistic citizenship and a means to democratize the public sphere.

'Art' will be studied as a site of contested representations and visions, embedded in power formations – themselves shaped by specific historical moments and geographical locations.

It is instructive and whimsical to consider an earlier attempt to organize culture. Just as PIs are cited as a contemporary aid to good judgement, Roger de Piles, a French academician, amplified the concept of rule, in the first decade of the eighteenth century, by devising a comparative list of artists appreciated according to four specific criteria. Composition, line (*dessin*), colour, and expression served as domains for artistic judgement in *Cours de peinture par principes* (1708) (see Barasch 1985: 310–77). This is essentially a numbers-driven approach to artistic appreciation – ranking artists in each of the four categories separately – with scoring according to a scale in which a score of 20 represented perfection. On the four categories of composition, design (or line), colour, and expression, Dürer scored 36 (8-10-10-8); LeBrun 56 (16-16-8-16); Leonardo 49 (15-16-4-14); Michelangelo 37 (8-17-4-8); Poussin 50 (15-6-17-12); Raphael 65 (17-18-12-18); Rubens 65 (18-13-17-17); and Titian 51 (12-15-18-6). What de Piles attempted was to give new meaning to rules as acknowledged criteria of judgement. Why, as regards purpose or motivation, we are not certain – possibly at the request of a patron, or for the sake of entertainment rather than for more serious purposes. Like PIs, which are provocative and suggestive, de Piles's distribution of scores makes us wonder what precisely the individual terms meant. Moreover, what does 'expression' mean if LeBrun scores 16, twice as much as Dürer or Michelangelo? According to art historian Svetlana Alpers (1995: 74), de Piles offers a nuanced account of how painting is to be viewed:

> First, in making the distinction Rubens/colour and Poussin/design, de Piles contributed the essential element to a binary structure of taste for art in France. The contrast between a view of Rubens and Poussin effectively divided pictorial taste and practice in France. Second, de Piles's defense of a definition of colour as exemplified in the paintings by Rubens gives a new emphasis to the viewer's experience of painting, and it does this in eroticized terms.

■ ■ ■

What is the proper role of the arts? Any response will always have a political hue, reflecting national tendencies and individual preferences concerning the role of state intervention. Indirect subsidies win favour in the USA, as it encourages individual decision-making of post-taxation income. Widening participation and social access initiatives have taken root in the UK under New Labour as part of a wider civil society agenda. Interesting arts and cultural developments are taking place in the UAE, namely Abu Dhabi and Dubai, with a potential to help shape perceptions of the Middle East. A common trait across nations has been the almost universal adoption of the relatively new language of cultural economics, not least of all economic impact studies, with its attention to factors supporting wealth creation and urban regeneration.

Chapter

3

BUSINESS AND THE ARTS

The business corporation, since its emergence in the mid-nineteenth century, has become a significant social institution. This is a theme pursued by Richard Eells (1967: vii) in *The Corporation and the Arts*, a project/book funded by the Rockefeller Brothers Fund: 'I found myself seeking to explain the interrelationship between the arts and the corporation as decisive institutions in our society'. Certain Americanisms populate the text like 'freedom of creativity and innovation' (in opposition to political totalitarianism of both the Left and the Right) and the language can be evocative: 'Artists and enterprisers at their best are among the prime questioners of our time, along with the philosophers and scientists'; 'They have a common goal in opposing the authoritarian suppression of questioners and the totalitarian pretense of monopolizing all innovation'; and 'All this entails heavy responsibilities both for the artist and corporate executive' (Eells 1967: 220–21). Yet the book retains value more than four decades later. For example, Eells (1967: 222) recognized a corporate-arts antagonism of conflicting cultures (materialism versus idealism), with a hope that 'out of hostilities there may yet arise a synthesis of great value'. This included reference to the spiritual dignity of art. Eells (1967: 284) proffered profitable reading for the corporate specialist in arts relationships: Matthew Arnold's *Culture and Anarchy* (1869), one of the foundation stones of liberal humanism, and the then contemporary work by Richard Hoggart, *The Uses of Literacy* (1957), which has become recognized as a pioneering work in cultural studies.

It is only more recently that 'the possibilities of corporate action in constructing support for cultural pluralism are greater in the areas of corporate policy than corporate giving', mooted by Eells (1967: 263), has been addressed. The lustre of the arts and associations with creativity and human expression can be attractive to businesses in enhancing relationships with customers, employees, and suppliers. The UK-based Business in the Community (BiTC) was established in 1982 to promote the concept that 'building a success business' includes 'improving your environmental impact', 'marketing with a cause', 'investing in a diverse workplace', and 'building healthy communities'.

This chapter starts by examining the roots of business support for the arts, which includes Eells's project (see Chong 2003). Business-backed initiatives in the USA and elsewhere to support prestigious arts organizations, initially through programme sponsorship, have become naturalized as part of plural arts funding. Yet critics appeared from the outset of the arts-business nexus, arguing against the privatization of public culture, and remain today. Next, the role of the arts in enhancing business relationships is discussed with reference to two prominent examples: corporate art collections; and contemporary artists collaborating with luxury brands, including recent initiatives of LVMH. Finally, business learning from the arts has taken root during the first decade of the twenty-first century, with attention on knowledge workers and the value of encouraging creative thinking in all types of organizations.

BUSINESS SUPPORT FOR THE ARTS

The American-based Business Committee for the Arts (BCA) – the first national, business-supported, not-for-profit organization that encourages business to support the arts and provides them with the services and resources necessary to develop and advance partnerships – was founded in 1967 as an initiative of David Rockefeller (in Gingrich 1969: xi; see also bcainc.org; Chagy 1970), chairman of Chase Manhattan Bank, who advocated business understanding and involvement in the arts:

> The modern corporate has evolved into a social as well as an economic institution. Without losing sight of the need to make a profit, it has developed ideals and responsibilities going far beyond the profit motive.

The public has come to expect corporations to live up to certain standards of good citizenship.

Today, the mission of the BCA 'is to ensure that the arts flourish in America by encouraging, inspiring and stimulating business to support the arts in the workplace, in education and in the community'. As such the BCA articulates multiple values of the arts as 'essential to the quality of life in the community'; 'a critical component in K-12 [kindergarten to grade 12] education'; 'good for business'; and as a means to 'affirm and celebrate who we are'. More specifically, six benefits to business from collaboration with the arts are noted: advance the business organization's strategic goals; reach new customers and markets; increase customer and employee loyalty; enhance the business organization's name recognition and its reputation as a concerned citizen of the community; enrich the quality of life in its operating community; and increase its (financial) bottom line.

At its outset, the BCA was answering calls put forward in the Rockefeller Panel Report (1965) that collective corporate action was needed to stimulate support in the arts, and Eells's text, *Business and the Arts* (1967), essentially a publicity document, provided a means for the BCA to communicate its message. The BCA articulated to S&P 500 firms the advantages of closer business dealings with the arts: improving corporate image, increasing sales, aiding recruitment, and attracting industry to an area were cited as direct benefits; at the same time, indirect business benefits to employees, the community, and society as a whole were also perceived. Social benefits came under the broad banner of corporate responsibility (e.g. helping to alleviate the problems of the under-privileged and the plight of the inner city). The seemingly diverse range of benefits reflected concerns being voiced during the 1960s: USA business corporations, like many established institutions, were criticized for being removed from the economic and social crises plaguing larger urban cities. Equally, there was a conspicuous wane in the confidence in American business. Arts sponsorship was presented as one relatively inexpensive way of regaining public support. From the outset, the general gist of the BCA has provoked criticism. Thomas Guback (1970: 132, 134) interpreted corporate sloganeering as 'the good community-minded citizen hid[ing] the ultimate nature of its policies', namely that profits may be counted 'in dollars as well as goodwill'; furthermore, he voiced concern over the formalization of a nexus in which 'the same men are running both spheres':

> While no sphere in society can remain entirely insulated from or insensitive to others, there is a difference between independently-activated response and the kind of cooperation bred and initiated by power and control. Especially now it is untenable that one institution should further extend its influence in monolithic fashion.

This was about the often undisclosed personal benefits to the senior executives, who make decisions about business support to the arts, such as accumulating social prestige and displaying so-called good taste (e.g. Bourdieu and Haacke 1995).

The BCA had high impact. It provided the model for like-minded organizations in other countries: the Council for Business and the Arts in Canada (CBAC), now Business for the Arts (BftA), was established in 1974; in the UK, the Association for Business Sponsorship in the Arts (ABSA), now Arts & Business (A&B), was established in 1976. Initiatives spread across the globe, including the European Committee for Business, Arts and Culture (CEREC) and Asian-based organizations in China, Japan, and Korea. Whereas the BCA was a lead organization at the outset, there is a case to suggest that the UK's A&B is now more engaged in fostering arts–business collaborations.

The founding director of ABSA, Luke Rittner, viewed the British initiative as based on elements of the BCA and the CBAC, with some variation. Unlike the American corporation which feels an obligation, almost a duty to support the arts and cultural life, business firms in the UK were pitched the sound commercial sense of supporting ABSA. Due to higher levels of state patronage, arts organizations in the UK were less dependent on corporate sponsorship (e.g. the Tate Gallery's first example of exhibition sponsorship did not occur until 1982, with support from S. Pearson and Son for an exhibition by the popular Victorian painter, Sir Edwin Landseer). Some were suspicious that initiatives by ABSA would encroach on public funding. ABSA distinguished itself through an interventionist role by administering government schemes designed to increase the level of business sponsorship. ABSA's name change to Arts & Business – with 'working together' as its strapline – reflects a desire to signal that the organization is involved in promoting collaborations beyond business sponsorship. A&B's current research agenda – investment and the funding landscape (i.e. 'a mixed-investment economy for culture is essential for its success and sustainability' particularly 'with a global recession embracing the world the investment and funding landscape in the UK'); culture and brand (i.e. 'arts partnerships as a good source of brand value for business, by aligning corporate brands with the values associated with a cultural output'); and creativity for competitiveness' (i.e. 'the arts offer one of the most dynamic ways to encourage people to think and behave differently') – strikes at the synthesis Eells mooted in 1967.

The links between business corporations and large, metropolitan-based public art museums are well established. For example, the inaugural meeting of the BCA, in January 1968, under the chairmanship of C. Dillon Douglas was convened at the Metropolitan Museum of Art (Met), where he was a trustee. Given the Met's stature, it attracted the most socially prominent and financially powerful individuals in New York. It is not surprising that the Met established the first 'Corporate Patrons Program', in the mid-1970s, a most visible venture under the auspices of its Business Committee. 'The business behind the art knows the art of good business' was the pitch for the Corporate Patrons Program, from an undated Met pamphlet, which served to promote the benefits of membership:

> Many public relations opportunities are available at The Metropolitan Museum of Art through sponsorship of programs, special exhibitions and services. These can often provide a creative and cost effective answer to a specific marketing object-ive, particularly where international, governmental or consumer relations may be a fundamental concern.

Critics consider museum–corporation relations as they have developed in the USA since the 1960s. Two decades ago in *Museum News* (January/February 1988), the role of promotions was recognized:

> In an era of heightened consciousness of public relations, image building is the most powerful incentive behind corporate museum patronage. Since sponsorship of temporary exhibitions provides the most exposure, it's not accidental that, historically, the biggest funders have been those with image problems.

In practice, arts organizations have seldom refused corporate sponsors based on the corporation's business activities. The director of the Tate during the ascendancy of corporate sponsorship, Alan Bowness (1980–88), included the following comment as part of a debate on arts sponsorship: 'We have only discriminated against sponsor-ship by tobacco companies partly because the government itself takes a different attitude to this form of advertising' (in Coombs 1986). Even now the exclusion criteria used by the FTSE4Good Index is limited to the traditional (and problematic) sectors of tobacco, defence, and nuclear power. The Association of Art Museum Directors (May 2007) recognizes that corporate sponsorship arrangements generate high publicity for business corporations and art museums:

> At the same time as museums have experienced unprecedented growth as cultural, educational and civic centers – serving more than one billion people

annually – American businesses have increasingly viewed art museums as venues for sponsorship both to serve the public interest and to address corporate relations and marketing goals. This circumstance provides obvious opportunities to art museums that seek to expand and diversify their base of financial support and to reach new audiences. At the same time, it presents challenges to ensure that the museum's educational mission is not compromised by external commercial interests.

Since the cancellation of a proposed solo exhibition at the Guggenheim in 1971 – viewed by many as an act of censorship by the museum – Hans Haacke (1981: 56) has devoted himself to exposing what he feels to be an unhealthy alliance between the arts and multinational enterprises:

In the 1960s the more sophisticated among business executives of large corporations began to understand that the association of their company's name – and business in general – with the arts could have considerable and long-term benefits, far in excess of the capital invested in such an effort.

Haacke's critique complements Erik Barnouw's *The Sponsor* (1978), and has much in common with what sociologist Herbert Schiller (1989) labels 'the corporate takeover of public expression'. Haacke (in Bourdieu and Haacke 1995: 17–18, 17) discusses patronage as 'a tool for the seduction of public opinion':

I think it is important to distinguish between the traditional notion of patronage and the public relations maneuvers parading as patronage today. Invoking the name of Maecenas, corporations give themselves an aura of altruism. The American term *sponsorship* more accurately reflects that what we have here is really an exchange of capital: financial capital on the part of the sponsors and symbolic capital on the part of the sponsored. Most business people are quite open about this when they speak to their peers. Alain-Dominique Perrin, for example, says quite bluntly that he spends Cartier's money for purposes that have nothing to do with the love of art (emphasis in the original).

Haacke seeks to highlight the contradictions inherent in the business-arts nexus, issues those most involved in forming alliances and collaborations feel are unimportant, or are quick to gloss over. According to Bourdieu (in Bourdieu and Haacke 1995: 1), Haacke has 'a truly remarkable "eye" for seeing the particular forms of domination that are exerted on the art world to which, paradoxically, writers and artists are not normally very sensitive'.

Consider three works by Haacke (*Art in America*, May 1990) – *On Social Grease* (1975), *MetroMobiltan* (1985), and *Helmsboro Country* (1990) – which seek to offer interventions, as he puts it:

The more the interests of cultural institutions and business become intertwined the less culture can play an emancipatory, cognitive, and critical role. Such a link will eventually lead the public to believe that business and culture are natural allies and that a questioning of corporate interest and conduct undermines arts as well. Art is reduced to serving as a social pacifier.

On Social Grease (1975) was an early attempt by Haacke to emphasize the extent to which initiatives by corporations in the arts originate 'from the public relations department of a company that wants to project an image of modernity, optimism, efficiency, and reliability' (Sheffield 1976: 122). Integral to the work, and framed as a plaque, on an august corporate edifice, was a pronouncement attributed to Robert Kingsley, an Exxon executive: 'Exxon's support of the arts serves as a social lubricant. And if business is to continue in big cities, it needs a more lubricated environment'. In *MetroMobiltan* (1985) Haacke sought to draw attention to unease he felt with a specific relationship, namely that between the Mobil Corporation and the Metropolitan Museum of Art. Nuanced references were made to the brochure distributed by the Met's Corporate Patrons Program and Mobil's activity in supporting recent exhibitions at the museum, including a show of ancient Nigerian art (1980) and works by New Zealand tribal artists (1984). At the same time, Haacke included as part of the piece the justification proffered by Mobil to opposition demands to terminate petroleum supplies to the South African police and military, as represented in text from *MetroMobiltan* (1985):

> Mobil's management in New York believes that its South African subsidiaries' sales to the police and military are but a small part of its total sales . . . Total denial of supplies to the police and military forces of a host country is hardly consistent with an image of responsible citizenship in that country.

In *Helmsboro Country* (1990), a similar play on names is used to draw attention to the links between Senator Jesse Helms, who opposed NEA funding to support exhibitions of works by both Robert Mapplethorpe and Andres Serrano, and Marlboro, the world's most popular cigarette brand, owned by Philip Morris, a corporate contributor to the electoral campaign of Helms. The sculpture, in the form of cigarette packet called Helmsboro, reflects this relationship. Moreover, Helms's attempt at arts censorship is set alongside Philip Morris's attempt to promote its support of the nation's founding beliefs by distributing copies of the USA Bill of Rights, which includes the First Amendment of the USA Constitution (1791), namely the freedom of worship, of speech, of the press, of assembly, and to petition the government.

From Haacke's perspective, there is the sense that multinational enterprises use the arts as a qualifier of character, hoping that symbolic associations with well-known arts institutions will be more important than the pragmatic description of what the firm produces, and its commercial relationships. Haacke has been phenomenally influential in the social critique of institutions. There are affinities to the political aesthetics of the Guerrilla Girls, Andrea Fraser, Fred Ward, and Carey Young. Haacke offers a conceptual framework to *Privatizing Culture: corporate art intervention since the 1980s* by Chin-tao Wu (2002) and *Culture Incorporated: museums, artists and corporate sponsorship* by Mark Rectanus (2002).

Corporate support is part of the plural funding mandates that many (national, regional, and local) governments seek to encourage in the face of competing demands for public subsidy in areas such as health, education, and social welfare. For example, the Association of Art Museum Directors has made the case, in several discussion documents during the first decade of the twenty-first century, that revenue generation is an investment in the public service of art museums. Arts organizations should not be viewed as subservient in fundraising and sponsorship negotiations with business organizations. Arts organizations are not coerced; rather a commercial transaction between two parties is at play. To be successful, it must be mutually beneficial: this is an issue of fit (or congruence). Following negotiations, a contract is signed between the business corporation and the arts organization for the exchange of agreed benefits and obligations – money or in-kind services or goods (such as labour or equipment) for an arts organization – over a period of time (e.g. one-off, one to three years, or three to five years are common markers). Both parties want to be able to measure the sponsorship: what is the cost to participate? What is the benefit from participation? The business corporation will assess the return to its sponsorship outlay – say in brand awareness – to ensure that a maximum benefit has been derived from the expenditure. Pro-active management is crucial. For example, UBS sponsored the reopening of New York's Museum of Modern Art in 2004 and the rehang of Tate Modern in 2006. This is consistent with UBS's then art banking arm. However, both sponsorship arrangements raised some concerns of aesthetic interference: MoMA allowed exhibition space for display of art from UBS's corporate collection; the size and location of the UBS corporate logo at Tate Modern intruded into the space for works of art. The AAMD (May 2007) has recognized the complexities associated with 'managing the relationship between art museums and corporate sponsors':

> In managing their relationships with corporate sponsors, art museums directors face an additional challenge. Some corporations may engage in unfavorable or unethical business practices, or may market controversial products or services. Others may seek to showcase products or services within a museum context or attempt to exert undue influence over the context of museum programming. The museum director and his/her board of trustees have the responsibility to determine whether sponsorship of museum programs by such businesses is consistent with the institution's interests and to act accordingly in accepting and managing – or rejecting – such sponsorship.

There is also a case to consider whether greater reliance on public (state) support is better.

The most significant impact of lead organizations like the BCA and ABSA/A&B, for example, in promoting business alliances has been to inculcate the current arts industry environment. For example, the BCA estimated total American business sponsorship of the arts in 1967 at $22 million; 30 years later the figure was $1.2 billion; in 2006, the figure was $3.16 billion. Business corporations feel comfortable supporting the arts and perceive value in collaborations: to advance the firm's strategic goals; to reach new customers and markets; to increase customer and employee loyalty; to enhance the firm's name recognition and its reputation as a concerned citizen of the community; to enrich the quality of life in its operating community; and to increase its bottom line. Arts organizations deem support by big business as an essential ingredient for financial success, which is often necessary for artistic projects to be realized. Moreover, arts organizations and artists recognize that they have lessons of value to businesses in developing greater creativity and intuition among a firm's employees and throughout a firm's operations.

Altruism and enlightened self-interest are two general arts–business positions. The altruistic stance addresses social benefits by recognizing that business corporations have 'assumed a central role in industrial society that the military organization or the religious community has occupied at other times and in other places' (Strum 1985: 158). However, corporations do not exist by divine right: 'The corporation like the Sabbath, was not made for its own survival. Its legitimacy depends on whether its meaning is truly representative of the meaning of life itself' (Strum 1985: 158). Philanthropic initiatives or charitable giving by publicly listed business corporations, such as setting aside a percentage of pre-tax profit to be donated to charitable organizations, have been supported by organizations such as the Committee Encouraging Corporate Philanthropy (CECP), self-characterized as 'an international forum of business [leaders] focused exclusively on corporate philanthropy', with a mission 'to lead the business community in raising the level and quality of corporate philanthropy', the Minnesota Keystone Program, and the UK-based Business in the Community (BiTC). Such corporate largesse – with corporate giving being direct benefits from funds disbursed to anyone other than shareholders – has been criticized by the neoconservative economist Milton Friedman (1962), who influenced so-called Reaganomics of the 1980s. Friedman interpreted business involvement beyond narrowly prescribed parameters of maximizing shareholder wealth – the corporate executive is an employee of the owners of the business, who seek profit maximization – as not only fiscally irresponsible, but potentially harmful to society. Corporate spending on social responsibility is a form of taxation, unless 'own self-interest' is a by-product of the expenditure.

With an enlightened self-interest perspective, the firm garners more tangible benefits without necessarily forfeiting broader societal concerns, since 'increasing sales and spreading goodwill will no longer be mutually exclusive objectives but can be goals which complement each other' (Mescon and Tilson 1987: 59). For example, BiTC has championed cause-related marketing: collaboration between a for-profit and not-for-profit in which a good cause is used to help market a good or service (e.g. transaction-based in the case of giving money to charity for each item sold). Friedman would appreciate that cause-related marketing is not philanthropic even though a not-for-profit is beneficiary; rather it is a subtler form of marketing. Environmental activist George Monbiot views the involvement of business in the areas of education, health, social welfare, and the arts – essentially the type of not-for-profit sectors sought in cause-related marketing initiatives – as a form of exploitation preying on deficiencies in public (state) support. Monbiot used his column in the London *Guardian* (31 July 2001) – in advance of the twentieth anniversary of BiTC, in 2002, with the Prince of Wales as president – to take BiTC to task for 'privatizing our minds' by 'reaching those parts of our consciousness untouched by conventional marketing': 'cause-related marketing is a new form of social control' used by the key members of BiTC, which he identified as 'Tesco, Safeway, Asda, Granada, Barclay's, Shell, BP, McDonald's, Diageo, and Whitebread', namely 'the companies most responsible for destroying small business and undermining our communities'.

Corporate social responsibility – with cause-related marketing as an example (see critique by Porter and Kramer 2002: 58) – is a reality, yet one which poses challenges for arts organizations, according to the SMART Company (2005: 14):

> First, businesses are looking more favourably on the arts activities that engage the community or address social problems. CSR professionals are more interested in funding community-based art, and concerned about charges of patronage or elitism, are moving away from traditional forms of corporate hospitality. Marketing professionals indicated a sensitivity to the emerging CSR environment to see the reputation benefits of including a community element to major arts sponsorship. Second, CSR has changed thinking in terms of evaluation. This move to greater transparency is forcing companies to prove the value of their spend on the arts – but the direct impact of the arts on society is often harder to prove than other good causes.
>
> Research shows that the arts sector faces stiff competition for funding from community budgets. Companies consider arts organisations to be less good at evaluating impact, and without the evidence for how arts activities benefit communities, it is hard for companies to justify significant funding.

Prioritizing social issues is essential for business corporations, according to Porter and Kramer (2006: 85): 'Social issues in the external environment that significantly affect the underlying drivers of a company's competitiveness in locations where it operates'. For example, ExxonMobil now views energy resources as more than oil and gas. (In a similar manner, British Petroleum uses the lower case 'bp' to position itself as an energy firm 'beyond petroleum'.) ExxonMobil engages in programmes to support education, health, and infrastructure (which includes health and safety) in communities in which the firm operates, namely developed countries like the USA and developing countries in Africa. Of ExxonMobil's community investments totaling $202.6 million in 2007, 'arts and culture' received only $8.8 million.

ARTS ENHANCING BUSINESS RELATIONSHIPS

Eells (1967: 289) noted that 'art pays': 'In its crudest form, this acceptance of art into the house of business is the corporate art collection'. Of course, much has changed in the intervening four decades. Damien Hirst has designed a collection, called 'Warhol Factory X Levi's Damien Hirst', using Levi's Original 501 jeans as a blank canvas, as part of The Warhol Foundation for the Visual Arts (with the final product priced at $80,000). It represented an attempt by three brands – not to mention the exclusive retailers – to collaborate for mutual benefits. Two categories of the arts enhancing business relationships are discussed in this section: corporate art collections, though conventional, remain important; and contemporary artists collaborating with luxury (fashion) brands represent an example of creative industries.

Corporate art collections

The act of collecting art and the contents of the art collection are important for corporations and professional business services (e.g. law, banking, accountancy, and management consultancy). The trend in corporate art collecting is mostly environmental as large offices have spaces to fill; at the same time, art humanizes the work environment. International Art Consultants (Harris and Flowers 2001), in a study on corporate art collecting commissioned by A&B, note that art within the working environment is 'a device for subtly reminding people about values and aims of the company' and serves as 'a stimulus for "engaged brain" thinking, contributing to a healthy office environment as a visual counterpoint to ever increasing technology in the workplace'. Bonhams, the third largest international auction house, addresses the utilitarian benefits of art within a corporate setting: a corporate collection can provide enormous marketing benefits and assist team identity and pride within the company; active involvement has brought about a popularization of corporate collections; and today's corporate collections are likely to have been built on the basis of, 'what's right for your brand?'. Bonhams, like Christie's and Sotheby's, recognizes the potential of corporate art collectors by offering a complete range of services: acquisitions, curatorship and management, valuations, sales at auction, private sales, and sponsorship and exhibitions.

Financial services institutions have used art as a point of differentiation and to address – at least before the current banking crisis – a somewhat staid, conservative, and uncreative image. Deutsche Bank through its 'Art at Work' initiative has amassed what is described as the world's biggest corporate collection, with 50,000 works of art in 1,000 branches. The collection is mainly affordable works on paper by contemporary artists produced after 1960; larger, more expensive works in main reception areas are a notable exception. Moreover, Deutsche Bank sponsors exhibitions, art fairs such as London's Frieze, and art museums, namely the Deutsche Guggenheim in Berlin and the Hara Museum of Contemporary Art in Tokyo. An American bank based in the City of London cites key characteristics of its corporate art collection: 'we buy what we like' has been a motivating theme; an art advisor is used alongside key buying guidelines, namely that works cost less than £10,000 each and that each purchase is by a twentieth- or twenty-first century British artist who is recognized or special in some way; the object is not to provoke questions such as what is art; works of art can be conversation pieces to set the tone of a meeting, but simply looking beautiful on the wall is also crucial; and 'the art collection strategy has never been one of let's make money, though recently some works which were sold – they no longer suited the mood – did well'. In order to remain viable a corporate collection needs to keep the following criteria in mind: emphasize 'the quality of the art in the collection' in order to have validity; have 'an underlying philosophy supporting the business objects'; ensure that the collection has a 'clearly defined scope'; consider how well the art is displayed such as integrating art into the architecture of the building; and consider cataloguing and documenting the collection and how it might be used for educational purposes. 'Is the collection financially robust and still developing?' is a final point, according to International Art Consultants (Harris and Flowers 2001).

In an age of changing corporate identities through mergers and acquisitions, corporate collections do come under scrutiny from shareholders, thus there needs to be a sound history of financial justification as well as flexibility regarding the collection's scope. 'Like private collections, corporate ones are constantly developing and often require disposals by sale', according to Bonhams. Lyon & Turnbull, the largest auction house in Scotland, has been successful in securing high-profile sales. The Drambuie sale in 2006 was one of the largest art sales in Scottish history with sales of £3.2 million. The collection had been led by three generations of the Mackinnon family, owner of Drambuie, the whisky liqueur brand, however falling sales of the liqueur meant that the company, now largely out of the family's control, engaged in a major sales of assets. In this case, works of art in the collection were viewed as inactive (or non-productive) assets – until they were traded for cash. The sale of the Deloitte Art Collection in 2008 raised £850,000. Deloitte inherited the former Arthur Andersen Art Collection in London in 2002, as part of the aftermath of the Enron scandal. Deloitte's decision to move offices in London – redecorating – invited the sale of art.

Contemporary artists collaborating with luxury brands

Crossover is often associated with mixing high art and popular culture. Examples from art music include the Kronos Quartet, Nigel Kennedy, Vanessa Mae, Yo-Yo Ma, the Opera Babes, Bond, and the contemporary opera, *Monkey: Journey to the West*, by Blur's Damian Albarn, in collaboration with director Chen Shi-Zheng and Gorillaz artist Jamie Hewlett, which premiered at the Manchester International Festival in 2007. Architect Frank Gehry has partnered with Tiffany & Co as part of the jewellery retailer's so-called democratic luxury initiative. Recent high-low fashion examples include fashion designers such as Stella McCartney and Karl Lagerfield collaborating with fast-fashion retailers such as UK's Top Shop, Sweden's H&M, and Spain's Zara. When art translates into fashion it is also an example of crossover, whereby two different disciplines are jumbled to create something new, fresh, and very marketable. A&B commissioned Ledbury Research (2007: n.p.) to study 'creative liaisons' between the luxury industry (e.g. brands like LVMH, Montblanc, BMW, Paul Smith, Laurent-Perrier, and Maxmara) and the arts:

> Luxury brands have for centuries been closely involved with culture and the arts. It's not surprising. The roots of most luxury goods are to be found in the hands of artisans. Today we more commonly call them designers. Though they could equally be perfumers or master distillers. Whatever we call them, artistry is their preserve.
>   . . . so it's little wonder that throughout history the commercial cousin has again and again been attracted to the unique, unfettered vision of the individual: a vision that inspires, challenges and illuminates. Such association has heightened their aesthetic and their perceived value.

Alcohol brands have sought the assistance of contemporary artists. As a most prominent example, each year since the end of the Second World War, Chateau Mouton

Rothschild has commissioned an artist to decorate its label (e.g. Jean Cocteau in 1947, Henry Moore in 1964, Picasso in 1973, Warhol in 1975, Keith Haring in 1988, Francis Bacon in 1990, and Robert Wilson in 2001). A similar label design initiative with living artists, Beck's Canvas, was launched by the beer brand – now part of the Anheuser-Busch InBev portfolio of beers including Budweiser and Stella Artois – in 1987, starting with Gilbert & George. Warhol was Absolut Vodka's first artist, in 1985, for what has become the well-known ABSOLUT ART campaign. Indeed its commercial and creative success has held to spoof advertisements by Adbusters. As an activist organization 'dedicated to examining the relationship between human beings and their physical and mental environment', Adbusters has sought to de-glamourize the consumption of alcohol, by drawing attention to the harms of excessive consumption such as impotence, hangovers, and death caused by drinking and driving.

ARTCO (artcollc.com) was established by art world insider Cary Leitzes, as part of the art boom of the mid-2000s, to partner brands with contemporary artists for creative collaborations:

> ARTCO is the vehicle for bringing together today's visionary artists and forward-thinking brands. ARTCO's expertise is in making the right connections between the two parties for innovative, creative collaborations that result in original, exclusive products, merchandise, ideas, concepts and more. It's where commerce and culture converge.
>
> The innovative ideas and themes resulting from these collaborations created a buzz, increased brand awareness and amazing new products that got customers shopping.

Clients include Pepsi Co, MAC Cosmetics, Banana Republic, DKNY, and Jones New York. As an exercise in global marketing, ARTCO assembled a group of twelve artists from different countries, who were commissioned to create original packaging for Pepsi addressing the cola brand's tagline, 'Create the life you want to live', for their respective country. ARTCO helped Banana Republic develop an arts initiative with 13 artists working in various media creating works, installed on a three-year rotating basis, throughout the retailer's 500 global stores. Noted for work that revolves around the concept of speed and its relationship to urban settings, Yoon Lee was commissioned by DKNY to create an original bottle design for two fragrances, Be Delicious and Be Red. Mass market clothing line Jones New York sought to reposition itself higher up the fashion market by working with artist Ryan McGinness to create a logo for a children's charity project.

Selfridges, in trying to position itself as a destination department store in London, has commissioned artists to create site-specific works: UK artists such as Sam Taylor-Wood and Julian Opie were the first ones, with more recent examples including contemporary Chinese artists such as Wang Qingsong and Song Dong. Rei Kawakubo, creator of the high fashion label Comme des Garçons, opened the Dover Street Market, a retail outlet set over six floors, in London's Mayfair, in the mid-2000s, with attention to what can be described as a curated display of clothes:

> I want to create a kind of market where various creators from various fields gather

together and encounter each other in an ongoing atmosphere of beautiful chaos: the mixing up and coming together of different kindred souls who all share a strong personal vision.

We hope to make DSM more and more interesting. I enjoy seeing all the customers coming to DSM dressed in their strong, good looking and individual way. I would like for DSM to be the place where fashion becomes fascinating.

In this regard, it is not dissimilar to the installations of contemporary artist Sylvie Fleury.

The most successful contemporary artists have been involved with high-profile collaborations in fashion, not least of all in the arena of limited-edition handbags such as Tracey Emin with Longchamp, Richard Prince with Louis Vuitton, and Julie Verhoeven with Mulberry. It is instructive to bear in mind that luxury brands are often part of global conglomerates: LVMH was created by the merger of Moët & Chandon and Henessey and Louis Vuitton in 1987; PPR was founded by François Pinault with brands now including Gucci, YSL, and Bottega Veneta; and Cartier, Van Cleef & Arpels, and Montblanc are owned by Richemont. (In this regard, Italian luxury brands like Giorgio Armani, Prada, Bulgari, Versace, and Ermenegildo Zegna are unusual for not being part of global conglomerates.)

The recent case of LVMH's Louis Vuitton brand is instructive. LV was dealing with an image problem, struggling to create a more contemporary identity with younger customers. LV's identifiable signature look – brownish colour leather handbags with tiled logos – was becoming stodgy and dull alongside fresh labels starting to compete in the handbag business. LV asked designer Marc Jacobs, also a prominent art collector, to update the line. Jacobs, sensing the growing popularity of Japanese art, sought a partnership with Takashi Murakami. At the time, Murakami was an emerging Japanese artist on the international art scene. Variously called Japan's Warhol or Japan's Hirst, Murakami founded KaiKai Kiki, a studio-factory practice, in 2001, for the production and promotion of works of art, the management and support of a select group of young artists (e.g. Chiho Aoshima, Mr., Aya Takano, Chinatsu Ban, Mahomi Kunikata, and Rei Sato), and the production and promotion of merchandise. Murakami's art reflects popular Japanese animations (anime) and comics (manga). Superflat was coined by Murakami to describe his art practice, namely a way to mimic the two-dimensional medium of his work.

The LV and Murakami partnership is not particularly contentious: it is essentially a commercial arrangement between a luxury brand and a contemporary artist. Murakami has also collaborated with Kanye West by designing the album cover of *Graduation* (2007). Moreover, there are links between West and LV: West references the luxury brand in 'Gold Digger' (2005): 'Cutie de bomb / Met her at a beauty salon / With a baby Louis Vuitton / Under her arm'; and West has designed a limited-edition collection of LV footwear.

The success of LV–Murakami is expressed by Ella Darcy (2007), a style-fashion blogger:

Murakami was a big reason I started to buy LVs. It started out so innocently, beginning with a pochette covered in cherry blossoms (pink on brown). Then I bought another one, in a different color (red on cream). I chased every future Murakami piece I could afford, from owning two cherry handbags (one of them a runway piece accented in bright red lizard – GORGEOUS!) and a wallet embellished with a panda. Not to mention the variety of clutches and wallets I bought with the colorful monogram on white canvas. (Never was a fan of the black canvas.) I even succumbed while on a trip to Italy. . . . I stood in the Venice LV store like a deer in headlights, and I HAD to buy. So I did (emphasis in the original).

The involvement of a public art museum such as the Los Angeles Museum of Contemporary Art (LAMoCA) with its Murakami exhibition (October 2007 to February 2008), including of the collaboration with LV, does raise issues regarding exhibition collaborations between American art museums and for-profit enterprises. The AAMD (March 2006) recognizes that such collaborations have become more prevalent:

> Proponents of exhibition collaboration with for-profit enterprises often make their case by citing changes in our global culture. Their argument is that 'education' and 'entertainment' as well as 'art' and 'experience' are becoming more and more fused. Moreover, the growing sense of cooperation between for-profit and not-for-profit ventures in many other aspects of daily life has further broken down traditional barriers between these kinds of organizations.

Yet the AAMD also warns of pitfalls:

> Most importantly, there are many in the museum profession who argue that the general public holds its tax-supported art museums to a standard that requires that fulfillment of mission will take precedence over short-term revenue generation.

Darcy (2007) opines on LAMoCA's ill judgement:

> While the curator at MoCA thinks that having the store within the exhibit breaks the barrier between low and high art, I don't know if I buy that. If that's the case, why are these bags costing $800–900 each? Why not lower the cost? And is it about art anymore when pieces right then and there are sale? Are the pieces on exhibit for sale, too?
>
> Also, why isn't MoCA getting a cut of the profits? MoCA isn't even charging LV rental space for the shop either. Maybe MoCA needs to invest in some finance guys to help them out here. Sounds like Bernard Arnault got his way and found another way to make money without giving anything up.

It goes without saying that LV is the big winner. Bernard Arnault of LVMH, in an interview with *Harvard Business Review* (Wetlaufer 2001: 118), emphasizes the importance of 'star brands', which he describes as being 'timeless, modern, fast growing and highly profitable'. Arnault believes that 'there are fewer than ten star brands in the luxury world' as 'it is very hard to balance all four characteristics at once

– after all, fast growth is often at odds with high profitability – but that is what makes them stars. If you have a star brand, then basically you can be sure you have mastered a paradox'. Of course, some fashion insiders contend that luxury in the hands of conglomerates stripes away the original basis of luxury associated with artisan production; moreover, craftsmanship by a family-owned business is much rarer. In the view of Dana Thomas (2007), Hermès, famous for its Birkin handbag, is the only genuine luxury brand. Thomas cites LVMH as an example of how luxury has lost its lustre. 'Louis Vuitton: a luxury brand is dead, a fashion brand is born', according to the *Luxe Chronicles* (22 May 2008).

The need to reinvent the brand as with the Murakami collaboration at LAMoCA is important, according to Arnault: 'a star brand is current – or you could call it fashionable. It is edgy, it has sex appeal, it is modern. In some ways it fulfills a fantasy. It is so new and unique you want to buy it. You feel as if you must buy it, in fact, or else you won't be in the moment. You will be left behind'. Bernard Catry (2003), programme director of LVMH's corporate university, has discussed the manufacturing of 'rarity' by luxury goods companies – like magicians pretending to do so by offering an illusion of scarcity – as a way to expand into new luxury market segments. 'Enticed by new sales perspectives, luxury firms started to shift from actual to more virtual supply constraints. This refers to the well-known limited edition or special series policies', according to Catry (2003: 13), who cites borrowing from the art world, where limited edition prints offer an opportunity to exploit the original.

BUSINESS LEARNING FROM THE ARTS

The so-called knowledge economy is supposed to be based on the advanced skills and capabilities of human resources (that is labour or employees). It is said that successful firms need to hire, train, motivate, and retain the best people. Even the UK's most politically progressive newspaper, *The Guardian* (24 May 2008), serves as a media vehicle for corporate creativity to be advertised. Creativity has been touted as a competitive advantage for all types of organizations. 'Creative thinking is one of the most precious resources we have', according to a recent advertisement by Shell: 'Inspiring creative thinking is fundamental to Shell's success as an energy company. We operate in a complex environment, where demand for energy is accelerating while supplies of responsible and sustainable energy are becoming increasingly difficult to secure. To overcome these challenges and deliver progress to our customers, we have to employ creative thinking and persistent problem-solving'. Not unlike the Shell example, Barclays Wealth's advertisement – in advance of the current financial crisis – cited Dorothy Parker: 'If you want to know what God thinks of money, just look at the people he gave it to'. A corporate prompt – 'Wealth. What's it to you?' – is followed by a proposed course of action:

At Barclays Wealth, we have always recognized that wealth means different things to different people. We can help you protect your wealth, grow it, use it, and pass it on. And, if like Ms. Parker, you are a passionate believer in philanthropic causes, we can even help you give it away.

Of course, such corporate sloganeering is ripe for parody. Artist Carey Young (2008) 'appropriates business ideas and techniques within her work in order to explore ideas of creativity, strategy, and progress':

> I have been collecting slogans about corporate creativity for the last decade. It's a little like building some vast textual graveyard of the imagination stone by stone, except this is no mausoleum: such slogans express corporate vision for the future, a desire to be associated with imagination, innovation, with artistic endeavour and the avant-garde new. This image of imagination allows firms to suggest they have a handle on the future, and as a result, a greater market worth. These slogans have not only accumulated on my computer like a virus, they are also everywhere outside it: in advertisements, on the TV, in public space, in our galleries. *Think Different. Invent. Imagination at work. Where imagination begins. It's not that hard to imagine.* A repetitive beat, an echo: the sound of the market's systems and images in endless call and response.
>
> The strange thing about these slogans is, in fact, that most are very hard to remember.

'One doesn't manage creativity. One manages *for* creativity', according to Teresa Amabile (2008: 102; emphasis in the original) of Harvard Business School, who has been a key advocate of the role of creativity within organizations. Creativity is a meeting point of three components, according to Amabile (1998): above-average abilities in terms of expertise and knowledge (technical and intellectual); creative thinking skills (how flexibly and imaginatively people approach problems); and task commitment or motivation (intrinsic as more important than extrinsic factors). There is an emphasis – as acknowledged by others working in the area, as well – that some degree of creativity can be unlocked in all employees: tap ideas from all ranks; encourage and enable collaboration; and open the organization to different perspectives. The work environment is important, according to Amabile (2002), if the managerial practice of creativity is to take root and flourish: there is a challenge of matching people with assignments; freedom means offering autonomy; it is essential to make the scarce resources of time and money available; design of teams needs to be mutually supporting and diverse, share excitement, generate a willingness to help team members, and recognize the uniqueness of other team members; supervisory encouragement is about avoiding negativity; and organizational support should encourage information sharing and collaboration. It is notable that Amabile (2008: 101) has *not* championed the arts in her articulation 'that creativity is essential to the entrepreneurship that gets new businesses started and that sustain the best companies after they have reached global scale'.

Management consultant Charles Handy has been a progenitor behind current interests in what and how the arts can improve business. In trying to look beyond capitalism, Handy (1997: 9) advocates 'Proper Selfishness': this 'search for ourselves' is an 'optimistic philosophy' based on the belief that 'we are ultimately decent people' and 'we best satisfy ourselves when we look beyond ourselves'. The arts are central to this journey of self-discovery, according to Handy, who believes that business can learn from the arts. Handy is not alone. The 'staff and organizational development' benefits through partnerships between business and the arts has grown significantly, according to the then creative director of A&B (Tim Stockil in Hadfield 2000: foreword):

> It has been driven, we believe, by an increasing awareness that creativity is one of the key differentiators of future business success. This growing realization has led many companies to explore ways of fostering and encouraging creativity and innovation in their staff.

A&B has commissioned several reports on arts and creativity during the first decade of the twenty-first century: *A Creative Education* (Hadfield 2000) offered a review of the role of arts and creativity in MBA and executive development programmes; how the arts can improve business by fostering creativity was discussed in *Creativity in Business* (Sandle 2004) and *(Re)Educating for Leadership* (Bewisck, Creamer, and Pinard 2004); and *Artful Development* (Stockil 2008) sought to answer 'how different art forms can address business issues'. A range of arts-based activities have emerged as suitable to engage managers to think outside of their daily experiences, according to Bewisck, Creamer, and Pinard (2004: 29):

> A single arts-based exercise or course can help skill development; continuing and challenging engagement with the arts can expand thinking and develop better problem solving. This is accomplished by increasing the emotional sensibility to both self and others through exposure to creative ideas and experiences that are foreign to day-to-day business life. These foreign experiences must be attended to with concentrated reflection, and this response must recur often enough to become accepted and typical behaviour with the arts. It then needs to be consciously transferred to other situations.

That knowledge is now viewed as a primary source of economic productivity – which is consistent with Richard Florida's creative class thesis – offers a partial explanation for the current attention on the arts as offering solutions to business. Howard Gardner (1983) has argued that individuals are made up of multiple intelligences, which has been adopted as a conceptual framework.[1] For example, Gardner is cited by Handy (1996: 60–63), who signals out the importance of 'interpersonal intelligence, the ability to get things done with and through other people', which is to suggest that creativity is linked to managerial leadership. The overall thrust is that intelligences may be developed or improved, hence the cases of Handy and the A&B-commissioned reports.[2] Indeed Ci: Creative intelligence (creative intelligence.uk.com) was established, in 2005, by Tom Stockil, formerly A&B's creative director:

> Nowadays, there is an ever-increasing interest in exploring creativity and the attributes or 'intelligences' that help people to be creative.
> So many businesses, anxious not to get left behind, started to look around to see who could help re-ignite the creativity of their people. Not surprisingly, many of them started to turn to the arts and artists – people whose work demands a continuous flow of creative abilities. Could business people learn from them? They could – and they do.

The sorts of processes and techniques used by artists, often honed over centuries of artistic endeavour, are precisely the processes that encourage creative intelligence. And creativity does not just relate to problem-solving. A creative approach to learning, leadership, management, interpersonal relations, culture, values, organisational development, communication, change or any other aspect of organisational life is what will distinguish the successful company from the failure in the 21st century.

Given Handy's populist appeal amongst the managerial classes, one is able to recognize his desire to reverse the accepted sequence such that the arts provide new insights for corporate managers.[3] For example, the first Arts & Business Week, as featured in the *Financial Times* (5 March 2001), focused on 'the idea that the creators of wealth and the creators of culture share ideas and experiences with the aim of precipitating more joint projects': 'Business guru Charles Handy will lecture on the importance of creativity in business, and executives will be encouraged to visit companies that have effectively used artists, from actors to dancers to painters, to improve productivity'. There was a decided accent on learning how so-called generators of culture can help to unleash the latent creativity of corporate managers, which raises the productivity level of corporations.

Meditations on organizations and the nature of managerial work have been a long-standing theme for Handy.[4] Adopting an increasingly self-referential perspective, a series of Handy's texts from the mid-to late 1990s – namely *The Search for Meaning* (1996), *The Hungry Spirit* (1997), and *The New Alchemists* (1999) – focused on the importance of the arts in times of structural transformation. To contribute (i.e. by making a difference to the world in some way) is, according to Handy, at the apex of his three-step approach to the search for meaning in life. But before one can start to contribute, one needs to find oneself. Handy believes that the arts provide a way to find oneself. This is a central theme in *The Search for Meaning*, which Handy (1996: 16) delivered as a keynote lecture in 1995 at the London International Festival of Theatre (LIFT):

> For me the theatre is a window on the world, as are all the arts. One does not have to be an expert in the theatre or any of the arts in order to get meaning from them. All you have to do is to sit, look, listen and, above all, think.

Two points seem to be implied by Handy: the unique individual (as spectator) is the focus of attention; and art, through its innate qualities, has the capacity to make one a better person. That works of art can perform a self-help role, or offer a guide to living, is pursued as a theme by Handy (1996: 66): 'We need a new dream of society where everyone is enabled to be an artist in this great game of life'.

This process of self-discovery is based on the notion that everyone is in some way a special artist. Consider the following passage by Handy (1997: 263–64), which is redolent with spiritual comfort:

> For me the *Resurrection* [by Piero della Francesca] carries a metaphorical meaning rather than a conventional religious one. I am free, goes that message, to break

free from my own past and to recreate myself. If I do so, I will be stronger and more sure. Even if my life up to now is counted as a failure by many, as was the life of the man in the painting, the best is yet to come. . . . The best is always yet to come if we can rise from our past.

There is no need to question the sincerity of Handy's sentiments. However, is there an emphasis on the excesses of contemporary society, namely an overtly self-referential perspective based on a simplified solace of immediate self-improvement?

The management truism that change is the only constant, suggests a link to the arts: 'Change is an inherent attribute of the arts. . . . Art is about changing the world and our perception of the world' (Stockil 2008: n.p.). However, what appears to be a return to the mystical power of art might be challenged as a reactionary position; at best, it needs to be viewed with scepticism. For example, sentimental beliefs regarding the therapeutic value of the arts have been raised by literary critic Harold Bloom in an interview with *Harvard Business Review* (Coutu 2001: 67):

HBR: One of the most vexing topics in business is change. What can you learn about change from literature?

Bloom: Business people are fooling themselves if they believe that the self can change easily. . . .

HBR: Are you suggesting that through change you become a better person – perhaps more caring, or even more productive?

Bloom: No, not at all. . . . At the same time, I believe that literature does have a fundamental truth to teach in regard to change: change always arises out of the unexpected. . . . By reading great literature, you can prepare yourself for surprise and even get a kind of strength that welcomes and exploits the unexpected.[5]

Bloom seems to suggest that change from reading literature is not direct; it cannot be exploited in a mechanistic manner, as associated with accounting techniques or popular guides to good living.

A somewhat quotidian rhetorical ploy is used by Handy to support his desire to see business and the workplace becoming more like theatre. Handy cites the admiration of a corporate manager following a performance by Cirque Plume: ' "Why do we have to bribe our people with so much money to work as well as this. Are we missing something?" ' (Handy 1996: 72). Many management gurus, as Gibson Burrell (in Alvesson and Willmott 1992: 69) notes, use a similar rhetorical trope to identify with the desire of upper management to channel and retain enthusiasm, skill, and adrenalin in the workplace; it is about seeking pleasure in the organization as a means to control producers.

Indeed the past decade has seen the growth of slick, multimedia shows, such as Cirque Plume, Cirque de Soleil, De La Guarda, and the Shaolin Wheel of Fire, in which technology is matched with acrobatics to create a new sophisticated form of circus, starring human beings instead of animals. But does Handy idealize the teamwork of arts organizations, and the notion that artists show great skill in the game of life? Two points are raised when one looks below the surface. First, is the principle of the performance fundamentally sound? This is essentially an issue of authenticity and a commitment to aesthetic integrity. Handy's corporate manager may well have made his comments in reference to the Shaolin Wheel of Fire: members of the troupe also perform extraordinary feats with flair and precision. Yet concern has been raised about what is perceived to be an uneasy mixture of ancient tradition and contemporary spectacle. Is there more to the Shaolin monks than circus tricks? Second, participation in making decisions has been challenged as a facet of all arts organizations: 'An orchestra is not a democracy but a dictatorship. The interpretation and presentation of this complex repertoire cannot be pieced together as a kind of consensus among the musicians', according to Henry Mintzberg (1979: 370).

What is behind the current experiment in business education with corporate managers learning from the arts? How have the arts been co-opted to perform a role in staff and organizational development?[6] A&B has commissioned several reports: *A Creative Education* (Hadfield 2000), *Creativity in Business* (Sandle 2004), *(Re)Educating for Leadership* (Beswick, Creamer, and Pinard 2004), and *Artful Development* (Stockil 2008). *A Creative Education* highlights that 'the arts provide rich and varied ways to complement management learning' (Hadfield 2000: 24). The general emphasis is that creativity is not only something restricted to so-called creative people, thus it is a matter of looking at new ways to foster those talents. Several strands of involvement are cited. First, business schools in the UK, including the London Business School (LBS), Cranfield, Henley, and Cass at City University (Hadfield 2000: Appendix 2), have started to incorporate the inculcation of so-called softer skills, including those associated with the arts and creativity as a means to encourage new ways of thinking by students. Notions of the leader as performer or conductor emphasize enhancing teamwork roles which are identified with successful companies. Second, in illustrating 'the practical applications of the arts in business' (Hadfield 2000: 13–22), attention is devoted to so-called high culture pursuits (with the inclusion of jazz being a noticeable exception), with generators including institutions of culture (like the Royal Shakespeare Company and the Royal Academy of Arts) and individual artists (e.g. musicians, actors, and poets) operating freelance consultancies. Corporations are represented by businesses associated with A&B (e.g. Orange, Starbucks, and Ernst & Young). Third, participants, according to examples, are 'senior executives', 'top middle managers', and 'promising employees' (Hadfield 2000: 22, 21, 16); in other words, workers with so-called elite identities. Creativity needs be applied by the employee to strengthen the commercial objectives of the sponsoring organization, according to Hadfield (2000: 16), as the case study of Halifax working with A&B reveals:

Halifax plc are keen to prepare *promising employees* for promotion. Under its Succession Planning Partnership Initiative, these employees, working in partnership with a personnel team, assess their developmental needs against ten core competencies. They then participate in project work and study programmes to facilitate their development. They are able to take time from their current roles, but have to demonstrate a *return on investment* through: presentation to their Regional General Manager to share their learning; and *enhanced performance* on returning to their existing roles.

A programme was developed with Richard Hahlo and Geoffrey Church, from the Royal National Theatre, who use their theatre skills to facilitate this learning (my emphasis).

As the Halifax example demonstrates, selecting employees to attend creativity workshops may be viewed as a retention tactic; it also represents a way for the firm to make better use of the intellectual capital and expertise of workers, which is controlled on an individual basis.

The market in creativity training, according to Sandle (2004) in *Creativity in Business*, has developed beyond Handy's advice to 'sit, look, listen and, above all, think'. Three types of artistic interventions are identified. *Role playing* involves artists – namely actors in this case – who had skills of direct relevance to business. *Total participation* offered business an opportunity to consider wider implications of the overlap between the skills that the arts had in abundance such as team work, communications, adaptability, flexibility, and passion. With *issue-based creative training* there is a case being made of an increasing range of issues that the arts could be used to address. 'The greatest strength of artistic interventions in a business context is the impact that they have on a personal level. Although business objectives can be based on changing a group's behaviour, for example, improving communication or the way a team works together, the motivation for change is most likely to come through an individual's experience of the training' (Sandle 2004: 9).

In *(Re)Educating for Leadership* (Beswick, Creamer, and Pinard 2004), two successful case studies of how the arts can improve business are recounted from business Unilever's Catalyst project headed by Alistair Creamer, a musician – and business education – Babson's MBA candidates are taught creativity by Mary Pinard, a humanities professor – with the approval of the Boston Consulting Group (as Ted Beswick is the BCG's historian). Unilever's new business strategy, adopted in 1999, sought to develop greater creativity and initiative among the firm's people and through its operating companies.[7] Catalyst was the name given to a project whereby artists and arts organizations would collaborate with Unilever – Lever Fabergé was the first division – to help address business issues in four areas: mindsets, behaviours, communication skills, and wider business initiatives. Pinard lead a creativity stream for MBA candidates at Babson, which has a strong focus on entrepreneurship. Managing ambiguity is a touchstone, according to Bewisck, Creamer, and Pinard (2004: 31), hence the role of poetry:

> The aesthetic perspective one must apply when understanding the arts is what can lead to change. Aesthetics can be a confusing world because it is sometimes explained as an appreciation of beauty, sometimes as an appreciation of the arts, and sometimes as a heightened perception through the senses.

The last sense of change is the key one from a business sense of usefulness. It is about empathy – to see from a different perspective – which may necessitate breaking away from the familiar and comfortable. This resonates with the view of Edgar Schein (2001: 81–83), of the MIT Sloan School of Management, on the role of art and the artist: 'art and artists stimulate us to see more, hear more, and experience more of what is going on within us and around us'; 'art does and should disturb, provoke, shock, and inspire'; 'the artist can stimulate us to broaden our skills, our behavioural repertory, and our flexibility of response'; 'the role of the arts and artists is to stimulate and legitimize our won aesthetic sense'; 'analysis of how the artist is trained and works can produce important insights into what is needed to perform and what it means to lead and manage'; and 'most important of all, the artist puts us in touch with our creative self'.

■ ■ ■

It is acknowledged that the presumed High Aesthete notion that the glory of art is in its utter uselessness has long gone. Utilitarian mandates are an important part of most aspects of society. From a conventional perspective, capitalism's reverential hat-tipping to the arts – say in the form of building a corporate art collection or by becoming a corporate sponsor – offers a public relations benefit to the commercial enterprise. (Of course, one is able to understand the pressure of arts organizations to chase plural funding sources, and it is an economic necessity of many working artists, musicians, and actors to supplement their artistic incomes.) There is the case that the corporate manager was promoted as the cultural hero of the twentieth century. But in many respects, this is not enough. Many corporate managers at the start of the twenty-first century desire to be viewed as cultivated men and women. In a secular world marked by democratic elections, it is recognized that the invitation for the corporate man to assume the role of the sage is enticing, according to Bourdieu and Haacke (1995: 41):

> Today, an increasing large fraction of owners and upper management throughout the world graduate from the best schools. Although they may not be great intel-lectuals, those who dominate the economic world, the owners of industry and commerce, are no longer the narrow-minded bourgeois of the nineteenth century. In the nineteenth century, artists such as Baudelaire and Flaubert could oppose the 'bourgeois' as ignorant or dim-witted philistines. Today's owners are, often, very refined people, at least in terms of social strategies of manipulation, but also in the realm of art, which easily becomes part of the bourgeois style of life, even if it is the product of heretical raptures and veritable symbolic revolutions.

But is it going too far to expect the arts to actually work for business?

But what are the ties that bind? The role of the BCA, a lead American lobbying organization, is examined; a critique which draws on Hans Haacke offers a sharp reminder that the arts may be used as a social lubricant to enable business to be conducted. The therapeutic value of the arts is gaining attention from business through promotion by the likes of Charles Handy and the UK's A&B. On the other hand, critics view this engagement as reactionary: it is based on conservative liberal humanist sentiments, and represents another form of social engineering to control workers.

SECTION II

Relationships with Stakeholders

4

OWNERSHIP AND CONTROL OF ARTS ORGANIZATIONS

Ownership and control of arts organizations implies issues of oversight and governance. The commercial sector of the arts, which is the focus of the first section, can be divided into two main categories: personal capitalism associated with owner-operated or closely held organizations; and managerial capitalism of large corporations either publicly listed or under private equity. The relationship between financial ownership and management control is a topic of long significance in corporate governance, in response to the rise of the publicly listed corporation during the twentieth century. To accentuate the relevance to arts management, attention is drawn to business models from commercial arts organizations: art market intermediaries, namely art dealers and auction houses; and a music company, EMI, acquired in 2007 by private equity firm Terra Firma. Pertinent issues regarding the corporate governance of not-for-profit arts organizations – namely the role of trustees in linking the governance and management functions of the organization through a 'chief executive' and the often knotty relationships associated with elite arts patronage – are addressed in the second section. In the third section, institutional isomorphic change is based on the work of sociologists Paul DiMaggio and Walter Powell, who contend that certain conditions result in the homogeneity of organizational forms and practices. How do institutional pressures make organizations within the same field such as art museums and opera houses resemble one another? 'Philosophies of philanthropy', a complementary appendix, addresses fundraising, a traditional view of philanthropy, and the emergence of so-called venture philanthropy.

COMMERCIAL ARTS ENTERPRISES

Commercial or for-profit enterprises, through two industrial revolutions, have been transformed from rural and agrarian to industrial and urban. Some of these developments, namely the separation of ownership and control in the rise of corporate capitalism, are instructive to better appreciate the currency of three categories of commercial arts organizations, which share profit as a bottom-line motive: owner-operated, publicly listed or quoted, and large private equity.

First, owner-operated enterprises include most art dealers, dance studios, independent record labels, and arts and cultural management consultancies (e.g. Lord Cultural Resources, AEA Consulting, and Morris Hargreaves MacIntyre). They are essentially small businesses with original founders, family members, or closely held retaining a continuing commitment to personal management of their business. It is therefore characterized as personal capitalism – the traditional sense of management-ownership – where financial ownership of the business is not separated from management control. The most successful are essentially entrepreneurial in that they represent the success of risk-taking: start small, prosper, and grow much larger within a relatively short period of time. In theatre, there are the examples of Andrew Lloyd Webber, Cameron Macintosh, and Ed and David Mirvish. David and Robert Heffel have been able to transform the art dealership founded by their father into Canada's largest auction house. Yet many small businesses, with a strong family-orientation, are not entrepreneurial in the sense of being risk-averse and staid.

Second, a public listing on a major stock exchange such as the New York Stock Exchange (NYSE) or the London Stock Exchange (LSE) is a key way to raise capital through investors (shareholders or stockholders who are the owners). This includes some of the most well-known media companies in broadcasting and entertainment such as British Sky Broadcasting, CBS, DreamWorks Animation, Sony, Viacom, Walt Disney, and Warner Music. Sotheby's, listed on the NYSE (under BID) as a specialized consumer service, represents a rare example of public listing for an art business; its direct rival Christie's is privately held (as are virtually all smaller auction houses).[1] A core theme in the case of the large, widely held, publicly listed corporation is the rise and entrenchment of managerial capitalism, namely the separation of ownership and control. In practice, passive shareholders, who gain a financial benefit from ownership (hence references to democratic capitalism), are separated from control over management decision-making that has devolved to salaried managers.

Third, private equity is, according to the British Private Equity and Venture Capital Association (BVCA), 'medium to long-term finance provided in return for an equity stake in potentially high growth unquoted companies'[2] – that is, capital and management combining to explore or exploit a business opportunity. Finance in return for an equity stake means that managers become owners. An unquoted company is one that is not publicly traded on a stock exchange. A start-up seeking investors is one common example of private equity. Another example occurs when there is a buyout of a publicly listed firm by a private equity firm. A prominent example from the commercial sector of arts and culture is the acquisition of music company EMI by Terra Firma in August 2007. Terra Firma is a private equity investment vehicle established by Guy Hands, who remains chief executive officer, in 1994.[3] Terra Firma, according to its Annual Review 2007 (n.p.), 'invests in large, asset-backed and complex businesses that have been overlooked, under-valued or misunderstood by the financial community'. In doing so, Terra Firma needs to 'add value through involving ourselves directly in the companies [we] buy' by 'working alongside management to overhaul the business both strategically and operationally'; 'This often involves introducing new initiatives, processes and procedures in order to change the behaviour and culture of a company'. Such initiatives have been controversial at EMI. It goes without saying that 'nurturing a business to a higher level of performance' is measured by financial return on investment; however, Hands (in Terra Firma's Annual Review 2007) suggests wider benefits of wealth generating, as a nod to corporate social responsibility mandates:

> In restructuring and reorganizing businesses, Terra Firma does, of course, also seek to make a return for its investors. However, it is often misunderstood exactly who gains from such investment performance. At Terra Firma, our largest group of investors are pension funds, both public and private, and the ultimate beneficiaries of strong investment performance are the members of those schemes.

Of course, others investors include insurance companies, sovereign wealth funds, and high net worth individuals. The investors are limited partners so are not involved in either the day-to-day affairs of the businesses or investment decisions, which is in the hands of general partners, who also have a financial stake as investors.

In all three categories of commercial enterprises in arts and culture, decision-making is often done with reference to audited financial statements – namely the balance sheet, income (or profit/loss) statement, and cash flow – and financial ratios – measuring short-term solvency (liquidity), long-term solvency (leverage or gearing), and profitability – are important to investors, creditors, and others.[4] In particular, publicly listed companies need to follow reporting regulations, which are monitored by the Securities and Exchange Commission (SEC) in the USA and the Financial Services Authority (FSA) in the UK. Stock market data is vital in the case of publicly listed companies as it is used to calculate key financial ratios, such as EPS (earnings per share) and the P/E (price/earnings ratio).[5] By its nature, the P/E ratio is a prospective ratio (as the stock market builds future prospects into the present share price). Privately held firms, whether small and owner-operated (like art dealerships) or large and involving institutional investors (such as EMI under Terra Firma), do not have to contend with share price movement, which they suggest offers a longer time horizon for decision-making.

Relationship between financial ownership and management control

The relationship between financial ownership and management control, which is part of contemporary decisions in corporate governance, has undergone dramatic changes. Adam Smith's *The Wealth of Nations* (1776) remains important when it comes to championing the role of capitalism. In particular, a passage in Book IV, Chapter II is often cited:

> He [every individual merchant] generally, indeed, neither intends to promote the public interest, nor knows how much he is promoting it. By preferring the support of domestic to that of foreign industry, he intends only his own security; and by directing that industry in such a manner as its produce may be of the greatest value, he intends only his own gain, and he is in this, as in many other cases, led by an invisible hand to promote an end which was no part of his intention. Nor is it always the worse for the society that it was no part of it. By pursuing his own

interest he frequently promotes that of society more effectually than when he really intends to promote it. I have never known much good alone by those who affected to trade for the public good. It is an affectation, indeed, not very common among merchants, and very few words need be employed in dissuading them from it.

The so-called invisible hand, interpreted as emphasizing individual and private initiatives in pursuit of profit, is considered by Smith – and his followers at the Adam Smith Institute – as the best way to maximize the common good.[6] Smith's world was one of many small and local merchants. Of course, the business context has changed since Smith's time. The first industrial revolution, of the eighteenth century with the development of textile mills, steam-engine power, and iron founding, meant a shift of labour-production to the factory. Two classes were created: the so-called bourgeoisie or capitalists as those who as individuals own or have ownership interests in the instruments of production and hire labour to operate these instruments; and the proletariat or workers (who operate as free labourers). The second industrial revolution, starting in the mid-nineteenth century, has been chronicled by the business historian Alfred Chandler (1977; 1990), who highlights the rise of managerial capitalism in the USA due to three-pronged investments in manufacturing, marketing, and management. Managerial capitalism is distinguished from personal capitalism, where personal management (of the owner-operator) is essential.

The separation of ownership and control, as a facet of the emergence of the so-called corporate enterprise system of capitalism, was first advanced by Adolf Berle and Gardiner Means in *The Modern Corporation and Private Property* (1932; revised second edition published in 1968), which remains a seminal text on corporate governance. By the late 1920s Berle and Means (1968: xv) noticed the growing dominance of the corporate form: increasing decision-making power in the control of corporate management, and the increasingly passive position of shareholders or stockholders (as interchangeable to denote owners of publicly listed corporations):

> The corporation becomes the legal 'owner' of the capital and thus has complete decision-making power over it; the corporation runs on its own economic steam. On the other hand, its stockholders . . . have and expect to have through their stock the 'beneficial ownership' of the assets and profits thus accumulated and realized, after taxes, by the corporate enterprise. Management thus becomes, in an odd way, the uncontrolled administrator of a kind of trust having privilege of perpetual accumulation. The stockholder is the passive beneficiary, not only of the original 'trust', but of the compound annual accretions of it.

Management as the uncontrolled administrator means that administrative coordination was better than market mechanisms – as proffered by Adam Smith – in enhancing productivity and lowering costs. The advantages of coordinating multiple units within a single enterprise could not be realized without a managerial hierarchy. Managerial hierarchy – increasingly technical and professional – becomes its own source of permanence, power, and continued growth. Over time, such professional structures of control become separated from ownership.

So-called Corporate America (or Big Business) grew to dominate branches and sectors of the economy, and in doing so, altered their structure and that of the economy as a whole. The result by the 1950s was a growing reliance on professionally trained managers: those at the operational level in charge of business functions like marketing, human resources, accounting, and operations; and so-called executives – including the chief executive officer and president (and other members of the senior management team) and the board of directors – who are charged with guiding the company towards profit.[7] This entailed an assault on the structures and habits of personal and familial enterprises. Share/stockholders, who are legal owners of publicly listed corporations, develop a passive relationship to their companies.

Institutional shareholders rather than private individual shareholders gain importance as corporations become larger with the number of shares increasing, according to Berle and Means (1968: xx):

> A very large number of shares are not held by individuals, but by intermediate fiduciary institutions [pension fund trusts maintained by corporations or groups of corporations for the benefit of employees and mutual funds, namely a portfolio of assorted stocks] which in turn distribute the benefits of shareholding to participating individuals.

There are at least two consequences, which continue to resonate (not least of all during the current financial crisis): the proportion of citizens in advanced capitalist societies who, to some degree, rely on the shareholding form of wealth has increased; and, at the same time, it has removed the individual still further from connection with or impact on the management and administration of these corporations.

Berle and Means (1968: xxvii) were able to articulate the value of publicly listed corporations to individual shareholders:

> Passive property – notably, stock – increasingly loses its 'capital' function. It becomes primarily a method of distributing liquid wealth and a channel for distributing income whose accumulation for capital purposes is not required. The corporation may, and indeed is expected to, retain earnings for the maintenance and enlargement of its capital plant and operations. The stockholders' right to spend the income from the liquid value of his shares as he pleases is guarded as a defense of his right to order his own life.

The wide distribution of shareholding is one way for the community to be better off. Berle and Means (1968: xxxv) also raised societal concerns about the responsibilities of corporations beyond a financial bottom-line to investors:

> Profits are an essential part of the corporate system. But the use of corporate power solely to serve stockholders is no longer likely to serve the public interest. Yet no criteria of good corporate performance have yet to be worked out. . . . Can criteria for good performance be developed to guide corporate management and inducements be provided to encourage the good? What chances would be needed

to make it true that action by corporate management in its own self-interest serves the public interest?

Private equity helps to form, develop, and reshape companies with high growth prospects, according to the BVCA (2004), and is a way for managers to become owners. This means a stronger link between financial ownership and management control. Private equity firms – equity securities in operating companies that are not publicly traded on a stock exchange – also make a claim to benefiting society via shared wealth creation. As private equity represents finance provided in return for an equity stake in unquoted companies, there is risk sharing. Private equity formats include buyouts and venture capital (at different stages such as launch, early development, or expansion of business). This includes start-ups seeking investors as with theatrical productions or independent film productions. Prominent private equity firms include Apax Partners, Bain Capital, the Blackstone Group, the Carlyle Group, CVC Capital Partners, and KKR. A typical private equity firm structure has a holding company established for the private equity partnership, which is the lead investment advisor for various funds. A private equity fund is established to raise money from investors (limited partners), such as pension funds, sovereign wealth funds, and high net worth individuals (who meet certain regulatory benchmarks as set, for example, by the SEC or the FSA), and partners of the private equity firm who also serve as owners of the fund. These funds are used to acquire, hold, and improve businesses (or investments). There is an eye to an exit at some point such as seeking a stock market listing or selling to another investor.

Private equity, as its name would suggest, often claims to distinguish itself from both public listing and debt financing. First, the private equity perspective is longer term so such investments are not subject to so-called artificial constraints of public companying reporting to meet compliance regulations. In contrast to stock price movement and the quarterly performance measures by which institutional investors may judge publicly listed companies, the investors behind private equity enterprises seek value over a longer time horizon. Second, raising money from debt (such as a bank loan) means that the lender has a legal right to interest on the loan and repayment of capital irrespective of the firm's success or failure. In contrast, private equity is invested in exchange for a stake in the business; as a shareholder, there is shared risk as the returns depend on the growth and profitability of the business.

Art market intermediaries

The purchase and sale of works of art in the international art market are primarily effected through numerous dealers, the international auction houses, smaller auction houses, and also directly between collectors. Much more art is traded through dealers than auction houses. Primary sales represent the first time a work of art is sold; this is conducted, in the main, by contemporary art (or primary market) dealers representing artists, with the selling price shared on an equal basis in most instances. Two peculiarities of the art market can be noted: very few established artists sell direct to buyers, which emphasizes the value of dealers in promotions and distribution; all buyers of art are potential sellers. As such, there is a large resale market for art via secondary market dealers or at public auction. Many primary market dealers also operate as secondary market dealers, particularly for the artists they represent. The traditional role of the auctioneer is as an intermediary between consignor and buyer (i.e. winning bidder): competitive bidding takes place in public; and auction results, namely low/high estimates and selling prices, are published, which means price transparency. On the other hand, according to auctioneers, transactions conducted by primary and secondary art dealers are not verifiable. Dealers operate in the same art market as auctioneers. The most prominent competitive factors impacting dealers include relationships and personal interaction between the buyer or seller and the dealer, the level of specialized expertise of the dealer, and the ability of the dealer to finance purchases of art.

Art dealing is a typical example of personal capitalism, that is to say an owner-operated enterprise. Risk-taking entrepreneurship is a necessary ingredient for success, particularly in contemporary art dealing, which is a dynamic, shifting economy. However, only a small number of contemporary art dealerships – led by the Gagosian Gallery and PaceWildenstein – have operated with a full-time staff complement in excess of 100. Indeed the vast majority operate with the equivalent of less than ten full-time staff. Art dealing can be considered a lifestyle business: it can provide a good standard of living and job satisfaction for the owners. The identity of the dealer – essentially the personality of the commercial gallery – tends to be reflected in the name of the business, a point that reiterates ownership equalling control. A limited lifecycle is assumed as natural: dealers exit the market (due to retirement or death), and new ones emerge. These new dealers may be the most ambitious, motivated, talented, or well-connected employees of established commercial galleries who want their own business. An emphasis on owner-operated management for all key decisions – including selection of artists to represent and final terms of sales with key private collectors and public institutions – and an absence of a professional management hierarchy places a limit to career progression working for another dealer. Moreover, the absence of risk when working as an employee for an owner-operator limits financial rewards (i.e. the bulk of the commercial gains accrue to the owner-entrepreneur).

Two unusual cases can be cited. First, the creation of PaceWildenstein in 1993, as a merger between Pace Gallery, a leading contemporary art gallery established by Arnold Glimcher in 1960, and Wildenstein & Co, a gallery founded in the nineteenth century dealing in Old Master and Impressionist paintings, was atypical, according to Carol Vogel, writing in the *New York Times* (29 October 1993): 'Mergers are highly unusual in the art world, especially ones that join two leading galleries run as family businesses and that cover totally different periods of art'. Second, there is usually little interest for art dealerships from external investors as the prospects for high growth are unlikely, thus Haunch of Venison achieved notoriety amongst other contemporary art dealers through its acquisition by Christie's in 2007. Haunch of Venison had been established, in 2002, by principals with art market experience: Harry Blain is regarded as particularly skilled in secondary market transactions; and Graham Southern was a former director of contemporary art at Christie's London. The purchase by Christie's, which is owned by François Pinault, a high profile collector of contemporary art, was not the first time an auction house purchased a dealer, though the stakes seemed higher. As an example of channel behaviour, Christie's was attempting to be more effective in how well it covers the contemporary art market: this means exploiting the skills and networks of Blain and Southern, and gallery venues in London, Zurich, and New York, to display contemporary art. It certainly hopes that it will be building a competitive advantage over its direct rival Sotheby's in meeting the needs of its clients.

Christie's and Sotheby's are the world's two largest auctioneers of authenticated fine art, antiques and decorative art, jewellery, and collectibles. Competition in the international art market is intense. A fundamental challenge facing auctioneers (or dealers) – as key intermediaries – is obtaining high quality and valuable property for sale either as agent or as principal. An auctioneer functions as an agent accepting property on consignment from its selling clients (consignors), though it is not typically known that the consignor is the primary client of the auctioneer.[8] The worldwide art auction market is concentrated: it has two principal selling seasons, spring and autumn, with sales in New York and London being the most important.

As a company listed on the NYSE, Sotheby's must disclose certain documents such as 'Form 10-K Annual Report' and the 'Investor Briefing' presentation to meet SEC regulations. Sotheby's also uses its 2008 Form 10-K return to make an early wry observation (on page 2) that the other international auction house, Christie's, is 'privately held, French-owned', an obvious contrast to its status as a publicly listed company in the USA. This suggests that both documents also have a publicity role: in the economic downturn, Sotheby's president and chief executive officer, William Ruprecht, and chairman, Michael Sovern, 'remain committed to delivering value to you, our *shareholders*, to our *employees* and to our *clients*' (my emphasis). It is telling that the stakeholders appear as shareholders first, followed by employees, and then clients. Whereas Sotheby's website focuses on the needs of prospective consignors and bidders, these (and other related) documents – located under 'investor relations' – are geared to current and prospective investors. The annual report and investor briefing are instructive in articulating Sotheby's business model and competition and risk factors.[9] Investors rank Sotheby's financial performance with reference to the prospect of future earnings: Standard & Poor's MidCap 400 (stock index) is one comparator; Sotheby's self-described peer group of luxury brands, Nordstorm, Saks Holdings, Tiffany & Co, and Movado, is another (Form 10-K 2008: 14). Investor enthusiasm can also have an impact on share/stock price. There was great news in the narrative portion of the 2007 Annual Report: 'a record year for Sotheby's'; 'consolidated sales were the best ever, rising 51 per cent to $6.2 billion'. However, the Investor Briefing (2008: 30) was identifying a cost reduction focus in the event of a downturn in the art market. Sotheby's art specialists – such as Tobias Meyer, principal auctioneer and worldwide head of contemporary art, Serena Sutcliffe, head of worldwide wine, David Silcox, president of Sotheby's Canada, and Lord (Harry) Dalmeny, director of house sales and heir to the Earl of Roseberry, whose 'role includes client liaison through which he has developed close connections with many of the leading buyers and dealers in this diverse field' – are key employees. They have essential client-facing roles in securing consignments and attracting bidders.

Sotheby's Investor Briefing (2008: 1, 2) seeks to tell a corporate story of growth opportunity and high differentiation: 'The auction business is core to Sotheby's franchise'; Sotheby's is 'a unique global franchise' with 'significant barriers to entry', namely 'client skills' and 'logistical and intellectual capital'. The reference to franchise, as a privilege or exceptional right granted to a corporation, at the outset strikes at what is noted in the summation of the Investor Briefing (2008: 34): 'continued focus on strategic investments; earnings and cash flow improvements; growing the loan portfolio to enhance earnings; and finding additional opportunities to "leverage" the brand'. Global wealth considerations are crucial, as expressed by Ruprecht and Sovern, in their joint letter to shareholders in the 2007 Annual Report:

> Our strategic focus on our top clients and on emerging markets significantly benefited our business. A few numbers reveal the full measure of the growth in our geographical reach. In 2003 our top buyers – those purchasing lots of $500,000 and above – came from 36 countries. In 2007 the number of these clients increased by 61 per cent over 2003 and they came from 58 countries.

The same statement also appears in the Investor Briefing (2008: 33). It reinforces an earlier point (on page 19), of focusing on the higher end of the auction market, by 'raising our per lot minimums to £3,000 / €4,000 / $5,000 globally' since 'in 2006, 47 per cent of our lot volume was at a hammer price of $5,000 or under', and 'those lots only brought 2.5 per cent of our total worldwide net sales'. On the other hand, Christie's website features 'New to the Market', with reference to New York and London, including objects listed under £3,000/$5,000. Some art market commentators suggest that Christie's, as a privately held firm, can afford to retain a stronger connoisseur orientation, even at the lower end.

The middle portion of Sotheby's Investor Briefing (2008: 6) is an articulation of the firm's business model, namely the importance of 'relationships – converting auction opportunities'. The auction segment consists of general auctions, auctions with consignor guarantees, and auctions with consignor advance loans. General auctions, which account for 85 per cent of auction sales, are based on Sotheby's traditional role of pure intermediation between consignor and buyer.[10] An auction with a guarantee – that is guaranteed sales price to the consignor even if the hammer price is less or the lot fails to sell and is bought-in – is a risk factor on the part of Sotheby's that the auctioneer will assume in a competitive market for attractive consignments. An auction with consignor advance loan is another inducement to secure an attractive consignment from a consignor who seeks cash in advance of an auction. The consignor advance allows a consignor to receive funds shortly after consignment for an auction that will occur several weeks or months in the future, while preserving for the benefit of the consignor the potential of the auction process.

In addition to auctioneering, there are related activities: brokering private purchases and sales of art, so-called private treaty sales; operating as a dealer in certain art sectors; and selling art-related financial services through Sotheby's Financial Services. First, private treaty sales are interpreted by some secondary market dealers as Sotheby's moving away from the traditional role of an auctioneer as a pure intermediary (or agency) between consignor and buyer.[11] Second, even more controversially, according to dealers, Sotheby's operates as a dealer through purchasing, in

2006, Noortman Master Paintings, one of the world's leading art dealers specializing in Dutch and Flemish Old Masters and French Impressionist and Post-Impressionist paintings.[12] Sotheby's Ventures acts as a merchant bank to create opportunities to acquire high value property for resale in partnership with important dealers. Third, Sotheby's Financial Services, a wholly-owned subsidiary for art-related financial services, exist to drive business for the auction segment; at the same time, profit is generated from the interest spread. Few traditional lending sources, even those with private wealth management capabilities, are willing to accept works of art as sole collateral as they do not possess the ability both to appraise and to sell works of art within a vertically integrated organization. Sotheby's believes that through a combination of art expertise and skills in international law and finance, they have the ability to tailor attractive financing packages for clients who wish to obtain liquidity from their art assets. There are two types of secured loans: consignor advances (as discussed above) and term loans. Term loans are general purpose term loans to collectors or dealers secured by an object not presently intended for sale. Term loans allow Sotheby's to establish or enhance mutually beneficial relationships with dealers and collectors and sometimes result in auction consignments. Secured loans are generally made with full recourse against the borrower. In certain instances, however, secured loans are made with recourse limited to the works of art pledged as security for the loan. To the extent that Sotheby's is looking wholly or partially to the collateral for repayment of its loans, repayment can be adversely impacted by a decline in the art market in general or in the value of the particular collateral. The current financial crisis, which has included a downturn in the art market, has led to a more cautious approach to the finance segment, including fewer guarantees and consignor advance loans.

Sotheby's Investor Briefing (2008: 34) seeks to allay concerns from a prominent case of price fixing, which occurred at the outset of the new millennium: 'Antitrust litigation is no longer a concern'.[13] Moreover, the former chairman of Sotheby's, Alfred Taubman, who was convicted, is no longer a controlling shareholder: 'Control of the Company now resides with all Sotheby's shareholders EQUALLY (all Class A shares)' (emphasis in the original). In its Investor Briefing (2008: 27), Sotheby's makes it clear that a 'corporate governance structure in line with best practices of public companies' and 'recapitalization has eliminated the risk that the Taubman's could sell their control stake to a third party'. Mistakes of the part have been corrected, hence a clean present, and an even brighter, prosperous future.

Music company

Terra Firma purchased EMI, one of the world's largest music companies, in 2007, and delisted EMI from the London Stock Exchange (see Terra Firma Annual Review 2007: 86–89; Maltby Capital Annual Review 2007). Maltby Capital was created by funds managed by Terra Firma to oversee the EMI investment. Terra Firma recognizes EMI as a brand steeped in heritage with recording artists such as the Beatles and Beach Boys, and recent talent including Gorillaz, Robbie Williams, Kylie Minogue, and Katy Perry. At the same time, Terra Firma noted EMI was a classic investment: 'cost-heavy, with value locked up in its assets' and 'operating in a market in transition' (Maltby Capital Annual Review 2007: 10).

EMI is presented as two divisions: EMI Music Publishing focuses on the acquiring, protecting, administering, and exploiting of rights in musical compositions, with revenue coming from licensing the right to use its music; and EMI Recorded Music represents recording artists spanning all musical genres; the business signs and develops artists, marketing and promoting them as well as distributing their music to retailers. EMI Music Publishing is an industry leader and highly profitable, according to Terra Firma, whereas EMI Recorded Music is deemed to be underperforming. EMI Recorded Music is thus the focus of restructuring by Terra Firma.

A shift to the digital consumption of music 'has been detrimental to the consumer-oriented Recorded Music business, but Music Publishing, which accounts for two-thirds of group profits, has been more protected through its more diversified revenue base' (Terra Firma Annual Review 2007: 86). Along with a shift to digital, according to Maltby Capital (Annual Review 2007: 17), music industry sales have also faced piracy (such as illegal downloads), changes to the retail outlets with the rise of supermarkets at the expense of specialist music retailers (comparable to what book-sellers face), and market fragmentation (including an erosion of traditional channels to market for consumers to discover music). However, such external market issues were compounded by 'important problems in its own business', according to John Birt, chairman of Maltby Capital (Annual Review 2007: 7), who identified internal factors eroding profitability: EMI Recorded Music 'has a culture where high expend-itures were at odds with the challenges it faced' which 'meant the company accepted as normal costs that should have been substantially cut back'; EMI Recorded Music's 'traditional way of working with artists . . . had become less fit for purpose' such that 'creative performance, as well as its financial performance, had begun to slide'; and 'the company's internal reporting, while data-rich, focused on traditional measures which could tell the company little about the major changes in its market place as they evolved' which meant that 'it provided insufficient information for fundamental metrics – such as artist profitability'.

In addition, EMI Recorded Music comprises two distinct activities: New Music, which finds and develops new artists, working with them to market and sell their music; and Catalogue, which markets work from past artists and the past work of current artists, packaging and marketing music already part of the EMI roster. New Music is likened to 'a venture capital business, often investing large sums of money in the risky process of picking artists, producing and marketing their work in the hope of eventually recouping the investment through sales', according to Maltby Capital (Annual Review 2007: 16), whereas Catalogue 'is an income basis with relatively low risks'. More importantly, it was noted that 'Catalogue was masking substantial losses in the New Music side of the business'. For example, 'of all the currently performing artists on its roster, 88 per cent made a loss for EMI Recorded Music' (Maltby Capital Annual Review 2007: 20). Controversy was sparked by the key focus on EMI Recorded Music's roster, which was viewed as bloated by Terra Firma (Annual Review 2007: 87):

> Currently EMI has more than 14,000 artists on its roster, of which just 200 account for half of revenues. It is actively working with 1,300 artists, but only a small number of these relationships are profitable. In the future, EMI will be more

selective in its artist relationships. It will also develop a broader relationship with its newer artists. EMI is financing the building of the artist 'brand' – the return on this investment will come through not only the sale of recorded music, but also from touring, licensing and other revenue streams.

Radical change to EMI Recorded Music's existing organization is proffered. This includes moving from standalone labels to a streamlined structure where labels are solely focused on A&R (Artists & Repertoire), the so-called engine room of New Music, and working more closely with artists on the creative process and on developing their long-term music careers. There is need to reduce headcount by 1,500–2,000 people, rationalize the existing artist rosters, and streamline the international market footprint, according to Terra Firma (Annual Review 2007: 87). A&R must improve 'the number of hit releases it achieves', an important measure of success, and historical practices such as 'creative concerns were frequently given more weight than the underlying economic rationale' are challenged (Maltby Capital Annual Review: 20). EMI Recorded Music was deemed to have weak governance and control: a cost structure that was not aligned to revenue levels; a business model that needed updating; and an organizational culture that was insufficiently focused on shareholder value. Costs savings of £200 million per annum are predicted, with 'the goal for EMI to become the most innovative, artist-friendly and consumer-focused music company in the world, while delivering the financial performance needed to build a sustainable business' (Terra Firma Annual Review: 86).

TRUSTEES AND ELITE ARTS PATRONAGE

As part of his definition of 'management of the arts', Colbert (in Towse 2003: 289) describes the board of directors (also trustees or governors) as 'a fundamental entity' for not-for-profit arts and cultural organizations.

> Concepts such as profit, per-share profit and market share have no relevance for a non-profit organization with a social and educational mission. Rather, the appropriate performance-measurement criteria must be centred on the achievement of the organizational mission.
>
> The roles and functions of the board of trustees thus extend well beyond financial considerations. Since a cultural organization is an institution with a social and educational mission and is financially supported by society as a whole, the primary responsibility of the board of trustees is to ensure that this mission is fulfilled. As a non-profit organization, it has no actual shareholders to hold it accountable. However, the society that provides the organization with funding can be regarded as its principal shareholder. The board of directors is thus responsible for safeguarding the organizational mission on behalf of this collective shareholder.

Colbert's contribution deserves elaboration and comment. First, in the absence of 'concepts such as profit, per-share profit and market share' motives with a financial return to investors, as is the case with commercial arts organizations (whether owner-operated, publicly listed, or private equity), the non-distributive mandate is a distinguishing characteristic of not-for-profits. Any net income – that is surplus of income beyond costs in any financial year – cannot be distributed as dividends to owners, which is to say that any surplus must be retained within the not-for-profit arts organization.

Second, 'the achievement of organizational mission' is core to the existence of not-for-profits. The board links governance and management functions of the arts organization through the equivalent of a CEO (chief executive such as director for art museums, or dual executives such as managing director and artistic director in the case of many performing arts organizations). Governance thus involves monitoring the organizational mission; in turn, monitoring entails relations with management (that is salaried staff charged with day-to-day operations including artistic programming), and relations entail rules of conduct and the clear definition of roles. The board needs to agree with the arts organization's CEO specific results that are directed towards the aim of the organization. In addition, the board needs to set limits to the latitude of the CEO. Mission constraint and conflict are considered inevitable – even for non-fatalists – when examining the institutional histories of many arts organizations. 'Since a cultural organization is an institution with a social and educational mission', which seem elastic at times, it can be a challenge to maintain a commitment to excellence and artistic integrity.

Third, that 'the role and functions of the board trustees extend well beyond financial considerations' counters the so-called 3Gs adage – give money, get money, or get off the board – of trusteeship, which views trustees of elite arts boards primarily as private sources of money. However, owing to mandated fiduciary obligations, trustees of not-for-profit arts organizations have an oversight responsibility for setting a strategic direction consistent with the organization's charter, by-laws, and mission and ensuring financial solvency. There is a necessity to recruit trustees with sound judgement and a commitment to the principles of arts organization as a not-for-profit organization in the public interest. Trustees with access or links to under-represented communities and not-for-profit experience can also be desirable.

Fourth, that not-for profit arts organizations are 'financially supported by society as a whole' is an instructive note that can be viewed as direct and indirect subsidies from the state. Not-for-profits can operate in the absence of, or very little, direct public funding, as is common in the USA, where indirect subsidies (via the taxation system) are more prominent to reflect an American aversion of allowing the state to gain control over arts and culture. The focus is on enabling private giving to arts organizations to take root and flourish. On the other hand, arts organizations can be in receipt of significant direct subsidy as has been more common in Europe.

Fifth, 'as a non-profit organization, it has no actual shareholders to hold it accountable', though 'the society that provides the organization with funding can be regarded as its principal shareholder' with the board charged with 'safeguarding the organizational mission on behalf of this collective shareholder'. This is about 'good governance and non-profit integrity', according to the Association of Art Museum Directors (June 2006), whose members are 'entrusted by the public to care for our shared artistic heritage', such that 'art museums are among the most trusted and respected public institutions in the world – resources for education and enjoyment

that provide lasting benefits to the people of the world'. Indeed, some arts organizations adopt a long time horizon such as 'in perpetuity for future generations', which
also emphasizes the societal dimension.

Political dimensions can be added to Colbert's description. Not-for-profit arts
organizations can be subject to fierce contestation over who controls the agenda,
particularly if the public benefit is encapsulated as part of the art organization's
mission. Forces of change are wide and not always limited to overtly political ones.
The stakes can be high, as curator Bruce Ferguson (in Greenberg, Ferguson, and
Nairne 1996: 177) makes clear:

> [T]he public museum, like the university and the church (all of which are what
> Althusser called 'ideological state apparatuses' like the family or the school), is
> under fierce and sometimes violent contestation over who controls its agenda and
> what its fundamental purpose is.
>
> This institutional and intellectual shift in the museum field is occurring both
> because of outside reforms like government agencies and philanthropic organiza-
> tions whose economic and social priorities have changed and because of internal
> forces which have to do with the inconstant nature of contemporary art in particu-
> lar and the changing roles of participants in the artworld, including patrons and, in
> particular, curators.

Moreover, there is the case that the art museum – Ferguson's focus – is a proxy for
many types of elite arts organizations. The AAMD (January 2007) has noted that 'in
the 150 years since the founding of America's first art museum, institutions and
collectors have built an extraordinary record of collaboration for the public good';
however, 'the relationships between museums and individuals – like all relationships –
have inherent challenges as well'. 'To ensure public benefit from their loans and
donations to museums by private collectors of works from their collections, museum
directors – in consultation with trustees and staff – weigh [certain] questions', according to the AAMD: is the work, in terms of content and quality, consistent with the
mission of the museum and the context provided by its permanent collections and
programmes? Is the collector an individual with a reputation of integrity whose
involvement enhances the museum's programme? Are the collector's motives transparent and acceptable to the museum? Are there restrictive conditions on the loan or
gift that place an undue burden on the museum? These are questions of agency
conflict that would call into question the core values of AAMD members such as
mission ('to serve the public through art and education'), *accountability* ('museum
directors are responsible to their trustees, staff, donors, and community for ensuring
that museums fufil their public service mission'), *integrity* ('meet the highest standards
of curatorial professional, and ethical integrity'), and *transparency* ('promote clarity of
purpose in action and openness in internal and external communications').

Two cases from the same UK arts institution, separated by two decades, illustrate
such challenges. Hans Haacke's *Taking Stock (unfinished)* (1983–84) was an attempt
to raise concern that Julian Schnabel, a hot artist for much of the 1980s (before
developing a reputation as a film director), had an exhibition at the Tate Gallery in
1982 based on works donated by the collector Charles Saatchi, who was also a

member of an influential patron's group at the Tate (see Chong 1997; Hatton and Walker 2000). In addition Haacke's work referenced UK Prime Minister Margaret Thatcher. As an adman *par excellence* Saatchi was illustrative of the broadening base of patronage beyond aristocratic elites. What links Saatchi to Thatcher, the Tate, and the international art world? Charles and his brother Maurice, who was made a life peer in 1996, were co-founders of Saatchi and Saatchi, the advertising firm that was crucial to the electoral success of the Conservatives under Thatcher in 1979. At the time, Charles, already an assiduous collector of contemporary art, was an active member of the Tate's Patrons of New Art, and a trustee of London's Whitechapel Art Gallery, a public institution. Tate's Schnabel exhibition, organized by the Patrons of New Art, resulted in a display of eleven paintings with nine owned by Saatchi (whose works would benefit from the provenance of a prestigious public art museum exhibition in any subsequent sale). A main point addressed ethics, namely the potential conflict of interest and loss of public trust. Haacke sought to make the various relationships more transparent by citing the role of Victorian values. The main image in *Taking Stock (unfinished)* is a portrait of Thatcher; the dual choices, of oil paint as a medium and the frame, were based on Victorian era works in the Tate Gallery, as a way to mimic her promotion of nineteenth century conservative policies at the end of the twentieth century. 'Of course, in their own way, the Saatchis are also Victorians. They match the young bourgeois entrepreneurs of the nineteenth century, relatively unfettered by tradition, without roots in the aristocracy, and out to prove themselves to the world', according to Haacke (in Bois, Crimp, and Krauss 1984: 24).

A more recent case of conflict of interest at Tate involved the purchase in 2006 of *The Upper Room* (1998–2002) by Chris Ofili, then an artist trustee, for £600,000. The Charity Commission, established by law as the regulator charities in England and Wales to increase the efficiency and effectiveness of charities and public confidence and trust in them, examined Tate's purchases of art produced by serving artist trustees.[14] In the case of the Ofili purchase, from his dealer Victoria Miro, Tate director, Nicholas Serota, argued that a quick decision had to be made to retain the work within a national collection, and that the price was less than the market value; moreover, Serota noted that the 250,000 visitors had viewed the work when it was on display between 2005 and 2006. The Charity Commission agreed that the purchase was in the best interests of Tate. However, in a press release (19 July 2006), Tate acknowledged the Charity Commission's 'criticisms of Tate's policies and procedures in relation to acquisitions of works by serving artist trustees and the processes for managing conflicts of interests'. Tate noted the implementation of a number of the Charity Commission recommendations: 'All acquisition of works by serving artist trustees will only be agreed with the approval by the Charity Commission. The trustees have also decided to refer gifts and pledges from artist trustees to the Commission for approval'; and 'Clear guidelines are being established on all transactions between serving artist trustees and Tate'. In addition, Tate's corporate governance would be strengthened: 'To add an independent member to their ethics committee which provides advice to the Trustees on ethical questions relating to Tate's range of activities'; and 'The cost of acquisitions made by Tate and the value of works given to Tate, will be disclosed annually in Tate's annual report'.

Who has the power and authority within arts organizations? What is the role of trustees in decision-making? What is the relationship between the board of trustees and professional staff (including the equivalent of the chief executive officer)? In the absence of a profit measure of performance, there are constraints on an arts organization's mission. This leads to challenges, if not conflicts, of how to balance competing interests – aesthetic appreciation, social welfare provision, or revenue generation, for example – in order to remain successful.

The board of trustees is crucial to the governance of arts organizations, as the board is vested with decision-making powers. As such, trustees have a privileged position. For example, within the category of volunteers – a form of unpaid staff crucial to the sustainability of arts organizations – trustees are situated at the top of any organizational chart. Strategic apex is a term used by Henry Mintzberg (1979) to designate the top of an organizational chart, charged with overall responsibility for ensuring the organization's remit is fulfilled, which entails three sets of duties: direct supervision, management of the organization's boundary conditions (i.e. its relationships with its environment), and the development of the organization's strategy. The strategic apex includes the board of trustees and the most senior salaried member of staff – CEO-equivalent such as the art museum director – who is formally accountable to the board of trustees. Working closely with the art museum director are senior personnel with titles like assistant, associate, or deputy director, chief curator, and chief administrative director.

Differences in direction and strategy between a board of trustees and (even successful) art museum directors can lead to a separation. For example, David Ross, former director of the Whitney Museum of American Art, resigned as director of the San Francisco Museum of Modern Art (SFMoMA) in 2001, where he had spent three years and $140 million building up the museum's collection of contemporary art, with acquisitions of works by Jasper Johns, Robert Rauschenberg, Mark Rothko, Francis Bacon, Alexander Calder, Chuck Close, and Frank Stella, to put the institution in the top ranks of museums of modern art in the USA. Elaine McKeon, chair of the SFMoMA board of trustees, according to the *New York Times* (18 August 2001), said that the executive committee and Ross had concluded negotiations 'that their paths had diverged at a time when a slow economy – particularly among the high-tech companies that are the backbone of Bay Area philanthropy – was forcing the museum to keep a tighter rein on its resources'. 'Our focus in the museum is on internal management, and Ross is focused on external matters, which he is a genius at', according to McKeon, who added:

What is good for the museum is not necessarily in his best interests. And we thought it was mutually beneficial if we parted. We are in a period, in an economy that puts the focus on management, on being fiscally responsible, financially responsible. It was a mutual parting of the ways, which was very friendly. So now David can get on with his life, and he can go do for somebody else what he did for us. But I have to think of our responsibilities.

Thomas Krens's resignation as director of the Guggenheim Foundation, after two decades at the helm, was a prominent art world news story. The board limiting the latitude of the director is a theme. According to a lead account in the *New York Times* (28 February 2008), Krens's resignation came three years after he triumphed in what has been described as a showdown with the Guggenheim Foundation's biggest bene-factor, philanthropist Peter Lewis. Lewis, who has donated about $77 million overall (nearly four times as much as any other Guggenheim board member in its history), resigned as a Guggenheim trustee after losing an argument that Krens was spending too much money and should focus more on the flagship museum in New York rather than on directing resources into developing Guggenheim satellites around the world. 'The New York museum is the center of the entire constellation', according to Jennifer Stockman, president of the board of trustees. This suggests that in resigning as director, Krens was responding to the changed mood of Guggenheim's board. 'This is something that Tom and the board decided together', Stockman added. Krens remains at the Guggenheim Foundation as a senior adviser for international affairs, overseeing the creation of a museum in Abu Dhabi to be designed by Gehry, which is an important project, which Stockman characterized as a 'natural transition'. In an interview with Spiegel, Krens (2008) responded to the events that led to his departure as director:

Spiegel: You established the Guggenheim brand, but also the Krens brand. Have you become too self-confident for the board of directors?

Krens: I'm sure that this played a role when I was the topic of discussion. But my top priority is the Guggenheim.

Spiegel: Peter Lewis was long the chairman of the museum's board of directors. But then he resigned because he felt that you were neglecting the original museum in New York.

Krens: Peter Lewis was my most important mentor early on, and he later came to the Guggenheim through me. He was the most generous donor in the history of the museum. I like him. That's all I can say about it.

Spiegel: You didn't take the criticism seriously?

Krens: Yes, I did, but I believe that the worldwide presence is a positive thing and that we should confront the challenges of a cosmopolitan world.

Trustees must act within parameters as articulated by an arts organization's charter, by-laws and mission statement; there may be additional structural constraints related to status as a charitable, not-for-profit organization. For example, the British Museum – a non-departmental public body, whose prime sponsor is the Department of Culture, Media and Sport (DCMS) – was created by the British Museum Act of 1753, which served as the governing document until the British Museum Act of 1963 and the Museums and Galleries Act of 1992.[15] The BM's trustees serve as the 'corporate body with the legal duty to hold the Museum's collection and make it available to our world audience' (with an important proviso, 'free of charge'). As another example, with reference to the USA, Henry Hansmann (1980: 62) notes that 'the purpose of the charter is primarily to protect the interests of the organization's *patrons* from those who control the corporation' (emphasis in the original). Trustees are asked to exercise effective control in order to fulfil their role as policy maker, management overseer, and performance evaluator. In practice, a smaller executive committee may decide major decisions for the full board to ratify, particularly in the case of arts organizations with large memberships (some elite arts boards in the USA are in excess of 50 trustees) to support fundraising.

It is not surprising that the dominant supervisory body in the USA, the business corporation, is familiar to invariably all trustees. Established to be self-perpetuating, such elite arts boards offer institutional stability, according to Hansmann (1980: 59), by exerting power in an uncontested manner:

> Thus a nonprofit corporation may have a membership that, like shareholders in a business corporation, is entitled to select the board of trustees through elections held at regular intervals. But the statutes typically do not make this a requirement, so that the board of directors may, alternatively, simply be made an autonomous, self-perpetuating body.

One particular reason for self-perpetuating bodies is the legacy of patronage by local and monied families. Critical to establishing many elite arts organizations, their support remains important: 'Elite patronage has changed very little over time. It is still the case, at least in the USA, that affluent individuals and wealthy donors continue to be the main source of unearned income for cultural institutions' (Blau 1991: 90). Such a system, which is most prevalent in the USA, has several consequences: socio-demographic sameness exists among trustees; ordinary members are excluded from electing trustees; boards are large in size; and there are no incentives for autonomous, self-perpetuating boards to proffer different models. However, the emergence of corporate managers as arts board trustees recruited for corporate affiliation and managerial professionalization have been noted (DiMaggio and Anheier 1990). For example, Francie Ostrower (2002: xvi) has examined elite arts boards representing opera houses and art museums in the USA:

> Elite boards are subject to two major, but often conflicting influences. One is rooted in trustees' class background, and the other is based in organizational needs of the large, complex institutions that they govern. The affluent men and women who serve on these arts boards attach class-based prestige and meaning to them and to involvement with art and arts institutions. These class-related values attract affluent people to boards and encourage large donations. As actual board members, elites do not abandon their class-based outlook. At the same time, however, organizational pressures and considerations come into play. Sometimes, class and organizational influences push in similar directions. Often, however, they are in tension. While class-based influences promote exclusivity and traditionalism, organizational needs often call for greater openness and change. Accordingly elites adapt.

In the UK, the trustees of national or prestigious arts organizations are often appointed from a pool known colloquially as 'the great and the good' of minor royals, major aristocrats, and those first in any line for knighthoods, namely ex-politicians, captains of industry, retired senior civil servants, and distinguished academics. In the case of many appointments to national arts and cultural institutions, an official process is used: the example the 25 trustees of the British Museum are appointed by Her Majesty (one), the Prime Minister (15), the Secretary of State via nominations by the presidents of the Royal Society, the Royal Academy, the British Academy, and the Society of Antiquaries of London, respective (four), and trustees of the BM (five). Unlike the situation in the USA, trustees in the UK have not been asked to become donors, as part of an appointment, or perform fundraising tasks. The situation is changing in the UK, though, with initiatives to encourage more private giving by individuals. (Such rhetoric of greater self-reliance in the arts and culture follows what has occurred in other arenas such as higher education.) Some UK arts organizations like the Royal Academy, which does not receive public subsidy for its programming of exhibitions, the Victoria & Albert Museum, and Tate have established fundraising arms in the USA. The Serpentine Art Gallery, which was able to capitalize on a close association with Princess Diana, has established an enviable reputation for generating private giving, with an invitation to its summer party being one of the most coveted of London's summer season.

Representative democracy is discernible in Canadian examples of arts boards. There has been a gradual shift from the USA model, of locale and private institutions, to public funding models. For example, the Montreal Museum of Fine Arts (MMFA) adopted a bilingual title, with the inclusion of Musée des beaux-arts de Montréal in 1960, to reflect the changing complexion of Quebec society, namely the so-called Quiet Revolution (about modernization and rising Quebec nationalism). In 1972 a partnership agreement was struck with the Province of Quebec to become the MMFA's prime source of operating funds, hence the change of status from a private institution to a publicly chartered independent corporation. In a similar manner, the Art Museum of Toronto, founded in 1900, changed its name to the Art Gallery of Ontario (AGO) in 1966 to reflect an expanded mandate – geographically from a city to the province and with education accorded a prominent position – by being incorporated as a provincial agency. The hybrid nature of board composition means that there are elected and appointed trustees. There is a nod to 'one member, one vote' democracy whereby ordinary members are able to elect trustees at an annual general meeting; in practice, however, candidates put forward by a nominating committee of the board are usually elected without substantial opposition. A state funding agency may appoint a minority number of trustees, as part of a funding agreement. These state-appointed trustees may be uncertain about whose interests they are supposed to represent: the government of the day, some concept of watch-dog for the so-called average taxpaying citizen, or as an independent trustee? Two studies were commissioned in the early 1980s following internal conflicts within the MMFA's board of trustees between state-appointed trustees – some who resigned – and those elected by the membership. In the early 1990s, an Independent Task Force of the Future of the AGO was created in response to the breakdown in normal negotiations between the AGO and its main public funding agency. Miscommunications between a state funding agency and a funded arts organization are not uncommon in Canada.

INSTITUTIONAL ISOMORPHISM

Is there sufficient homogeneity of form and practice amongst opera houses or art museums to suggest that they represent a distinct institutional form? Can the same be said of other arts organizations? This issue of institutional isomorphic change – the role that institutional pressures make organizations within the same field resemble one another – has been examined by sociologists Paul DiMaggio and Walter Powell. Unlike Max Weber, to whom an explicit reference is made in their 1983 essay, 'The iron cage revisited', which is part of studies in new institutionalism (Powell and DiMaggio 1991), DiMaggio and Powell (1983: 147) contend that 'bureaucratization and other forms of organizational change occur as the result of processes that make some organizations similar without necessarily making them more efficient'. They argue that bureaucratization and other forms of homogenization emerge out of the structuration of organizational fields. The desire is not to explain variation among organizations in structure and behaviour; rather Powell and DiMaggio seek to understand why there is such startling homogeneity of organizational forms and practices. Isomorphism 'is the concept that best captures the process of homogenization'; it is 'a constraining process that forces one unit in a population to resemble other units that face the same set of environmental conditions' (DiMaggio and Powell 1983: 148). They identified three mechanisms by which institutional isomorphic change takes place: *coercive* (i.e. the power of dominant organizations and the state to coerce conformity in structure and practices), *mimetic* (i.e. the drive to imitate seemingly successful organizations to try to achieve similar success or merely to look acceptable), and *normative* (i.e. the role of professionals and their networks in demanding and producing similarities in background and orientation).

First, coercive isomorphism results from both formal and informal pressures exerted on organizations by other organizations upon which they are dependent, and by cultural expectations in the society within which they function. The greater the dependence of one organization on another, or the greater the centralization of an organization's resource supply, the more similar it will become to the dominant organization or resource supplier in structure and focus. Many conventional arts organizations, like art museums and opera houses, have internalized the external bureaucratic environment by incorporating in their structures administrators responsible for retailing, fundraising, corporate sponsorship, grant applications, and marketing. This suggests that arts organizations grow administratively and hierarchically in complex environments that are abundant in resources. Transactions within a complex environment increase the tendency of the organization to formalize and amplify its administrative functions. With reference to non-profit arts organizations in the USA, sociologist Richard Peterson (in DiMaggio 1986: 175) has described the internal and extraorganizational factors that 'typically operate in concert, mutually reinforcing the drive toward formal accountability and increasing the need for arts managers with the orientation and skills of art administrators'. Internal factors – growth in size, increasing task complexity, organizational life cycle, and the cost disease associated with Baumol and Bowen – have been working to encourage greater bureaucratization in individual organizations, according to Peterson (in DiMaggio 1986: 169). Extraorganizational factors are important because institutional funders (whether government bodies, private foundations, or corporate sponsors), private patrons, or the market (as regards earned income and audience figures) increasingly hold arts managers formally accountable for actions taken in the name of the arts organization.

The funding environment is the culprit, according to McKinsey & Co: 'All organizations – for profit or not – are shaped by those who fund them' (Lowell *et al.* 2001: 148). For example, internet start-ups reflect the complexion of the venture capitalists who provided capital funding. Non-commercial organizations have fared less well: 'Nonprofits typically rely on grants and donations' (Lowell *et al.* 2001: 148). Most donors take 'a project-based rather than an organization-building approach to philanthropy' (Lowell *et al.* 2001: 149); and corporate sponsors also tend to focus on specific programmes. This means that non-profits are discouraged from investing in organizational infrastructure (e.g. information systems, staff development processes, and adequate management capacity). Managers may spend too much time following the money by adding programmes to obtain a particular grant even if the fit to the organization's mission is not great. The last Conservative government in the UK (under John Major) introduced a semantic change whereby citizens of public services were reconceptualized as consumers, which led many arts organizations to write visitors' charters to comply with the new ethos. Likewise, the availability of new funding in the UK from the National Lottery in the 1990s, with the new millennium in sight, meant that arts organizations had to learn to apply for this money. Large amounts were directed into capitalizing public arts projects and events. Organizations without substantial reserves or income found it harder to apply, especially since no funding was set aside for maintenance or lost revenue. Most recently, New Labour via the DCMS has put pressure on national arts organizations to address a range of extra-artistic concerns such as social inclusion, lifelong learning, and economic regeneration of local communities, which critics have labeled as the instrumentalization of arts and culture policy.

Second, mimetic isomorphism results from standard responses to uncertainty, given that uncertainty represents a powerful force that encourages imitation. An organization will model itself after organizations it perceives as successful, the more uncertain the relationship between means and ends or the more ambiguous its goals. The institutional formation of the V&A – as the Museum of Manufacturers and later the Museum of Ornamental Arts – in the direct aftermath of the 1851 Great Exhibition, directed attention to decorative and industrial arts. In Philadelphia, following the 1876 Centennial Exhibition, itself based on the success of the Great Exhibition, the Pennsylvania Museum and School of Industrial Arts (now the Philadelphia Museum of Art) was created with the UK example in mind, namely with the value of the industrial arts deemed as educational and commercial. Likewise, the (English) Arts and Crafts movement was an important influence on decorative arts in Montreal. The Montreal Museum of Fine Arts is explicit in acknowledging decorative arts alongside painting and sculpture. In a more assured manner, Nicholas Serota conceived what became Tate Modern with reference to existing leading museums of modern art, namely so-called urban models of MoMA in New York and the Pompidou Centre in Paris; at the same time, he desired the humanistic benefits of a so-called rural model of a museum of modern art, such as the Louisiana Museum of

Modern Art, outside of Copenhagen. Tate Modern was supposed to combine the benefits of both urban and rural models while ensuring that visitors were cognizant of a particular experience of looking at art in London.

Much of the homogeneity in organizational structures stems from the fact that, despite a search for diversity, there is relatively little variation from the pool of generally acceptable alternatives. Large arts organizations choose from a relatively small set of international accountancy and management consultancy firms. Under the conventional wisdom that institutions trust institutions, corporate sponsors (as represented by S&P 500 or FSTE 100 firms) tend to have similar business aims and look for equally blue chip (or elite) performing and visual arts organizations for relationships. Morgan Stanley's sponsorship of 'The First Emperor: China's Terracotta Warriors' (2008) exhibition at the British Museum reflects the growing significance of China as market for financial services, and the networking opportunities from an exhibition that attracted the most senior government officials from China and the UK. As a way to support its credentials in the area of private wealth management, Swiss-based UBS has sponsored Art Basel; in addition it sponsored the reopening of New York's MoMA and the second rehang of the permanent collection at Tate Modern. More controversially, BMW and Armani have been involved in separate exhibitions directly linked to sponsorship agreements at the Guggenheim. This strengthening arts–business nexus has provoked institutional critiques by visual artists like Hans Haacke and Carey Young and cultural critics such as Chin-tao Wu. Fundraising practices used by the wealthiest private universities in the USA have been adopted by elite arts organizations in the USA and the UK. Capital projects remain a catalyst for rejuvenation, galvanizing support, and serving as a rallying point for key supports, with many viewing endowment funding – notwithstanding events of the current credit crisis – as a source of financial stability to arts organizations.

Third, normative isomorphism stems primarily from two aspects of professionalization: the resting of formal education and legitimation in a cognitive base produced by university specialists; and the growth and elaboration of professional networks that span organizations and across which new models diffuse rapidly. Elite academic recognition still matters: it has been assumed that directors of national (art-based) museums in the UK – that is the British Museum, the National Gallery, Tate, the V&A, and the National Portrait Gallery – will have studied at Oxbridge or the Courtauld Institute of Art; reading art history at Williams College has a similar significance in the USA.[16] There is a particular result from the two aspects of professionalization, according to DiMaggio and Powell (1983: 154):

> It creates a pool of almost interchangeable individuals who occupy similar positions across a range of organizations and possess a similarity of orientation and disposition that may override variations in tradition and control that might otherwise shape organizational behaviour.

The filtering of personnel is an important mechanism for encouraging normative isomorphism. 'Many professional career tracks are so closely guarded, both at the entry and throughout the career progression, that individuals who make it to the top are virtually indistinguishable' (DiMaggio and Powell 1983: 154). Furthermore, according to DiMaggio and Powell (1983: 155):

> The professionalization of management tends to proceed in tandem with the structuration of organizational fields. The exchange of information among professionals helps contribute to a commonly recognized hierarchy of status, of center and periphery, that becomes a matrix for information flows and personnel movement across organizations. This status ordering occurs through formal and informal means.

■ ■ ■

Every so often – though not that often – a stir is caused by an arts and culture article. Writing in the *New York Times* (3 December 2000), Roberta Smith sparked a national debate amongst art museum directors when she challenged them to ensure that objects on display are treated as works of art:

> Today's museums are under attack from art-theory ideology on one side and commerce on the other. In their exhibition programs, at least, they often behave less and less like museums – that is, places where the goal is the visual, largely private experience of art objects. More and more they are in danger of becoming places where larger social and historical patterns are either consciously or unconsciously played out, where people of all ages are given cursory lessons in history and morality, or where consumer desire is stoked by merchandise orchestrated into artful displays that may or may not be sponsored by the maker of that merchandise.

The integrity of art museums was called into question. Two exhibitions, both from 2000, were cited as being seriously flawed to the point of compromising the aesthetic mission of public art museums: 'Giorgio Armani' at the Guggenheim New York had the effect of turning Frank Lloyd Wright's building into a department store; and the Los Angeles County Museum of Art (LACMA) was refashioned a historical society with 'Made in California: art, image and identity 1900–2000'. Leading members of the Association of Art Museum Directors replied with *Whose Muse?* (2004), edited by James Cuno (2004: 73), now president of the Art Institute of Chicago, who articulated that museums behave in a manner to retain the public trust:

> For in the end, this is what visitors most want from us: to have access to works of art in order to change them, to alter their experience of the world, to sharpen and heighten their sensitivities to it, to make it come alive or new for them, so they can walk away at a different angle to the world.

Moreover, the AAMD has sought to articulate the role of art museums within contemporary society: though not part of the market, they cannot avoid the impact of the market.

On the other hand, commercial arts enterprises – for-profit in orientation – are part of the market. The types of questions posed as part of 'the future of capitalism' (e.g. ft.com/capitalism) discussions, such as appropriate levels of corporate governance and managing levels of risk, loom large. Shareholder value (as opposed to short-term maximization) still matters, but there may be greater attention to the means of how, such as pleasing customers, motivating employees, and improving goods and services. Trust, which is predicated on long-term relationships, matters more. Communications between corporate managers and shareholders, as the financial owners, need to be enhanced.

APPENDIX: PHILOSOPHIES OF PHILANTHROPY

Fundraising has, as a traditional form of philanthropy, been vital to not-for-profit arts organizations. This has included writing cheques to finance capital projects such as new buildings and supplementing endowment funds. Yet during the last decade, the rise of venture philanthropy, an attempt to combine characteristics associated with venture capital to traditional philanthropy, has gained attention. This has included some so-called old economy versus new economy rhetoric associated with the dot-com era of the late 1990s.

Peter Drucker (d. 2005) and Henry Drucker (d. 2003) were not related, but both proffered foundational points on the philosophy of fundraising. Successful fundraising can help to safeguard arts organizations against future cuts in subsidies, yet Peter Drucker (1990: 41) voiced some concern about too much attention to raising money:

> Almost by definition, money is always scarce in a nonprofit institution. Indeed, a good many nonprofit managers seem to believe that all their problems could be solved if they had more money. In fact, some of them come close to believing that money-raising is really their mission.
>
> But a nonprofit institution that becomes a prisoner of money-raising is in serious trouble and in a serious identity crisis. The purpose of a strategy for fund-raising money is precisely to enable the nonprofit institution to carry out its mission without subordinating that mission to fund-raising.

What he seems to be tackling is goal displacement. Artistic excellence is difficult; it can be displaced by goals such as fundraising targets that can be achieved, or are easier to measure. One knock-on effect is a disproportionate increase in fundraising staff relative to professional, arts-based staff. Moreover, fundraising has become a continuous process, with annual campaigns alongside project-based ones.

Fundraising may be an instrument to engage and energize donors; it is about strengthening an existing interest in what the arts organization is doing so that the donor develops an emotional connection. It is not unlike the precepts of successful branding. Oxford Philanthropic was established by Henry Drucker in 1994 as a management consultancy to advise not-for-profit organizations on developing strategies for major fundraising programmes. (In its obituary, on 7 November 2003, the London *Guardian* noted that Henry Drucker 'was widely recognized as one of the founding fathers of modern fundraising in Britain. He headed a team which, over six years, raised some £340m by 1994 for Oxford, the most successful British university fundraising campaign to date'; Oxford Philanthropic is no longer in operation.) In a *Financial Times* interview, from 1997 (6/7 December), Drucker discussed private giving by individuals and fundraising, in spiritual terms:

> Fund-raising can liberate the donor.
>
> The most successful fund-raisers in the world, measured by dollars raised, are American universities. But the vocabulary, the arguments, are all Protestant arguments. It's about inspiration, changing the world, and personal destiny. The language of fund-raising I teach is really a version of Protestant theology.

Two points require further comment. First, most of the elite universities in the USA are private, not-for-profit institutions. Endowments are crucial to understanding the sustainability of the best American universities. For example, before the current credit crunch, 75 had endowments in excess of $1 billion. Fundraising skills honed at places like Harvard, Brown, Princeton, and Duke are being transferred to the most prestigious arts organizations in the USA. At the time of Drucker's *FT* interview, Oxford Philanthropic was attempting to replicate this pattern in the UK: half of the consultancy's 30 organizational clients were universities; visual arts and art music organizations accounted for an additional one-third. Second, liberal humanism issues help in understanding the role of Protestant theology. Can the transformative value attributed to giving be viewed as a form of reification? Moreover, a subtle point has been mooted that the devotion of Americans to capitalism and religion is peculiar to the USA: 'it is religion in this country to refute Marx', according to literary critic Harold Bloom (in Coutu 2001: 68), who believes that the American religion 'is an indigenous religion with almost nothing in common with European Protestantism'. Apart from taxation benefits, which influence charitable giving in the USA, 'freedom of democracy' issues need to be considered. Unlike the situation in Europe, giving in the USA to self-selected 'good causes' represents a way for Americans to express themselves.

What united Peter and Henry (the two Druckers) was a belief that much of humanistic service, which includes the arts along with education, health, and social welfare, is better due to private giving generated via fundraising; this is viewed in opposition to reliance on public funding. This suggests that ideology may play a more significant role than tax concessions to explain giving in the USA and Canada relative to Europe. A requirement to raise funds means that those who give show a greater commitment to the institution; and institutions need to upgrade, improve, and innovate to remain attractive to donors.

The pyramid is a powerful visual symbol for fundraisers. It represents something to ascend such as a corporate organizational chart; or possibly another mountain to climb. Whatever metaphor is used, the pyramid has segmentation markers. In a similar manner, many business organizations use pyramids to distinguish multiple layers, from all customers at base level to so-called partners at the apex. (Major airlines are a prime example of using rewards and loyalty as part of segmentation tactics.)

The fundraising pyramid encapsulates two principles. First, there is a small group of top donors who provide the bulk of monies gifted. The so-called 20/80 rule is a benchmark emphasizing that a relatively small proportion of donors – say 20 per cent – account for the vast bulk – say 80 per cent – of the total funds raised. These high maintenance givers are difficult to cultivate in any formulaic manner, which is to say that one-to-one engagement is required. Second, fundraisers need to find incentives to encourage individuals to ascend the pyramid. Asking for a specific gift in relation to the individual's ability is said to improve the rate of return. Once a suggested donation has been received, the donor falls into a category that the arts organization should seek to cultivate: how to encourage the donor to upgrade the gift? A reworking of Abraham Maslow's psychological hand, from the 1940s, is in evidence. Maslow's basic hierarchy of needs pyramid has five levels of need, ranging from lowest order to highest order: survival and safety, human interaction, love, affiliation, and self-actualization. One is deemed to become more spiritually enlightened at higher levels of the pyramid. This is similar to the three-stage journey of self-discovery posited by Charles Handy (1997): those who do not strive to the summit in 'a search for meaning', namely to make a contribution to society, sell themselves short; too many individuals, once they satisfy basic survival needs, are content to remain at the middle stage of identity, which may accrue through a position in marriage or career.

Cynics interpret the pyramid model as exploiting individual insecurities about being excluded or not belonging to a group. The tactics of television evangelists, with their mixture of bullying and coddling, provide an obvious example. All the leading luxury brand owners understand the power of emotion. Additionally, the USA Securities and Exchange Commission notes that so-called pyramid schemes are a type of fraudulent activity:

> Participants attempt to make money solely by recruiting new participants into the program. The hallmark of these schemes is the promise of sky-high returns in a short period of time for doing nothing other than handing over your money and getting others to do the same.

Money coming in from new recruits is used to pay off early-stage investors, but at some point the scheme gets too big, and the promoter cannot raise enough money from new investors to pay earlier investors – eventually the pyramid will collapse. Bernard Madoff's Ponzi scheme is a current example, albeit on a grand scale.

There is a need to identify and articulate the range of project packages for each campaign to raise funds. Notwithstanding this constant, there are noticeable trends. First, the shift from fundraising to *fund development* is promoted as more than semantic. But is it in practice? Fundraising is about asking for money because the need is so great (i.e. going around with a so-called begging bowl). On the other hand, fund development is about *people* development; that is, creating a constituency in tune with the organization's mission. As such, the ultimate goal of fund development is enabling donors to see their support of the institution as personal self-fulfillment. There is also the general educational benefit of strengthening the mission of the enterprise. Second, an emphasis on generating funds to supplement an endowment recognizes that a properly managed endowment – invest in a manner to grow the capital and live off the interest – offers greater financial stability than a reliance on public subsidy (which is subject to changing political tides) or even commercial operations (which can fluctuate depending on the popularity of programming). A private source of income can offer artistic independence (as suggested by Virginia Woolf in the case of writers who are women). Third, seeking money from individual donors for operating purposes now competes with fundraising for capital projects. The tendency to seek outside money for special projects remains important. Yet more and more of the money required by not-for-profit organizations is for operating purposes (e.g. covering staff wages through endowed positions, a common practice at elite universities with named chairs). More pressing as a practical matter is the need to coordinate an increasingly heady stream of activity that requires ongoing face-to-face appeals to high net worth prospects. Capital projects occur with greater frequency so that a decade is viewed as a long time between major building projects. Ongoing (e.g. year-to-year) campaigns are used to generate much needed operations revenue; furthermore, they serve to remind individuals of the multitude of ways that the institution can benefit from one's generosity.

The social capital associated with being a board member of a leading arts organization would appear to remain high. So-called contracts of giving – with explicit expectations of giving by trustees – were identified to be in use by the end of the twentieth century at some prestigious arts organizations in the USA: $100,000 per annum at the Whitney Museum of American Art, the New York City Ballet was asking $25,000 which was level pegging with the Museum of Fine Arts, Boston (see, for example, *WSJ*, 7 May 1999). Carnegie Hall is a reputed pioneer amongst arts organizations by examining the financial assets of prospective board members as part of the selection process. The general criticism is that such a view of board members – essentially as walking wallets – emphasizes fiscal concerns of art organizations above all else. On the other hand, so-called new money Americans (including self-made HNWIs in their thirties from financial services or high technology) see no taboo in talking about money; however, they may lack the cultural capital associated with inherited wealth. One way to alleviate this source of discomfiture is to make unwritten codes more transparent: 'At various points in history, etiquette books were produced to show the newly rich appropriate table manners. This new openness is the institutional equivalent of showing where to find the dessertspoon', according to Peter Dobkin Hall, the then director of Yale's Program on Nonprofit Organizations (*WSJ*, 7 May 1999).

The first constituency in fundraising is the institution's own board. Raising money is a social process that revolves around the fundraising committee. A figurehead is appointed as patron. From a perspective of generating funds, there is a need for trustees to take an active part in raising money (by giving themselves and persuading others to give). A board member needs to be able to respond to the following when making a pitch: how much are you going to give yourself? It is important to cultivate pace-setting donations, which is done during the so-called quiet phase. This important stage ends when the monetary goal of the fundraising campaign is released to the public. A so-called public campaign is often measured in people not money: this stage is about generating moral support from a wider constituency; however, it is accepted that only a relatively small amount of money will be received.

One illustration of how the stakes have been raised is that becoming a member or friend of an arts organization is about purchasing a service, not an act of philanthropy or making a donation. At base level, benefits need to be explicit. The casual visitor, in considering an annual membership, may do a mental cost–benefit analysis as part of the decision-making process. For example, with the opening of Tate Modern in 2000, Tate decided to revise its membership scheme along lines associated with a restaurant menu: in 2009, a base membership at £57 can be complemented with a guest pass by adding £24 (for all four Tate locations), London private view pass (£24), St. Ives pass (£5), and Liverpool pass (£5). Patrons levels of silver (£1,000–£4,999), gold (£5,000–£9,999), and platinum (£10,000) represent higher levels of membership (i.e. where 'friends' become 'Friends'): one is assumed to be more in tune with the organization's core aims and enjoying concessions becomes less important. At the same time, personal contact with works of art and artists and more intimate access to the institution become crucial. Various stages are visible at the MFA, Boston. Governance is via a two-part structure: at the apex is the board of trustees (25–43 members); in order to talent-spot potential trustees, a second-tier body, called the board of overseers (with a maximum 120 members), was created. In addition, the MFA Council was formed for those in the intermediate stage of post-university, late youth (e.g. aged 25–40); these so-called young associates, who are recognized by many arts organizations as tomorrow's trustees, are attracted to the social life and network potential of an elite arts organization.

The cases of Alberto Vilar and Eli Broad are instructive as both highlight some of the pitfalls of over-reliance on a major donor with bargaining power. First, Vilar emerged in the late 1990s as an international patron of opera. Strings were attached to Vilar's largesse – 'he likes to see his name writ large' – so that there was the Vilar Floral Hall at the Royal Opera House, the Vilar Grand Tier at the Metropolitan Opera, and the Alberto Vilar titles for opera were said to represent a new system of multi-language translation; moreover, 'he has also argued that donors should get bigger programme billing than composers' (London *Daily Telegraph*, 23 May 2001). At the time, Vilar was cited as merely the most recent self-made man turned arts patron, so it was not surprising that his operatic investments were strategically interlinked and based on cultivating social relations. His fall from grace – imprisoned for securities fraud – meant longer term repercussions beyond mere embarrassment for his favoured opera houses.

Second, the following statement appears on the Broad Art Foundation website:

> Underscoring the Broads' profound commitment to public museums and to the city of Los Angeles, Eli and Edythe Broad and the Los Angeles County Museum of Art (LACMA) in 2003 announced the Broads' $60 million donation to create the Broad Contemporary Art Museum (BCAM) at LACMA. This unprecedented gift encompassed three philanthropic goals: to ensure LACMA's crucial role in the presentation of modern and contemporary art in Los Angeles; to bring a great architect to LACMA to help redress its architectural and functional problems; and most importantly to catalyze and advance the growth of Los Angeles as a global capital of contemporary art. The Broads' gift was their largest gift to a single arts institution and the largest donation ever made to LACMA.

The Broad Contemporary Art Museum at the Los Angeles County Museum of Art, which opened in February 2008, is viewed as an act of patronage by a LACMA trustee since 1995 and one of the leading collectors of contemporary art. Yet Broad's decision – announced one month before the opening of what has been described as a museum-within-a-museum – to have his 2,000-odd work collection remain with his foundation, rather than being donated to LACMA, has been criticized in the *New York Review of Books* (Martin Filler, 20 March 2008):

> The parties who acceded to Broad's de facto privatization of a big chunk of LACMA – the cultural equivalent of a leveraged buyout, or taking a public company private – have done a grave disservice to the taxpayers of the county, who,

whether they like it or not, will be footing the bill for much of Broad's monument to himself. . . . art world veterans agree that Eli Broad pulled off an enviable deal for approximately $60 million.

At the outset of the new century, Henry Drucker (2000) considered the potential of developments in philanthropy taking root in the USA:

It is possible to hope that, intelligently adapted and applied to the UK, this metaphorical creature ('venture philanthropy') could importantly aid the not-for-profit sector in two ways: it might offer an additional, new way of giving which would attract substantial sums of money from newly wealthy people; and it might provoke wider change through its poignant and convincing critique of some aspects of the present pattern of giving.

In doing so, Drucker cited the pioneering work on venture philanthropy of Christine Letts at Harvard's Kennedy School of Government. To better understand which venture capital practices could be put to use by the not-for-profit sector, Letts and colleagues hosted a meeting with leaders of foundations, not-for-profit organizations, and venture capital firms. An article in *Harvard Business Review*, in 1997, helped to promote venture philanthropy, including the identification of some relevant venture capital practices: risk management, performance measures, closeness of the relationship, amount of funding, length of the relationship, and the exit (Letts *et al.* 1997).

Newer terms to philanthropy have been suggested: *investment* in lieu of donation or grant (as in investment partner or investee rather than grant recipient or grantee and investor rather than donor); *high engagement* means active investing and monitoring; the need for funded projects to have *high impact* addresses a requirement to measure performance, hence a *social return on investment; scalability*, which comes from internet start-ups, refers to selecting basic models that can be scaled up to increase the social impact; the potential to become self-sufficient is a factor of *capacity building*. However, Andrew Clark, writing in the *FT Magazine* (23/24 February 2008), also recognizes the potential limitations of venture philanthropists in the arts: 'The arts work on the basis that you employ the best available and let them get on with it, whereas businesspeople and bankers operate within a set of strict management controls'; 'It's the difference between being driven by the profit motive and being vocational . . .'. Clark continues:

If you start from those very different standpoints, whenever a decision is taken there will be tension between the two. The focus in the arts is content; for donors from the business world it's as much about presentation. The audience they have in mind is their peer-group – people who think like them and judge the world by the same criteria.

Not unlike attempts to attract support as part of a company's corporate social responsibilities, where the arts trail behind social causes in the areas of health, education, and welfare, traditional arts organizations such as art museums, orchestras, opera companies, and ballet troupes have struggled to hang on to the attention of donors in the competitive arena of venture philanthropy (McGee 2006). Potential venture philanthropists may see arts organizations as sites of aesthetic pleasure, thus less directly relevant in changing lives compared to cancer research, famine relief, or the alleviation of poverty and homelessness in metropolitan cities. In order to create a new pool of donors/investors, it is necessary to create new audiences. But, how to connect them to the activities of arts organizations?

Of course, there are inspirational examples of high aesthetic achievement. Artangel (artangel.org.uk) is able to make a claim that it

has pioneered a new way of collaborating with artists and engaging audiences in an ambitious series of highly successful commissions since the early 1990s. We've created a reputation for producing work that people really want to see and for which they often travel miles to experience.

This commitment to the production of powerful new ideas by exceptional artists has been at the forefront of changing attitudes and growing expectations amongst both artists and audiences.

Beyond the white walls of the gallery, the black box of the theatre or the darkened interior of the cinema, there are other forms of expression where the relationship between artist and place is of primary importance. This is a relationship which Artangel actively explores in events where context and content are often indistinguishable. An artist's response to the qualities and conditions of a particular place is central to the development of a project. And finding the right place is an integral part of the commissioning process we undertake.

A prominent work is Rachel Whiteread's *House*, in which the artist made a cast of a Victorian terraced house in London's East End, which was completed in autumn 1993. Created as a public sculpture, which won high praise as one of the most ambitious sculptures made by an English artist in the twentieth century, the work was demolished in January 1994 (as intended by the artist). Screening *The Cremaster Cycle* (cremaster.net), a series of five films written and directed by Matthew Barney between 1994 and 2002, in London's Ritzy Cinema in 2002 is another high profile event, according to Film Forum:

An art world phenomenon eight years in the making, Barney's epic cycle of birth and sexual differentiation melds genres as diverse as the Busby Berkeley musical, the gothic Western, and operatic spectacle, encompassing Celtic myth, Masonic initiation rites, motorcycle races, obscure historical references, high fashion, lush music, and category-defying imagery, as it spans half the globe, from Boise to Budapest, with Barney himself popping up as a tap-dancing satyr, a naked magician, a giant, and serial killer Gary Gilmore.

The commissions of Artangel are due to patrons, with many art world insiders listed: Company of Angels (£750 per annum or £500 for each of four years) with gallerists (e.g. Sadie Coles, Stephen Friedman, Alison Jacques, Barbara Gladstone, Michael Hue-Williams, Nicholas Logsdail, Victoria Miro, Stuart Shave, Graham Southern, Timothy Taylor, and Angela Westwater), museum directors (e.g. Mark

Jones, Sandy Nairne, and Nicholas Serota) among the 167; Special Angels (£5,000 per annum) with private dealer Ivor Braka among the 13; Artangel International Circle (a small group of committed benefactors based around the world who make a five-year commitment at a substantial level of support) which includes Iwan Wirth (collector and dealer behind Hauser & Wirth) and Anita Zabludowicz (collector and founder of art space 176); and Artangel America with 501(c)3 status for tax-relief benefit to America donors. Artangel's aesthetic decision-making of commissioning projects is beneficial, particularly in an art world often fixated with objects for sale (the so-called commodity fetish). Moreover, the desire for experiences between artists and audiences, including the relationship between artists and places, has not been compromised by commissioning decisions. Many of the projects – not least of the examples of Whiteread and Barney – are challenging, but also engaging.

5

ARTS CONSUMPTION
AND CONSUMERS

Arts consumption and consumers places an emphasis on the demand for the arts. What stimulates demand for the arts? Who are arts consumers? Consuming the arts can operate on several levels. Appreciators (spectators) are a core category as regular participants of the arts. They can be distinguished from non-appreciators, who do not include the arts as part of their regular basket of consumption goods and services. What accounts for arts consumption at the level of appreciation is discussed in the first section of the chapter. The interests of cultural economists and sociologists researching the arts both emphasize the cultivation of taste with different explanations. Cultural economics, as advanced by George Stigler and Gary Becker, emphasizes utility (satisfaction) maximization such that taste for the high arts is a form of addiction. The late Pierre Bourdieu is viewed as a pioneer in the sociology of art, with Paul DiMaggio, Howard Becker, Raymonde Moulin, Richard Peterson, and Vera Zolberg as other prominent contributors. The second section examines the pressing and complex issue of audience development: initiatives to encourage genuine audience development at the local level often confront structural barriers to widening arts participation. Advanced and more engaged levels of arts consumption – building on appreciation, which may lead to arts patronage such as commissioning contemporary operas or collecting fine art and antiques – is addressed in the third section. From a historical perspective, these are forms of elite recreational activity that require wealth. Attention on demand for the arts both counters and complements the focus on the supply side of the equation, namely building and strengthening the supply of artists and performing and visual arts organizations.

Consumption and consumers is an obvious reference to the management function of marketing. 'Art becomes a process which goes through the endless manufacture of objects produced, new or used, exhibited or forgotten', according to contemporary art curator, Achille Bonita Oliva (1988: 40), 'in which the artist intervenes to rescue the object from the first chain of *ordinary consumption* and to put it into a higher chain, that of *aesthetic consumption*' (my emphasis). 'Marketing and the arts', as a complementary appendix, examines the dual role of marketing and the arts: 'marketing for the arts' (or arts marketing) – essentially the modified application of marketing management principles (e.g. Philip Kotler) to the arts – is core to arts management (e.g. Kirchberg and Zemblyas 2009; Colbert in Towse 2003); and critical or interpretive marketing perspectives of 'the arts for marketing' have taken root (e.g. Brown and Patterson 2000), including the contribution of contemporary artists.

ARTS APPRECIATION AND TASTE FORMATION

The position of cultural economists has gained less attention in the literature outside of economics relative to the sociological explanation. Cultural economists focus on experience and exposure in taste formation (see McCain in Towse 2003), with George Stigler and Gary Becker providing a starting point with an influential paper, 'De gustibus non est disputandum' (Latin maxim 'there is no disputing about tastes'), in the *American Economic Review* (1977). 'We are proposing the hypothesis that widespread and/or persistent human behavior can be explained by a general calculus of utility-maximizing behavior, without introducing the qualification "tastes remaining the same" ' (Stigler and Becker 1977: 76). In particular the notion of maximizing satisfaction – a key element for economic thought – is used to understand arts consumption: 'In a word or two, the activity of art is a maximizing activity. Without that assumption, economics has no place in the study of art or anything else', according to William Grampp (1989: 8). Appreciating art is a cultivated taste: preferences are shaped by consumption experiences as an adult. A taste for art is acquired – or discovered – and the rate of arts consumption increases over time with exposure, according to Stigler and Becker (1977: 77–78):

> Tastes are frequently said to change as a result of consuming certain 'addictive' goods. For example, smoking of cigarettes, drinking alcohol, injection of heroin, or close contact with some persons over a appreciable period of time, often increases the desire (creates a craving) for these goods or persons, and thereby cause their consumption to grow over time. In utility language, their marginal utility is said to rise over time because tastes shift in their favor.

In this case, one can refer to arts consumption as 'addictive' – that is, the arts consumer attempts to maximize satisfaction. Arts consumption increases with an ability to appreciate art, which is a function of past arts consumption, thus satisfaction arises over time. Stigler and Becker (1977: 79–80) acknowledged the role of education: 'The effect of exposure on the accumulation of music capital; might well depend on the level of education and other human capital. . . . This would explain why educated persons consume more "good" music (i.e. music that educated people like!) than other persons do' (emphasis in the original). The role of education is crucial in the sociological explanation of arts appreciation.

The sociological approach to the understanding of the predisposition to art and cultural consumption – which is at odds with the standard Kantian aesthetic philosophy in which the purity of aesthetic contemplation derives from so-called disinterested pleasure – owes much to Bourdieu and Darbel's *L'amour de l'art* (1969; translated in 1991 as *For the Love of Art*), which is based on a series of visitor (audience) surveys at various French art museums in the 1960s.[1] The work challenged the 'myth of innate taste'; it set out to define the social conditions which made this experience – Kant's phrase that 'the beautiful is that which pleases without concept' – and the people for whom it is possible (art lovers and so-called 'people of taste'). 'Free entry is also optional entry' or a 'false generosity', according to Bourdieu and Darbel (1991: 109–13), as it is 'reserved for those who, equipped with the ability to appreciate works of art, have the privilege of making use of this freedom'. That high arts consumption, such as attending opera performances or visiting public art museums, is closely linked to educational level (whether measured by qualifications or length of schooling) and secondarily to social origin remains an important conclusion. Indeed it has been validated by more recent studies in countries with a different sociopolitical and arts funding contexts to France (which is discussed below).

Bourdieu's *La Distinction* (1979; translated in 1984 as *Distinction*) – with the subtitle, 'a social critique of the judgement of taste' – continued the general thesis of the earlier text by emphasizing formal education and the family. 'To the socially recognized hierarchy of the arts, and within each of them, of genres, of schools, or periods, corresponds a social hierarchy of the consumers. This predisposes tastes to function as markers of "class" ', according to Bourdieu (1984: 1–2). A three-zone model of cultural taste, representing a hierarchy of tastes and preferences which correspond to education and social class, is proffered: *legitimate* (e.g. the *Art of Fugue* or the *Concerto for the Left Hand*, or in painting, Breughel or Goya); *middle brow* (e.g. minor works in the major arts such as *Rhapsody in Blue*, or, in painting, Utrillo, Dubuffet or even Renoir); and *popular* (e.g. choice of work of so-called light music or classical music devalued by popularization, such as the *Blue Danube*, and especially, songs totally devoid of artistic ambition). Moreover, according to a British commentator, Paul Greenhalgh (in Vergo 1989: 86):

> It was clear by 1900 that the higher arts were perceived by the middle class as a kind of cultural duty – a form of work which was necessary to maintain status – and that art of any kind was barely perceived at all by the working classes. Therefore, not only was the relation between education and pleasure problematic, but also the boundaries of what properly constituted pleasure.

Bourdieu's work on the sociology of cultural consumption is more important for some sections of society than others: 'It is, however, within the dominant class, the bourgeoisie, that symbolic struggles are most apparent and most severe. It is here that the definition of cultural legitimacy is fought over' (Jenkins 1992: 142).

The science of taste and cultural consumption is examined by Bourdieu (1984) with the following postulate in mind: 'A work of art has meaning and interest only for someone who possesses the cultural competence, that is, the code, into which it is encoded'. An autobiographical account by Dillon Ripley (1969: 140), secretary of the Smithsonian Institute (1964–84), near to the end of *The Sacred Grove* offers some impressions of his early experience with museums:

> My own philosophy of museums became established at the age of ten, one winter when we were living in Paris. One of the advantages of playing in the Tuileries

Gardens as a child was that at any one moment one could be riding the carousel, hoping against hope to catch the ring. . . . Another moment and one could wander into one of the galleries of the Louvre. I still remember one day I found the ship models . . . Then out to the garden again where there was a patch of sand in the corner to build sand castles. Then back to the Louvre to wander through the Grand Gallery.

There was no essential difference in all of this. The juxtaposition was natural and easy. No threshold of tiredness and lack of concentration was reached. It was as easy as breathing in and out.

This suggests that Ripley learned to master the code as if it were play. His obituary in the *New York Times* (13 March 2001) makes reference to his education – BA Yale and PhD Harvard – and family background: 'Though born to wealth and privilege [his great grandfather was founding chairman of the Union Pacific Railway], Mr. Ripley had a common touch, which he brought to his work at the Smithsonian'. Yet not everyone is so fortunate, according to Bourdieu (1984: 2):

A beholder who lacks the specific code feels lost in a chaos of sounds and rhythms, colours, and lines, without rhyme or reason. . . . Thus the encounter with a work of art is not 'love at first sight' as is generally supposed . . . [rather] the art-lover's pleasure presupposes an act of cognition, a decoding operation, which implies the implementation of a cognitive acquirement, a cultural code.

Successful mastery of the code to gain artistic competence, according to Bourdieu, requires use of scarce resource time. First, there must be economic means to invest in educational time; this marks differential class access to different levels of education. Second, the development of cultural practice and artistic production has become more complex in its coding; the requirement that one is *au fait* with a wider and wider range of cultural references – not least of all because much contemporary art is self-referential – has meant that one needs to devote more and more time in order to remain competent, or use money to recruit advisors who can supplement one's own taste and time commitment.

Arthur Danto (1964: 581) made the following observation with reference to Warhol's *Brillo Box* (1964), a reproduction of a Brillo box, which was exhibited in the same year:

What in the end makes the difference between a Brillo box and a work of art consisting of a Brillo box is a certain theory of art. It is the theory of art that takes it up into the world of art, and keeps it from collapsing into the real object which it is (in a sense of *is* other than that of artistic identification). Of course, without the theory, one is unlikely to see it as art, and in order to see it as part of the artworld, one must have mastered a good deal of artistic theory as well as a considerable amount of the history of recent New York painting (emphasis in the original).

To appreciate Warhol's work, Danto implied that one required knowledge of Duchamp and of post-Second World War painting in New York, namely Abstract Expressionism and the rise of Pop Art. A progenitor of Pop Art in the UK, Peter Blake, writing in *Art World* (December 2007/January 2008), has made a similar case for Damien Hirst: he 'has pretty much brought the possibilities of two main branches of abstract painting to a conclusion'. First, Color Field painting, associated with Kenneth Noland and Ellsworth Kelly, is set alongside Hirst's spot paintings, 'which work on a formula, and in a way there is nowhere you could go after that with Color Field painting'. Blake adds: 'With the spot paintings, you know exactly what you'll get; you could almost choose the colours. You are getting a made-to-measure, readymade abstract painting that couldn't be more beautiful'. Second, Hirst's spin paintings, which were 'created by pouring paint on to a revolving surface, are completely random, which is what the Abstract Expressionists in the main were attempting to do – it's certainly what Jackson Pollock was trying to do', according to Blake, who continued: 'Again, with the spin paintings, you get an absolutely beautiful work'. 'This doesn't mean that to make an abstract painting after Hirst is invalid', according to Blake, 'but that he brought what was going on to a conclusion at that point'.

Likewise, the following exchange between two friends in *Art*, by French playwright Yasmina Reza (1996: 24), emphasizes that conditions exist for the aesthetic appreciation of so-called legitimate art:

Marc: Are you going to have it framed?
Serge laughs discreetly.
Serge: No! . . . But, no . . .
Marc: Why not?
Serge: It's not supposed to be framed.
Marc: Is that right?
Serge: The artist doesn't want it to be. It mustn't be interpreted. It's already in its setting. (*He signals Marc over to the edge.*) Look . . . you see . . .
Marc: What is it, Elastoplast?
Serge: No, it's a kind of Kraft paper . . . Made up by the artist.

Contemporary artists invite ironic gestures. For example, conceptualist photographer Tom Hunter, who has a strong affinity for Hackney, a depressed borough of London, used an artist residency at the National Gallery to create works for an accompanying exhibition, 'Living in Hell and Other Stories' (December 2005 to March 2006). Explicit visual references to Old Master paintings in the NG collection are reconstructed to address local tabloid press headings. Thus '*The Rokeby Venus*' (1647–51), which the NG describes as 'the only example of a female nude by Velázquez', is staged in Ye Olde Axe with a pub stripper – representing a vanishing tradition of (male) working class entertainment – posing as Venus. As part of a (successful) campaign by the NG and the National Gallery of Scotland to raise £50 million to keep Titian's *Diana and Actaeon* (1556–59) on public display, Hunter recreated the scene with a semi-nude Kim Cattrall as Diana. The aesthetic practice of Kent Monkman, a Canadian painter and performance artist of Aboriginal descent, inverts the works of two of Canada's most well-known artists, Paul Kane (1810–71) and Cornelius Kreighoff (1815–72): he updates the historical representation of painting from the mid-nineteenth century – a post-colonial nod – along with a very witty homosexual undertone of queering colonialism. As another example of cultural competence and consumption, consider the intentionally provocative comment by the occasional opera director Jonathan Miller (London *Guardian*, 6 August 1998): 'If you perform *Il Trovatore* with Pavarotti, and you attract an audience of the sort that applauds when the curtain goes up, then you know that you've committed a deeply vulgar opera'. These examples reinforce Bourdieu's point that mastery is required to appreciate a work of art; moreover, money alone is not enough to acquire taste and aesthetic acumen.

The general thrusts of *For the Love of Art* and *Distinction*, in terms of schooling exerting a determining influence and social inequities of inheriting cultural capital from one's parents, have been validated by researchers in Anglo-American countries. This addresses a main criticism of Bourdieu's thesis that it was particular to French sensibilities of the 1960s.

Sociologist Paul DiMaggio has been at the forefront in examining the role of the arts in the USA. DiMaggio and Useem (1980: 59) have considered the factors at the root of one's disposition to the arts and cultural participation:

> Although there were variations between several fields of the arts . . . the pattern of high educational attainment being linked to attendance held for every field of the arts we studied. (Visitors to science, history, and natural history museums were noticeably less well-educated, although they were more similar to the arts audiences studied than to the public at large.) Art attenders were much more well-educated than the public at large whatever the art form, whether performances took place indoors or outside and whether admission or tickets were expensive or free.

Furthermore, 'a substantial amount of evidence indicates that educational attainment is strongly related to the arts and cultural involvement and that education is a better predictor of such involvement than are occupation and income' (DiMaggio and Useem 1980: 62). Schuster (1991: 2, 43) corroborates the chief findings of DiMaggio and Useem: 'The audience for the arts [in the USA] was more highly educated, was of higher occupational status, and had a higher income than the population as a whole'; and he adds that 'while short-term changes in the audience profile may be attained through very visible and popularly attractive exhibitions or programs, it is much more difficult to sustain these changes over a longer period of time'. This is consistent with more recent research findings published by the NEA (2004: 24), based on the 2002 Survey of Public Participation in the Arts:

> More than any other demographic factor, going to arts events and art museums is hugely correlated with an individual's educational attainment. Education is much more predictive of arts attendance than household income, for instance.
>
> In turn, educational attainment is a proxy for many other factors including early introduction to the arts through parents and schools, formal arts training, proximity to art offerings, and a number of social factors.

'When modified to account for sociohistorical context, Bourdieu's theory can be used to excavate social class differences in contemporary American consumption' (Holt 1998: 22).

Race has been a prominent issue in the USA, which makes the research of DiMaggio and Ostrower (in Prankratz and Morris 1990) enlightening. The consumption by black Americans of so-called European cultural products is lower than for whites, with the proviso that the 'effects of race on these activities, however, are dwarfed by those of educational attainment and are often less than those of income, gender, or place of residence'; more importantly, their study supports 'the applicability of the notion of capital, as developed by Bourdieu in research on historically unicultural France, to multicultural United States' which confirms 'the utility of viewing patterns of artistic taste and consumption as quasi-rational responses to incentives for investment in capital culture, and of interpreting cultural capital as symbolic information about social membership required by persons with complex and extended social networks', according to DiMaggio and Ostrower (in Prankratz and Morris 1990: 130, 131, 132). The research conducted by John Falk (1998: 40) into museum attendance in the USA reveals that race is not the key factor:

African-American leisure behavior is very similar to European-American leisure behavior, though tremendous differences in leisure behavior exist within the African-American community. Whereas black-white differences exist, and there are some, race does not emerge as the best variable to explain them.

Falk (1998: 41), like Bourdieu, identifies social origins:

One of the best predictors of whether an adult will go to a museum is whether he was taken to museums by his parent when he was a child. . . . Historically, many minorities, recent immigrants, and the economic under-class had less opportunities to visit museums as children than the more affluent majority population.

Briton Nick Merriman has criticized Bourdieu's exclusion of psychological factors in preference for sociological ones; however, Merriman (1991: 82) concluded that Bourdieu's shortcomings were less problematic in certain cases when considering the situation in the UK:

A contributory factor must be Bourdieu's concentration on art galleries where, we have seen in the case of the Tate Gallery and the Victoria & Albert Museum, visitors are much more highly educated and of a higher status than in more general museums, and where arguments about cultural and class divisions are easier to make.

The classification of museums by subject matter has invited a hierarchy. Museums of archeology and natural history were prominent at first, in the nineteenth century; however, the present situation is marked by the art museum as the 'paradigm of the museum experience', according to Ludmilla Jordanova (in Vergo 1989: 24). This illustrates a class structure of museum objects and museums themselves, with the non-utilitarian being more highly valued from an aesthetic perspective. In theatrical productions, a similar ranking takes place with musicals ranked lower than plays in terms of artistic merit and intention.

It has been suggested by Nicholas Penny, now director of the National Gallery, that Bourdieu and his adherents 'smugly explain away the complex relationship with the past which great collections and the museums of the [nineteenth] century reveal' (*LRB*, 21 December 1989). Even those in sympathy with Bourdieu's position, such as Garnham and Williams (1980: 222), have deliberated in public:

> There seems to us (and this is very much a question of tone, nuance and attitude) to be a functionalist/determinist residue in Bourdieu's concept of reproduction which leads him to place less emphasis on the possibilities of real change and innovation than either his theory or his empirical research makes necessary.

Due to the constraints of individual arts organizations to respond to the conclusions provided by socio-demographic profiling at the macro-level, many have turned to individual psychology to better understand the behaviour of attenders and non-attenders. For example, lifestyle analysis (or psychographics) is based on the assumption that marketers can plan more effective strategies if they know more about their target markets in terms of so-called attitudes, interests, and opinions. Entrance fees may be viewed as a *subjective* barrier to visiting museums, according to research conducted in Europe: 'Conscious lifestyle choices represent *actual* barriers to museum visits, not the amount of entrance fees. This agrees with Bourdieu and Darbel's analysis' (Kirchberg 1998: 9; my emphasis). This is consistent with findings on arts consumption in the UK that 'as a barrier to attendance price appears to have only a limited influence; there are many other factors which affect the decision to attend' (Feist in Fitzgibbon and Kelly 1997: 261). Pricing is complex. Opera is expensive so that even £50 – near the high range for popular musicals in London – does not guarantee an unobstructed view at the Royal Opera House. On the other hand, the Wallace Collection – London's equivalent to New York's Frick Collection, with the finest display of Old Master paintings in a single exhibition room, is merely five minutes away from the main retail artery of Oxford Street – is free.

From an American perspective, it has been noted that 'most studies have shown the demand for attendance at the live performing arts to be price inelastic' (Heilbrun and Gray 1993: 94). This means that consumers of such services are not especially sensitive to changes in price. On its own, the decision to (re)introduce so-called free entry to the permanent collections of the designated national museums (based in London) is not enough to entice a socio-demographic mix that replicates the UK population at large. Are many non-attenders rejecting arts and culture offers prior to a consideration of price? What other barriers exist? How are they being addressed? At the same time, many existing attenders who can afford to pay an entry tariff – say even £10, which is less than a West End London cinema ticket and much, much less expensive than attending a Premier League football match (if tickets are available) – are being subsidized.

Possibly more important than price are so-called emotional barriers. Is the institution perceived to be threatening or unwelcoming? Viewing the building as exterior space, contemporary architects of art museums – building types in their own right –

try to avoid imposing grandeur and monumentality (Markus 1993). This reflects a changing aesthetic of how the art museum wants to be perceived. For example, the Philadelphia Museum of Art's building opened in 1926 and became known as the Philadelphian Acropolis; the Griffin, a fabulous creature with an eagle's head and wings and a lion's body, continues to protect the institution. Yet there was a missed opportunity to exploit popular culture links to Sylvester Stallone's working class hero in *Rocky I* (1976), who makes a triumphant run up the stairs of the PMA, to widen the visitor base. The Pompidou Centre, on the other hand, which opened in 1977, stands out as 'a turning-point in the design of museums by stating the case for the *desanctification* of art' (Davis 1990: 42; my emphasis), with riding its escalator and dining in the rooftop George restaurant listed as key activities for tourists in Paris.

From an American perspective, Marilyn Hood (1983) has been influential in advancing research from leisure studies to better understand why people do or do not attend museums, and how to attract people who do not already attend. She identifies five profile attributes of pleasurable or satisfying leisure experiences: the opportunity to learn, social interaction, the challenge of new experiences, participating actively, and feeling comfortable in one's surroundings. 'Such characteristics are shared by people of all races and ethnicities, incomes, education levels, and ages, regardless of sex', according to Falk (1998: 40), who contends that Hood's first point, the opportunity to learn, is consistent with Bourdieu's findings:

> The primary reason most people attend museums, whether by themselves or with their children, is in order to learn. That is a major reason why museum-going correlates so highly to a level of education. That is not because one needs a college degree to think learning is important. It is because individuals who think learning is important are more inclined to pursue higher education than those who don't. Individuals who value learning seek it in many forms through higher education; by watching educational television; by reading books, magazines, and newspapers; and by visiting museums.

With research interests similar to Hood, but working in the UK, David Prince (1990: 166) believes that non-attenders are 'a legitimate part of the potential audience' and that their perceptions of arts organizations as both 'social institutions and visit destinations' need to be considered. Prince (1990: 166), like Hood, stresses that 'attitudes and life values are more useful analytical devices for understanding the problem' of non-participation; however, he is more willing to concede that attitudes and life values 'are themselves mediated by class factors . . . peer group and culture self recognition and allegiance'.

Levels of arts participation include absolute level of consumption, rates of participation, and frequency of participation (see, for example, McCarthy, Ondaatje, and Zakaras 2001). One can cite rising arts attendance figures for many individual arts organizations. At the same time, the habit of arts participation is not evenly distributed throughout the population, as indicated by classical music and museum attendance in the USA: 'Over one-third of people with education beyond college went to at least one classical performance in 2002, compared with 4 per cent of adults with just a high school education' (NEA 2004: 22); 'Although museum attendees look a lot like the total population in most respects, they differ in two important ways: they are better educated and have higher incomes' (McCarthy, Ondaatje, and Zakaras 2001: 50). The importance of word-of-mouth as a communications tool for arts organizations leads to social replication: the more friends and family members one has who participate in the arts the more likely one is to follow suit.

AUDIENCE DEVELOPMENT

Arts managers who are interested in broadening the audience base are confronted with a truism: change in audience composition is a slow, resistant process. The Lila-Wallace-Reader's Digest Fund commissioned RAND Corporation (McCarthy and Jinnett 2001) to examine the innovative ways arts and cultural organizations attract new audiences, reach a larger share of existing audiences, and deepen the involvement of current participants. Encouraging new audiences is about genuine audience development; marketing can help arts organization get more of the same (that is a larger share of existing audiences); and marketing and development initiatives are about helping to strengthen relationships with current participants (including the so-called ladder of higher annual membership levels and to donor status categories associated with fundraising). A consumer behaviour model is proffered with stages of decision-making, namely an individual's background followed by three stages, perceptual, practical, and experience, to indicate factors that influence an individual's decision to participate in the arts. Background – which includes socio-demographic characteristics (such as education and income), personality factors unique to the individual, an individual's past experiences, and the individual's social/cultural identification – help to shape a person's perceptions about the arts. In many respects, McCarthy and Jinnett (2001: xi) cover the ground of Bourdieu *et al.* from the sociology of arts and Stigler and Becker *et al.* from cultural economics:

> The current research literature on arts participation offers these institutions little guidance for their participation building efforts. This literature has two major drawbacks. First, it oversimplifies the process an individual goes through in deciding to participate in the arts, failing to take into account that the process involves more than one decision and that different factors determine the outcomes of each decision. Arts institutions thus are not provided with enough information to determine what strategies may be appropriate for encouraging the participation of those who constitute their target populations. Second, it emphasizes individuals' socio-demographics rather than their motivations and attitudes, thereby failing to provide the practical guidance institutions need if they are to influence people's participation behavior. An arts institution cannot, after all, influence an individual's background characteristics.

There is an acknowledgement of barriers to participate as some individuals, because of their background and attitudes, are disinclined to participate in the arts.

Changing the perceptions of non-attenders is central to the first stage: attitudes toward arts participation result from personal beliefs about arts participation and perceptions of social norms towards arts participation. Outreach programmes, often managed via educational arms of arts organizations, are central. There is a moral imperative of social responsibilities to make the arts available to a wider cross-section of society; at the same time, there is political capital especially for elite arts organizations in receipt of substantial public subsidies. The London examples of Tate Modern and the Royal Opera House are illustrative. Situated in the depressed London borough of Southwark, Tate Modern has assumed a leadership role in trying to engage with local youth and young adults: Tate Forum, based on the participation of those aged 16–18 years and living in Southwark, is an art group that also serves as a focus group; Tate Tracks was based on popular recording artists setting tracks to a work in the permanent collection that could only be heard at Tate Modern, thus Roll Deep on Anish Kapoor, Graham Coxon on Franz Kline, and the Chemical Brothers on Jacob Epstein; and two Long Weekend events in May. One outcome is support for Tate Modern's expansion to coincide with preparations for the London 2012 Olympics. The chief executive of the ROH, Tony Hall (ROH Annual Review 2007/08: 17–18), highlights new technology:

> Broadening our appeal through the deployment of new media in an appropriate and strategic fashion is a key aspect of our widening access strategy. . . . Our presence online in forums such as Facebook and YouTube has proved wildly popular with the number of hits every day demonstrating how important it is to reach our audiences of every age using relevant media. This year we will beam live and recorded performances into cinemas in both the UK and North America, extending to further areas of the globe in the near future. . . . While there is no substitute for the unique experience of attending a live performance at the Royal Opera House, the democratisation of our art forms via new media is a development that we wholeheartedly embrace and will continue to pioneer.

If one controls for education as a factor, effects of arts socialization – arts education classes and more general exposure to the arts – are particularly important in explaining differences in participation rates among the less well educated.

The second stage – intention and decision to participate – includes several decisions, including where, when, and how. Arts organizations can address these practical issues in various ways: touring and off-site programming, extended opening hours, online presence and information, and tactical pricing or sales promotions. Experience – the third stage – includes participation and reaction to the experience. If the experience is unpleasant, which may include a psychological discomfort of being apart from the rest of the audience, there may not be a repeat visit. Consider the assumed etiquette for listening to art music, according to the then artistic director of the London Philharmonic Orchestra, Serge Dorny (London *Daily Telegraph*, 5 October 2000), who was appointed director general of the Lyon National Opera in 2005:

> To the first-time concert-goer, the unwritten codes of music appreciation can seem as demanding as Tamino's initiation rituals in Mozart's *The Magic Flute* – get

to your seat before the music starts, sit still, listen in silence without rustling the programme or tapping your feet, and don't on any account applaud between movements. If you have a music degree, you're off to a good start. If you haven't, and your motivation is pure pleasure, then you may feel that you are in the right place at the wrong time.

There is an unresolved dichotomy between aesthetic excellence and access. Does widening the audience base need to be at the expense of having an educated audience? Lack of knowledge of a particular art form raises interesting issues. Is there a responsibility on the part of performing and visuals arts organizations to provide background information to complete neophytes? What level of visual or musical literacy should an arts organization assume on the part of its audience? What are the implications of focusing on the quality of experience of arts participants as consumers?

For example, Acoustiguide, the leading firm in the supply of audioguides to museums, emphasizes its value in supporting interpretative goals, which may be important to making the experience of non-habitual visitors more rewarding. But is access enhanced? Moreover, are audioguide users given sufficient tools to develop their own appreciation of art? Or do they remain dependent on the museum's products for their knowledge and feelings of privilege? Ressa Greenberg (1987: 107) has offered an instructive critique:

> The true educational function of Acoustiguide and similar tours, then, is not a democratic one. Quite the contrary, as Pierre Bourdieu has demonstrated in the 'Aristocracy of Culture' chapter in *Distinction* and his earlier *L'amour de l'art*. One learns to yearn and later to demonstrate the requisite Kantian disinterest of the true initiate. One learns to spend one's time looking, while listening, supposedly in pursuit of knowledge, all the while lusting for the chimera of privilege imparted by the voice on the tape.

This supports a belief that most visitors aspire less to professional competence than to what Bourdieu calls 'status-induced familiarity' with legitimate culture. Institutions like products that support untapped markets; the audioguide, as a popular, mid-market gadget, fits this bill. Those who are unable (or unwilling) to spend that most luxurious of commodities – time – in pursuit of a passion, are addressed by the audioguide: so-called highlights of a permanent collection or temporary exhibition can be covered in a reasonable period of time. As an ancillary service, audioguides generate cash in a more cost-effective manner than traditional methods (e.g. tours by education staff members or volunteers) by exploiting advances in technology; and, like other consumer products driven by technology such as mobile telephones, audioguides continue to become more aesthetically appealing to users.

The regression of listening to art music – a theme Theodor Adorno (1973) raised in the 1930s and 1940s – continues to be addressed. Pianist Charles Rosen (*NYRB*, 20 December 2001) cites first principles of acculturation:

Learning to sing and learning to play the piano have been supplanted today by collecting records. This is a disquieting development that is already affecting the future. The audience for serious music has become increasingly passive, and there is no longer an important body of educated listeners experienced in the making of music that can act as a bridge between the general public and the professional.

The popularizing of art music has led to accusations of aural wallpaper: so-called listeners tune-in to classical music stations, but do not really listen; bookstores play classical music to add an aura of educated sophistication. On the other hand, dwindling audiences for art music has depressing consequences: the language of the classical and modern canon (say from Beethoven and Bach to Schoenberg and Stravinsky) is so unpleasant to those accustomed to a diet of MTV music videos that it can be used to shift undesirable youths from unattended car parks and shopping malls.

ART COLLECTING AND COLLECTORS

There is a growing body of literature on the cultures of collecting, which is an intensely involving and engaged form of consumption.[2] Numerous categories can be cited. Memory and meaning in the case of family-based objects passed from one generation to another, which is core to the *Antiques Roadshow* television programmes on both sides of the Atlantic. There is social interaction of children – mainly boys – and cards. Art as a means to display wealth and gain social status – with the aesthetic and spiritual value of art and its cash worth in the marketplace – is a theme with long associations. The role of art dealer Joseph Duveen and monied America collectors such as Andrew Mellon is well-known (see, for example, Blom 2002: 124–36), and serves as a backdrop to the plot of Simon Gray's *The Old Masters* (2004), which addresses some ethical issues of the art market (in the 1930s), including Duveen's relationship with art historian Bernard Berenson. French philosopher Jean Baudrillard, with a contribution from 1968, was included in *The Cultures of Collecting* (Elsner and Cardinal 1994). Adam Lindemann (2005) included fellow collectors as key contemporary art market players alongside art dealers. Collectors can be private individuals, public institutions (e.g. art museums and university collections), or commercial institutions (e.g. corporate collections). There is a longstanding and complex relationship between private collectors and public institutions (Brooke 1989; Cuno 2004; AAMD January 2007).

Collecting is about the gathering together and ordering of objects, which is distinct from object organization. A distinction is made between collecting and terms such as accumulating, possessing, and hoarding. Is collecting a form of commodity fetishism? Or does collecting exist independently of capitalism? In the *Financial Times*'s 'How to Spend It' magazine (September 2008), Tamara Salman, Liberty of London's creative director, talks about her collection:

About two years ago, my partner found Ray Caesar's work on the internet [raycaesar.com] and thought it would appeal to me – how right he was, and I've become somewhat obsessed. Caesar is a British artist living in Canada – he's a very strange person who sometimes thinks he's a dog. He paints digitally, and his warped imagination produces an extraordinary mix of vivid colour, innocence and almost pornographic macabreness, in the context of a surreal Victorian Gothic fantasy, that I find completely inspirational. I've always collected creepy antique dolls' heads, and their moulds, that look rather like his figures.

I've collected five of his works – they are prints, but in small editions, and they are becoming much harder to get hold of. My favourite shows what looks like two Victorian girls whispering together, very chocolate-boxy until you realize that have horrible lobster hands.

I researched the late Victorian culture in which Arthur Liberty flourished and was drawn to his subversive side. Caesar's work has the same feel and somehow fits with everything at Liberty. We shot the autumn campaign in New York, in the avenue that leads to the Woolworth mansion, which looks like a Caesar painting.

Salman begins by noting that Caesar is a contemporary artist who 'paints digitally'. There is a case that many contemporary artists who exploit technological advances in mechanical reproduction are able to make objects in an interesting manner – the artist becomes an 'exclusive consumer of anonymously produced and continually circulating things' (Groys in Grunenberg and Hollein 2002: 56). The artist or producer is a marked absence in the consumer behavior research of Russell Belk *et al.* (1988), who examined collectors and collecting using a data collection procedure not dissimilar to allowing collectors to talk about their collection. Indeed, as Grunenberg (in Grunenberg and Hollein 2002: 17) has noted, in reference to art and consumer culture: 'Meaning is created not just by *what* we buy, but also *where* and *how* and what happens to the product once it is in our possession' (emphasis in the original).

In an article published in *Advances in Consumer Research* Russell Belk *et al.* (1988: 548–53) proffered eight propositions about collecting, which are instructive alongside Salman's ruminations. First, 'collections seldom begin purposefully'. Salman 'discovered' Caesar through the gift-giving of her partner. Indeed the gesture of the gift is one of caring, a form of intimate social interaction, which anthropologist Mary Douglas explored in *The World of Goods* (1979). In *The Gift*, Lewis Hyde (1979: xii) addresses the work of art as a gift – 'which moves the heart, or revives the soul, or delights the senses, or offers courage for living, however we choose to describe the experience' – that places a constraint on the market economy of merchandising. The issue of art and friendship – as opposed to a disagreement over aesthetic taste – is central to Yasmina Reza's play *Art* (1994), as the purchase of a work of contemporary art by Serge causes a rift with his close friend Marc, who perceives his friend's budding art collector status as becoming a different person (see the fifth point below). Second, 'addiction and compulsive aspects pervade collecting', which is a point that economists would also note. Salman notes that she has 'become somewhat obsessed' with Casear, and has 'collected five of his works'. Third, 'collecting legitimizes acquisitiveness as art or science'. Salman notes a level of skill to collect 'small editions' that 'are becoming much harder to get hold of'. Fourth, 'profane or sacred conversions occur when an item enters a collection'. The profane, as common and mundane, and the sacred, as extraordinary and special, are brought together under the rubric of collection. Salman describes Caesar's work as 'completely inspirational'. The objects are removed from commodity exchange – that is until they are sold – as Marc Shell, in *Art and Money* (1994), noted how money becomes art. In the case of art objects, they do not have ordinary utilitarian roles to lose, yet can be exchanged for money. Fifth, 'collections serve as extensions of the self'. Salman makes a strong link between her career as creative director of a leading fashion brand and collecting. The media vehicle of the *Financial Times* to declare her collection of Caesars means high visibility. Self-definition is highly dependent upon our possessions: 'In a materialistic society, the quality and quantity of our possessions are broadly assumed to be an index of our successfulness in life in general. Self-definition is highly dependent upon our possessions, according to Belk (1995: 87): 'In a materialistic society ... the effects of superior knowledge, tenacity, monetary resources, cleverness, or luck'.

A similar message is communicated by Raymond Moulin (1987: 82): 'Part of the pleasure of collecting lies in risk and competition. Collectors gamble on paintings and artists the way racing enthusiasts gamble on horses or market enthusiasts on stocks. ... It is an elite recreation, a game in which the losers are presumably those without culture of artistic taste'. Sixth, 'collections tend towards specialization'. Salman notes that she has 'always collected creepy antique dolls' heads, and their moulds, that look rather like [Caesar's] figures', and Caesar also fits with her research interests in 'late Victorian culture'. Seventh, 'post-mortem distribution problems are significant to collectors and their families'. Keeping one's collection intact may be a way to gain a sort of immortality. The opening in 2008 of the Thomson Collection at the Art Gallery of Ontario is a recent example of the late Lord Kenneth Thomson's private passion – including the collector's eye (and that of his dealer-advisor) – on public display. The rise of private art foundations – with many as initiatives by collectors focusing on contemporary art – has raised concerns of operational sustainability and the diversion of works of art away public institutions. When public institutions collect, through donations and via an acquisitions budget, they are shaping popular taste and cultural memories. Eighth, 'there is a simultaneous desire for and fear of completing a collection'. Jean Baudrillard (in Elsner and Cardinal 1994: 23) has drawn attention to a collection's 'incompleteness, the fact that it *lacks* something ... one needs such and such an absent object' (emphasis in the original).

The 2002 Survey of Public Participation of the Arts (NEA 2004: 44) includes 'owning art': 'There are dramatic differences between those reporting that they own art and those who do not. About one-third of respondents in households making more than $75,000 per year report owning original art. People aged 45 to 64 are more likely to own original art than other age groups'. Arts Council England has a scheme – Own Art – 'designed to make it easy and affordable for everyone to buy contemporary art': up to £2,000 can be borrowed to buy art at approximately 250 participating galleries (with the loan repaid in ten monthly, interest-free instalments). Note that under £3,000 is the positioning of the Affordable Art Fair.

The *World Wealth Report*, an annual joint publication by Capgemini and Merrill Lynch since 1998, identifies the range of personal wealth using terms derived from banking: from the mass affluent at the low end to ultra high net worth individuals (UHNWIs). HNWIs – individuals with more than $1 million in investible assets, according to private wealth management segmentation – have always been core to arts patronage. There is an ultra (U) category for individuals or families with investible assets in excess of $30 million. New collectors come from the entrepreneurial super-rich class. Many are based in the USA – as indicated in the *ARTnews* list of top collectors – but international dimensions are more important than ever with the rise of HNWIs and UHNWIs from the emerging economies of Russia, India, China, and the Middle East.

The rise of the mass affluent segment has been chronicled (Nunes and Johnson 2004; Silverstein and Fiske 2004). The term was first used in retail banking: for example, HSBC Premier starts at £100,000 annual gross salary. How to persuade the mass affluent to spend part of their discretionary income – that is income after paying out for taxes, operating expenses, and savings – on the arts? It has been noted that the mass affluent as art buyers are consumers with eclectic tastes not connoisseurs. As such dealers need to think more like retailers. A narrative (or compelling story) is needed for each art object. Too much choice can cause confusion – deemed 'the paradox of choice' (Schwartz 2004) – so editing is needed. Shopping as a leisure experience needs to be accommodated. There is a need to reassure neophyte buyers who may be nervous with clear pricing and education. Consumers want to be individuals and the home is key for self-expression.

■ ■ ■

Consumption addresses demand, which is also to acknowledge that supply increases and suppliers are competitive. Arts consumption operates on various levels. There are arts attenders (also spectators or appreciators) who can be distinguished from non-attenders. Education and social origins are key to understanding arts consumption according to sociology of art research, while the notion of addiction and maximizing satisfaction are posited by cultural economics.

That marketing practices have little genuine impact on audience development is often not disclosed. Widening the base of support, as measured by socio-demographic profiling, is a political issue of social inclusion. What are the barriers to effective access and entry? Some are identifiable, yet more complex is how arts organizations should communicate to their current and prospective audiences. Does the popularity of the audioguide, as an access and interpretative device, aid its users to develop critical skills to look at art? Where do the visually or musically literate fit in? Can arts organizations continue to think of programming geared at so-called educated audience members?

Collecting art may be a progression of involvement from appreciating art through museums and exhibition venues. Sufficient discretionary income is needed to collect, though. Chapter 7 on 'Financial Investing in the Arts' adds another level of consumption, including art as an unregulated financial instrument of interest to investors (looking to diversify their asset base) and speculators (seeking a quick return).

APPENDIX: MARKETING AND THE ARTS

'Marketing' is, according to a dictionary of modern thought, 'now widely held to be the most important of industrial and commercial disciplines' (Bullock and Trombley 1999: 504). In no small measure, this is due to the valorization of the consumer at the heart of marketing philosophy. Marketing discussions often emphasize the role of the marketer, the person doing the marketing. Can so-called skills-will-travel marketers add genuine value to arts organizations? Yes, according to an article in the *Harvard Business Review*: 'One can learn the key characteristics of a product in a few weeks, but market awareness and marketing expertise take years to master. Once gained this expertise can be applied to many products or market contexts' (Andreasen 1982: 106). Of course, such an assertion raises the hackles of non-marketing mindsets in arts organizations such as curators, musicians, and dancers. For example, Gareth Morgan (1993: 24) likens marketers to *peacocks* (i.e. all show and no real substance), *penguins* (i.e. always well-dressed and not very intelligent), or *Irish setters* (i.e. very good looking but not very intelligent).

Are marketers the promoters of images rather than the creators of value? This is the type of question posed when considering the two perspectives of 'marketing and the arts'. The arts marketing literature adopts a position that marketers help to widen choices available to arts consumers and to enhance the overall quality of the arts experience. Interpretative marketing researchers have responded in a backlash: 'Certainly there is no shortage of marketing-made-easy books for the arts community', according to Brown and Patterson (2000: 17). These critics believe that the current marketing position is not progressive enough. They desire to shift the emphasis from 'marketing the arts' (or arts marketing) to 'the arts for marketing' (see Brown and Patterson 2000: 18–19). The arts for marketing includes engaging with the marketing content of artistic artifacts, and applying the tools and techniques of artistic appreciation to marketing institutions and ephemera such as advertising and promotional campaigns. Representations of marketing and consumption-related phenomena can offer alternative perspectives on the principles and practices of marketing management.

Arts marketing

The 'national arts marketing project' of the USA-based Arts and Business Council describes 'marketing as a *process* by which you come to understand the relationship between your *product* and your *customer*' (artsandbusiness.org, accessed 13 May 2009, emphasis in the original). Arts marketers tend to define arts marketing as about people, thus the core question: who are these people? Rather than replicating what is already available in arts marketing textbooks, there is a focus on interpreting the principles of marketing management, particularly ones promoted as instructive to performing and visual arts organizations. Furthermore, the complex relationship between marketing initiatives and audience development is addressed.

Marketers, say those involved in sales, advertising, public relations, media, and consultancy, for example, have a double role: they represent a commercial system; and they become actors in a process of commodity exchange (see Enis, Cox, and

Mokwa 1991). Marketing offers firms an opportunity 'not just to experience the sweet smell of success, but to have the visceral feel of entrepreneurial greatness', according to Theodore Levitt (1960: 56). Marketing orthodoxy, as such, suggests that this inter-play between company and customer within the context of competition helps to generate national wealth creation. At the same time, in order to succeed, marketers need to be myth-makers: what fiction is to be created? What story needs to be told to get the customer to believe your USP (unique selling proposition)?

The work by pioneers in the field of marketing – including Peter Drucker, Theodore Levitt, and Philip Kotler – started to be articulated during the 1950s and 1960s in the context of rising consumerism in the USA. Sophisticated advertising imagery helped to inculcate consumerist values, with advertising no longer selling a product; it was selling a way of life and set of values (Ewen 1988). Marketing ortho-doxy offers a 'positivistic view of the world' (Morgan in Alvesson and Wilmott 1992: 136), which is prefaced on the central role of the consumer in relationship to the organization. Fifty years ago, Drucker (1954: 52) was advocating single-minded, if not quasi-spiritual observations, in *The Practice of Management*: 'There is only one valid definition of a business: to create a satisfied customer'; and 'The customer is the foundation of a business and keeps it in existence'. In a celebrated *Harvard Business Review* article, Levitt (1960: 56) posited that 'the organization must learn to think of itself not as producing goods and services but as *buying customers*, as doing the things that will make people *want* to do business with it' (emphasis in the original).

What do relationships mean to marketers? Using the notion of transaction, Kotler (Kotler and Levy 1969; Kotler 1972) has promoted marketing as a pervasive social activity. According to Kotler, marketing is specifically concerned with how transac-tions are created, stimulated, facilitated, and valued. He distinguished three levels of marketing consciousness. First, marketing is defined in terms of market transaction; namely, buyers and sellers meeting to exchange goods (see, for example, Bartels 1968; Bagozzi 1975). Second, two parties may meet to exchange things which are of value to them (e.g. political parties and voters) so that every organization (whether market-based or not) should be conceived as producing something of value for a client or customer. Third, Kotler raised the stakes by arguing that a higher state of marketing consciousness exists: marketing applies to an organization's attempts to relate to all its publics, not just its consuming publics. The things-of-value are not limited to goods and services, and money; rather, they include other resources such as time, energy, and feelings. In what has become an iconic statement (see Glenn Morgan in Alvesson and Willmott 1992; Brown 1995), Kotler (1972: 52) went so far as to posit marketing 'as a category of human action indistinguish-able from other categories of human action such as voting, loving, consuming, or fighting'.

Kotler has not been alone in letting the rhetoric rip. Terms like loyalty manage-ment, relationship marketing, and customer relationship management are cited as offering a new management mindset about how firms are trying to engage with customers. By way of analogy, marketing orthodoxy acknowledges a shift from mar-keter as hunter (e.g. focusing on the immediate sale) to the marketer as gardener (e.g. cultivating relationships). So-called new marketing treats each customer as unique and aims to match his or her requirements. There is an emphasis on engendering loyalty, to the extent that marketers talk about the lifetime value of the customer accruing to the firm.

Managing heterogeneity is the essential basis behind understanding the importance of market segmentation, which is a process by which the total market is divided into distinctive groups. Consider the pioneering statement of market segmentation by Wendell Smith (1956: 3):

> Segmentation is disaggregative in its effects and tends to bring about recognition of several demand schedules where only one was recognizable before . . . market segmentation . . . consists of viewing a heterogeneous market (one characterized by divergent demand) as a number of smaller homogeneous markets in response to different product preferences among important market segments. It is attributable to the desires of consumers for varying wants.

The conventional wisdom is that marketers must decide which market segments to enter and design a marketing programme – that covers elements of the marketing mix including product attributes, advertising, pricing, and channels of distribution – to suit the requirements of the selected target segments. The benefits from market segmentation – including better matching of customer needs, enhanced profits, enhanced opportunities for growth, retention of customers, targeted communications, stimulation to innovation, and market segmentation share (Doyle 1998: 68–70) – seem too enticing to ignore. From a commercial perspective, only a limited range of consumer products invite mass marketing (i.e. a single message that has the potential to appeal to the entire market). Yet the misapplication of market segmentation occurs. There may be too much emphasis on demand level: by concentrating on the heavy user, the marketer ignores the potential for increased usage by light users or non-users. Developing socio-demographic profiles of alternative segments is not unproblematic as there may be missing variables (such as associated with lifestyle analysis); moreover, it may be difficult to translate socio-demographic profiles into actionable marketing programmes. Following the identification of segmentation variables, a firm must decide those segments it aims to target. This entails evaluating the relative attractiveness of the segments: size of the segment, its growth rate, profit potential, and its fit to the core capabilities of the firm are some of the conventional factors marketers take into account. The aim is to choose groups of customers (targets segments) who will offer a so-called lifetime of value for the organization. (Relationships with banks often last longer than marriages!)

Philip Kotler (in Drucker 1990: 58) labels 'STP marketing' as instructive to all types of arts organizations, by which he means segmentation, targeting, and positioning have a generic applicability. The current emphasis is on micromarketing; that is, looking at establishing more refined market segments. Segments-of-one is an extreme example of personalization: this position of customer intimacy is supposed to change what the firm does in response to customer input and past behaviour by the customer.

If one believes Briton Keith Diggle (1984: 19), 'arts marketing' was coined by him in 1970. However, there is much to suggest that the application of corporate marketing management techniques to American not-for-profit organizations in health care, education, social welfare, and the arts was gaining support by the late 1960s (see, for example, Kotler and Andreasen 1975; Kotler 1979). By refining Kotler's notion that transaction is a core concept of marketing, Benson Shapiro (1973) helped to set the tone of marketing in non-commercial contexts. Shapiro identified two constituencies (or customer segments): *donors* provide resources; and *clients* receive resources. Some individuals are both donors and clients, as is the case with loyal and generous arts patrons, yet Shapiro was right to recognize that facilitating the exchange relationships becomes more complex than traditional buyer–seller transactions. The so-called bottom line of the non-commercial organization requires a twofold process: serving *client* groups is a prime objective (mission), yet this is only possible if mutually-satisfying exchanges exist with *donor* groups (funding).

In the foreword to *Marketing the Arts* (1980), Kotler (in Mokwa, Dawson, and Prieve 1980) identified four major interrelated marketing challenges: attendance stimulation, audience development, membership development, and fundraising. Attendance stimulation, cited as the first major challenge, has an immediate and direct impact on attendance figures, a main yardstick to measure organizational success. There is a choice, according to Kotler, between *broadening* (i.e. 'trying to bring serious art to more people') or *deepening* (i.e. 'developing a more coherent experience for those who are already interested in the arts') the audience base. (Of course Kotler's broadening should be viewed as two separate paths: more of the same as measured by socio-demographic profile; and diversifying the existing audience base.) Membership development served an important linking role; getting one to join as a member represents the first stage of a more formal and potentially stronger bond. Finally, revenue from fundraising activities complements attendance and membership revenue. For example, 'Awards for Marketing Institutional Excellence' by the American Association of Museums fall into four categories: awareness building, attendance generation, crisis management, and merchandising excellence.

It is not surprising that ideas associated with Kotler, as one of the seminal thinkers behind the formation of marketing management, have been adopted by arts marketers. Indeed, Kotler's publications list includes marketing for the performing arts (Kotler and Scheff 1997) and museums (Kotler and Kotler 1998). Other contributors to 'marketing for the arts' textbooks include Danny Newman, Alvin Reiss, François Colbert, Elizabeth Hill, Fiona Combe McLean, Bonita Kolb, and Ruth Rentschler.

Early arts marketers who are grouped with Diggle include Americans Danny Newman and Alvin Reiss. Newman was an early advocate of promotion and price to stimulate demand; he believed that it was possible to increase the market by emphasizing activities associated with selling. *Subscribe Now!* (1977) was the emphatic and evocative title of Newman's handbook: performing arts organizations were encouraged to attract more subscribers with a downgrading of occasional ticket-wicket patrons. Reiss was equally bullish and vigorous in a practitioner-oriented text, *Cash In!* (1986), which bore the descriptive subtitle, 'funding and promoting the arts, a compendium of imaginative concepts, tested ideas and case histories or programs and promotions that make money'. (Perhaps such texts – not unlike school mailings to alumni – take on an insistently cheery, exclamation-mark-strewn tone because they are really about raising money, which does not invite irony!)

It was with a 'greater broad-mindedness . . . entrapping those slothful, fickle, single-ticket buyers who I may sometimes for haste give up on', according to New-man (Diggle 1984: 1), that Diggle sought to expand on his work. Like Newman, Diggle had a background as a performing arts marketing consultant, which helps to explain why he suggested that museums ought to consider selling advanced-entry tickets. Diggle (1984: 38) believed it was possible to introduce a theatrical flavour to the experience of museum goers:

> [I]f attendance at an art gallery or museum were defined by date or time, and even given a stated duration, it would take on the character of a performance something that begins at a certain time and ends at a certain time – the idea of a limited capacity would be suggested and so there would be *something* to buy and a reason for buying it *now* ('If you don't buy it now, you might not get in') (emphasis in the original).

Museum blockbusters are driven by sales. While the notion of spectacle is not new – think of the 1851 Great Exhibition held at London's Crystal Palace – the contemporary museum landscape is more indebted to the attendance-shattering success of the 'King Tut' exhibition (which toured the USA and Canada in the late 1970s and early 1980s). There has been optimism and museum growth: capital expansion projects are deemed necessary in order to secure large-scale travelling exhibitions. The prospect of higher attendance figures would entice corporate sponsors; moreover, sales from ancillary services (e.g. shops, cafes, and audioguides), not to mention admissions revenue, would flourish. Museums hoped to become more financially self-sufficient; broadening the appeal to museums was also viewed as a benefit. Art market hyper-activity and expanding links between culture and tourism added grist to the museum mill of the 1980s and 1990s and has continued to do so in the 2000s. Not even the current credit crunch may cause a reversal in the rallying cry associated with building projects.

The general popularity of blockbusters, as major cultural events with an access-ible social cachet, seems to suggest that the sales-oriented approach has some relevance. Promotional hype – or marketing communications – serves to raise expectations, and heighten anticipation on the part of prospective spectators. It also allows the institution to gauge the sales potential.

In discussing culture in the marketplace, Paul DiMaggio (1986: 88) strikes at a concern dear to marketers:

> We know rather little about why some art forms do well on the market and some do poorly. It is not enough to say that popular forms survive and unpopular ones fail: what this assertion ignores is *the power of market segmentation*. Markets are created by entrepreneurs; they do not exist in nature. Thus American popular radio became dramatically more innovative and diverse when the radio industry began segmenting markets by age, ethnicity, region, and race (my emphasis).

Marketing analysis from retailing and other industrial sectors seems to suggest that art museums need to identify two distinct types of audiences: *potential donors* who often become members; and *the general public* who attend museums to be entertained and educated (Blattberg and Broderick in Feldstein 1991: 327). A case has been made that there should be two different museums to cater to two distinct audiences: a *mass marketing museum* designed to appeal to the public at large; and a *boutique museum* aimed at the donor and potential donor (Blattberg and Broderick in Feldstein 1991: 337). However, conventional market segmentation seems to be a solution fraught with difficulties when applied to arts organizations. One can appreciate the emergence of a clash of cultures, or confrontation of ideologies. For example, the then director of a prominent art museum in the USA was 'disturbed' by 'the possibility or the necessity of museums addressing two very different kinds of audiences': it 'may possibly undermine the whole mission of a museum, which is to bring as many people as you can get in an art museum to experience direct contact with a work of art' (Anne d'Harnoncourt, the then director of the PMA, in Feldstein 1991: 36–37). A more recent and sensitive initiative at segmenting is advanced by Tate, based on socio-demographic and psychographic variables: *intellectual* visit versus *social* visit. Intellectual visitors are classified as *aficionados* (visual arts professionals looking for inspiration and escapism), *actualizers* (non-visual arts professionals seeking inspiration), *sensualists* (non-visual arts professionals, culture vultures seeking emotional experience), *researchers* (visual arts professionals on research visits), and *self-improvers* (people developing their visual arts knowledge). On the other hand, social visits are made by *families* (mixed age groups, with social and educational motivations), *social spacers* (people meeting or visiting with others, wanting to make the place their own), and *site seers* (mainly tourists who have identified the gallery as a destination site). In particular social visitors are cited as offering the greatest potential for growth. For example, both Tate Britain and Tate Modern used a marketing campaign, 'Create Your Own Collection', to attract social spacers.

Marketing attention tends to be in keeping with the contention of Diggle (1984: 43) that arts organizations 'are looking for audiences and the money that comes from audiences . . . drawing audiences from those already favourably disposed'. Arts organizations grapple with the issue of audience development: how to balance up the socio-demographic profile of their audience members in order to be more representative of the general population. Quotas are not viewed as being instructive (as they can emphasize the relativist position that equates cultural equity with merely valuing differences in race, sex, and class). Reducing the ability to cater to the needs of the well-informed (i.e. core or primary) spectator is not recommended. But how to respond more positively to the needs to other groups? Should arts organizations think about addressing two very different kinds of audiences? Such a segmentation strategy would mean that members representing a more diverse audience could be offered a separate product. But would changing the product to fit what the audience wants abrogate aesthetic and ethical responsibilities? Merely to cater to aesthetic taste preferences of current spectators would result in arts organizations becoming predictable and narrow in their breadth and perspective. Regular visitors (or frequent attenders) are familiar with the institution and feel psychologically comfortable in the surroundings because it is part of their lifestyle. How to entice wider participation, as measured by cultural diversity?

In its *Final Report*, the Independent Task Force on the Future of the Art Gallery of

Ontario (1992: 26–27) cast significant doubt on the contribution of marketing practices to genuine audience development:

> After extensive consultation, the Task Force is of the opinion that although marketing may be of primary importance in increasing audience, it is not the key to broadening audience.

A case for cultural diversity was made by the Task Force:

> [T]he only way the Gallery can broaden audience is to make a clear commitment to cultural diversity. This means not only multilingual devices, but strong educational opportunities for the young to interact with the Gallery's collections and with the attitudes and ideas which have shaped the making of that art, concerted efforts to exhibit and collect contemporary art which comes from non-majority cultures, partnerships with ethno-racial professionals who work out of a different aesthetic, special incentives for membership and volunteer involvement and an emphasis throughout the programming of the Gallery on providing access for non-traditional audiences as participants in the Gallery as a cultural institution relevant to their needs.

Cultural diversity is not a theme raised by Bourdieu in an explicit manner, yet it does strike at issues of real and perceived exclusion.

Audience development can be approached in two distinct ways, according to DiMaggio (in DiMaggio 1986: 88), based on ideas proffered by Augustin Girard. First, classical dissemination is aimed at democratizing institutions that have historically been supported by urban elites. If a proactive education policy makes the arts more accessible, the continuing inroads of mass high education particularly in the USA, Canada, and the UK, should assist. Even usually rarefied cultural organizations like Glyndebourne engage in touring opportunities to broaden the opera company's reach. Indeed Glyndebourne's educational outreach programmes received arts council funding. The internet has the potential to reach possible new audiences, but few institutions think of using the internet as an alternative to an on-site visit; rather the current emphasis is on offering information and as a preview prior to making a visit. There is the case, though, that the social constituency for the distinction between high and popular culture – formed due to elites desiring a prestigious culture they could dominate and call their own – is eroding. Second, access becomes less difficult by broadening the definition of the arts. Should efforts to support and develop creative industries be emphasized? There is already a blurring of the distinction between not-for-profit and commercial enterprises in the arts. Popular musicals have been staged at the London's subsidized theatres, not least of the National Theatre, before being transferred to the commercial West End. Commercial galleries mount exhibitions that rival, in scholarship and aesthetics, what publicly subsidized arts venues offer. Barriers to effective access or entry operate on various dimensions. Physical barriers are being addressed in many jurisdictions, though there are limitations to renovations to older buildings (which is particularly pronounced in the UK with buildings of architectural or historical merit). Disability is an obvious point, so transportation should also include the distance one needs to travel and the associated costs. 'Market solutions will do nothing to address problems of access for persons with little discretionary income; problems of diversity and survival of art forms without large markets; or, indeed, most of the other values with which cultural policy is concerned' (DiMaggio in DiMaggio 1986: 89). A case needs to be made that arts organizations help to nurture a citizenry equipped to make informed choices in a democracy.

The arts for marketing

Early arts marketers like Diggle, Newman, and Reiss were consultants who emphasized promotional activities to increase audience figures. The direct hand of Kotler is noticeable in texts on marketing the performing arts and museums. Moreover, he has shaped the current band of so-called academic marketers who are interested in the arts. A controversial issue for many large and prominent arts organizations is market segmentation (an organizing principle for retailers and restaurants, for example). There is a concern that an explicit decision to have different offerings for different types of visitors would require a fundamental rethinking of the role of arts organizations in society.

The application of marketing as presented in standard textbooks is fraught with difficulties, even though marketing the arts (or arts marketing) represents a growing sub-sector. As an inversion, 'the arts for marketing' represents an interpretative marketing to disentangle core concepts. 'Art and aesthetics are increasingly firing the marketing imagination', according to Brown and Patterson (2000: title page). This has resulted in a growing body of writing on the arts adopting critical marketing perspectives (Brown and Patterson 2000; Schroeder 2005; Holbrook 2005; Bradshaw and Holbrook 2007; O'Reilly and Kerrigan 2010). So-called critical management studies that took root in the 1990s is also part of the intellectual lineage, according to Glenn Morgan (in Alvesson and Willmott 1992: 136): 'The market itself remains a realm of freedom, in which choice and the sovereignty of the individual consumer remain paramount. For Critical Theory, however, the myth of market freedom and with in the myth of marketing itself need to be unpackaged', according an entry on marketing.

Several examples of the arts for marketing are raised. Komar and Melamid drew attention to the citizen reconceptualized as consumer through greater emphasis on marketing research techniques. Carey Young's claim for institutional critique, as part of an artist's role and identity, is raised by New York's Poster Boy, who challenges the promotion of brand equity, and dissent is part of the aesthetic practice of Czech artist David Cerny.

Consider the following definition – see marketingpower.com, the site of the AMA – approved by the American Marketing Association:

> Marketing research is the function that links the consumer, customer, and public to the marketer through information – information used to identify and define marketing opportunities and problems; generate, refine, and evaluate marketing actions; monitor marketing performance; and improve understanding of marketing

as a process. Marketing research specifies the information required to address these issues, designs the method for collecting information, manages and implements the data collection process, analyzes the results, and communicates the findings and their implications.

The Russian-born visual arts team of Komar and Melamid interpreted consumer research data (based on a telephone poll of 1,001 American adults answering 103 questions, and interviewing by focus groups) compiled by a Boston market research firm, with sponsorship from the National Institute (an offshoot of *The Nation* magazine), as the basis for their exhibition, 'People's Choice: The Polling of America' (1994–95), about aesthetic preferences and taste in painting (see diacenter.org/km). Intending to discover a true 'people's art' by surveying popular taste in painting, they created two art works: a tiny (e.g. paperback-sized) abstract canvas entitled *America's Most Unwanted*, embodying the sharp geometrical forms, mostly mustard yellow and red, with a darkening to black around the edges, supposedly least appreciated by the general public; and *America's Most Wanted*, a medium-sized, blue-skied lakeside vignette populated with humans (including a central figure of George Washington) and two deers, all allegedly comprising the nation's most-favoured elements. Of course, the raw statistical data cannot dictate such images; rather, these paintings could only arise from a sensibility well-acquainted with pictorial conventions. For example, *America's Most Unwanted* makes reference to Russian Constructivism with its 'aura of godless geometric mysticism and socialist utopianism' (Vine 1994: 118), which is not perceived to be ideologically sound in the USA. The Hudson River School, including the theme of Manifest Destiny, is referenced by *America's Most Wanted*.

What is represented by this jocular meddling of art and marketing? Making art is one of the last areas of 'democratic-consumer' society to be subjected to opinion polls. Melamid (diacenter.org/km) has described the concept for the project:

In a way it was a traditional idea, because faith in numbers is fundamental to people, starting with Plato's idea of a world which is based on numbers. In ancient Greece, when sculptors wanted to create an ideal human body they measured the most beautiful men and women and then made an average measurement, and that's how they described the ideal of beauty and how the most beautiful sculpture was created. In a way, this is the same thing; in principle, it's nothing new. It's interesting: we believe in numbers, and numbers never lie. Numbers are innocent. It's absolutely true data. It doesn't say anything about personalities, but it says something about one's ideals, and about how this world functions. That's really the truth, as much as we can get to the truth. Truth is a number.

Polls have become ubiquitous markers of contemporary public opinion and taste in advanced economies. But is there only the illusion of dialogue? Can polls serve as an index of value? Polling is fraught with distortions, eliciting truncated opinions. Preferences are elicited only in the abstract. Moreover, there is the argument that polls serve as an escape from real understanding of complex issues. Cynical observers argue that polls now serve as a tool for the *seduction* of public opinion.

The methodology underpinning Komar and Melamid's paintings, based on so-called scientific viewer-demand information, has links with America's ideological war against communism during the 1950s and 1960s, according to David Ross (1995: 76), the then director of the Whitney Museum of American Art:

Many modern polling practices are an offshoot of cold war computer war-games developed to simulate battle scenarios in accordance with shifting variables. Just as advertising has been touted as a consumer society's bulwark against communism and fascist perversions of mass psychology, so the market-probability research as emerged from anticommunist war-gaming came to be seen as a way of keeping the free world one future ahead of the evil empire. The depth of attitudinal polling that has led to today's virtually daily tracking of neighborhood psychographics is the very essence of cold war democracy. New management, corporate symbolism, spin surgery, deep agenda-setting – these are the PR tools that helped to preserve our sacred liberties in the struggle against totalitarianism.

Komar and Melamid exaggerate the mechanics of cultural production by numbers to such a degree that its absurdity becomes devastatingly apparent, according to Ross (1995: 72–73):

Long intimate with bureaucratic thought and practice, their work feeds off a withering familiarity with the arts of the modern state: its procedures for manufacturing consent, and its facility for squeezing every possible drop from the rhetorical fruits of communism and democracy while exhibiting little evidence of either ideal.

A sense of wry humour and irony is apparent in their work: 'There is a truth in every joke', according to Melamid (in Meyer 1994: 142). Questions are raised and left unanswered. Is their approach to aesthetic value based on scientific truth different from one generated from cultural taste? Just how many other things – subjected to market research – get so drastically misrepresented? What kind of society is produced that lives and governs itself by focus groups and exit polls?

Lampooning the obsession with demographics and target marketing can no longer be directed solely at Americans. Komar and Melamid's project began on the web, in 1995, under the auspices of the Dia Center for the Arts, and has expanded to more than a dozen countries. Results of surveys in other countries are highlighted by similarities with the American polls. This broaches ideas about the universality of art. Can one talk about a homogenization of tastes and standardizing what is on offer, namely the globalization of markets?

Carey Young explores the parameters of institutional critique. 'Soft power is', according to Young (2003), 'a problematic but challenging descriptor, one of those potentially useful terms that could offer an open door to those politically-motivated artists able to slip through the door':

1. Most corporations now operate in the realm of the dematerialized and the transient, their value gauged by intangible assets such as brand equity and intellectual

property. Any protest aimed against them would be at its most powerful if con-
ceptualized to operate within the same conceptual, electronic/digital realm.
2. No clear standards yet exist for 'ethical' products or services. Corporations typically seek to appear responsible via PR spin rather than taking on any morally or
ethically-induced changes to their usual operations.
3. In uncanny echoes of the artistic avant garde, businesses proclaim their ability to
innovate, and attempt to remain as 'cutting edge', as creative as possible in the
attempt to reinvent themselves, regroup or to find new ways of cutting costs, in an
era of shrinking markets and ever-swifter competition.
4. Dissent is commodified: companies aim to 'manage' or even recruit activists on to
their company board in order to neutralize them; marketing to the consistent desire
for transgression within fashion, an ad campaign for a fashionable brand of jeans
features scenes of anti-capitalist protest; the most revered business thinkers exhort
managing directors to think like 'revolutionaries' in order to become strong leaders.

Young notes that she is 'attracted to exploring how the artist's role, agency and identity
could or might need to change in response to the collapsing categories between
business, politics and culture'. Examples of such engaged artists are provided by New
York's Poster Boy and Czech-based David Cerny (in a project for the European Union).

New York's MTA (Metropolitan Transit Authority) and the NYPD view graffiti
(i.e. drawing or writing scratched on a wall, or like space, without the permission of
the owner of the property) as a form of vandalism, hence a criminal act. Poster Boy –
either an anonymous guerrilla artist or as part of a collective – emerged in 2007 in
New York using scratchiti (i.e. a style of graffiti of etching logos onto glass or plastic)
to alter, intervene, and invert commercial advertisements on New York's subway
platforms as a way to reclaim what ought to be public spaces. 'Poster Boy's work
straddles two boisterous artistic sub-cultures: street art and culture jamming', according to a recent profile (London *Guardian*'s 'Guide', 17–23 January 2009). Street or
urban art includes UK's Banksy, a darling of the art auction world in 2007 and 2008,
and Shepard Fairey of 'OBAMA HOPE' fame, with earlier examples, from the 1980s,
such as Keith Haring. Culture jamming is part of the agenda of Adbusters to invert
the branding messages of corporate communications through satire. An advert for
Puma shoes with Usain Bolt, a star of the Beijing 2008 Olympics, is recreated by
Poster Boy, who etched McDonald's 'Golden Arches' and added an anti-consumerist
message, 'McDorse the World'. In another example, with a stronger political critique,
the logo for the Iron Man brand of video games is given a different positioning
message: 'IRAN = NAM'.

Artist David Cerny (davidcerny.cz) was commissioned by the Czech Republic, for
its presidency of the European Union (January to June 2009), to create a work of art.
The idea, according to Milena Vicenova, the permanent Czech representative to the
EU, was that 'making fun of prejudice destroys it most efficiently' (*Financial Times*,
16 January 2009). It is instructive to remember that the current EU project is a
response to the European-inspired wars on European soil during the first half of the
twentieth century and the resulting communist regimes that divided the continent.
The initial focus on western European integration has been expanded in the post-
communist period to include central and eastern European nations.

With a budget of approximately €375,000 (10 million Czech koruny), Cerny was supposed to collaborate with one artist from each of the 27 EU-member nations. Each artist would depict his or her country using common stereotypes or prejudices. The result is *Entropa* (2009), a large (16 sq. m.) installation designed for the Council of Ministers building in Brussels; its 27 parts are held together by snap-out plastic parts similar to those used in a modelling kit. Some are whimsical: a nation marked by the word *grève*, or strike (France); made of Lego (Denmark); lying within an Ikea flatpack (Sweden); a group of Catholic monks erecting the rainbow flag of the gay community (Poland); a building site (Spain); and an empty space intended to signify absence (UK) to denote the country's Eurosceptic tendencies. There is a stronger punch behind others: a flooded land with minarets poking through as a possible comment on the nation's simmering religious tensions (the Netherlands); a lump of gold on sale to the highest bidder (Luxembourg); a Dracula-inspired theme park (Romania); a rudimentary Turish lavatory, with references to the Ottoman Empire (Bulgaria); and an autobahn arranged as a swastika (Germany). Yet, following complaints, it was revealed that Cerny created *Entropa*, including the creation of fictitious statements and biographies for 27 artists. A hoax against EU bureaucracy? A comment on the EU's detached decision-making? Henry Kissinger's foreign affairs quip, 'Who do I call if I want to call Europe?', springs to mind. Art critic Michael Archer (London *Guardian*, 14 January 2009) was supportive:

> A lavish combination of toilet jokes, jaded national stereotypes, mild offensiveness, post-colonial chippiness and jingoism presented in the form of an outdated schoolboy hobby, Entropa ticks all the boxes we could want. A large-scale Airfix kit of Euro-parts, it provides us with everything we need to assemble, if not the Europe we may wish for, at least the one we're presently saddled with.

Creny has defended his installation: 'I am seriously pro-European. It would be a great pity if Europe would not be able to take this as a bit of satire and irony. If we are strong as Europe, it should be OK for one nation to make fun of other nations' (London *Times Online*, 14 January 2009). This strikes a note with an editorial in the *Financial Times* (17/18 January 2009) supporting Cerny: 'It offers a golden opportunity to bring Europeans closer to their remote Union, whose motto hereafter will become: "We can take a joke" '.

■ ■ ■

In his celebrated 1939 essay, 'Avant-garde and kitsch', the high modernist art critic Clement Greenberg (1961: 10) highlighted the rise of kitsch, an ersatz culture, 'destined for those, insensible to the values of genuine culture, who are hungry nevertheless for the diversion that only culture of some sort can provide.' Greenberg (1961: 10) elaborated:

> Kitsch is mechanical and operates by formulas. . . . Kitsch is the epitome of all that is spurious in the life of our time. Kitsch pretends to demand nothing of its customers except their money – not even their time.

Did marketing become the new kitsch during the latter half of the twentieth century, which bore witness to the ascendancy of marketing as a mass cultural phenomenon?

6

MANAGING FOR EXCELLENCE AND ARTISTIC INTEGRITY

Human resources management (HRM) strategy focuses on the role of personnel policies in enhancing and strengthening productivity and corporate culture, according to a standard definition, with the belief that 'these practices are designed and implemented with the expectation that they will lead to a more stable, satisfied and productive workforce, facilitate the socialization, training and evaluation of incumbents, and sustain an equitable, or fair, system for allocating pay and mobility opportunities' (Steffy and Grimes in Alvesson and Willmott 1992: 181).

There is a tendency, which includes standard HRM textbooks, to focus on tracking a series of generic HRM functions. First, *selection* means so-called fit between the person and the position. Second, *performance appraisal* is about monitoring performance to ensure capacity to meet responsibilities. Third, *rewards* can be intrinsic (i.e. internal to the individual such as job satisfaction or being part of a work group) and extrinsic (i.e. often material attractions such as monetary rewards of salary and potential bonus, fringe benefits, size of office). Fourth, *development* (or progression) is about encouraging personal development, ensuring best practice (health and safety and equal opportunities), and skills enhancement. Fifth, *grievance and disciplinary procedures* in the cases of so-called problem employees, which is a form of risk assessment to mitigate wrongful dismissal claims, is of particular concern. This representation of HRM poses some image problems. There remains a perception – not least of all by employees within organizations – that HR managers are non-productive and driven by bureaucratic mandates. Many consider labour–employer (or industrial) relations to be unappealing.

A typical arts management course unit addresses contracts, labour, and employee relations as primary components of HRM, which highlights that HRM is about 'addressing issues as they emerge' (Steffy and Grimes in Alvesson and Willmott 1992: 181). This includes union–management disputes in the arts, which impede the creative act from reaching audiences. For example, the Society for London Theatre (SOLT), the trade association that represents the producers, theatre owners, and managers of the major commercial and grant-aided theatres in central London, includes a section on 'industrial relations':

The Society plays a major role in industrial relations with Equity (the actors' union), the Musicians' Union and the Broadcasting Entertainment Cinematograph and Theatre Union (BECTU). The Society is responsible for collective negotiation on behalf of its members on the minimum rates of pay and conditions, and gives advice on a range of employment matters relating to the engagement of artists, choreographers, designers, directors, musicians, box office and front-of-house staff and technicians.

The Society plays an active role in mediating and settling disputes concerning employment and contractual matters.

When industrial relations fail, the ramifications can be widespread. The recent strike by the 12,000 members of the Writers Guild of America (WGA), the official union representing writers in the film, television, and new media industries, is a prime example (BBC News, 13 February 2008). The strike began on 5 November 2007 and lasted three months; it is estimated to have cost the Los Angeles-based film and television industry around $733 million, with the wider economy losing around $1.3 billion. (The last major WGA strike in 1988 lasted 22 weeks, costing the industry an estimated $500 million.) The strike concerned residuals: writers wanted a new contract with film and television studios that gave them more money when their work got sold on DVD or downloaded or streamed online; a negotiated settlement sees writers receiving a percentage of the profits generated.

However, the new language associated with human capital management emphasizes a shift from the employee as paid, free-labour – as distinguished from serfs, in being able to make a choice of employee and being paid – to people being our most important asset. This is an attempt to address the importance of intellectual capital rather than fixed assets. The organization at the outset of the twenty-first century is considered to be a flexible network of knowledge workers, thus the model of management advanced at the outset of the twentieth century by Henri Fayol (namely planning, organizing, coordinating, commanding, and controlling) is no longer suitable, according to Henry Mintzberg (2004). Arts organizations, in particular, need to maintain a commitment to excellence and artistic integrity.

Several topics are addressed in a chapter that addresses managing for excellence and artistic integrity. First, organizations are social systems. Yet conflicting rhetoric is detected: there is attention devoted to an organization's people (i.e. employees) as essential to commercial success, which is consistent with human capital management on work motivation, organizational culture, decision-making, and group dynamics; at the same time, restructuring (and complementary management terms) often have the same result of fewer employees. Michael Eisner provides insights on managing creativity at Disney during his 20-year reign. Second, Nicholas Serota, director of Tate, and Quintin Ballardie, artistic director of the English Chamber Orchestra, provide instructive profiles of arts leaders who help to elucidate Gareth Morgan's 'imaginization' concept. Third, growing out of organizational psychology, leadership studies have emerged during the last two decades as a sub-discipline of management studies. At the same time, there have been trenchant criticisms of the romanticized conception of leadership. For example, Mintzberg makes a case for engaged management. Fourth, 'parallel administrative hierarchies' are viewed through the successful attempt of bifurcatation at the Philadelphia Museum of Art and the failed attempt at the British Museum. A complementary appendix on 'Personal development in arts management' raises issues of how the notion of a career has changed, not least of all for arts and cultural workers. Some points on intellectual, personal, and social capital are proffered.

ORGANIZATION AS SOCIAL SYSTEM

Core to industrial sociology, which has an entrenched position within management studies, is the notion that the (business) organization is a social system with workers and managers as industrial member-citizens. Elton Mayo's experiment, in the late 1920s to the 1930s, at the Hawthorne plant of the Western Electric Company in Chicago, asked a basic question: what influences the behaviour of workers? The assumption, based on Frederick Taylor's research on the principles of scientific management, from 1911, stressed economic incentives (i.e. workers were economic men seeking to maximize material rewards) and environmental conditions (such as heat, lighting, rest breaks, etc.). Mayo's Hawthorne Experiments noted the importance of social factors: the influence and satisfaction gained from membership in cohesive work groups; and the role of leadership, especially from direct line managers (such as foremen and supervisors). One outcome of Mayo's research has been the rise of the so-called Human Relations School, which emphasizes the importance of face-to-face, small group relations, supervisory leadership, opportunities for direct personal participation in group activities, and that the workplace is a place to help develop social skills by offering possibilities to belong to cohesive and small groups with a common purpose (see Perrow 1986). An example is the work of Herzberg (1968), who highlighted the significance of *motivation* factors such as achievement, recognition, the work itself, responsibilities, advancement, and personal growth that can lead to positive satisfaction and motivation. In the case of art museum directors, this can include contact with works of art, autonomy, and relations with colleagues at other institutions (DiMaggio 1988: 30). Those working in contemporary visual arts venues could also include collaborations with artists. Herzberg differentiated motivation factors from *hygiene* factors such as company policy, supervision including the relationship with the supervisor, and work conditions that if employees are not content with them will lead to dissatisfaction and demotivation.

Yet there is conflicting rhetoric on the treatment of employees. A positive perspective is promoted by individual organizations. Unilever, one of the leading business corporations advocating the role of creativity within organizations, addresses human capital. 'Our Values → Our People' is a way for the company to articulate that its 'community is shaped and led by its people, who operate creatively within a framework of shared values and business goals'. Other key points can be noted: 'Because our people are fundamental to the way we do business, they're at the centre of everything we do' (e.g. professional fulfillment, work/life balance, ability to contribute equally as part of a diverse workforce); 'We grow as a company by growing our people. This insight is behind all our efforts to keep our people fulfilled and committed'. 'Conducting our business with integrity' is core to being 'guided by values and standards' which 'are set out in our corporate purpose and given practical application in our code of business principles'. Embracing difference is part of a diversity agenda which 'means more than physical diversity – gender, nationality, style, race and creed'; 'It's about us – creating an environment that inspires different individuals to contribute in their own different ways within a framework of shared values and goals'. More specially, 'We strongly believe in creating an environment which fosters creativity and engenders powerful team commitment – an environment where differences are valued and where people can fully realize their true potential'.

On the other hand, restructuring is a contested term used to capture a large number of processes incorporating organizational change. It is one of the major themes in the reshaping of work and organizations and took root during the last 15 years of the twentieth century (see, for example, DiMaggio 2001) and continues during the first recession of the twenty-first century. The general causes of restructuring include technological advances whereby workers are replaced, as opposed to increasing their productivity by enlarging their skills base. In the case of subsidized arts, a general desire in most advanced economies to see decent public services without over-straining the taxpayer means getting by with fewer resources from the public purse. In theory, restructuring is aimed at carving away layers of corporate fat, jettisoning under-performing business units, and raising asset productivity. Yet there appears to be a predictable sameness to restructuring as it is applied: 'Masquerading under names like refocusing, delayering, decluttering and right-sizing (one is tempted to ask why the "right" size is always smaller), restructuring always has the same result: fewer employees' (Hamel and Prahalad 1994: 6). Managers in the middle of the organizational hierarchy – formerly safe white-collar employees – are particularly vulnerable to losing their jobs when organizations decide to restructure.

If 'intended reductions in personnel' is a working definition of restructuring, this raises the question of when to stop: where is the dividing line between cutting fat and cutting muscle? 'Too few companies have made the transition from restructuring to building. Unless they do, it is only a matter of time before they will be restructuring again', according to Michael Porter (1987: 22). Restructuring in practice can be 'a means of dealing with the failure of past strategies' (Porter 1987: 22). Indeed, given the labour-intensive nature of many arts organizations, there is a primary focus on labour costs as a way to reduce the overall budget. As management reform, which involves keeping the same old departmental structure (more or less), but hoping to do more with fewer people, it is fraught with difficulties, according to Hamel and Prahalad (1994: 11):

> Downsizing belatedly attempts to correct mistakes of the past; it is not about creating the markets of the future. The simple point is that getting smaller is not enough. Downsizing, the equivalent of corporate anorexia, can make a company thinner; it doesn't necessarily make it healthier.

There are charges that all the talk about so-called human capital does not square with what may appear to be indiscriminate axing of jobs. Critics of restructuring cite work intensification for those who remain in the organization. Plummeting morale, higher levels of stress, and job insecurity of the remaining employees (e.g. the so-called walking wounded or carping critics) are not uncommon results; there is also the risk that those with the best skills and knowledge may accept other opportunities in order to escape the organization. On the other hand, downsizing and restructuring can be about eliminating redundant skills and acquiring new ones. This means an emphasis on changing the functional requirements of the organization as opposed to cutting costs.

The Walt Disney Company marked the one hundredth anniversary of its founder's birth in 2001. Walt Disney is celebrated as one of the major brand builders of the twentieth century, yet the leadership of Michael Eisner, who assumed the dual roles of chief executive officer and chairman of Disney in 1984, has been instrumental. Disney had been a faltering brand following the death of its founder in 1966. Indeed, Eisner assumed the helm by preventing the break-up of the Disney empire: it was being stalked by an unfriendly suitor, Saul Steinberg, one of the leading corporate raiders of the 1980s, who wanted to sell the studio and keep the theme parks. However, it was a stockholder revolt in 2004 led by Roy Disney, nephew of the founder, in light of a hostile takeover bid by Comcast, that resulted in Eisner being stripped of his role of chairman, though he remained CEO until he resigned in 2005. (Eisner remains on Disney's board of directors.) Disney's market value of $57.4 billion at the time of Eisner's departure needs to be viewed against $2 billion when Eisner took over; revenue also increased approximately 2,000 per cent, from $1.5 billion to $30.8 billion. Under Eisner, Disney became a major film studio. The enhanced financial performance metrics are due to a pragmatic approach to managing creativity, according to Eisner (in Wetlaufer 2000. 117), who was interviewed for *Harvard Business Review*:

> We are always looking for creative solutions to problems – and solutions that cost less money. Remember we still run a business; art and commerce go together. I often quote Woody Allen saying, 'If show business wasn't a business, it would be called show'. Everything we do must not only be creatively responsible but also fiscally responsible, whether we are talking about an acquisition or a corporate financing or a scene in a movie. And in the end, the most creative and sound solutions will emerge. Finding a solution is, by definition, a creative act.

Disney is a factory churning out things for people to buy, but surrounded by myth. Uncle Walt, in his studied avuncular persona, promoted himself as a big bee gathering pollen in order to spread it, flower to flower. He invented the job title, imagineer, to describe the multi-skilled workers who combined a creative force with engineering know-how to design the original Disney theme park in 1955. A similar perspective is adopted by Eisner (in Wetlaufer 2000: 116) who views senior managers as 'editors of other people's work':

> In fact, we consider that our job. We're editors of architects, we're editors of screenwriters, and we're editors of sports shows. We don't just come up with ideas. We listen to other people's ideas, and we tweak them, change them, refine them, and hopefully improve them.

Eisner (in Wetlaufer 2000: 119) believes that the success of Disney owes much to institutionalizing an environment for directed creativity: 'Discipline is part of creativity. . . . Discipline is good for the creative process, and time limits are good. An infinite amount of time to do a project does not always make it creatively better'. At the same time, Eisner (Wetlaufer 2001: 120) emphasizes the role of 'common sense' (essentially akin to good judgement, but he makes a concerted effort to differentiate it from 'audience research'):

> For some reason, a lot of people in the creative industries think that you should come up with lots of great ideas and then subject them to audience research. But most audience- or customer-research is useless. Exit research is fine, even helpful, and a good thing. Audiences are honest generally on what they have just seen, but prospective research is ridiculous. If you conducted interviews after the movie Titanic came out, everyone would have told you they wanted another movie about a love affair and a sinking ship. But common sense tells you that if you made another movie like that, everyone would say, 'Not again!'.

Guarding the Disney brand was an underlying responsibility for Eisner. For example, animated films, from the era of *Snow White and the Seven Dwarfs* (1937) and *Pincocchino* (1940), have been resurrected with more recent successes such as *The Little Mermaid* (1989), *Beauty and the Beast* (1991), *The Lion King* (1994), and *Pocahontas* (1995). So-called pencil mileage may be garnered from animators; moreover, there is a huge windfall from product tie-ins (including theme parks and network and cable television). Indeed, the Walt Disney Company has been cited by McKinsey & Co (see Court *et al.* 1999) as a prime example of developing a 'diversified' brand: the initial brand platform can be leveraged to move into other opportunities. Diversified brands attempt to cultivate a so-called 'golden thread' so Disney is about 'wholesome fun' for all ages; Disney builds 'high credibility' personalities led by Mickey Mouse; moreover, it leverages Disney aggressively by developing multiple theme park sites tied to feature films, hotels, and other merchandising.

IMAGINING ORGANIZATIONS

Gareth Morgan (1993: 276) adopts an anti-mechanistic approach to exploring organizations. What he labels 'imaginization' – a combination of 'imagination' and 'organization' (with no reference to Walt Disney's 'imagineering') – encourages one to become a skilled interpreter of actual situations (a form of reflective practice), and serves as a mode of personal empowerment and an approach to change:

> [It] seeks to mobilize the potential for understanding and transformation that rests within each and every one of us. It seeks to challenge taken-for-granted ways of thinking and, in the process, open and broaden our ability to act in new ways.

'Imaginization' builds on the principle that people and organizations tend to get trapped by images that they hold of themselves and that genuine change requires an ability to see and challenge self-images in some way. Two images are striking: *strategic termites* and *spider plants*. Strategic termites are managers who seek to generate major organizational change in difficult situations. Strategic termites have clear aspirations about what they would like to achieve, but work in an open-ended manner. Like termites, they are opportunistic in their approach to change; they are strategic in the sense that decisions and actions are always guided by an overall sense of purpose and direction. Strategic termites are viewed as valued managers within organizations as they 'create substantial change by making small, significant changes that attract interest and attention of those immediately involved, allowing the character of the new organization to emerge' (Morgan 1993: 52). As an image, spider plants are used to represent the desire of organizations to be more flexible and innovative. The umbilical cord (like those of a spider plant) serves to reconcile the contradictory demands of creating decentralizations while supporting accountability and control. Decentralization offers local units power and autonomy for some kind of self-organizing activity; at the same time, a measure of central control is retained.

Nicholas Serota and Tate

The example of Nicholas Serota, who was appointed as director of the Tate Gallery – now called Tate – in 1988, is instructive (see Chong 1999 for an earlier discussion). On the one hand, he had the conventional education (Haberdashers' Askes' School, Cambridge, and the Courtauld Institute of Art) and social origins (the son of a Labour life peer appointed by Harold Wilson) one associates with the director of a national museum dedicated to art. His counterparts in the USA are similar in profile, according to research conducted by DiMaggio (1988) for the NEA.[1] On the other hand, Serota's experience was based on exhibiting contemporary art – Arts Council of Great Britain (1970–73) and then directorships at Oxford's Museum of Modern Art (1973–76) and London's Whitechapel Art Gallery (1976–88) – without the responsibilities associated with managing a permanent collection. Serota (in Papadakis 1991: 92) has discussed his first major project, to rehang the permanent collection:

> It is important that when you come to the Tate and look at twentieth century art, you should be conscious of the fact that you are in London and not in Paris or New York: that is to say I think people come hoping that they will see how British art plays a part in the broad story of international twentieth century art. I think that the re-hanging has helped to reinforce the part that British artists have played, not so much in the sense of coming third in the race, but in the sense of the interchange of ideas across the Channel or across the Atlantic, or now back across the Channel. We are an island and it is very interesting to see how artists have reacted to what is happening in continental Europe and America.

The rehang of the permanent collection was a curatorial-driven project initiated in 1990 under the banner 'New Displays', with sponsorship from British Petroleum. Serota (in Wilson 1990: foreword) has articulated how New Displays set out to establish 'three new principles' for the presentation of the collection. First, with a 'simple chronological path' the visitor can view art from the Tudors to the present day; the evolution of British art until Impressionism is chronicled, at which point connections between British and foreign art are made. Second, 'within the general sequence' particular galleries are set aside for selected artists and themes – on a rotation basis – to be examined more thoroughly. Third, 'the wish to diversify the conventional patterns and readings' of art accounts for the display programme called 'Cross-current': occasional exhibitions comprising works from the permanent collection are devised to provide opportunities for persistent art historical themes or ideas to be traced over a period of time. However, the wide political significance of New Displays cannot be overstated. With an aim 'to break the rigid divisions between British and Foreign, Historic and Modern', which had formed at the Tate Gallery's Millbank site, direct references were made to the situation in New York (MoMA) and Paris (Pompidou Centre). As competitor cities to London, both had museums dedicated to modern art, which indicated an absence that should be corrected. Space limitations were addressed in an innovative manner. Serota was afforded a marketing opportunity to renew the permanent collection each year by treating it like a temporary exhibition. This was communicated as a commitment to new audiences, particularly non-visitors. The overtly political purpose of the rehang was recognized from the start by informed observers: 'By making such grand and generous use of available space, it argues the absolute necessity for the building of a new and separate gallery wholly devoted to modern art' (McEwen 1990: 61). The rehang should be read as the opening salvo by Serota, at the outset of his directorship, to operate two Tate sites in London. Serota (in McEwen 1990: 46) suggested as much at the time of the first rehang: 'Waiting for the new buildings would simply take too long . . .'.

In 1992, the trustees of the Tate began to consider looming dates of significance – the centenary of the Gallery in 1997 and the new millennium – and institutional initiatives. A 'family of galleries', first mooted in 1988, gained importance: the Tate desired identifiable outstations by presenting the national collections of British and Modern art to audiences outside of London. Tate Gallery Liverpool – now Tate Liverpool – opened in 1988 as part of a major urban regeneration project of Albert Dock; and Tate Gallery St. Ives – now Tate St. Ives – was opened in 1993. (Plans for an outstation in Norwich, so-called Tate of the West, were dropped.) Moreover, the trustees announced a decision to pursue a separate site for the proposed Tate Gallery of Modern Art (now Tate Modern) for international modern and contemporary art, and at the same time the Millbank site – in keeping with the original intention of Henry Tate – would be relaunched as the Tate Gallery of British Art (now Tate Britain, home to British art from 1500 to the present day). 'One collection', it was reiterated by the trustees, would mitigate concerns that a national collection would be broken.

The discussion to convert the disused Bankside Power Station into a museum of modern art was announced in March 1994. Two other sites were on the final list; however, Bankside offered advantages: it provide space for current needs and space for future expansion; the local council of Southwark was positive to the museum project; and Bankside was viewed as 'the most doable'. The Swiss partnership of Herzog & de Meuron was selected in 1995 to lead the project of converting a disused power station into a museum of modern art. The Bankside bid was accepted by the

Millennium Commission as one of London's landmark projects. At the same time, plans were accepted to expand and refurbish the Millbank site.

Serota's goal of Tate Modern was realized in 2000, a decade after New Displays. The role of the museum of modern art has been discussed by Serota (1996: 55) in terms of traditional antinomies of interpretation and experience:

> The best museums of the future will ... seek to promote different models and levels of 'interpretation' by subtle juxtapositions of 'experience'. Some rooms and works will be fixed, the pole star around which others will turn. In this way, we expect to create a matrix of changing relationships to be explored by visitors according to their particular interests and sensibilities. ... Our aim must be to generate a condition in which visitors can experience a sense of discovery in looking at a particular movement, rather than finding themselves standing on the conveyor belt of history.

The blurring responsibility for contemporary British art between the two London sites, as both can claim curatorial responsibility, has been less problematic in practice than first perceived by commentators. As director of Tate, with four sites, Serota is chief executive and accounting officer, with a devolved management structure, including a deputy director (Alex Beard) and directors at Tate Modern (Vincente Todoli) and Tate Britain (Stephen Deuchar). Not all attention is focused on Tate Modern, given that the Turner Prize – established in 1984 as an annual art award to celebrate new developments in contemporary art, namely 'a British artist under fifty for an outstanding exhibition or other presentation of their work in the twelve months preceding' – remains at Tate Britain.

It is instructive to consider that a particular art world moment occurred in the 1990s: London of the so-called Young British Artists (YBAs) – with Damien Hirst's 'Freeze' exhibition of 1988, organized with fellow postgraduate students at Goldsmiths College, University of London, under the tuition of Michael Craig-Martin, cited as a starting point – became the centre of international attention (see Chong in Robertson 2005: 84–102). Indeed Craig-Martin (London *Guardian*, 11 April 2009) cites Thatcherism as a catalyst: 'art students by necessity became more self-assertive in their efforts to survive' which included the 'Freeze' exhibition.[2] London's rise meant a momentary deflection away from New York for the first time since 1945.[3] Along with artists living and working in London, other constituent players emerged and developed international stature. New dealers like Jay Jopling (White Cube) representing Jake and Dinos Chapman, Gilbert & George, Damien Hirst, and Sam Taylor-Wood, and Sadie Coles representing Angus Fairhurst, Jim Lambie, and Sarah Lucas, for example, quickly developed reputations. Charles Saatchi's role as a lead collector – based on his own engagement with contemporary art from at least the mid-1980s when the first Saatchi Gallery was opened – was high impact, including the 'Sensation: Young British Artists from the Saatchi Collection' exhibition mounted at London's Royal Academy in 1997, which brought the new art of the YBAs to a wider, non-specialist audience. Fergus Henderson's St. JOHN restaurant, which was opened in 1994, served as unofficial canteen. The visual arts were an integral part of so-called Cool Britannia – national boosterism for export sales associated with the creative industries including music (e.g. Oasis and Blur) and fashion (e.g. Paul Smith, Alexander McQueen, and Stella McCartney) – that New Labour was able to exploit in the 1997 General Election alongside D:Ream's single *Things Can Only Get Better* (1994). The social ties of Cool Britannia are represented in one of the emblematic works of the period: Julian Opie's design for the cover of *Blur: best of*, which appeared in October 2000. Blur – Damon Albarn and Dave Rowntree, who studied at Goldsmiths, plus Alex James and Graham Cox – formed in 1989. Their first album, *Parklife*, was released in 1994. A digital drawing of Opie's Blur cover was purchased by the National Portrait Gallery in September 2001, which is a remarkably quick entry for both the musical band and visual artist to official state recognition as culturally significant. Opie, who graduated from Goldsmiths in 1979, is represented by Nicholas Logsdail's Lisson Gallery, arguably the most revered contemporary art dealer in London following the retirement of Anthony d'Offay, and Alan Cristea. London's lack of a contemporary art fair of importance was filled in 2003 by the Frieze Art Fair, which attracts publicity akin to London Fashion Week, and is attended by major private and institutional collectors. Christie's and Sotheby's have organized contemporary art auctions, as part of Frieze week activities, to capitalize on spending power on display.

Serota has been able to capitalize on this unprecedented interest in contemporary art production through the administration of the Turner Prize. Such a prominent position has made Serota a likely target. Serota (in Grant 2003: 52) has responded to accusations that his personal taste dominates Tate:

> Museums have to make selections. Choices are made all the time, and you can't duck those choices. They establish the frame through which we look at the very recent past. Later generations can make corrections, and that may be more or less expensive to do; generally more expensive, because we may have failed to collect some of those things that have become regarded as important. But you can't evade the responsibility of taking a view.

Critics against what they perceive as institutionalized conceptual art include David Lee, editor of *Art Review* until 1999, and the Stuckist group 'against conceptualism, hedonism and the cult of the ego-artist', who posit that 'artists who don't paint aren't artists'.

Serota has the support of Tate trustees, with Tate Modern considered one of the early cultural success stories of the twenty-first century. Indeed Tate has taken pride in celebrating its achievement in establishing a museum of modern art in London:

> Tate Modern has transformed a previously underdeveloped area of London and has helped give the city a new image as a leading centre of contemporary culture. It has become a key landmark for London, while its programme and architecture have won international acclaim.
>
> Since 2000, more than 30 million people have visited Tate Modern – it was designed for 1.8 million visitors annually, but has reached an average of 4.6 million visitors over recent years. Understandably, there is huge pressure on public facilities; and more space is needed to maintain and develop our programme.

Furthermore, Project Transforming Tate Modern, aimed at establishing the full potential of the entire Tate Modern site and surrounding areas, has been developed by a design team led by architects Herzog & de Meuron. The revised plans for the new development of Tate Modern (from press release dated 31 March 2009) were granted planning permission by Southwark Council:

> The proposed new building will be an extraordinary and unique addition to London's townscape. There have already been great regeneration benefits for the area following the opening of Tate Modern at Bankside. It is anticipated that Tate Modern 2 will further contribute to, and form the focus for the future regeneration of this area. The application can be strongly recommended for approval.

The project is due to be completed in 2012, one of the key cultural projects to coincide with the London Olympics, at an estimated cost of £215 million (at 2012 prices).

The chair of the Tate trustees, in the 'Foreword' to Tate Report 06/07, strikes at the heart of widening access imperatives:

> By 2015 we aim to make three significant changes in our work. We will present a wider range of views across all our programmes, from major exhibitions and Collection displays to education programmes, gallery interpretation and online content. By implementing our Diversity Strategy and achieving its milestones, we will bring diversity into everything we do, from programmes and the people we work with to the very way we think. And we will increase the extent of our work beyond the walls of our buildings, growing our international programmes, our presence on the web and our education work.

The chair elaborates by reference to Tate's assets:

> We will do this by continuing to work closely with artists and staff, many experts in their field, who provide the creativity, determination and ambition for which Tate is renowned. And we will use our other great asset, the Collection, as a vehicle for change. In a challenging environment we will find ways to grow and develop the Collection because with the right acquisitions and displays, we can present a more diverse range of art, offer many more viewpoints and share our work more widely with audiences around the world.

It is instructive to note that 'artists and staff' – 'who provide the creativity, determination and ambition' – precede 'the Collection' – 'a vehicle for change' – as Tate's assets.

Quintin Ballardie and the English Chamber Orchestra

'In simple terms, the overriding priority in the commercial world is the need to make a profit and be good; in the subsidized one, it is the need to be good' (Eyre 1998: foreword). Yet this seems to devalue the role of individual initiative and enterprise prior to the establishment of arts quangos during the last 60 years. Must artistic excellence and market forces be viewed as oppositional? Are there not distinct advantages for an organization to operate under the banner of private support and public access?

The English Chamber Orchestra (ECO), which has organizational roots dating back to the post-1945 surge in baroque music, presents an innovative case of artistic entrepreneurship throughout the latter half of the twentieth century (see Chong and Trappey 2001). According to Leopold de Rothschild, founding chairman of the ECO Music Society: 'It is an enterprise governed by market forces and reliant on public demand for the excellence of its musicmaking' (ECO 1983: 9). The vision and ethos of Quintin Ballardie, current artistic director, principal violist, and moving spirit of the ECO, remains steadfast to founding principles of the orchestra: 'We believe very strongly in free enterprise. It is up to us to make it work and make money, if possible, as well as making great music'. He champions that the ECO should remain 'privately held'. The 'private' nature of the ECO creates an obstacle in being eligible to receive public funding. The non-distribution constraint, a primary characteristic of not-for-profits, is not maintained as a surplus, if any, may be divided amongst two uses: ploughed back as retained earnings to support the activities of the organization; and/or paid as a dividend to the shareholders. Ballardie draws an annual payment as a director equivalent to the salary of an assistant arts administrator; he adds that his main source of income comes as full-time player in the orchestra. Moreover, the orchestra has a particular orientation, according to Ballardie (Chong and Trappey 2001):

> It is run on a completely different basis from any other orchestra in the world. The four London symphony orchestras – London Symphony Orchestra, London Philharmonic Orchestra, Royal Philharmonic Orchestra, and The Philharmonia – contract their players and rely heavily on government subsidy. All our players are freelance; we have no such thing as a written contract, though it is understood that they will give the ECO work first call. There is no such thing as public money without strings. We have to produce the best product. I find that pressure stimulating.

The ECO cannot be a role model for all arts organizations, yet there is a great deal to suggest that it offers an alternative path: the orchestra has managed to cultivate an enviable artistic record, with a paramount commitment to national and international excellence in performance, while being able to generate sufficient revenue (in lieu of direct public subsidy) to remain an ongoing concern. While other arts organizations have engaged in intense competition for arts council recognition and public grants, the ECO is proud to announce a certain independence: 'The orchestra receives no support from Arts Council England' is included as part of its programme notes. Through fiscal conservatism, the ECO has focused on staying in business by making great music for its audiences, including having recorded over 1,200 works.

Quintin Ballardie has been described as a 'benevolent despot' with 'incredible energy', 'absolute devotion', and 'fantastic ears for talent'. The role of the musician-entrepreneur is crucial to understanding Ballardie's position at the ECO. With the title of artistic director, he is modest in describing himself: 'I am basically a viola player and I suppose a very good fixer. Those are my real skills, and that is what I enjoy doing' (Chong and Trappey 2001). Ballardie's role as a player – he was the principal viola of the London Philharmonic Orchestra between 1963 and 1971 at the same time as principal viola of the ECO – means that 'there is no "them and us" feeling in the ECO: I am "them", I am the chap who runs the show, but I am also one of "us" '. It goes without saying – but needs noting – that the ECO cannot help but reflect some of the cantankerous entrepreneurial spirit, disposition, and independence of its founder. Indeed, Ballardie's strong views on running an orchestra run counter to many assumptions regarding job security, participatory decision-making, and government subsidies.

First, Ballardie is not a conductor. Unlike most chamber orchestras established and maintained by conductors to further their careers, according to Ballardie, the ECO does not exist to further his cultural ambitions as a conductor. (The performance record of the orchestra also indicates that the orchestra has not been used to highlight Ballardie as a solo violist. Indeed Ballardie is largely absent on the ECO website.) Yet as an unabashed cultural entrepreneur, Ballardie takes credit for the overall success of the orchestra, including the appointment of players. (As part of its status as a full-time orchestra, the ECO has first call on a specific set of musicians, who are appointed by Ballardie.) 'A good ear at picking the talent', according to Ballardie, is his most important skill. Indeed Ballardie is from an older generation of successful arts entrepreneurs, stressing that he has no management background; what he knows about orchestral management was learned on the job, including skills developed as a manager of orchestras for theatrical productions in London's West End.

Second, the players do not have full-time contracts with the ECO, which is to say that they are self-employed musicians. Whereas in many instances, the hand of the accountant forces such a decision, Ballardie recognizes the central role of the players: 'An orchestra is the sum of its musicians, and this applies especially to a small ensemble of the ECO's calibre. Many members of the orchestra are distinguished chamber and concert soloists in their own right'. This implies two things: that the ECO is an ensemble of possibilities, with the contribution of each player having an impact on the overall quality of the performance; and that the ECO is confident enough in its retention capability to support its players – independent of their association with the orchestra – in developing solo careers and forming small ensembles (such as woodwind quintets, trios, and the like). Even though the players are not bound to the ECO by contract – about 30 are needed for a typical performance – they are willing to allow the orchestra to have first call on loyalty. The payment of 'good fees' provides a financial incentive; performing with some of the world's finest musicians and conductors is also important. (According to Pauline Gilbertson, the ECO's administrative director, fees offered by the orchestra are not exceptional – the top end of the BBC Symphony Orchestra range is £40,000 per annum – but higher than the London average and well above the promulgated Musicians' Union rates for engagements.) London's position as one of several international centres of music, essentially an issue of clustering, means that the ECO is able to draw on a rich pool of talent.

Third, the ECO is not democratic in that it does not operate with a player's board for collective decision-making. 'In an ideal world', according to Ballardie (Chong and Trappey 2001),

it is right that an orchestra should be self-governing; however, there are just too many problems. After all, why should players, artists in their own right, be saddled with responsibilities many of which they are not trained to cope with. I find that they appreciate someone who will not only take care of them but also take the very difficult decisions which are needed from time to time. They want to be able to moan and groan and blame someone, and I suppose I fulfil that function. All I know is that I admire and respect beyond measure their collective ability.

Empathy is included in Ballardie's toolkit: as a player he feels confident in recognizing the particular problems facing fellow players; there is also the sense of shared experiences, as he plays alongside the other musicians on stage.

Fourth, the artistic direction has remained in the ECO's hands under the general direction of Ballardie. Artistic activities have to pay: owing to a lack of public subsidy, private sponsorship assumes greater importance. This provides a certain amount of commercial pressure, but it also offers Ballardie freedom to see the orchestra develop in a way based on artistic possibilities offered by the players. For example, the orchestra is only on its third so-called permanent relationship with a conductor. Prior to Ralf Gothóni's appointment, the music critic of the *Financial Times* (12 May 2000) noted the good fit:

> Gothóni first conducted the orchestra in Finland in 1997, and what began as love-at-first-sight seems to be developing into a long-term affair. Their London concert eighteen months ago suggested a partnership made in heaven, as the orchestra responded to Gothóni's inspirational direction with playing that transcended questions of style or authenticity.

Gothóni succeeded Jeffrey Tate, who was conductor between 1985 and 2000; and there was a brief relationship in 1961 with a young Colin Davis. During the period of three decades when the orchestra was without a principal conductor, the ECO relied on a succession of three orchestra leaders (Emanuel Hurwitz, Kenneth Sillito, and José-Luís García) who took an enormous amount of responsibility for maintaining and developing the orchestra's style and standards; at present, Stephanie Gonley is leader.

ON LEADERSHIP STUDIES

Being a leader or displaying leadership qualities is now assumed to be part of many job descriptions. It may represent an inflation of terminology, where being a manager is no longer sufficient. Giving 100 per cent is no longer enough; one now needs make a public declaration to offer 110 per cent to be viewed as sufficiently self-motivated and committed. The relationship between management and leadership – executive decision-making as a process within organizations – deserves comment. Leadership is different from management, according to John Kotter (1990), though they are complementary systems of action. This reflects some very common complaints on leadership and management within organizations: we are over-managed and under-led; or we have strong leadership, but weak management. Management is coping with complexity, planning and budgeting, organizing and staffing, controlling and problem solving, which has direct references to Fayol. On the other hand, according to Kotter (1990), leadership is coping with change, setting a direction, aligning people, and motivating and inspiring. This has much in common with Michael Porter (2006), who concluded a presentation on strategy to the American Association of Museums by emphasizing 'the role of leaders': lead the process of choosing the organization's unique position (i.e. the choice of strategy cannot be entirely democratic); clearly distinguish strategy from operational effectiveness; communicate the strategy relentlessly to all constituencies; maintain discipline around the strategy, in the face of many distractions; decide which competitor changes, technologies, and customer trends to respond to, and how the response can be tailored to the organization's unique position; and measure value and progress against the strategy.

Cultural leadership has the potential to grow. For example London's City University, one of the progenitors of arts management, has just started an MA in Cultural Leadership in conjunction with the Cass Business School which 'seeks to strengthen *self-awareness* and cultivate the *interpersonal skills* needed to build, motivate and empower teams in order to turn *vision* into reality' (emphasis in the original). Moreover, leadership is not restricted to one job title within the organization: 'Underlying this is a conviction that leadership must be developed at all levels within organisations' (emphasis in the original). The 'ambition is *to provide MBA-level professional development specific to the cultural sector*, combining business school teaching with guest speakers and case studies from the cultural sector and creative industries' (emphasis in the original).

Mintzberg (2004: 6) takes a differing view from Kotter and Porter, and even possibly from the MBA orientation of cultural leadership at City University: management and leadership are interchangeable, as managers have to lead and leaders have to manage. 'Management as a practice' is proposed by Mintzberg (2004: 10). 'There is no "one best way" to manage; it all depends on the situation'. The practice of management is characterized by ambiguity. In doing so, he posits engaging management to offset two prominent and dysfunction styles: calculating and heroic. 'Management practice is about pull', according to Mintzberg (2004: 39), as 'what is needed is a particular situation'. There is a need to make a commitment to society. Mintzberg (2004: 274) on engaged management – 'closest to craft, engaging managers connect on the floor; they are less inclined to deem from detached offices' – in contrast to heroic management.

That organizations are complex and managing complex organizations requires a deep knowledge of context. This chimes with Eisner (in Wetlaufer 2001: 124), who places attention on situational analysis in discussing leadership at Disney:

> I have come to the realization that there is no right and wrong with leadership. There is no exact formula. The right style of leadership varies by industry, by person, by the people you are leading. It is unrealistic to think that one leader's way is necessarily the only way.

Moreover, Eisner identified four leadership roles he used in managing creativity. First, *leading by example* 'also means showing a combination of enthusiasm and loyalty to the institution, and it certainly means demanding excellence in the organization'.

Second, *being there* means having contact and exposure and being available. As the organization gets larger, a 'team of leaders' needs to help run the organization. Eisner focuses on the 40 people on whom he has an impact every day: 'I'm very available to them. And I try to get out there as much as possible'. Third, *being a nudge* means that 'sometimes all good ideas or good people need is an advocate who won't shut up'. It is about avoiding ideas falling through cracks or getting mired in bureaucracy. Fourth, *being an idea generator* means that the 'leader in a creative business should be creative'.

Does the rise in leadership reflect a belief that organizations – not least of all arts organizations, if the proliferation of interest in cultural leadership is any indication – need a particular breed of individual called leader? Certainly leadership studies has made inroads in the last two decades as a sub-discipline of management studies. An instructive starting point is 'The romance of leadership', a powerful critique in *Administrative Science Quarterly*, which remains instructive after approximately 25 years (Meindl *et al.* 1985: 78):

> In our view, the social construction of organizational realities has elevated the concept of leadership to a lofty status and level of significance. Such realities emphasize leadership, and the concept has thereby gained a brilliance that exceeds the limits of normal scientific inquiry. The imagery and mythology typically associated with the concept is evidence of the mystery and near mysticism with which it has been imbued.

The executive is the one who 'bears the moral freight of organizations in society' according to Charles Perrow (1986: 73), in his analysis of complex organizations. So-called good leaders are democratic (not authoritarian), employee-centred (rather then production-oriented), and concerned with human relations (as opposed to bureaucratic rules). 'There is a belief that good leadership will lead to high morale, and high morale will lead to increased effort, resulting in higher production', according to Perrow (1986: 85, 88), who notes that 'the nonpersonal decisions [i.e. "mundane factors such as the market, technology, competition, or organizational structure"] appear to have more effect than decisions as to how to lead people'. Perrow (1986: 88) continues by questioning assumptions about the genuine impact of leaders on organizations:

> There is some confusion here, since we are prone to say that an organization has done well because of exceptional leadership. What we generally mean is that the decisions made with regard to organizational structure, type of product or service, quality control, new technologies, and so on have been good decisions, not just that the leaders have summoned an extra ounce of cooperation and motivation from the followers or been helpful in planning the workers' tasks or in teaching them skills.

This is similar to a point mooted by Meindl *et al.* (1985: 96):

> The romanticized conception of leadership suggests that leaders do or should

have the ability to control and influence the fates of organizations in their charge. This assumption of control and the responsibility it engenders is a double-edged sword: not only does it imply giving credit for positive outcomes, but it also entails laying blame for negative ones.

Meindl *et al.* (1985: 100) make an interesting conclusion by commenting on the role of followers and 'follower-ship' within organizations:

> And, if our analysis is correct, the continuing infatuation with leadership, for whatever truths it yields about the qualities and behavior of our leaders, can also be used to learn something about the motivations of followers. It may be that the romance and the mystery surrounding leadership concepts are critical for sustaining follower-ship and that they contribute significantly to the responsiveness of individuals to the needs and goals of the collective organization.

The range of writing on leadership during intervening period, since Meindl *et al.* (1985), has been wide: it includes academic journals such as *The Leadership Quarterly*, with organizational psychology and management science as academic bases, analysis of so-called business celebrities such as Bill Gates, Richard Branson, Robert Murdoch, Steve Jobs, and Michael Dell (Guthey, Clark, and Jackson 2009), and populist books on leadership, which range from *In Search of Excellence* (Peters and Waterman 1982) to *The Leadership Secrets of Genghis Khan* (Man 2009). (A wry reviewer of Genghis Khan has suggested that someone is probably writing a management book on the inspirational genius of Adolph Hitler!)

PARALLEL ADMINISTRATIVE HIERARCHIES

Many arts organizations offer a good illustration of what Mintzberg (1979) describes as the emergence of 'parallel administrative hierarchies'. Two sets of salaried employees have contested the management of many large and established arts organizations: the *operating core* (i.e. those performing the basic work of the organization such as curators, musicians, or actors); and the *support staff* (i.e. those who aid the functioning of the operating core outside the basic flow of the operating work such as fundraisers, marketers, accountants, and retail managers). Specialist members of the operating core (e.g. curators in art museums) have power because of their expertise concerning 'professional operations'. The operating core is 'at the heart of every organization', according to Mintzberg (1979: 24), and is responsible for securing the inputs, transforming inputs into outputs, distributing outputs, and providing direct support to the input, transformation, and output functions. In the case of support staff, power resides in administrative offices, which suggests that 'one must practice administration, not a specialized function of the organization, to attain status' (DiMaggio 1986: 12). An organization's 'attempt to encompass more and more boundary activities in order to reduce uncertainty, to control its own affairs' is reflected in the size and scope of support units (Mintzberg 1979: 32). Historically and traditionally, the ethos of the art museum has posited the curatorial departments at the core of the organizational structure (not unlike academic departments in universities): this in effect invited many curators to manage their departments like separate medieval baronies. In lieu of curatorial cooperation, many were ready for turf wars regarding the display of the permanent collection and the schedule of temporary exhibitions.

At the same time, one can cite substantive change within 'professional bureaucracies' (or 'collegial' organizations dominated by skilled workers who use procedures that are difficult to learn yet well defined), namely the rise of the power of the administrator or manager who is not part of the operating core. Non-specialist professional managers – those bracketed by Mintzberg's support staff component – have grown in importance and influence owing to issues of funding and education mandates, which necessitates an attempt to disseminate the arts to wider segments of the population.

Power flows to those professionals who care to devote their effort to doing 'administrative' as opposed to 'professional' work. It has been suggested by Adorno (1978: 97) that complex and prosperous environments will augment cultural bureaucracy:

> The dialectic of culture and administration nowhere expresses the sacrosanct irrationality of culture so clearly as in the continually growing alienation of administration from culture – both in terms of its objective categories and its personal composition.

The professional administrator derives power from serving key roles at the *boundary* of the organization, between members of the operating core and interested parties on the outside, including funding sources. For example, a managing director (coming from a background in finance, law, accountancy, or management consultancy, for example) may be hired to work alongside the chief aesthetic officer, with a mandate to 'open out the institution' and 'take a hard look at how money gets spent'.

Management structures can influence the direction of arts organizations. What values are represented? Bifurcated management structures exist in many diverse types of organizations. The French talk of 'co-habitation', when the president and prime minister represent political parties of different ideological stripes. University halls of residence in England often have a bursar in charge of management, with a warden responsible for welfare and pastoral care; if residents liken the bursar to an 'iron fist', the warden is the 'velvet glove'. To have dual executive roles is the assumed practice in many art music organizations. Bifurcated management structures with dual executive roles, of a president in the top administrative position, working alongside a director with authority over aesthetic matters, has been the practice in many performing arts organizations in the post-impresario era. In the case of art music organizations, a general manager and conductor divide responsibilities. The Metropolitan Opera has a general manager (Joseph Volpe from 1990 to 2006 and now Peter Gelb) and a conductor (Joseph Levine is in charge of music). This was explicit in the four-part television series *Naked Classics* (January 1997 on Channel 4 in the UK): part III focused on the Met's general manager Joseph Volpe and part IV examined the role of the then conductor Zubin Metha. For example, Quintin Ballardie is artistic director of the English Chamber Orchestra; Pauline Gilberston is administrative director.

The situation for visual arts organizations has been different with an emphasis on one executive position, called director, who conventionally has direct experience with art (and artists in the case of contemporary visual arts organizations). There are some exceptions which are instructive. Following the departure of Thomas Hoving as director of the Metropolitan Museum of Art in 1977, the Met decided to adopt a bifurcated management structure. That the career mobility of curators or art historians to the office of director was perceived as less certain was an expressed concern. For example, in the pre-Hoving period, it was assumed that directors of elite art museums would have educational qualifications in art history and professional training as curators or art historians, with managerial training acquired on the job. At the time, a number of prominent museum people were opposed to bifurcation, arguing in the main that there ought to be one chief executive, who progressed through the curatorial ranks. According to the then director of the Cleveland Museum of Art (Sherman Lee in *ARTnews*, October 1977):

It's a misapplication of quite different thinking into an area that is quite different by philosophy and by purpose from a business enterprise. . . . The fastest way to destroy art is to make it like everything else, homogenize it, make it part of the profit-making setup.

The appointment of Philippe de Montebello, as the Met's director, who remained in post until 2008, has not seen populism materialize. He has expressed views on museum management in the *Financial Times* (1/2 December 2001):

We do not compete with Disney theme parks, with rock concerts. We would be silly to do so. There always has been a solid core audience for high culture. I don't think it has diminished. Its expectations are different from those who enjoy popular culture, who seek quick fixes and instant gratification.

Indeed many do not realize that the Met even has a president.

The case of bifurcation at the Philadelphia Museum of Art from 1982 to 1997 is instructive. Following the departure of Jean Sutherland Boggs as director, the board of trustees felt that the PMA had two individuals within the corporate fold who could make a dual structure work: Robert Montgomery Scott, a leading lawyer in Philadelphia and a trustee since 1965, was appointed president; and Anne d'Haroncourt, curator of twentieth century art for a decade, was appointed director. The relationship lasted 15 years until Scott's retirement in 1997, when d'Haroncourt assumed sole executive responsibilities as director and chief executive officer. Mutually-supporting reasons account for why another president was not appointed to succeed Scott: by the early 1990s, there was already internal questioning amongst staff members whether bifurcation had run its course; management structures and systems were much stronger than they had been during the directorship of Boggs, who was recognized by the trustees, at the time, as requiring a senior administrator to offer support; and, most importantly, d'Haroncourt was receiving offers for top museum posts in the USA and expressed a desire not to have another president at the PMA. It would appear that the PMA adopted bifurcation as a means to deal with a specific institutional circumstance, with the benefit of being able to tap good, local talent, as opposed to treating bifurcation as an organizational panacea.

There was a short-lived and unsuccessful – albeit animated and amusing – attempt of parallel administrative structures at the British Museum (BM), at the turn of the century, with a managing director, Suzanna Taverne, hired as a corporate business manager to work alongside the director, Robert Anderson. Taverne, with substantial experience in merchant banking and media, was hired in 1999 to offer additional management and financial support to the director, a traditional curator figure. At the time of Taverne's appointment, she was proffered as the future of UK's national art museums. However, when it emerged, in 2001, that she would not be appointed director upon Anderson's retirement, she decided to leave the institution. Selective excerpts of an interview Taverne gave to the London *Sunday Times* (9 September 2001) have been quoted with relish: 'There is this priesthood of curators, who look after the relics. There's this notion that only they can be the intermediaries between the relics and the public. They carry this sacred flame of the institution – the museum'; she went on to comment on the photos of the BM's past museum directors, 'Look at them. All white males'. For its part the BM abandoned the experiment of having dual executives. A director with curatorial authority and managerial capability along with active leadership and strategic vision, what is perceived to be the ideal candidate, was sought.

A manager-scholar, Neil MacGregor, successful director of the National Gallery (1987–2002), was appointed as the new director of the British Museum in 2002. Viewed as a talented museum curator, MacGregor also came with a record in raising money and mounting crowd-pleasing exhibitions. There is much to suggest that MacGregor has rejuvenated the BM (which has included declining an opportunity to become the director of the Met following de Montebello's retirement); moreover, he is leading the 'North West Development' project, which is of fundamental importance in delivering the BM's four objectives (i.e. to manage and research the collection more effectively, to enhance access to the collection, to invest in our people, and to increase self-generated income). The 250th anniversary of the BM, in 2009, provided an apposite occasion for MacGregor (2009 BM anniversary lecture; *Financial Times* 'The Diary', 17/18 January 2009) to celebrate the institution's achievements and contributions. MacGregor reemphasized the BM's position as 'the first national museum in the world opened free of charge "to all studious and curious persons" ' and 'the private collection of every citizen in the world', which is to say that the BM is remains a public institution with free entry and a commitment to make its collections available to greater and more diverse audiences. The BM is 'in the position where we have to address the whole world, and in a new way', according to MacGregor, who adds that the BM can use objects and the information available to 'construct an image of what we don't experience'.

One often thinks that a museum director good at diplomacy is successful at courting favour with current and prospective donors; however, MacGregor has engaged in tactful negotiations with other countries to foster an exchange of ideas and objects. Indicative of this intercultural connectedness is an impressive series of exhibitions, held during 2008 and 2009, on leaders and rulers – Qin Shihuanghi (reigned 221–210 BC) as 'The First Emperor: China's Terracotta Army', with the

Morgan Stanley as corporate sponsor; 'Hadrian: Empire and Conflict', based on the Roman Emperor (reigned AD 117–38), with British Petroleum as corporate sponsor; and 'Shah 'Abbas (reigned AD 1587–1629): The Remaking of Iran' in partnership with the National Museum of Iran and the Iranian Cultural Heritage, Tourism and Handicrafts Organizations and in association with the Iran Heritage Foundation – is a tangible result to the benefit of the BM, including its esteem in the eyes of major cultural authorities and governments outside of the UK. The UK benefits from such exhibitions – what some deem cultural diplomacy – though MacGregor is aware not to compromise the BM's independence from government. Core to MacGregor's message of the BM as a public institution is retaining public trust.

■ ■ ■

In many respects arts and cultural organizations should be at the fore of current discussions on human capital management given a commitment to excellence and artistic integrity. Indeed some of the initiatives of Arts & Business – as raised as part of Chapter 3 – have suggested ways that business can learn from the arts. At the same time, an encroachment of newer values associated with non-aesthetic performance measures – including the instrumentalism of the arts and culture, as discussed in Chapter 2 – make arts and cultural organizations even more complex to manage and lead. Experimentation with different executive management structures – not least of all questions surrounding what constitutes legitimate authority – is one manifestation which is likely to continue. Certainly there is more mileage for those interested in exploring the intertwined relationship between management and leadership. One senses a moral earnestness and fascination with leadership. As such the emergence of cultural leadership – initially broached in Chapter 1 – can be viewed as part of broader concerns. Guidance is sought from leaders, which raises questions on the moral purpose of leadership, the role of followers, and whether there is too much importance granted to the influence of leaders.

APPENDIX: PERSONAL DEVELOPMENT IN ARTS MANAGEMENT

At the start of the twenty-first century, the changing economic organization is draw-ing attention to flatter hierarchies, more ambiguous job descriptions, and fewer rules. Research predicts that 'the career, as an institution, is in unavoidable decline'; and the 'social division of labour into discrete professions and careers is obsolete' (Flores and Gray 2000: 9, 18). At the same time, 'knowledge production' is promoted as essential if it can be used to build a sustainable advantage that can be leveraged across products, according to Walter Powell (in DiMaggio 2001: 35). For those in the arts, related issues of professionalization and career mobility are raised. Discussions about professionalization can be interminable and often painful, yet they continue to be raised by some arts workers. Viewed from a sociological slant, professionalism con-cerns 'a form of self-organization that enables practitioners of an occupation to defend the importance of their contribution and the legitimacy of their decisions' (DiMaggio 1988: 52). Furthermore, according to Ehrenreich and Ehrenreich (1979), the so-called professional-managerial class has assumed the accoutrements of professionalism, with organizations to advance the interests of the field; more importantly, they have come to conceive themselves as possessing special skills, and their work as deserving professional respect.

Consider the apprenticeship recollected by John Murdoch (1993: 326), who was assistant director (collection) at the V&A Museum before being appointed director of the Courtauld Institute Art Gallery in 1993, where he remained until 2002, when he became director of art collections at the Huntington Library, in California:

> In his last months [1974] as Keeper Graham instituted for me a twice weekly private session, two hours long, in which he systematically took me through the collection of miniatures, of which I had no previous experience. For each artist there was something distinctive, the shape of the ear, perhaps, or more often something more minute, such as the way in which the shadow under the eye was drawn, or the outlining of the nose, or the shading of the background. He used a hand-held lens and knew exactly what he was looking for in each object. . . . It was only years later that I realized what Graham was doing, that I was being inducted into a specific tradition of connoisseurship, and that there was, within it, an apostolic succession at the V&A (Murdoch 1993: 326).

Murdoch goes on to outline how Graham Reynolds, who had joined the V&A in 1938, was inducted into the 'specially difficult and arcane field of miniatures, which is studied only at the V&A' by Carl Winter (1906–66); in turn, Winter, a great connois-seur, had joined as an assistant keeper in 1931, when the towering personality of the department was Basil Long (1881–1937), who had been in the department since 1906 and had a string of major catalogues to his credit including 'the monumental *British Miniaturists* of 1929, which is still standard'. According to Murdoch, he came across a newspaper obituary of Long in the departmental library: it noted that after graduating from the University of Heidelberg in the late 1890s, Long went off to Milan, where he studied the methods of the great Giovanni Morelli (1816–91). The 'tradition of objective art historical scholarship to which I was inducted in my turn in 1974', according to Murdoch, can be traced back to Morelli, rightly considered as one of the progenitors of the discipline of art history, hence 'an apostolic succession at the V&A'.

In many respects, Murdoch's induction and mobility at the V&A was not unusual for museum professionals of his generation. Duchamp scholar Anne d'Harnoncourt spent virtually her entire professional career at the PMA, where she was director and chief executive officer at the time of her untimely death (aged 64) in 2008; Philippe de Montebello spent most of his curatorial life at the Met, including a long span as director from 1977 to 2008. Joseph Volpe started at the Metropolitan Opera as a stagehand in 1964 and rose through the ranks to the position of general manager in 1990, which he kept until 2006. But is this system of organizational work, marked by relative security, clear hierarchies, and linear, upward progression within an organization or sector, any longer available for those entering arts organizations at the start of the twenty-first century?

Is the notion of the career, the binding together of phases of a working life to shape a coherent narrative from it, now fading from view? Changes shaping organizations have been identified. First, rather than jobs, projects become more important (Powell in DiMaggio 2001). Work is organized around a team or work group charged with responsibility for a project. There is merging of conception and execution (with design and production running on parallel tracks). From a positive light, (Powell in DiMaggio 2001: 57), 'workers are increasingly authors of their own work'. In order to make organizations more dynamic, Douglas Hague (1993) suggests a rule-of-thumb for senior managers: stay five years in the job; do not remain more than ten years in the organization. On the other hand, job or work intensification may be behind the language of participation. Is the 'new flexibility liberating or imprisoning' (Powell in DiMaggio 2001: 58)? Of course, some workers will have grown accustomed to job structures heavy with unskilled positions, antiquated job titles, and an acceptance of high absenteeism.

Second, flattening hierarchies and the spread of networks make it more important to develop a latticework of collaborations with so-called outsiders (Powell in DiMaggio 2001). From a personal perspective, creating a record of achievement becomes even more important as a way to encourage people to trust you and collaborate with you. 'When you stop learning in a job, you begin to shrink', according to Peter Drucker (1990: 154), who recommends taking a volunteer job with an organization (as a way to repot oneself). Yet such collaborations are not uncontroversial from an organizational perspective as blurring the boundaries of the firm 'makes it difficult to know where the firm ends and where the market or another firm begins' (Powell in DiMaggio 2001: 58).

Third, cross-fertilization among industries means leveraging distinctive capabilities across fields. How to manage the relationship: 'the execution – compete or collaborate with a dazzling array of rivals and partners – is complex indeed' (Powell in DiMaggio 2001: 62). The case of the Guggenheim Foundation with its growing tentacles raises issues associated with franchising a cultural brand. Musical theatre has learned a great deal from Hollywood in making a certain type of performing art attractive to mass audiences. Are developments that encourage cross-fertilization among industries harmful or positive for consumers, or creators?

Arts and cultural workers more than workers in other sectors of the economy will feel the impact of the decline of conventional career structures and the rise of knowledge-based production. A current *curriculum vitae* that can be emailed instantaneously is advised. Managing online data, not least of all content on social networking sites, is important as tracking techniques and online searches are becoming common.

Competency sharing is grounded in the spirit of reflection, which Mintzberg (2004) views as helping to develop an engaged manager. With this in mind, personal development may be viewed as enhancing three forms of capital: intellectual, personal, and social. First, *intellectual* capital is usually associated with formal education and qualifications, but it ought to be considered more broadly to include acquiring new skills throughout a working career. This can be addressed by highlighting a recent work-related achievement: what skills were required? Also quantify the benefit the achievement had to the firm.

Second, *personal* capital focuses on one's emotional growth as a person. Self-reflection appears in many common interview questions (as indicated by a cursory review of large recruitment agencies). What is the most difficult situation you have faced and how did you tackle it? (It appears that this is gauging your definition of difficult and your approach – hopefully logical – to problem-solving.) What are your strengths? (No excuses for not having prepared this one.) What are your weaknesses? (This is another set-piece. Stating 'none' is not an option; indeed, it may lead to further problems.) In addition examples are asked in a series of questions: when you have worked under pressure, when your work was criticized, when you disagreed with your boss, when you have not got on with others, and when you have been out of your depth. Likewise, group dynamics appear: what kinds of people do you like working with? What kind of people do you find it difficult to work alongside?

Third, *social* capital emphasizes the developing of a network of personal relationships, best if such contacts are fostered by shared values and trust. Such social networks (e.g. school and university alumni associations) are often maintained for non-economic reasons, yet can affect economic outcomes. Social networks plays a role as prospective employers and employees prefer to learn about one another from personal sources whose information they can trust. Sociologist Mark Granovetter (1973, 1983) has proffered 'the strength of weak ties': close friends tend to move in the same circles so there is an overlap of information. However, acquaintances – those we have weak ties to – know people we do not, and thus more novel information can be received.

Selling oneself to a prospective employer, business partner, or funder has affinities with the challenges of persuading senior peers (Conger 1998). First, it is important to establish *credibility* through expertise, which may be from demonstrated track record of sound judgement and accomplishments, and *relationships* (that is being trusted). Second, identify *common ground* with the audience, which is about understanding the audience – essentially an issue of empathy – and looking to see how they can benefit from you. Third, reinforce your position with *vivid language*, by using examples, stories, metaphors, or analogies, and *evidence* such as numerical data. Fourth, and finally, *connect emotionally* to the audience.

SECTION III

Wealth and the Economy

7

FINANCIAL INVESTING
IN THE ARTS

■ ■ ■ ■ ■ ■ ■

Consuming the arts can progress from appreciation – such as visiting art museums in the case of the visual arts or attending the theatre in the case of the performing arts – to greater engagement. With the financial means this may include investing in the arts. Investing in the visual and performing arts is a broad category of activity with varying motivations. Financial investments in any particular market sector are fraught with challenges. As the Ponzi scheme is entering everyday discourse, it is worthwhile to note the perils of speculation based on crowd psychology. Charles Mackay (2003), in *Extraordinary Popular Delusions*, which first appeared in 1841, examined three financial scandals, including what has become known as Tulipomania: an incident from seventeenth-century Holland, which has some affinities to the arts – not least of all recent works by living artists sold at auction – when people went into debt collecting tulip bulbs. Of course, collecting ceased when a sudden depreciation in the value of the bulbs rendered them worthless (except as flowers). Fred Kelly and Philip Carret both wrote books on financial speculation that were published shortly after the crash of the stock market in 1929. 'After vanity and greed, perhaps the most malign influence to one making money from the market is the Will to Believe', according to Kelly (2003: 14), who addressed the psychology of speculation. In a similar vein, Carret (2004: 8) noted: 'It is quite impossible to draw a sharp line and say of those on one side, "These are investors!" and those on the other, "Those are speculators!" '. Whereas gamblers make decisions based on hope, 'speculators are those who use brains' to find 'hidden weak spots in the market', according to Carret (2004: 10), who considers the speculator to be 'the advance agent of the investor'.[1]

The availability of risk capital is one reason for entrepreneurial activity. Wealth is certainly a key characteristic to be able to invest in the visual and performing arts. It ranges from the so-called mass affluent (i.e. annual gross income in excess of $100,000 as used in retail banking), at the low end, to ultra high net worth individuals (i.e. investible assets in excess of $30 million as used in private wealth management). There are also complementary and competing investment vehicles where passion plays a part role: fine art, theatre, and film sit alongside fine wine, classic automobiles, and thoroughbred racehorses (see the Appendix on 'Alternative passion investments').

Patrons of fine art have always included the rich and powerful. Even with the rise of the public art museum – making appreciation of art more widely available, relative to the (by definition) restricted access to private art collections – collecting art is still considered an elite recreational activity. The demarcation between collecting and speculating in fine art is not always clear: 'Speculation is amusing. Because good taste and good investment go hand in hand, the speculator qualifies as a connoisseur by the profit he earns' (Moulin 1987: 99).

Cats – the longest running musical in the history of either London's West End or New York's Broadway – is often cited as a case of commercial success in theatre for the investors. Andrew Lloyd Webber announced the closing of the London production of *Cats* following a final performance on 11 May 2002, its twenty-first birthday. *Cats* was innovative: traditional theatre investors and producers would not touch Lloyd Webber's project, based on T. S. Eliot's *Old Possum's Book of Practical Cats*. Cameron Macintosh, who agreed to produce it, had to seek investors at £750 per subscription to raise the £450,000 needed to open the show in 1981. Investors have been well rewarded: every £1.00 invested has seen a return of £56.67, which means £42,500 for an initial subscription of £750 (London *Daily Telegraph*, 16 January 2002). It goes without saying that producers with a record of long-running and successful shows will reward the loyalty of their original investors in subsequent investment opportunities.

Film is listed as one of 'five performing arts' in a collection of essays originally published in the *New York Review of Books* (Silvers 2001); however, the contributor, Garry Willis (in Silvers 2001), notes that a case against film as art boils down to one or more of four complaints: movies are commercial; they are collaborations, more committee work than the responsibility of a single artist; they are technological products; and they mix genres. Such attributes, coupled with the glamour associated with Hollywood, make film ripe as an alternative investment vehicle. An example is IndieVest (2009), an independent film studio, financier, and distributor in the USA with a member community of private investors, which describes itself as 'connecting film and capital' by offering a turnkey operation from pre-production through to distribution (with a guaranteed domestic distribution of 1,500 theatres).

It is instructive to note that rates of return on investment in the arts can be measured beyond the financial (or economic) exchange value for money. There is an aesthetic yield (or psychic return) of pleasure based on connoisseurship and cultural patronage, which has been interpreted as a method for social elites to feign a disregard for commerce. There are also social benefits that can accrue to the owner: it signals one's income level, cultural erudition, or attitude to novelty and risk.

Finally, the economics term fungibility deserves mention. Fungibility is a characteristic of an asset that describes its interchangeability (or mutual subscription) with other individual assets of the same type. Assets with this characteristic – as in the phrase 'a dollar is a dollar' no matter where it came from, where it is located, or what you plan to buy with it – simplify the exchange process as interchangeability assumes that everyone values all assets of the class as the same. Fungibility is distinct from liquidity (i.e. ease of converting an asset into cash). Richard Thaler (1985; 1999) examines mental accounting as the set of cognitive operations used by individuals and households to organize, evaluate, and keep track of financial activities. Thaler

(1999: 202) was drawing attention to irrational decision-making, including his own: 'My own thinking about mental accounting began with an attempt to understand why people pay attention to sunk costs, why people are lured by bargains into silly expenditures, and why people will drive across town to save $5 on small purchases but not a large one'. An example dealing with fine wine (Thaler 1999: 191–92) is discussed in the appendix with reference to a recent advertising campaign by a prominent wine merchant.

FINE ART INVESTMENT FUNDS

Characteristic of speculation in a booming art market has been the quickness with which works sold in the primary art market appear at auction. A prime example – and possibly the climax of the bull market – was Damien Hirst's exhibition/auction of new works, 'Beautiful Inside My Head Forever', at Sotheby's London on 15/16 September 2008 which totalled £112 million. (The first day of the sale coincided with the collapse of the investment bank Lehman Brothers. Hirst's share from the two-day sale was £95.7 million.) Another development in the recent art boom – which is more internationally diverse than the art boom of the 1980s – has been interest in art as an alternative asset for investment purposes.

Noting the structural differences that exist between the workings of the securities and art markets is an instructive starting point before examining two key examples – art market price data and art funds – that represent the growing industry built on art investment aspirations. Structural differences between the workings of the securities and art markets suggest that the art market, due to the internal qualities of art and the external market for trading in art, is not an efficient market, according to William Baumol (1986: 10–14), in an influential article on 'art investment as floating crap game' published in *American Economic Review*. The qualities in weighing an art purchase – authenticity, quality, rarity, condition, provenance, and value, according to the Art Dealers Association of America, a leading trade association – mean that each art work, even similar themes by the same artist, is unique, which is to say imperfect substitutes. On the other hand, the inventory of a particular stock (share) is made up of a large number of homogeneous securities, all perfect substitutes for one another. A work of art's 'uniqueness' means that the owner holds a monopoly on that work of art; in contrast, a given stock is held by many individuals who are potentially independent traders on the near perfectly competitive stock market. There is no organized marketplace where trading in a given stock can take place frequently – like the NYSE or NASDAQ in New York or the LSE or AIM in London – for trading in art. Art is traded – that is to say bought and sold – via dealers and auction houses. But such trades in a particular work of art are marked by infrequency – as the holding period can be measured in years and decades. Hence lower levels of liquidity for art. One consequence of low trading volume is greater price fluctuations. The price at which a stock is exchanged is, generally, public information; on the other hand, the price at which an art work is traded is frequently known only to the parties immediately involved. Price data is limited to public auction sales, though the precise arrangements between the auctioneer and the consignor – such as consignment charges or guarantees[2] – are not disclosed. More significantly, there is incomplete sales data as sales through dealers (operating in the primary and secondary markets) and private treaty sales by auctioneers are excluded.

'Only those critics who have succeeded as instruments for the redistribution of general tastes seem really to have been in a position to profit from their judgement', according to Baumol (1986: 14). Moreover, the equilibrium mechanism is weaker in the art market. In the case of a stock, its 'true' (equilibrium) price is known, at least in principle: it is the stock's pro rata share of the discounted present value of the company's expected stream of future earnings. But, for a work of art, the true equilibrium price is difficult to gauge. For an economist, Baumol (1986: 14) makes an amusing observation on the non-financial returns of art (i.e. aesthetic yield or psychic benefits):

> Ownership of art works may well represent a very rational choice for those who derive a high rate of return in the form of aesthetic pleasure. They should not, however, let themselves be lured into the purchase of art by the illusion that they can beat the game financially and select with any degree of reliability the combination of purchase dates and art works that will produce a rate of return exceeding the opportunity cost of their investment.

Opportunity cost can be organized into several categories: investment returns in an alternative asset, transaction costs from buying and selling, and carrying costs. Transaction costs associated with buying and selling art are higher than for other financial instruments. A risk premium, which might be covered by carrying charges for insurance, security, and conservation, needs to be deducted from any apparent rate of return. Proper insurance can be a chief annual carrying cost. Yet providers like AXA, Chubb, and Hiscox with specialist knowledge in art highlight that insurance – at a fraction of the cost of the art – is a necessity for any art owner. It is also important to gauge the changing value of art: for example, Gurr Johns, established in 1914 with offices in London, New York, Paris, and Munich, operates as a firm of valuers and fine art consultants, independent of any auction house or dealer.

Organizations such as Artprice, Artnet, Art Sales Index, and Art Market Research offer international art market data based on auction prices. The reputation of contemporary artists, based on exhibitions and collections, is tracked by Kunstkompass and Marek Claassen's Artfacts. ArtTactic was created by Anders Petterson to offer financial analyst-like reports for contemporary art investors. Art price data based on auction sales, such as by Artprice, Artnet, and Art Sales Index, offers transparency and can be a general pointer on art market conditions. However, one needs to be wary of using so-called art indexes as a proxy for the actual price that a work will achieve at auction or with a dealer.

Many so-called art indexes show the average price paid for an artist's or movement's works over a given period. But, as noted above, works of art are not interchangeable: artists can have different periods of critical reception; both the provenance of the work and its physical condition can impact on value; moreover, limited transactions can cause distortions. It has been noted that average prices are being shown not price/earnings ratios. What is needed for a proper index is repeat sales data. This means tracking the actual changes in the sales price of a work of art.

Such a task is not easy as the only sales data available in a verifiable, transparent manner is through the major auction houses. As such, a major deficiency of the major art market price databases is the inability to access primary market sales by dealers – a major gap given the boom market for contemporary art – secondary market sales by dealers, and private treaty sales by auction houses. An upward bias also exists as works *bought in* at auction – that is fails to sell at auction when the *reserve* is not reached – are excluded.[3]

How do rates of return on investment in art compare with returns elsewhere? What are the main determinants of the prices of art works? In an attempt at art market innovation, Jianping Mei and Michael Moses, two finance academics at New York University, examined repeat sale auction prices. Mei and Moses (2005; 2002) conclude that art outperforms fixed income securities as an investment, though it significantly underperforms stocks in the USA; art should be viewed as a risk-reducing strategy rather than a return-producing strategy; as a diversification tool, investors in art should not be looking at short holding periods; and price estimates for expensive paintings have a consistent upward bias over the long-term of 30 years in an examination of the relationship between auction estimates and the long-term performance of works of art.[4] However, it is important to bear in mind that the Mei Moses data set is limited. It is based on 13,000 price pairs, or repeat sales, from auctions (initially only at Christie's and Sotheby's in New York). The original three collecting categories, American Paintings 1700–1950, Impressionist and Modern, and Old Masters, have been expanded to include two more, Post-War and Contemporary and Latin America. This means that the art market attention on contemporary art is not addressed. The general weaknesses associated with price indexes remain: transactions conducted by dealers are excluded, which is a striking exclusion in the case of contemporary art where primary market sales via dealers are crucial for introducing the work to the art marketplace; upward price bias is built into the selection process as only successful works are included since works bought in at auction are excluded.

Art funds represent an example of structuring a vehicle to invest in art, with investors pooling resources, which help to diversify holdings. Popular examples of pooling resources in other sectors include mutual funds and real estate investment trusts (REITs). Art funds are structured like private equity funds. Two categories benefit from art funds: those who provide the capital that allows acquisition of art (limited partners); and those who manage the fund (general partners) by drawing on a range of advisors and specialist service providers. 'It is arguably not realistic to talk of an art investment fund industry', according to Bruce Arnold (2009) of Caslon Analytics, who considers whether 'art investment funds are more accurately characterized as trading mechanisms', which is to say: 'Strip away the gesso, glitter and genuflections at Sotheby's or another upmarket venue and art investment funds involve the same patterns of speculation found in commodities as unromantic (and potentially lucrative) as pork bellies, oilseeds or copper ingots'. Arnold notes two trading strategies by art funds: the first is to trade recognized major works by established artists, where there is a finite supply; the second is to acquire, hold and then sell works that are more clearly undervalued, which is riskier as it depends on successful forecasting of what will be recognized as of value in the future.

The success of the British Rail Pension Fund (1974–89) is often cited by supporters of art as an investment. A growing demand for more sophisticated financial instruments also spurred the growth of private equity and hedge funds. Investment in art – as part of a booming art market – as sexy can be cited (Arnold 2009). However, art funds remain largely uncharted territory, with a patchy record since the first ones were launched in the 2000s. (The Fine Art Fund, which is based in London, is cited as the most successful story. On the other hand, Dutch bank ABN Amro departed from the art fund marketplace in 2005, one year after announcing its entry; and USA-based Fernwood Art Investment, which received high media attention, including a Harvard Business School case study, floundered and closed in 2006.) Arnold (2009) acknowledged activity and excitement: '2007 and 2008 saw announcements that several art funds – often badged as "unique" or "the first" – were being launched and would provide fortunate investors with returns of around 15 to 20 per cent along with opportunities for portfolio diversification'. A degree of healthy scepticism is plainly evident: 'In practice some of the announcements are unlikely to be followed by substantive establishment of a fund, particularly a fund that generates stellar results for investors rather than managers'.

Philip Hoffman (see Robertson and Chong 2008), a qualified accountant and formerly of Christie's, is chief executive of The Fine Art Fund (TFAF) Group, which was established in 2004 to raise $350 million to invest in museum quality art: 'Given the phenomenal interest in art as an asset class, TFAF was established as an investment vehicle for art, including oil on canvas paintings, works on paper, and sculpture, from the thirteenth century to the present'.[5] Objectives in assessing a work's potential 'include growth of 40 per cent in one year or tripling of value in three years' with 'works bought in the range $300,000 to $5 million, with an average of $600,000 per work'. The minimum investment is high at '$250,000 and investors are committed for at least three years'. Trading costs are kept to a minimum by 'mostly buying and selling privately, so cutting out the transaction costs associated with auctioneers'; moreover, the fund 'is able to move opportunistically, for example, by buying from distressed sellers'. Alongside the main fund, Hoffman notes that 'co-investment is another method as it allows a group of investors to buy a specific work or works with a short holding period, that is mostly one or two years, in mind'. Most of the works in TFAF are stored in Geneva or out on loan to art museum exhibitions. Fund members can pay a rental charge of 1.25 per cent of the work's insured value in order to display a work at home.

Other art funds are in various stages of development. Meridian Art Partners launched an emerging art markets fund in 2008. Meridian Art Partners (MAP) was established by Andrew Littlejohn and Pamela Johnson, both formerly of Phillips de Pury in New York, with headquarters in New York.[6] MAP's first product, the Meridian Emerging Art Markets Fund, was launched in 2008: it is a five to seven year closed-ended limited partnership open to accredited investors worldwide, with a minimum investment of $250,000; an annual management fee of 2 per cent is levied and a capital gains charge of 20 per cent of any gains over 6 per cent. Littlejohn and Johnson believe the fund's focus – on contemporary art from emerging art markets throughout the world, including but not limited to Africa, Asia, India, Latin America, the Middle East, and Russia (though the fund will also include a small allocation of established Western contemporary art) – will capitalize on current and future art market opportunities and that it will support emerging art markets and their constituent artists; moreover, non-Western investors may be more willing to take risks in making investments. The basic business model is similar to TFAF, with emerging markets – for both the art and investors – being a point of differentiation.

V22, based in London, is a contemporary art organization which includes a permanent collection, a gallery and artist studio, and project spaces. The V22 Collection is a body of contemporary art which grows on the recommendations of a variety of art experts and its core artist ownership base.[7] Shares in V22 started trading on the PLUS Markets in August 2006.[8] As an investment vehicle for art, it differs from an art fund: investors buy shares in a publicly listed firm that is building a contemporary art collection; also artists are involved in controlling the future direction of V22. V22 shares can be bought or sold through a stockbroker, though it is recognized that there is much less trading on PLUS Markets. The selection process, coordinated by Tara Cranswick, a practising artist who worked at the Saatchi Gallery, is implemented in two stages: artists will only be considered for selection if they have a proven track record of at least five years, or are represented by a contemporary dealer, or have work in a major collection; and artworks for the collection will be recommended by an advisory panel comprising collectors, critics, artists, dealers, curators, and regional agents, with a belief that this method will attract more artists and create a varied and well-rounded collection.

'The problematical nature of art investment funds and the absence of readily identifiable public funds (i.e. models for emulation and for benchmarking) has meant that there are no operational guides or manuals about setting up and managing a fund', according to Arnold (2009). Three lifecycle stages typically exist for private equity funds such as art funds: fundraising, investment strategy, and exit.

First, fundraising involves soliciting investment from likely prospects of high net worth individuals. The process of fundraising, which may involve informal contact between peers and formal road show presentations, may take a year or more, though most commitments appear to be made within six months. A challenge for art funds is convincing investors of the track record of the fund manager, often schooled in the fine art market, in managing complex financial instruments. Establishing credibility can be the result of expertise – being able to demonstrate a track record of sound judgement – and trust based on prior relationships with individual prospects. There is a need to identify common ground which requires empathy – making an emotional connection – with the prospects: how do they benefit? Fundraising involves reinforcing a position with vivid language (e.g. examples, stories, metaphors, and analogies) and evidence (e.g. numerical data). Lord Gowrie (in Goodwin 2008: foreword), former chairman of Sotheby's Europe and great raconteur, is chairman of TFAF board.

Second, investment involves acquisition of one or more assets (works of art) by the fund manager. Hoffman explains the selection process with an emphasis on due diligence: 'A strong internal regulation process is critical for investor confidence. The due diligence process is very important. TFAF makes investments using a 20-point process (e.g. how does the proposed price for the work compare with similar works, provenance, condition of the work, market conditions for buying, etc.). Everything needs to be documented'. TFAF has five art buyers: two for Old Masters, one for Impressionists and Modern, one for Modern and Contemporary 1960–85, and one for Contemporary 1985–2005. The decisions of the art buyers are aided by three art advisors – Old Masters, Impressionists and Modern, and Modern and Contemporary – who are able to factor in forthcoming exhibitions. The art buyers, art advisors, fund board, and fund managers are involved in different stages of the purchase approval process.

Third, successful exit strategies matter. This means speedy, trouble-free, and lucrative sale of the work or works of art in the fund. Exceptional profits are dependent on fortune and the selection of what proves to be a winner in the short (one to three years) to medium (three to five years) term.

Investors in art funds in the UK, USA, and Switzerland, the main trading centres for art, will not benefit from rules and regulations made for the protection of investors. For example, TFAF Group notes that its investment funds are not recognized collective investment schemes for the purposes of the UK's Financial Services and Markets Act 2000; investors in the investment funds do not benefit from the rules and regulations made for the protection of investors, nor from the Financial Services Compensation Scheme. Shares in art funds – as private equity funds – are not dealt in or on a recognized or designated investment exchange nor is there a market maker in such shares. As such, it may be difficult to dispose of one's shares other than by way of redemption – which often exacts a discount (or penalty) to the investor. In the case of V22, publicly traded on the PLUS Markets, the level of trading activity may be low making liquidity an issue.

The low level of regulation associated with buying and selling art means that it is avoided by institutional investors such as pension funds. So-called advisors and buyers – essentially art market insiders – may have multiple financial stakes in any transaction for a fund that would fall foul of corporate governance benchmarks (of accountability, public disclosure, and transparency) for S&P 500 and FSTE 100 firms. At the same time, the relative inefficiency of the art market offers significant opportunities for shrewd and well-informed private investors. As such art can have a place in a private investor's portfolio allocation (with some promoters suggesting 1–10 per cent). A financial advisor can help to gauge one's current level of exposure to alternative asset classes as there is no correct portfolio allocation for art to gain diversification benefits. For example, Hoffman recommends that 'a diversified portfolio has 5 per cent invested in art (as the majority of art sectors have a low correlation to stocks and bonds)'; and for a $1 million investment in art, he recommends '$500,000 in an art fund, $300,000 in a co-investment, and $200,000 devoted to a private (home) collection'. Furthermore, there is a need to consider how to invest over different works to diversify the overall art investment portfolio. Market timing is important, which is to say not to buy at the height of a market. Being able to minimize transaction costs adds to the investor's financial return. Finally, if aesthetic pleasure is derived from art works, it may serve as a discount to the required financial rate of return.

THEATRE ANGELS

Equity financing, whether from venture capital or an angel investor, is not easy money: some degree of autonomy and control may be lost to investors. On the other hand, debt financing is essentially a loan (often from a bank): the loan has to be repaid (with interest within a stated period of time) and assets of some sort must be pledged. Financial indicators and ratios may be used as part of the decision-making process by investors and lenders of money (see, for example, Vogel 2001: 354–57). However, many of the measures – cash flow and private market values, price/earnings ratios, price/sales ratios, and book value – are most appropriate for entertainment industry investments of publicly listed companies. One measure, debt/equity ratio, is a basic statement of the amount of debt the firm has compared to its level of equity. To investors or lenders, this ratio is important because it indicates the amount of money available for repayment in the case of default. The ability to service debt depends on projected cash flows, which can be volatile.

The Society of London Theatre (SOLT) is the trade association which represents the producers, theatre owners, and managers of the 50 major commercial and grant-aided theatres in central London.[9] One of the services offered by SOLT is its so-called angels list, which puts private individuals who have expressed an interest in investing in London theatre in touch with SOLT-member producers who are seeking investors for new productions. The angels list is important in helping to stimulate entrepreneurial activity. Investing in theatrical productions is an example of private equity financing: it provides an opportunity for third-party financing to be made available to enterprises not quoted on any stock exchange. Motives behind the funding of theatre are 'much more speculative and entrepreneurial than in any of the other [traditional performing] arts' (Vogel 2001: 328).

The financing and development process for theatre resembles that used for films, hence some references to IndieVest. Angel investors (or backers) seek opportunities which support financial and personal objectives. Theatre angels usually have an advanced appreciation of theatre, possibly even some professional knowledge. Investing in a theatrical production is one way to get more involved. Closeness or access can play an important part in the decision-making process of angels. This can mean geographic reach as angels will want to see the production at one of the touring venues. Moreover, angels want to know with whom they are dealing, thus attention is devoted to the track record of the director and lead actors; straightforward information on the producer, arguably the most important player in the equation, can sometimes be more difficult to secure. 'Ultimately, most people that become film investors choose a particular film investment opportunity that they have identified as a feature film project that can potentially generate general audience acceptance in the marketplace – offering potentially significant profits' (IndieVest 2009: para 6).

IndieVest (2009) offers the insider enticement of executive producer status: 'Members who have chosen to become an Executive Producer of a particular film investment opportunity will also enjoy premium VIP seating at their film's premiere and a cocktail reception after the premiere with members of the case. As well, Executive Producers will be able to attend the set while their particular film is shooting and enjoy other "Executive Producer only" perks' (para 19), namely being 'listed individually in the end credits under IndieVest Executive Producers' (para 20). By way of context, the 'Explainer' column (20 February 2009) of online magazine *Slate* (slate.com) answered 'what does a Hollywood producer do, exactly?' The producer shepherds the film from start to finish. 'In a typical arrangement, the producer develops an idea or script with a writer and secures the necessary rights. He often hires the director, supervises casting, and assembles a crew. Additionally, the producer oversees the budget and then coordinates the postproduction work—everything from editing, to commissioning music, to encouraging the film's stars to plug the movie on talk shows'. 'An executive producer often owns the rights to a book or story idea or secures at least 25 percent of the film's budget'. The latter, as a source of funding, is the IndieVest scenario. 'Executive producers rarely have creative or technical involvement and are often caught up with several projects at once'. Further down the producer hierarchy is the ' "co-executive producer" title [which] applies to studio executives or distributors who have a limited financial stake in the project. A co-producer works under the producer and often helps with casting, financing, or postproduction. The line producer is on the set at all times to supervise the budget but has little or no creative input'.

SOLT requires a two-stage process before being added to the list of angels: a leaflet, 'Information for Prospective Investors in West End Shows' is dispatched to prospective angels; a letter must be posted to the Legal Officer at SOLT 'confirming that you have read this leaflet and understand the risks involved'. SOLT makes explicit the speculative nature of investing in theatre:

> You should be aware that commercial theatre is a high risk business and that the majority of productions probably fail to recoup all the capital invested. In this event, you will not receive the return of the original investment.
>
> It is therefore advisable to seek professional advice before any investment is made.

The successful producer is king. Many producers already have their own so-called stable of investors who are given first option to invest in their shows and you should know that established producers of the long-running and successful shows in the West End, such as the hit musicals, are unlikely to use the Society's list as their loyalty lies with their original investors. However, the existence of the Society's Angels list does mean that SOLT producers can send their invitation to invest to a wider group of people if they wish to do so – those that they know have expressed an interest in backing shows. There is no Broadway equivalent of SOLT's angels list; indeed Broadway producers tend to shy away from soliciting smaller investors.

In the case of film investment, applications for IndieVest (2009) membership require vetting (paras 2, 3, and 22), according to SEC rules and regulations for securities in the USA: an accredited investor is 'a natural person who has net worth, or joint net worth with the person's spouse, that exceeds $1 million at the time of purchase' or 'a natural person with income exceeding $200,000 in each of the two most recent years or joint income with a spouse exceeding $300,000 for those years and a reasonable expectation of the same income level in the current year'. Membership starts at $2,950 per year which includes access to feature film projects seeking funding (para 23). However, to become an IndieVest independent film executive producer – that is by investing in one or more independent film opportunities (para 4) – requires substantially more as 'private placement offerings generally have a $50,000 unit minimum (para 5).

Each theatrical production is unique. Yet the contents of any document from producers inviting investment have similarities. Three examples of private placement memoranda for West End productions – by different producers – received in 2008 are instructive. 'It is my pleasure to invite you to invest in our forthcoming production' of a new comedy that 'has already picked up heat in the press' (Production 1). 'I am delighted that we will be co-producing' a 'compelling drama' that 'has not been revived since its original production at the Haymarket in 1972' (Production 2). 'A great big joyous musical based on a successful film', it 'is an upbeat love story'; 'have a look at the investment papers' with an invitation for 'full units at £20,000' (Production 3). All three make risk factors explicit:

> Production 1: Investors must bear in mind that investment in a theatrical production is extremely speculative. Investors may not get back all or any part of the money amount invested. Consequently, no one should invest more than he or she is prepared to lose.
>
> Production 2: Theatrical production is an inherently risky business. Contributions to the Production will involve a higher level of risk than most other financial transactions and there is no probability, but only a possibility, that contributors will get back the amount which they contribute.
>
> Production 3: Investment in theatrical productions is highly speculative and carriers a special degree of risk. Investment in the production will involve a higher level of risk than most other financial transactions and there is no probability, but only a possibility, that investors will get back the amount which they invest.

Production 2 adds: 'The contribution to the Production will not be covered by any compensation scheme'. Production 3 notes that 'any investment in the production is not transferable and as there is no market for investments, it may be difficult to an investor to obtain reliable information about the value of the investment or the extent of the risks to which the investors is exposed'. Production 1 notes the illiquid nature of the theatrical investments: 'Income from investment may fluctuate in value in money terms depending on the degree of box office success. There is no recognized market for the investment and therefore investors are unlikely to be able to sell an investment' (Production 1). In a similar manner, investing in film productions is marked by high risk factors: 'Like all private placements, an IndieWest (2009) feature film investment opportunity is illiquid and cannot be readily sold' (para 7); 'Film investments are risky and difficult to predict' (para 16); and 'IndieVest film investments are speculative in nature, involve a high degree of risk, and are only appropriate for investors who can afford to lose some or all of their entire invested capital' (para 17). However, Production 1 concludes the risk factors section by accentuating the non-financial aspects of being a theatre angel: 'BUT ALWAYS REMEMBER THAT INVESTING IN SHOWS CAN BE FUN' (emphasis in the original).

Some terminology is useful: the *producers* – often it is more than one individual or firm – intend to present a *play* in the cases of Production 1 and 2 and a *musical* in the case of Production 3 at a West End *theatre* with a capacity of around 400 seats for Production 1, approximately 700–900 seats for Production 2, and around 1,400 seats for Production 3. The presentation of the play/musical at the West End theatre is called the *production*. Production 2 will be presented at a regional theatre – with a financial stake as one of the co-producers – and then tour the English provinces prior to a proposed West End presentation. The *cast* or *actors* are contracted to appear in the production. In the case of Production 1, the *director* and *author* are the same. As Production 2 is a revival, the producer has been granted all necessary rights in the play to mount the production by a company who act as literary agents for the *author*.[10] Production 3 is more complex: the *creators* are the *authors* of the book which led to a motion picture distributed by a major *Hollywood studio*; moreover, the *director* and *choreographer* from the *original production* are engaged in the transfer of the musical to London from the country-of-origin. Details of other members of the creative team – *designer, lighting designer, and sound designer* – who have agreed to work on the production are attached as part of all sets of documentation. *Net profits* of the production refer to box office income available to the production after paying or providing for all *weekly running expenses*, including royalties due to the *royalty participants* will be applied as to 100 per cent towards repayment contributions until *recoupment of the costs of production*. Post-recoupment, the net profit of the production shall be divided 40 per cent to the producers and 60 per cent equally to the subscribers (contributors) for Productions 1 and 2; half each in the case of Production 3.

In a similar manner, film investing, according to IndieVest (2009: para 11), has a selection process prior to the release of a private placement memorandum. First, as a minimum hurdle, there is an absolute requirement for compelling, character-driven projects with unique stories. Second, once the initial benchmark is met, there is a need to fine-tune scripts, reach agreements with writers and directors, establish below-the-line-budgets, and cast for on-screen talent. Third, commercial metrics are used to address film distribution and marketing costs; finance teams analyse the commercial viability of each project (e.g. track record of the talent involved and comparable domestic and foreign releases). Moreover, to avoid a liquidity crisis calling halt to the production, 'all capital necessary to complete a project – from pre-production through to distribution – must be placed in segregated escrow accounts prior to pre-production commencing' (para 12).

Production 1 will be capitalized at £250,000 (the *capitalization*); Production 2 at £475,000; and Production 3 at £4 million, which represents the larger budgets of musicals versus plays. (Advertising and publicity at £65,000 account for a substantial proportion of the pre-production costs of £213,000 for Production 1. In the case of a musical like Production 3, pre-production advertising and publicity is £650,000.) Investment is available in units of £2,000 for Production 1; £5,000 for Production 2; and £20,000 for Production 3. All three stipulate *no overcall* from the investor. This means that investors will have no liability in excess of their agreed investment. However, in the event that the production costs exceed capitalization, the producers shall be entitled to raise or contribute the additional monies required: 'with a consequent dilution of the profit participation of the investor' (Production 1) and 'no part of the contributors' share of 60 per cent of net profit will be payable to a supplier of additional money' (Production 2).

Estimates for Production 1 are provided in the placement memorandum for illustration purposes based on a theatre capacity of 413 seats and a run of 16 weeks. The amount to recoup is £213,000. The net box office, based on eight performances with ticket prices between £25 and £45, is £98,000 per week. Fixed weekly running costs are £29,000. Production 1 is based on 'an exceptional West End theatre deal . . . whereby rather than paying a traditional rent and contra, the theatre will receive 25 per cent of Net Weekly Box Office Receipts, which will be capped pre-recoupment of £15,000 (moving up to £17,000 post-recoupment)'. At an average of 60 per cent financial capacity of the theatre, the capitalization could be recouped in 18 weeks; at 50 per cent, the capitalization could be recouped in 47 weeks; at 80 per cent, the capitalization could be recouped in 8 weeks. The weekly running costs are approximately 30 per cent of the projected financial capacity of the theatre, which means that the production will make a loss in weeks where income falls below this figure.

Production 2 is contingent upon successful negotiation with a West End theatre management to enable a West End opening in a theatre of the capacity (700–900) on which the estimates are based. (If no theatre is secured within the specified timetable, all subscriptions will be returned in full.) The amount to recoup is £381,000. Production 2 has a similar ticket pricing with a box office capacity of £207,000 based on a seating capacity of 780 and a run of 14 weeks. The fixed weekly running costs are £71,000. It is estimated that at 55 per cent of weekly box office capacity, the West End production will recoup in 13 weeks; at 60 per cent capacity in 10.25 weeks; at 70 per cent capacity in 7.75 weeks; and at 80 per cent capacity in 6.25 weeks. Before recoupment it is estimated that the production breaks even at 53 per cent of weekly box office capacity.

Musicals operate on a bigger scale. Ticket prices for musicals tend to be higher, ranging from £20.75 to £60.75 rising to £65.75 at weekends in the case of Production 3, which is based on larger seating capacity, of 1,400 seats on sale per performance, with an assumption of eight performances per week. At 100 per cent capacity, and with fixed weekly running costs of £205,000, the estimated net box office receipts will be £425,000. The weekly breakeven pre-recoupment is a weekly box office of 54 per cent. The number of weeks to recoup for a musical is longer than for a play: even at 100 per cent box office capacity, 22 weeks will be required; whereas 90 weeks – nearly two years – is required to recoup, based on 65 per cent box office capacity. Traditionally, successful musicals run longer than plays; this has the potential for higher return on investment. Production 3 is banking on a fortuitous transfer of the original production.

There is a *royalty pool* based as a percentage of *weekly operating profits*: 12.5 per cent (Production 1); and 12.25 per cent (Production 2). In the case of Production 3, there is a note that 'the Producers have not yet finalized arrangements with the royalty participants and so there can be no assurance that such arrangements will be agreed'. The net profit is spilt as 60 per cent to contributors (investors) and 40 per cent to producers (both Production 1 and 2); half each in the case of Production 3. In the case of a revival, the co-producing theatre is part of the royalty pool: 1.5 points in the royalty pool for Production 2. In the case of musicals, there may be more royalty demands than for plays. For example, in Production 3 pre-recoupment royalties are payable to the Hollywood studio and music publishers at an estimated 7 per cent of net box office receipts; and, as Production 3 is a transfer of an original musical, 'a royalty of 4 points in the royalty pool [is paid to the] licensor and original producer'. Finally, a payoff, as a return on investment (if any), is made to investors after weekly running costs and royalty payments are paid. For a contribution of £5,000, the contributor is entitled to a net profit of 0.631 per cent (Production 2). Investors are paid after running costs together with royalty participant share and retention of a sum to judged appropriate to meet contingencies (Production 1).

In the case of feature film investments, each IndieVest Picture is organized as a limited liability company specially set up to make a particular feature film. 'Generally, after our Executive Producer Members have been paid back their entire investment and a premium return, Executive Producer Members then generally receive 50 per cent or more of the net profits of the project, with Filmmakers generally receiving 40 per cent of the net profits and IndieVest Pictures generally receives the remaining 10 per cent' (para 10). Film has a much longer time horizon relative to theatre: 'A film investment opportunity may begin generating a return on investment within twelve months after financing, however, it would not be unusual for two years or more to pass before a project sees a significant return on investment' as 'many factors come into play, including the length and commencement of the production schedule, the availability of specific talent, the length of post-production and the seasonal feature film distribution patterns' (para 13).

Though the private placement memorandum is approved for the purpose of the UK's Financial Services and Markets Act 2000, this does not reduce the need for investors to scrutinize the proposed financial instrument. 'Such approval is to allow producers to comply with the requirement of the legislation and may not be regarded as an endorsement of the project' is noted in all three cases. There is an important caveat about the estimates and schedules proffered in the private placement memorandum: *estimates are distinct from a forecast.* 'These figures are for illustration only and are not forecasts. It should be emphasized that these figures are based on best estimates and may be subject to change' (Production 2). Moreover, these figures are current estimates based on current expectations and may vary when negotiations are complete. The *estimates may be different from actual outcome* so that investors recoup less quickly and the point at which profits become payable may come later *if at all.* The role of risk – and the commensurate reward potential – is what distinguishes saving from investing. Even the financially literate will have a difficult time reviewing theatrical productions: how to separate the shoddy, second-rate, and over-priced from genuinely attractive vehicles? How to compare the goods on *all* the stalls? Thus a general caveat emptor note: 'If you have any questions about this investment, you are advised to speak to a solicitor and a qualified financial advisor' (Production 1).

■ ■ ■

Both art investment funds and theatrical investments by angels are risky financial vehicles with little protection to claim compensation for any losses. Art investment funds, with minimum entry stakes at around $250,000, are about financial returns. Moreover, investors in an art investment fund are not involved with the decision-making process, which is placed in the hands of professional investment managers. On the other hand, theatre angels seem to invite insider access (to the theatre) as a drawing card. The financial points of entry for theatrical investments are much lower; moreover, there is a clear indication that most financial investments in theatrical productions will not be recouped. Theatre angels focus on two key markets, London's West End and New York's Broadway, with limited potential to grow. Art investment funds, though much less developed, have the potential to develop as the art market grows.

In order to spread risk, theatre angels do not need to invest alone.[11] Theatre investment clubs, essentially a group of like-minded people who pool their money to make investments, can operate with members studying different investment proposals, with a vote as to which ones to back. Pooling funds with other investors is one way to diversify holdings and hence spread risk (e.g. if five angels each stump up £5,000 – often investments are available in £1,000 to £5,000 units for plays – there is the possibility to invest in five to ten different theatrical productions, whereas a lone angel could only back one or two productions). IndieVest (2009) recommends diversification: 'Utilize portfolio theory to better manage and potentially further reduce investment risk, creating a greater opportunity for upside potential. Members should plan to make their film investments in several different projects of differing types over time' (para 18).

APPENDIX: ALTERNATIVE PASSION INVESTMENTS

'Passion investments' is a term used in the *World Wealth Report*, a document produced by Capgemini and Merrill Lynch (2008). Of course, passion in this sense denotes strong enthusiasm for the investment. It also implies more than just a financial return on investment. As a complement to investing in fine art, theatre, and film – discussed in the main part of the chapter – fine wine, classic automobiles, and thoroughbred racehorses are considered. Fine wine and classic automobiles are sectors represented by the leading auction houses. Thoroughbred horseracing has been called the sport of kings – think Royal Ascot or the Dubai World Cup – and is part of the *World Wealth Report's* sports investment category (which includes sports teams and sailing).

Several sources are used. This includes interviews from Robertson and Chong (2008) with Simon Staples, sales director at Berry Brothers & Rudd, which is Britain's oldest wine and spirit merchant, having traded at the same London shop since 1698; and Tim Schofield, head of motoring at Bonhams, which has unrivalled experience in the sale of collectible motor cars, motorcycles, cycles, and aircraft with offices in London, Paris, and San Francisco (as the heritage of Bonhams motoring department can trace its roots back to Brooks, the specialist collectors' motoring auctioneer founded by Robert Brooks and James Knight in 1989). The British Horseracing Board (BHB), the governing body for horseracing in the UK, provides information on owning a racehorse as part of its responsibility to market and promote horseracing.

Pleasure, product, and process serve as three broad markers for the discussion of fine wine, classic automobiles, and thoroughbred racehorses as alternative passion investments.

First, pleasure, as about sensuous enjoyment as a chief object of life, is crucial to understanding how the alternative passion investments are marketed. According to Staples, 'Wine gives so much pleasure; great wine and great food at the end of the working day. Wine is meant to be enjoyed. All wine knowledge in the world can be distilled into one simple question: is it good to drink? At more than £100 a bottle, the issue is less about taste and more about kudos'. He cites the influence of the USA-based wine critic Robert Parker (erobertparker.com), who devised a 100-point scoring system: 96–100 is 'an extraordinary wine of profound and complex character displaying all the attributes expected of a classic wine of its variety' such that 'wines of this caliber are worth a special effort to find, purchase, and consume'; and 90–95 is 'an outstanding wine of exceptional complexity and character . . . these are terrific wines'. Parker's qualification – 'The numerical ratings are utilized only to enhance and complement the thorough tasting notes, which are my primary means of communicating my judgments to you' – is sometimes lost, though. One impact of Parker, particularly in the USA, is that 'wines which score above 90 points have shown the greatest appreciation in value', according to Staples. A case in point is a recent offer in the *Financial Times* (February 2009) in partnership with Lay & Wheeler: '2004 Château Langoa-Barton Cru Classé St-Julien / *Awarded 90 points by Robert Parker, this is a wine not to be missed* / Buy 2 cases (24 bottles) at £22.50 per bottle and save £36.00 (Normal list price £24.00 per bottle)' (my emphasis). Of course, there are other recognized wine critics: the international business press includes Jancis Robinson

(*Financial Times*), who rivals Parker, and Brenda Gaiter and John Brecher (*Wall Street Journal*). Michael Broadbent, who founded Christie's Education's wine course, Andrew Jefford, Hugh Johnson, and Serena Sutcliffe, head of Sotheby's wine department, also have prominent positions in the international wine world.

That pleasure derives from intimate participation is evident in horseracing and classic automobiles. *The Thrill of Ownership* (2006), the title of the BHB's practical guide to owning a racehorse, opens with enthusiastic glosses: 'We're in it for fun. But winning is an enormous thrill'; 'When I go racing I can feel the excitement as soon as I see the runners in the paper. The adrenaline really starts pumping'; 'The buzz of having a runner in a race is second to none, you just can't beat it'; and 'We've had a great deal of fun [from ownership] without spending a fortune'. Naming one's race-horse – and registering it with Weatherby's – and choosing the racing silks (colours) to be worn by one's jockey are symbolic rights of involvement accorded owners, alongside the practical benefits of prize money and raceday privileges (such as special facilities dedicated to owners). 'There is a real "fun factor" in collecting and enjoying classic motors, which may be the most pleasurable of alternative investment classes' according to Schofield, who cites that 'runs and races (on public roads and private circuits) can broaden friendships' with 'lots of events globally'.

Second, what to buy? This can be challenging as specialist knowledge is often needed. Though many people drink wine, building a wine cellar or investment port-folio is more complex. 'Wine is a minefield', according to Staples. He describes Berrys as being best at French Bordeaux, which remains the cornerstone of the trade in fine wine (in the key markets of London, New York, and Hong Kong). The main districts of Bordeaux are Médoc (the most important), Pomerol, Saint-Émilion, Graves, and Sauternes. The 1855 Official Classification of Bordeaux, as part of the Exposition Universelle in Paris, established five divisions or growths, known as the *grands crus classés*, from premier down to cinquième, of the top red-wine-producing châteaux of Bordeaux. White wines of Sauternes were divided into two subcategories. There has been only one official change: Mouton-Rothschild was promoted to premier grand cru classé in 1973. The first growth châteaux – Lafite-Rothschild, Mouton-Rothschild, Margaux, Haut-Brion, and Latour – remain the benchmark of excellence. Great wines in limited supply include Pétrus (£3,000 per case which quickly rises to £10,000) and Le Pin (approximately 500 cases per annum at about £10,000). Staples notes some non-French, attracting high prices with strong collector bases, have emerged: Italian super Tuscans, Californian cult wines, and branded Australians. Super Tuscans emerged in the late 1980s outside the official premium Italian wine designations, DOGC and DOC, as Bordeaux varieties were used. Most are still are sold as *vino de tavola* or table wine, though Sassicaia – a proprietary name for a Cabernet Sauvignon/Cabernet Franc blend – has its own DOC status, Bolgheri Sassicaia. Cult wines is an American term used to describe largely Cabernet Sauvignon wines produced in small quantities by California's Napa Valley wineries such as Araujo, Colgin-Schrader, Frog's Leap, Grace Family, Harlan Estate, and Screaming Eagle. Australians emphasize the producer (as the brand) rather than the source of the grapes, with notable successes like Penfolds Grange Hermitage and Penfolds Bin 707 Cabernet Sauvignon.

Andrew Jefford (*FT*'s 'Investing in Wine' section, 10 June 2006) proffers the three

As of amount, ageability, and appeal as key criteria, with Bordeaux as a key choice. Amount means 'sufficient quantity to develop an international identity and reputation' among the world's wealth who 'need names to recognise and stocks to buy'. Bordeaux has a 'tradeable mass gives it the vital market presence'. 'An assured ageing trajectory' is the second criterion: 'It must set off on a route that will take it from the charm and challenge of youth towards a modulated and seductive middle age and eventually towards an old age of invariable harmony and occasional sublimity', which is viewed as a good description of good or great Bordeaux. Third is the requirement 'that a wine has universal and enduring aesthetic appeal', with Jefford adding, 'note the word enduring'.

'There is much knowledge in the public domain for classic motors', according to Schofield, and opportunities exist 'to purchase a highly competitive and eligible entry (race ready condition)'. He notes that 'the great variety of historic sportscar events around the globe – such as Le Mans Classique, Goodwood Revival, and Monaco Historique Grand Prix – are key drivers of consumer demand and market popularity'; as such, 'a well-document provenance (including events and repairs) enhances value'.

Relationships are important in horseracing: this includes making a choice of racehorse and developing one that is competitive. Racehorses can run on the flat or over jumps. (Flat racing includes celebrated challenges like the American Triple Crown – the Kentucky Derby, the Preakness Stakes, and the Belmont Stakes – and racing takes place globally, including England, Ireland, and France (in Europe), Dubai, Japan and Hong Kong, and Australia.) There are three different ways to buy a racehorse: privately, claiming and selling races, or at public auction (via specialist bloodstock auctioneers in the UK such as Tattersalls or Doncaster Bloodstock Sales). The BHB (2005) notes that 'it is important to enlist the support of a trainer or bloodstock agent' as 'they will have a thorough knowledge of how each purchasing method operates and help you buy the correct horse'. 'The quality of advice you receive at this stage is likely to have a major influence in your future success'. (A bloodstock agent usually charges 5 per cent of the purchase price as a fee.) Choosing a trainer is 'the most important relationship' an owner will have, according to the BHB (2005): a 'personal rapport' with a trainer is crucial 'as the key to the enjoyment of racehorse ownership is the direct involvement with the sport, and the more an owner feels at ease discussing their horses with the trainer, the greater the sense of involvement'. Moreover, the BHB (2005) notes that legal advice is strongly advised on drawing up a co-ownership agreement (including a sample agreement along with a list of specialist solicitors and details of industry related bodies).

Third, what is the process of making a passion investment? How to make a purchase? Wine is classified by UK Inland Revenue as a so-called wasting asset so it does not incur capital gains tax. There are three points in time to buy wine, according to Staples. First, *en primeur* (or wine futures) is the process of buying wine in the summer after the harvest but not actually receiving it for another 18 months, when it is bottled and released onto the market. Second, when the wine is physically available, which is usually two to three years after the vintage. Third, ten years before the wine is ready to drink. One investment strategy is to buy five cases *en primeur*: drink two and sell three. As a wine merchant, Berrys is often a willing buyer. 'The opening *en primeur* price is almost always considerably cheaper than the future price for the wine on the open market; *en primeur* can also be the only way to secure wines that are available in very limited quantities', according to Staples, who adds that 'in building a cellar, red Bordeaux remains key: in the main, buy the greatest wines from the greatest vintages'. Buying *en primeur* requires storing wine in a bonded warehouse: the advantage is that the purchase is ex-VAT (17.5 per cent) and ex-duty (UK duty is £1.29 per 75 cl bottle for still wine); the disadvantage is that the owner is not able to take physical possession as part of an in-house cellar.

An advertisement for Berrys' Cellar Plan features two bottles of Lafite-Rothschild 1996 each set aside key (rhyming) terms to wine collectors, 'profit' and 'quaff it', with a communal message: 'Pleasure. An altogether more profitable investment'. The pitch for fine wine as an alternative asset continues: 'Everywhere investment advice. It's enough to drive one to drink. Far better the tried and tested Berrys' mantra of drink some, save some. With so much at stake, we believe it essential to invest in assets that, regardless of market performance, will always go down well'. Such a promotional pitch is core to Thaler (1999), who discusses the mental accounting of wine collectors, including those who buy wine *en primeur*. When a bottle of the wine – whose value has increased – is later consumed, what happens? According to Thaler (1999: 192), 'the typical wine connoisseur thinks of his initial purchase as an investment and later thinks of the wine as free when he drinks it'. Berrys' mantra is an example of 'mental accounting that transforms a very expensive hobby into one that is "free" ', according to Thaler (1999: 192).

Keen to attract new collectors, Berrys has an instructive website (bbr.com) including a pronunciation guide and 'ten tips for investing in fine wine': deal only with established and reputable merchants, but shop around for advice and prices; buy your wines in bond so that duty and VAT are not payable up front as this will maximize your investment; buy unmixed sealed cases, in original wood if possible, as these will be worth the most; expect to invest over a five year period, but be ready to sell if advised; buy as close to the opening price as possible; buy parcels of five cases or more whenever possible; invest at least £5,000 if you are looking for serious returns; do not blindly buy just the big names – they may have less profit potential; listen to your wine merchant; make sure you know the provenance and storage history of any wine you buy as this will seriously affect the market price; and take out insurance so that your wine is fully covered at market price rather than the price you paid for it. The more active wine collector can now access more price data using the London International Vintners Exchange (Liv-ex; liv-ex.com), which includes interactive tools in order to manage a cellar collector like a stock portfolio. (Liv-ex was established in 1999 to allow a trading and settlement platform for the world's major trade buyers and sellers of fine wine. Though private collectors cannot trade, they can join to have access to a database of prices.)

Whereas involvement with wine and classic motors can be pursued on an individual basis, the financial stakes for individual entry can be higher for racehorses. Sole ownership is one category of racehorse ownership, with a sole owner responsible for the purchase of the horse, as well as running costs of keeping the horse in training and racing. (It is possible to purchase a racehorse in the UK for less that £20,000. The average running cost for keeping one horse in training in the UK is approximately £20,000 per annum, though the actual cost will vary depending on the choice of trainer.) 'Co-ownership' (or as commonly known as the syndication) of a racehorse is becoming 'a very popular route into ownership', according to the BHB (2005), as it 'involves participation of more than one owner'. There is a diversification of financial risk; moreover, it may offer a cost-effective point of entry for first-time owners to gain knowledge of how the sector operates. Co-ownership is available in several formats – joint ownership, racing partnership, company ownership, leasing, and racing clubs – which offer varying less of commitment (BHB 2005). Joint ownership can consist of between two and 12 individuals, all of whom must become (or already be) registered owners. It is the nearest to sole ownership. Racing partnerships, which consist of two to 20 individuals (of whom at least two must become, or already be, registered owners) are of three types: trainer managed, independent group (often a social group of friends), or professionally run partnership. The trainer managed and professionally run partnership offer so-called hassle free racehorse ownership (so there are similarities to investing in fine art funds and theatrical productions). A racing partnership may last two years, which gives a trainer sufficient time to get a feel for a horse's abilities and assess the horse's performance with an eye to deciding to go forward or dissolve the partnership. Racing clubs 'offer a low priced introduction into racehorse involvement' as participation is based on a one-off annual subscription fee (approximately £100 to £500). By becoming a member of a racing club, one 'receives the benefits of the club, but is not entering into racehorsing ownership directly' (BHB 2005).

The BHB (2005) notes that 'The basis of any co-ownership should NOT be marketed to you as an investment opportunity. The predominant purpose of any co-ownership should be for recreation and enjoyment' (emphasis in the original). Other sources note that one recoups an investment by having a racehorse that finishes in the top five, as typically the winning horse takes 60 per cent of the listed purse; 20 per cent to second place; 12 per cent to third; 6 per cent to fourth; and 2 per cent to fifth. The Nakayama Grand Jump in Tokyo, one of the world's richest races, has a total purse of ¥170.4 million (approximately $1.893 million) with the winner taking ¥80 million (approximately $888,000) and prize money down to tenth place. Winning races also increases the value of the racehorse as a breeder, which is to say that pedigree matters a great deal.

■ ■ ■

The idiomatic phrase 'whatever rocks (or floats) your boat' – do what makes you happy – is apt to characterize passion investments of fine wine, classic automobiles, and thoroughbred racehorses. In many cases, the pure financial return on investment will pale in comparison to other financial instruments. In this regard there is a return to the issue of pleasure.

GLOBALIZATION AND THE ART WORLD

■ ■ ■ ■ ■ ■

The chapter title, Globalization and the Art World, needs to be unpacked. The art world is based on a core-periphery orientation with social networks that bind key players. Artist and critic Martha Rosler (1997: 20–21, n. 1), writing in *Art Bulletin* on money, power, and contemporary, offers a 'thumbnail definition' of the '*high* art world' as

> the changing international group of commercial and nonprofit galleries, museums, study centers, and associated venues and individuals who own, run, direct, and toil in them; the critics, reviewers, and historians, and their publications who supply the studies, rationales, publicity, and explanations; the connoisseurs and collectors who form the nucleus of sales and appreciation; plus the artists living and recently dead who supply the goods (emphasis in the original).

She continues with an identification of the core art world: 'This art world, if it needs to be said, is based on the advanced industrial countries of the West, along with outposts like Australia and the quasi-Western country of Japan'. Economies of agglomeration with core-periphery patterns remain. However, the market for con-temporary art – in terms of production, distribution, and consumption – has become more globalized in the decade since Rosler's article appeared. New York and London are global centres for the art market. Other core art market centres include EU cities like Paris, Amsterdam, Madrid, and Milan. Post-unification Berlin has developed a reputation for artists. Non-EU Switzerland – namely Geneva, Zurich, and Basel – is notable for the same reasons private banking is attracted to the country. Hong Kong, since its return to China, has already established itself as a trading centre (for some Chinese art categories and wine). In the Middle East, the United Arab Emirate's Abu Dhabi and Dubai and the Qatari capital Doha have taken lead roles as cultural hubs.

Any discussion of globalization – which is pursued in the first section by address-ing power brands and the experience economy – invites a clash of opinions.[1] Refer-ences to globalization in the art world has parallels to what is occurring from a geopolitical perspective. This may mean neologisms like Chindia or Chimerica to signal rising powers of the twenty-first century alongside the current hegemony of the USA, or an acronym like BRIC (Brazil, Russia, India, and China) to indicate the rising wealth of emerging countries with large populations. French philosopher Nicolas Bourriaud is the curator of 'Altermodern', theme of the Tate Triennial 2009 at Tate Britain: '*A new modernity is emerging*, reconfigured to an age of globalisation – understood in its economic, political and cultural aspects: an altermodern culture' (emphasis in the original).

Two art world examples under globalization are discussed. First, the emergence of art dealers, largely based in New York, London, and several European art capitals, capitalizing on contemporary art as an important sector has occurred. There is a case that these dealers – characterized as powerhouse, super, or mega to indicate influence and size, with the Gagosian Gallery at the fore – have become market markers. The dual success factors, of a so-called good eye (or aesthetic judgement in selecting the right artists to promote) and social networks with access to private collectors and public institutions, remain important. Second, in a related manner, so-called superstar art museums have also sought ways to attract audiences and promote identity. In the post-Cold War environment, arts organizations, like fast-food conglomerates, need satellites and franchises to make a profit, hence the need to invade so-called empty cultural spaces. The case of the Guggenheim Foundation since the late 1980s has been a contentious case of ambitious global expansion. The opening of the Guggenheim Bilbao in 1997 is not the first Guggenheim initiative of expansion, but it has remained the most successful to date. Moreover, the most recent interest in Abu Dhabi by the Guggenheim and the Louvre – in separate projects – can be considered as part of an overall strategy of the UAE to become a leader in the visual arts. Some view it as a welcome sign; on the other hand, critics suggest imperialist ambitions behind such attempts to establish global brands, with art as a handmaiden of cultural tourism. Both art world examples benefit from reference to the 'economics of superstars' thesis proffered by Sherwin Rosen (1981) where relatively small numbers of people earn enormous amounts of money and dominate the activities in which they engage. The combination of imperfect substitution and joint consumption technology make it possible for talented persons – those with so-called box office appeal – to command both very large markets and very large incomes.

POWER BRANDS AND THE EXPERIENCE ECONOMY

In everyday English, a brand can be likened to reputation (i.e. what is generally said or believed about a person's or thing's character); this means that branding is a plan for earning that reputation, and for making sure that consumers know about it and believe in it too. At the outset of the new millennium, the V&A Museum mounted an exhibition on the rise of brands and branding: 'The brand is a prefix; the qualifier of character. The symbolic associations of the brand name are often used in preference to the pragmatic description of a useful object', according to the curator Jane Pavitt (2000: 16). The ethos and language of branding, as integral to contemporary managerial discourses (see Brighton 2002), pervades our everyday lives in catchphrases: Coca-Cola is 'The Real Thing', 'Just Do It' with Nike, and BMW offers 'The Ultimate Driving Machine' which is 'Sheer Driving Pleasure'. This is consistent with the stance of marketing guru Philip Kotler (1999), who considers that the art of marketing is largely the art of brand building. Branding as a form of corporate storytelling is a more prosaic characterization by James Twitchell (2004), an English professor who has investigated various aspects of commercial culture. Brands matter if one assumes the contention, as advanced by David Aaker (1991; 1995; Aaker and Joachimsthaler 2000) and the brand consultancy Interbrand, that most important assets of any business are intangible and comprise the firm's brand equity. This means that the brand is a source of competitive advantage and future earnings.

That 'some brands become icons', according to Douglas Holt (2003: 43, 44), is a form of 'myth making':

> People have always needed myths. Simple stories with compelling characters and resonant plots, myths help us make sense of the world. They provide ideals to live by, and they work to resolve life's most vexing questions. Icons are encapsulated myths. They are powerful because they deliver myths to us in a tangible form, thereby making them more accessible.
>
> When a brand creates a myth, most often through advertisements, consumers come to perceive the myth as embodied in the product. So they buy the product to consume the myth and to forge a relationship with the author: the brand. Anthropologists call this 'ritual action'.

Of course, there is a case that the consumerist association of branding stripped away the sacredness of icons and the supernatural associated with myths. Closer to the point might be 'inventing tradition', as used by historians (Hobsbawn and Ranger 1983: 1): it includes 'both "traditions" actually invented, constructed and formally instituted and those emerging in a less easily traceable manner within a brief and dateable period – a matter of a few years perhaps – and establishing themselves with great rapidity'. Indeed, Wally Olins (1989: 7) – co-founder of brand consultancy Wolff Olins, now owned by Omnicom – cites Hobsbawn and Ranger's concept of invented traditions as relevant to the corporate identity strategies of all types of organizations:

> The identity of the corporation must be so clear that it becomes the yardstick against which its products, behaviour and actions are measured.
>
> This means that the identity cannot simply be a slogan, a collection of phrases: it must be visible, tangible and all-embracing.
>
> Everything that the organization does must be an affirmation of its identity.

Power brands, according to McKinsey & Co (Court *et al.* 1997), are marked by 'personality' and 'presence'. Personality means extending beyond a functional relationship to the consumer so that he or she develops an emotional bond to the brand. Giving power brands a personality – not unlike what one associates with friends and family – is a form of anthropomorphism. Presence, or high visibility and recognition that is attractive to consumers, in the marketplace is often due to national or international scale. Firms focus resources on brands with strong 'appeal' (i.e. strong current performance and prospects for sustained growth) and 'scale' (i.e. potential to justify large investment in technology, innovations, and communications). Exploiting brand value, according to McKinsey & Co (Court *et al.* 1999) can be via either 'focused' or 'diversified' brand leverage. Focused brand leverage – Amazon for books and Starbucks for coffee are good examples – is about owning and broadening a particular category; the brand captures all occasions of consumption. Diversified brand leverage – Disney is a prime case – sets out to create a 'golden thread' (i.e. core to the brand, such as Disney's focus on wholesome fun for the entire family); this includes building high-credibility personalities (such as Mickey Mouse) and lever-aging aggressively (from animation to theme parks and co-branding arrangements with multinational enterprises).

Global marketing and branding coalesce in the management term glocal: firms seek the advantages of scale such as *global reach* while seeking to ensure relevance through *local touch* (such as expressed in the popular HSBC campaign, 'The world's local bank'). Consolidation has taken place in many commercial sectors, including the creative industries, with attention to reducing complexity, streamlining operations, improving cost effectiveness, and enhancing profitability. The auction sectors within the UK (e.g. The Fine Art Auction Group's Dreweatt brand and Edinburgh-based Lyon & Turnbull's marketing alliance with Freeman's) and Canada (e.g., 'Sotheby's in associ-ation with Ritchies' – until recently – and 'Joyner Waddington's Canadian Fine Art' compete with Heffel in bi-annual auction sales) have seen consolidation. Music com-panies not least of all EMI (under Terra Firma) want to focus on a smaller number of recording artists who have the potential to develop profitable global platforms.

Theodore Levitt's influential 'globalization of markets' thesis was published in *Harvard Business Review* in 1983. He made a polemical argument that some inter-preted as a case for standardization: make the same things on offer in the same way everywhere, to gain economies of scale from standardizing production and market-ing, with an emphasis on low prices for consumers. 'Firms must learn to operate as if the world were one large market by ignoring superficial regional and national differences', according to Levitt, who believed that consumer preferences were con-verging (hence a homogenization of tastes) alongside a growing demand to consume (that is the pluralization of consumption):

> Cosmopolitanism is no longer the monopoly of the intellectual and leisure classes; it is become the established property and defining characteristic of all sectors everywhere in the world. Gradually and irresistibly it breaks down the walls of economic insularity, nationalism and chauvinism.

Technology was cited as the primary agent of change – as it continues to be from a business management perspective – that drives the world towards a converging commonality of human preferences. The impact of Levitt's thesis, which remains a standard reading on marketing and management curricular, led Harvard Business School (2003), Levitt's academic home until his death in 2006, to reassess it 20 years later. Malleability of consumer preference, which is to say that the market is what organizations make of it, not what they find remains an important point raised by Levitt. This means catering to demand-side preferences and looking at ways to maxi-mize supply-side economics of simplicity. Certain cases allow for the globalization of markets thesis to be realized, such as luxury consumer products and affluent consumers in industrialized and emerging nations. Art collecting makes an explicit appearance in the tenth edition of *World Wealth Report* (Capgemini and Merrill Lynch 2008) as a so-called passion investment.[2] International auctioneers have sought to expand to emerging art trading centres such as Hong Kong and Dubai. Even public art museums have sought to reach outside of their country-of-origin.

Many cultural regeneration initiatives focus on the physical transformation of urban spaces often aligned to wider rebranding and repositioning interests. The Guggenheim site in Bilbao, a formerly depressed area, is represented as a primary example of revitalization and transformation via architecture and regeneration, hence a significant development. It is a powerful metaphor for the contemporary way to do cultural business, namely by becoming an international tourist destination. As there can be ambiguous relationships to local populations as well as other parts of the arts fabric, the economic benefits (e.g. measured by tourism and investment) can be highly contested. Critics suggest that urban renewal based on cultural projects often benefit corporate interests more than people living in the local area. Moreover, concern has been raised regarding the standardization of cultural attractions. For example, 'Nagoya/Boston Museum of Fine Arts' is a joint venture between the Museum of Fine Arts, Boston and the Chamber of Commerce of Nagoya – art from the MFA's permanent collection, in the form of two five-month loan exhibitions each year and five-year exhibitions, including objects from its extensive Japanese art collection, in return for Japanese cash of '$50 million in payments spread over the life of a 20-year-plus pact' (*NYT*, 18 April 1999). A museum building in Nagoya, integrated as part of a hotel complex, was opened in 1999. This illustrates how international patterns of economic wealth have an impact on the identity of museums. The MFA views this alliance as the first in a series of international satellites; indeed it is one of the few art museums in the USA possessing a sufficiently large collection to consider multiple outposts. Employing the permanent collection in such a manner sidesteps deaccessioning; moreover, it allows the institution to argue that more of its art works are on display to larger audiences.

More recently, Simon Anholt has proffered the importance of branding a country, 'which if intelligently and responsibly applied, can bring real benefits to countries as they compete and collaborate in the global community'. 'Public diplomacy' has been advanced by Anholt: 'governments need to present their policies to entire populations, not just in private to other governments; the way that they present the whole country (its products, its culture and its people as well as its government's policies) to the outside world'. For example, 'Istanbul, a city of the four elements' was selected by the European Commission as a European Capital of Culture in 2010. Istanbul, as representing Turkey, 'would function as a bridge connecting Europe to its East. It is a living example of the meeting of civilisations. It has been at the crossroads of European civilizations for centuries and it has learned to "live difference" ', according to the Selection Panel for the European Capital of Culture, which convened in 2006, to make the selection for 2010. On the other hand, some claim that Turkey's candidacy for European Union membership is hampered by its association to the shadow cast by the Ottoman Empire, a population that is predominantly Muslim, and shared borders with Syria, Iraq, and Iran. Modern Turkey was founded as a secular democracy in 1923, and Turkey has been closely aligned with the West as a founding member of the United Nations, and a member of NATO (since 1952) and the OECD (1961). Turkey's prospective membership in the EU, which formed in 1992 as a successor to the European Economic Community (EEC), established in 1959, has been a source of much debate. Culture has been proffered as a way to declare Western (a code for Christian) credentials. 'Turks: a journey of a thousand years (600–1600)' (2004) at London's Royal Academy of Arts would fall within Sotheby's remit of auctioning historical documents of value and beautiful examples of craft and calligraphy produced in a region spanning from Spain to India, covering almost 1,500 years of Islamic history. The Sakip Sabanci Museum in Istanbul has mounted important exhibitions on Turkey's relationship in Europe, including 'Picasso in Istanbul' (2005), which was characterized as 'among the most politically loaded international art exhibitions anywhere in the world', according to Jackie Wullschlager (*FT Magazine*, 19/20 November 2006), as 'playing host to Picasso demonstrates Turkey's European credentials', 'Master Sculptor Rodin in Istanbul' (2006), and 'Voyage to the West: the 70 year adventure of the art of Turkish painting (1860–1930)' (2009), in which the 'Turkish art of painting in the Western sense is being interpreted anew' by including 'works by painters such as Jean-Léon Gérôme and Gustave Boulanger, who were the teachers of the first generation of Turkish painters in Paris'. An inaugural auction sale of contemporary Turkish art, as a separate category, at Sotheby's London in March 2009 was successful: with 73 lots comprising paintings, photographs, sculptures and installations showcasing original work by 53 artists, the sale raised in excess of £1.3 million. In advance of status as 2010 European Capital of Culture, Istanbul seeks to 'rebrand itself as a global style capital' (*How to Spend It*, May 2009).

Pine and Gilmore (1998: 97–105), co-founders of Strategic Horizons, proffered 'the experience economy', which has affinities to leisure and tourism studies. 'While prior economic offerings – commodities, goods, and services – are external to the buyer, experiences are inherently personal, existing only in the mind of an individual who has been engaged on an emotional, physical, intellectual, or even spiritual level'. What is the level of customer participation: passive (i.e. consumers do not affect the performance) or active (i.e. customers play key roles in creating the performance or even that yields the experience)? What is the connection, or environmental relationship, that unites consumers with the event or performance: absorption (i.e. engrossing one's attention) or immersion (i.e. involve deeply as part of the action)? Paco Barragán, in *The Art Fair Age* (2008), uses the example of Art Basel Miami Beach – an offshoot of Art Basel, which opened in December 2002 – to epitomize the emergence of art fairs in the early 2000s as 'Urban Entertainment Centers (UECs)'. In doing so, Barragán draws on the work of Pine and Gilmore to view the art fair as staging an experience. Of course, there has always been a performative element to the art world: the term art scene suggests both parts in a drama to be performed and celebrity notions of being seen. In the case of Art Basel Miami Beach, elements of the chorus to Will Smith's 'Miami' (1998), which strike the celebratory social scene of south Florida, are part of the experience: 'Party in the city where the heat is on / All night on the beach til the break of dawn / Welcome to Miami (bienvenido a Miami) / Bouncin' in the club where the heat is on / All night on the beach til the break of dawn / I'm going to Miami, welcome to Miami'. This suggests that a successful art fair as UEC is more than a trade show (as a meeting place between leading dealers of contemporary art and collectors). There is intense networking to generate sales and to build and sustain relationships. Status as a collector at Art Basel Miami Beach means being part of a desirable network; there is a case that the high prices for contemporary art regulate access into the art world. Art Basel Miami Beach is part of branding Miami as an elite cultural destination for art and design. The emergence of satellite art fairs parallel to Art Basel Miami Beach, led by NADA (New Art Dealers Alliance), has been an indicator of success and buoyant market conditions, with assumed art world competition to become part of an elite core.

Theme the experience, according to Pine and Gilmore: a well-defined theme is concise and compelling and drives a narrative story line that captivates the consumer. Art Basel Miami Beach, as an extension of Art Basel, has been able to capitalize on an attractive location (Miami in December) for elite dealers and prominent collectors. At the other end of the spectrum, the Affordable Art Fair (AAF), which operates in the USA, the UK, and Australia, positions itself at an entry level with all works on display for under £3,000 (or $5,000). 'Curate, don't just decorate', from an early promotional campaign, sets the tone. The vast majority of contemporary art fairs, situated between Art Basel and the AAF, need to establish a brand position relative to other fairs: this includes competitive entry selection criteria (i.e. peer review of assess quality of exhibiting dealers) to ensure dealers and artists from a variety of countries for a global orientation, which is considered appealing to collectors. Staged entry access to elite contemporary art fairs – not just a private view before the general public, but how privileged is private view – can be used as markers of social distinction. A cultural programme, to balance the commercial imperatives of an art fair, can include a curated section, including performance art and large-scale installations that many consider highly creative, seminars and round table discussions, book launches, etc. Private lounges at art fairs sponsored by investment banks during the boom years of the mid-2000s – UBS at Art Basel and Deutsche Bank at Frieze, for example – followed the segmentation models of airport lounges and VIP sections in clubs.

Commercial-oriented zones have taken root in art museums. Any ideological debate on the pros and cons of museum shops has longed passed in an era of plural funding, or at least reduced public subsidy. The tourism factor is crucial as souvenir shopping is part of the experience. There is a need to mix in memorabilia, according to Pine and Gilmore (1998), as physical reminders of an experience which generally sell at price points far above those commanded by similar items that do not represent an experience. The 'do not touch' aspect of a museum visit may be relieved by the museum shop. Multiple provisions, at various locations and price points, for food and drink are increasingly important to contain spectators. There has been a marked change within art museums in promoting food and drink as part of the experience. In 1988 the V&A was rebuked for its promotional campaign, 'an ace caff with a rather nice museum attached', produced by Saatchi & Saatchi, to launch the opening of the Henry Cole Wing. The reference to the new restaurant was supposed to make the museum more inviting to a target segment of so-called twenty-something Londoners. Yet rather than being viewed as whimsical and urbane, the advertising copy was interpreted as a crass attempt to make the museum more popular as a social site. In contrast, the reopening of New York's MoMA in 2004 included many comments, such as references to the availability of upmarket French-American food and drink at MoMA's fine-dining restaurant, The Modern, which is in partnership with Danny Meyer's Union Square Hospitality Group. The Modern has a separate street-level entrance – entry to MoMA is not required and access is extended beyond MoMA's opening hours: 'The art and food are utterly complementary. The better the food, the more intense the museum experience. . . . I would love it if The Modern [which also has two private dining rooms] emerges as one of the great restaurants in New York', according to MoMA director Glenn Lowry (*NYT*, 27 October 2004). Engage all five senses, according to Pine and Gilmore (1998), as the more sensory stimulants that accompany an experience, the more effective and memorable the experience can be. Of course, this may pose the question of whether art provides any existential experiences anymore: how are visitors able to feel or sense the specific character of the place where the museum is located (which applies to the permanent collection with which the museum works as well as the store) (Gerber, Wismer, and Moser in Walliser-Schwarzbart 2003)?

DEALERS AS MARKET MAKERS FOR CONTEMPORARY ART

Chief to understanding the structure of the art world is the importance of networks, that is to say, complex sets of social and economic relationships, which can include cooperation and competition. The theme of networks in the contemporary art market has been advanced by sociologists such as Raymonde Moulin, in her pioneering study of the French art market (first published in French in 1967, and translated into English in 1987) and Howard Becker (1982).[3] This is not surprising: art is an aesthetic (essentially non-utilitarian) object that is thinly traded in a low regulatory environment, often as an elite recreational pursuit; moreover, contemporary art has the additional market characteristics of unlimited supply and greater opportunities for key players to shape taste. In addition, a globalized art market that is marked by low regulation invites entrepreneurial activity to take place. It is not possible to measure with any particular accuracy the entire international art market or to reach any conclusions regarding overall competition. Most players – dealers and auction houses as the key intermediaries – are privately held firms so do not report annual totals for revenues or profits as part of audited financial statements released to the public, and any amounts reported may not be verifiable.

Economic sociologist Mark Granovetter (1985), in a paper published in the *American Journal of Sociology*, has examined how economic action is embedded in structures of social relations. Though no reference is made to the art world, what Granovetter (1985: 490) puts forward is an instructive framework:

> The embeddedness argument stresses instead the role of concrete personal relations and structure (or 'networks') of such relations in generating trust and discouraging malfeasance. The widespread preference for transacting with individuals of known reputation implies that few are actually content to rely on either

generalized morality *or* institutional arrangements to guard against trouble' (emphasis in the original).

Embeddedness is implied in 'The artist's reserved rights transfer and sale agreement' (Projansky and Siegelaub 1971) – 'special awareness of the current ordinary practices and economic realities of the art world, particularly its *private, cash and informal nature*, with careful regard for the interests and motives of all concerned' (my emphasis) – that was proffered in the early 1970s as a way for contemporary artists in the USA to gain greater economic benefits from the resale of their works. In particular, the agreement drew particular attention to the central role of the dealer, who 'knows all the ins and outs that go down in the business of the art world' as a link between artists and private and institutional collectors. However, the failure of the agreement to take root also indicates the preference of dealers for social relations rather than institutional arrangements to mediate complex transactions.

Granovetter (1985: 490) identifies benefits of 'information from one's own past dealings with that person': 'it is cheap'; 'one trusts one's information best – it is richer, more detailed, and known to be accurate'; 'individuals with whom one has a continuing relation have an economic motive to be trustworthy, so as not to discourage future transactions'; and 'departing from pure economic motives, continuing economic relations often become overlaid with social content that carries strong expectations of trust and abstention from opportunism'. Granovetter (1985: 491) notes that a preference for social relations, as 'a necessary condition for trust and trustworthy behavior', rather than institutional arrangements is not without opportunities 'for malfeasance and conflict'. Three main categories are identified. Each is applicable to the art world. First, 'trust engendered by personal relations presents, by its very existence, enhanced opportunities for malfeasance'. *The Art Newspaper* cites periodic cases of so-called confidence rackets or embezzlement involving dealers and curators. Second, examples of fraud through schemes like bid rigging rely on internal levels of trust amongst the collaborators (so-called honour among thieves). An informal history of auction houses is not complete without anecdotes of bid rigging by dealers. Of course, the most celebrated example may be the price-fixing between Christie's and Sotheby's. Third, in the absence of sustained social relations, disorder could result. In an atomized state, this would result in 'desultory dyadic conflicts' (Granovetter 1985: 492). A form of this is channel conflict between auction houses and dealers when there is a perceived breach in accepted codes of behaviour: for example, auction houses buying dealers and engaging more aggressively in private treaty sales has resulted in art dealers supporting art fairs as a way to compete and excluding the participation of art dealers associated with auction houses. However, there has not been a war, which is consistent with Granovetter's analysis that conflicts are relatively tame unless each side can escalate it by calling on substantial numbers of allies in other firms.

Network relationships in the art world are represented in 'The Art Eco-System' of arts consultancy firm Morris Hargreaves McIntyre (2004) as a 12-point flow between two institutions, art school and the public art museum:

1. Artists attract recognition of peers;

2. Exhibition curated by artists or freelance curator and representation in small publicly funded gallery;
3. Activity attracts critical attention;
4. Attracts attention of dealer;
5. Attracts private collectors;
6. Dealers build artists' reputation through sales including international art fairs;
7. Dealer builds critical endorsement through exhibitions/sales in small publicly funded or regional independent galleries;
8. Purchase or exhibition in major public gallery;
9. Legitimization adds value and status to collector and profit to dealer and artist;
10. Collector lends to public gallery;
11. Collectors' discernment is endorsed – invited onto boards of galleries; and
12. Collectors bequest collection to galleries.

It is at art school that artists first attract the recognition of peers. The market making abilities of the dealer, who has a central position in the model, is essential to the circulation of art. Both aesthetic taste and social networks are requirements for successful contemporary art dealing. The finish is represented by the public art museum as an idealized final resting place for art enhances the status of the artist, collector, and dealer. It is important to acknowledge that the commercial art market relies on publicly funded institutions – art schools in educating artists and public art museums serving as a record of taste and a starting point for art historical analysis – as markers of aesthetic quality. One might also include the important role of not-for-profit exhibition spaces from small art-run centres serving the local community to kunsthalles (or institutes of contemporary art) with international reputations that serve a vital role in exhibiting works of artists (as an artist who is not exhibited has no reputation). Dealers and private collectors benefit from these publicly funded institutions as it reduces the search costs associated with decision-making: which artists to represent and/or collect?

Contemporary art in the marketplace now has several circulation patterns: primary sales, secondary sales, and tertiary sales. Primary sales represent the first time a work of art is sold; this is conducted, in the main, by public art dealers, also referred by some as gallerists, who operate commercial gallery (or retail) spaces that are open to the public.[4] Being identified as a public dealer – as opposed to operating as a private dealer[5] – is a prerequisite to exhibit at many leading art fairs. Gallerists or primary market dealers focus on artist representation and promotion; as such dealers and artists tend to divide the sales price on an equal basis in most instances. Distribution is necessary for artistic success: an artist who is not exhibited is not known and will not be collected. It is the role of the dealer to promote his or her artists, as it is rare for an established artist to sell direct to collectors. Some dealers have exclusive representation agreements with artists. On the other hand, some artists have different dealers in different geographic locations, though there is often a lead dealer, who manages the selling price of the artist and mitigates channel conflict amongst the dealers and price arbitrage by buyers. In the case of in-demand or hot artists – the dealer creates so-called waiting lists (which is a method to gain control over buyers).

Secondary sales represent all subsequent resales of a work that take place through dealers. Most primary market dealers also operate in the secondary market, especially in the case of artists they represent. Some dealers will try to enforce a right of first refusal when a buyer (collector) wants to sell, which is about gaining control over where the work is placed (and how the artist is priced). Public auctions represent a tertiary sales market, which is important to the art market system: competitive bidding takes place; and auction results, namely low/high estimates and selling prices, are published. This means price transparency, which is crucial to the creation of art market price data, as transactions via dealers are private and not verifiable. Characteristic of speculation in a booming art market has been the quickness with which works sold in the primary art market appear at auction. A prime example – and possibly the climax of the bull market – was Damien Hirst's exhibition/auction of new works, 'Beautiful Inside My Head Forever', at Sotheby's London on 15/16 September 2008 which totaled £112 million.[6]

Aesthetic taste is needed to select artists to represent and/or collect. The work of living artists – a temporal marker by definition – is challenging to assess, as there is an unlimited supply of varying quality (see Abbing 2002).[7] In the current environment, degree qualification from a leading art school is one indicator of a young artist's potential. As such, successful artists show a career pathway not dissimilar to that of corporate lawyers, investment bankers, and art museum directors, namely crucial entry portals based on elite educational qualifications (see Galenson 2005): Yale School of Art, the Rhode Island School of Design, the School of the Art Institute of Chicago, CalArts, Cranbrook, and Cooper Union, for example, in the USA; Goldsmiths (University of London), the Slade (University College London), the Royal College of Art, the Royal Academy School, the Glasgow School of Art, and the schools of art of the University of the Arts (namely Camberwell, Central Saint Martins, Chelsea, and Wimbledon) as key in the UK. Yet many leading dealers will want to see a track record of success, following art school, before agreeing to represent an artist. Most leading dealers of contemporary art tend to limit the number of artists under representation to a figure (say between 20 and 40) that allows a degree of artist–dealer interaction. Very few dealers, with the Gagosian Gallery and Jay Jopling's White Cube as notable exceptions, represent more than 40 artists. Not unlike major record companies using independent record labels as so-called research and development to scout and groom new talent, the best emerging dealers who appear at art fairs parallel to the main ones devoted to contemporary art (e.g. Art Basel, Frieze, and Art Basel Miami Beach) may lose the most commercially successful artists to leading dealers (see working list below). The lack of contractual arrangements between artists and dealers – a conventional aspect of the art world – offers flexibility to both sides to end relationships, though both artists and dealers cite mutual trust as key to a successful relationship.

Collectors of art are of two main categories: institutions such as public art museums, private art foundations/museums, or business corporations; and private individuals. Of course, some private collectors, such as those cited by *ARTnews* in its annual review, behave like institutional collectors. Patrons of art have had an important contribution to the history of civilization. The formation of public art museum collections, in the USA and Europe, has relied on the beneficence of individual art collectors (Bazin 1967; Impey and MacGregor 1985; Pointon 1994). It is likely that the taste of private collectors will continue to inform public institutions; however, we are witnessing the growth of private museum projects by leading art collectors of contemporary art such as Eli Broad (Los Angeles), Charles Saatchi (London), François Pinault (Venice), Guy Ullens (Beijing), and Daria Zhukova (Moscow). Whether these initiatives will survive the death of the founder-collector – in the tradition of Peggy Guggenheim (Venice), Isabella Stewart Gardner (Boston), Henry Clay Frick (New York), and the first four Marquesses of Hertford and Sir Richard Wallace (London) – is too early to determine.

The goal of art is to find a home; indeed provenance is a term used to denote ownership history of the work since it was created. The idealized repository of art is the museum, as this often serves as a precursor to entering the primers of art history. With this in mind, the significance of the term 'museum quality' is better appreciated: it is used by dealers and auctioneers to signal works of the highest aesthetic value – that is to say, worthy to be on display in a public art museum. In some cases, a dealer or auctioneer will reference a comparable work in a public collection for the purposes of indicating comparative value (with aesthetic or intrinsic value being translated into American dollars or euros). Such rhetoric is geared to appeal to private collectors, which is ironic as the formation of the public art museum, such as the Louvre, as distinct from private collections, is cited as an example of a democratizing institution (see Carrier 2006; Cuno 2004). Dealers prefer to place works with private collectors who have expressed intentions to donate works to public collections: in the first instance – the primary market sales – the dealer does not need to discount the selling price for a private collector beyond 10 to 15 per cent (whereas a museum may require a more substantial cut of 25 to 40 per cent); and the work should not enter the secondary market if it is donated to a museum, which also enhances the reputations of both artist and dealer.

Wealth is a key hurdle separating two groups of fine art consumers: appreciators (spectators) and collectors. Appreciators of fine art fall within the sociological explanations emphasizing the cultivation of taste first posited by Pierre Bourdieu (1984): education attainment (as measured by length of time in full-time education or highest qualification) and social origins (that is the role of parents) are key predictors.[8] From having a high participation rate visiting art museums, those with sufficient discretionary income may want to own works, with the most desirable objects being ones that could belong in a museum collection. Collecting fine art is, from a historical perspective, an elite recreational activity. Adopting the marketing language of financial services, the target segments range from, at the bottom end, mass affluent – a new term from retail banking to denote individuals earning in excess of $100,000 per annum (see, for example, Nunes and Johnson 2004; Silverstein and Fiske 2004) – to ultra high net worth individuals (UHNWIs), which is part of the conventional language of private wealth management to indicate individuals or family groups with investible assets in excess of $30 million. (The category of connoisseur collector, operating on a limited budget, is a dying breed!) Many are based in the USA, yet international dimensions are of growing significance with the rise of HNWIs and UHNWIs from the emerging economies of China, India, Russia, the Middle East, and Latin America.

Any list of top contemporary art dealers is bound to be subjective, though the following 25 have been selected via representation at leading art fairs and consultation (see Chong in Harris 2010).[9] They are listed alphabetically in three groups based on primary location (New York, London, or continental Europe), with some having multiple sites in the same city or multiple cities. New York leads the way with Mary Boone Gallery (Mary Boone, 1977; two sites), Cheim & Reid (John Cheim and Howard Read, 1997; one site), Paula Cooper Gallery (Paula Cooper, 1968; one site), Gagosian Gallery (Larry Gagosian, 1983; seven sites), Gladstone Gallery (Barbara Gladstone, 1980; three sites), Marian Goodman Gallery (Mariam Goodman, 1977; two sites), Lehmann Maupin (Rachel Lehmann and David Maupin, 1996; two sites), Luhring Augustine (Lawrence Luhring and Roland Augustine, 1985; one site), Matthew Marks Gallery (Matthew Marks, 1990; three sites), Metro Pictures (Janelle Reiring and Helene Winner, 1980; one site), PaceWildenstein (Arnold and Marc Glimcher and Guy Wildenstein, 1993 as joint venture between Pace Gallery and Wildenstein & Co; four sites), Andrea Rosen Gallery (Andrea Rosen, 1990; two sites), and David Zwirner (David Zwirner, 1993; three sites). London is also very important with Albion (Michael Hue-Williams, 2004; two site units 2009), Sadie Coles HQ (Sadie Coles, 1997; two sites), Haunch of Venison (Harry Blain and Graham Southern, 2002; purchased by Christie's in 2007; three sites), Lisson Gallery (Nicholas Logsdail, 1967; one site), Victoria Miro Gallery (1985; one site), and White Cube (Jay Jopling, 1993; two sites). Other leading dealers accentuate the continuing importance of continental Euorpe: Contemporary Fine Arts (Bruno Brunnet, Nicole Hackert, and Philipp Haverkampf, 1992, Berlin), La Galerie Chantal Crousel (Chantal Crousel, 1980, Paris), Hauser & Wirth (Ursula Hauser, Iwan Wirth, and Manuela Wirth, 1992, Zurich), Yvon Lambert (Yvon Lambert, 1966, Paris), Galerie Emmanuel Perrotin (Emmanuel Perrotin, 1989, Paris), Spruth Magers (Moinka Spruth and Philomene Magers, 1998, Berlin).

New York and London remain central as represented by the powerhouse selection: approximately two-thirds operate in New York, 40 per cent operate in London, and thus far two – Gagosian and Haunch of Venison – operate in both. Paris (four dealers), Berlin (three dealers), and Zurich (two dealers) represent a second group of significance. Only three dealers – Chantel Crousel (Paris), Emmanuel Perrotin (Paris and Miami), and Contemporary Fine Arts (Berlin) – have operations in neither New York nor London. Within key markets like New York and London, property, often referenced as the process of gentrification, is never far from art market concerns. For example, SoHo, as hub of the New York art world since the 1960s, started to give way to Chelsea in the 1990s (following the relocation of the Dia Art Foundation in 1987). The decision of Paula Cooper, one of the first SoHo dealers, to move to Chelsea in 1996 was highly symbolic. Lehmann Maupin opened in SoHo in 1996, moved to Chelsea in 2002, and opened a second space, in 2007, in the Bowery, home to the New Museum of Contemporary Art, which is being touted as a new cultural hub. The YBA scene, led by Hirst and associated with 'Cool Britannia' London of the 1990s, saw the emergence of the East End as a site for contemporary art (both production and distribution). For example, White Cube's decision to leave its original site at Duke Street, in Mayfair's West End, for Hoxton Square in 2000 excited much attention; in 2006 White Cube returned to the West End (Mason's Yard, which is near Duke Street, with 12,500 square feet of exhibition space), and now operates two galleries in London.[10]

Twelve of the powerhouse dealers opened galleries before the mid-1980s and remain highly competitive. This is one indicator of the importance of establishing and maintaining relationships with artists and collectors. That a majority of these dealers are women, namely Paula Cooper, Mary Boone, Marian Goodman, Barbara Gladstone, Chantel Crousel, Janelle Reiring and Helene Winner (Metro Pictures), and Victoria Miro, suggests greater gender balance in primary market art dealing. However, successful market entry in contemporary art dealing, accentuating the role of entrepreneurship, is also evident. Eleven dealers established in the 1990s have risen to the top rank, with a representative distribution of art market centres as home locations: New York (Cheim & Read, Lehmann Maupin, Matthew Marks, Andrea Rosen, and David Zwirner), London (Jay Jopling and Sadie Coles), and continental Europe (Contemporary Fine Arts, Hauser & Wirth, Emmanuel Perrotin, and Spruth Magers).

Two enterprises formed since 2000, Haunch of Venison (est. 2002) and Albion (est. 2004), are worth note, particularly in the current financial crisis. As part of the market boom for contemporary art, both hired former museum directors and well-known architects to launch new sites in New York: Robert Fitzpatrick (ex-Museum of Contemporary Art Chicago) and Steven Learner Studios in the case of Haunch of Venison; and Albion secured David Ross (ex-Whitney Museum of American Art and San Francisco Museum of Modern Art) and David Adjaye.

The acquisition of Haunch of Venison, established by Harry Blain and Graham Southern, by Christie's, which is owned by the prolific contemporary art collector François Pinault, in 2007, is not usual. As such, it provoked disapproval by other contemporary art dealers, who feel an encroachment onto their territory of the art market. That is to say private treaty sales (i.e. a form of behaviour in which an auction house extends beyond pure agency between consignor and competitive bidders to performing a role more akin to a dealer) of contemporary art, through the skills and relationship networks of Blain and Southern, and museum quality exhibition venues in London, Zurich, and New York. Christie's is attempting to be more effective in how well it covers the contemporary art market, with the hopes that it will be building a competitive advantage over its direct rival Sotheby's. Whereas Haunch of Venison remains buoyant, Michael Hue-Williams's Albion, which operated in London and New York, has had to recoup: 'We're retrenching right back to a smaller operation in London. This kind of gallery isn't sustainable in the current environment. It's a very tough climate. No one has experienced this before. Everyone is under enormous pressure', according to Hue-Williams (cited in Bloomberg, 8 May 2009). This followed an earlier announcement of the closure of the New York site. Albion London was located in a building project of Foster + Partners. Albion (16,000 square feet), which afforded Hue-Williams (theartnewspaper.tv, 4 November 2008), who started as a secondary market dealer in the late 1980s, an opportunity to establish a 'production house with an open book on offer to artists' (such as Ai Weiwei, Cai Guo-Qiang, James Turell, and Zhan Wang) to create large-scale works for a monumental interior space. Albion exhibited Zhan Wang's 'Scholar Rocks' in 2008, with *Rock Number 59* (2005–6) on prominent display at the British Museum, in the Great Court, including the note: 'Lent by the artist with the support of Michael Hue-Williams'. Furthermore, Hue-Williams, writing in *The Art Newspaper* (25 January 2008), suggested that contemporary Chinese art available at auction distorts our understanding of Chinese art production. It is anticipated that Hue-Williams will relocate to a smaller site in London's West End.

Larry Gagosian, who started as a dealer in Los Angeles in the early 1980s before relocating to New York in 1986, is cited for his impact in the contemporary art market boom during the last fifteen years, namely expanding the scale of his operations with multiple gallery sites, first in the USA and then in Europe, and a bigger roster of the leading artists (with 98 'artists exhibited' listed, including Hirst, Jeff Koons, Takashi Murakami, Richard Prince, Ed Ruscha, Cindy Sherman, and Cy Twombly and the recently dead such as Francis Bacon, Joseph Beuys, Alberto Giacometti, and Andy Warhol). For example, Gagosian moved from the West End, where he started in London in 2000, to King's Cross (12,500 square feet designed by Caruso St John) in 2004, citing the issue of scale as a reason for the move: certain artists need a larger structure, and there is an opportunity to mount major exhibitions and display works for sale.[11] For example, 'Pop Art Is . . .' (2007) was conceived as 'a major exhibition to mark the fiftieth anniversary of Richard Hamilton's visionary definition of Pop Art' with 40 artists represented: from the first generation such as Hamilton and artists associated with Leo Castelli such as Ed Ruscha, who is represented by Gagosian (following the death of Castelli), 'to subsequent generations of artists who have traced and extended Pop Art's varied legacies' (such as Koons, Hirst, Murakami, and Prince). Gagosian's exhibition, with approximately half of the works marked NSF (not for sale), coincided with Frieze 2007 – including a helicopter above the art fair with a banner announcing the exhibition title and location, hence 'Pop Art Is . . . Gagosian' – and related exhibitions at the Hayward Gallery and the National Portrait Gallery. Such exhibitions lend scholarly and intellectual credibility to the commercial gallery, imbuing it with a gravitas that enhances the brand. Enhancing the brand means helping the buyer to make a purchase and price premiums. Gagosian's second exhibition in Moscow, 'for what you are about to receive', coincided with the September 2008 opening of the Garage Centre for Contemporary Culture, an initiative of Daria Zhukova (with the support of Roman Abramovich). Seventy sculptures were on display: from Calder to Koons, from (David) Smith to Serra. That is art Russians would buy. Most recently, Gagosian opened an office in Hong Kong.

Powerhouse dealers have grown in physical size, which is perceived as presence: ten have gallery sites in different cities; and eight have multiple sites within the same city. 'Much like its artists, David Zwirner has experienced extraordinary growth. In 2002, the gallery moved to 525 West 19th Street in Chelsea. Four years later, in 2006, it expanded from 10,000 to 30,000 square feet, adding spaces at 519 and 533 West 19th Street, allowing the gallery to mount three independent, full-scale exhibitions simultaneously'. Victoria Miro also highlights her physical size: 'In 2000 she moved to an 8,000 square feet former furniture factory in the northeast. In October 2006 the gallery expanded further opening Victoria Miro 14, a 9,000 square feet exhibition and viewing space adjacent to the original gallery. Today the gallery is one of the largest commercial spaces in London'. Likewise Emmanuel Perrotin, who wanted an opportunity to be less French (which is to suggest that he is faltered by references as the French Gagosian), opened a 15,000 square feet gallery, located near the Rubell Family Collection, to coincide with Art Basel Miami Beach in 2005. This represents the hyper-competition for visibility and reputation in order to attract and retain artists and collectors in a globalized art market. Yet additional space is also curatorial. Andrea Rosen opened Gallery 2 to coincide with her tenth anniversary, in 1999: '... infusing the gallery with one-time projects enhances the vocabulary, meaning, and impact of the gallery's agenda ... this program allows us the freedom to show, for instance, a single piece by an artist or a single body of work by an artist we would not otherwise have the opportunity to show, an exhibition of historical works ...'; and Mary Boone notes that she has 'mounted historical shows' and 'the gallery in this manner functions as a kunsthalle or project space'. Four of the seven dealers with a single location – Lisson, Paula Cooper, Metro Pictures, and Chantal Crousel – have long-established reputations, and may not want to be part of a perceived supermarket-type of an approach to art.

Many powerhouse dealers acknowledge and promote their role in the careers of artists they represent. In doing so, they seek to situate their own contributions within the recent historical context of contemporary art. Mary Boone makes it clear, including her current role in the secondary market, that she was influential in promoting many of the leading painters of the 1980s such as Julian Schnabel, David Salle, Francisco Clemente, and Jean-Michel Basquiat. Marian Goodman notes that her gallery 'has played an important role in introducing European artists to American audiences and helping to establish a dialogue among artists and institutions working internationally'. For example, in 1977, she 'opened her gallery with the first exhibition of Marcel Broodthaers in the USA (organized before his death in 1976)'. In a similar manner Jay Jopling discusses the formation of White Cube in 1993 'as a project room for contemporary art. Although it was one of the smallest exhibition spaces in Europe, it was arguably one of the most influential commercial galleries of the 1990s'. Longevity at an elite level of primary market dealing includes the cultivation of new artists. Metro Pictures is able to note that original gallery artists like Cindy Sherman and Robert Longo remain, while adding artists in the 1990s such as Tony Oursler, and more recently in the cases of T.J. Wilcox, Olaf Breuning, and Paula Olowska. Likewise Victoria Miro who combines 'established names with younger talent' by representing 'four Turner Prize nominees: Ian Hamilton Finlay, Peter Doig, Isaac Julien, and Phil Collins and two winners, Chris Ofili and Grayson Perry'; moreover, 'with an acclaimed eye for great and innovative artists, she is also renowned for nurturing young artists'. Finally, Nicholas Logsdail, in discussing Lisson, is able to articulate four phases of advanced curatorial practice: 'it was one of a small number of pioneering galleries in the UK, Europe, and the US to champion a generation of artists who were transforming the way art was made and presented, focusing on an idea or concept behind an artwork over expressive or descriptive aims' (e.g. Sol LeWitt, Lawrence Weiner, Donald Judd, Dan Flavin, Carl Andre, and Art & Language); it promoted the New British Sculptors, such as Tony Cragg, Richard Deacon, Shirazeh Houshiary, Anish Kapoor, Julian Opie, and Richard Wentworth, who came to maturity in the early 1980s; in the 1990s 'a more diverse group demonstrated a poetic conceptualism of images and language' (e.g. Rodney Graham, Douglas Gordon, Jonathan Marks, and Christine Borland) while other artists (e.g. Tony Oursler and Jane and Louise Wilson) 'used the media of video and sound to create heightened vision and social constructs of their age'; and a new generation has emerged in the first decade of the twenty-first century (e.g. Gerard Byrne, Santiago Serra, Tim

Lee, and Christian Jackowski) 'who explore the structures of representation and cultural value from global perspectives'.

It goes without saying that new dealers will emerge from New York, London, and continental Europe to replace the current big beasts. What is more interesting is the potential to see the emergence of contemporary art in Asia – specifically China, India, Japan, and Korea – with reference to both artists and art dealers. Contemporary Chinese artists such as Zhang Xiaogang, Ai Weiwei, and Cai Guo-Qiang became darlings of auction sales during the mid-2000s, led by Christie's and Sotheby's; prominent non-Chinese collectors namely Uli Sigg, Guy Ullens, and Charles Saatchi served as early adopters (or influential trendsetters and endorsers). Sales prices of works by modern (MF Husain and SH Raza) and contemporary (Subodh Gupta and TV Santosh) Indian artists also spiked, driven by buyers living in India and NRIs (non-resident Indians). The creation of contemporary art investment funds, mainly in India and Korea, also attracted financial speculators. The example of Japan's most visible artist, Takashi Murakami, is of interest. Murakami, who is likened to Hirst, started Kaikai Kiki, an art production company, which includes Chiho Aoshima, Rei Sato, and Aya Takano. Dealers as owner-operated businesses suggest a limited lifecycle and, hence, opportunities for new ones to emerge. AICON, Bodhi Art, and Nature Morte have expanded operations outside of India, but have not been invited to the leading art fairs. ShanghART, Beijing Art Now, and Red Gate have appeared at leading contemporary art fairs, though some Chinese artists have established relationships with leading dealers in New York and London. As Indian and Chinese dealers represent a narrow range of artists, their potential to grow appears stymied. Arario and PKM are looking to break through, even though Korean artists are less well known internationally. Of the Asian dealers, Japanese ones such as Tomio Koyama, Koyangi, and ShugoArts are the most global in outlook when measured by representation of artists and attendance at art fairs.

Certain questions about contemporary art from Asia arise. Cities in China (Beijing and Shanghai) and India (Mumbai and New Delhi) will assume greater art world significance as New York and London slowly cede power. What market conditions for contemporary art help to account for the distribution of certain artists from Asia? Are there particularities associated with the operations of Asian dealers? Is it necessary that Asian dealers adopt established art market codes of practice? The opening by PaceWildenstein of Pace Beijing (22,000 square feet in a former munitions factory) in August 2008, in the 798 Art District near the Ullens Center for Contemporary Art, is one the first prominent entries into a non-Western market by a contemporary art dealer based in New York or London. What is required if Beijing's 798 Art District seeks to rival New York's Chelsea in influence?

LEVERAGING ART MUSEUMS FOR AUDIENCE AND IDENTITY

'Individuality' is a core value of members of the Association of Art Museum Directors:

Each museum has a unique identity, and its collections and programs serve the distinctive interests of the community. Museum directors have the responsibility and freedom to exercise sound professional judgment in ensuring that their museums are responsive to local interests while adhering to the national standards of quality for which the AAMD's members are recognized.

Stephen Greenblatt (in Karp and Lavine 1991: 42) suggests that the pursuit of individuality is bound within 'two distinct models for the exhibition of works of art': 'resonance' (politics) and 'wonder' (poetics). Each presents a different treatment of the art object and its relationship to the spectator. Resonance is 'power of the displayed object to reach out beyond its formal boundaries to a larger world, to evoke in the viewer the complex, dynamic cultural forces from which it has emerged and for which it may be taken by a viewer to stand'. This is associated with new historicism. There is a greater focus on the art object as a resource for the spectator to make sense of it. On the other hand, wonder is about the 'power of the displayed object to stop the viewer in his or her tracks, to convey an arresting sense of uniqueness, to evoke an exalted state'. This represents the conventional position of museums, grounded in the Kanatian idealization, of individual masterpieces. The art object is considered to be source material of intrinsic value. Greenblatt (in Karp and Lavine 1991: 54) concludes that the two models are not mutually exclusive: 'almost every exhibition worth viewing has elements of both . . . a strong initial appeal to wonder . . . that then leads to resonance . . . for it is easier in our culture to pass from wonder to resonance than from resonance to wonder'.

Where it has been assumed that brand positioning is about differentiation (i.e. what is different or better than alternative offerings), it is important to establish a 'frame of reference', which signals the goal they can expect to achieve by using the brand, and to develop 'points of parity', namely the qualities consumers consider 'legitimate and credible' for a brand to be considered competitive within a frame (Keller, Sternthal, and Tybout 2002). 'Superstar museum' is used by cultural economist Bruno Frey (1998) to describe a particular category of museum: a must for tourists, which suggests high brand recall or recognition; attracts large number of visitors as such a headline figure of popularity serves to measure success in the absence of financial performance metrics; houses in its permanent collection famous artists and art works (as found in art history texts); the architecture of the museum building is an artistic feature, which has fostered a starchitect-designed mindset as an essential ingredient for museum development projects; and commercially aware of both internal revenue spaces for merchandising and catering and external impact measures on the local economy. It goes without saying – but needs to be reiterated – that the Guggenheim Bilbao, which opened in 1997, was manufactured to be a museum with high brand values to generate popular appeal (see Twitchell 2004; Cuno 2004; Carrier 2006). As a key cultural project to regenerate the disused port town of Bilbao, in the Basque region of Spain, it represented a partnership of several brands. Architect Frank Gehry's museum building remains the key drawing card. The opening also featured Jeff Koons, who created *Sky Puppy*, a large-scale public sculpture. Koons, who is represented by Gagosian, has modelled for Hugo Boss. In turn, Hugo Boss, one of the Guggenheim's major corporate sponsors – including the Hugo Boss Prize, a biennial award established in 1996 to recognize a significant achievement in contemporary art – is keen to advance the German-based fashion label in the USA. The success of the project has given rise to the so-called Bilbao Effect, namely that an industrial town can be transformed into a tourist mecca; in many respects Bilbao changed the perception of culture.[12]

Though the Solomon R. Guggenheim Foundation was established in 1937, the emergence of the Guggenheim brand really dates from 1959, when Frank Lloyd Wright's spiral building was opened as the Solomon R. Guggenheim Museum. In 1979, the Peggy Guggenheim Collection – which had been established in 1951 in Venice – came under the control of the Guggenheim Foundation. Thomas Krens arrived at the Guggenheim Foundation in 1988 as chief executive officer, and he remained in post until 2008. A significant part of Krens's legacy at the Guggenheim – and the impact on the museum world – has been to question and challenge the ideals and principles that gave rise to the public art museum. This has included expanding the conventional boundaries of the museum beyond one physical site, which includes operations outside of the country-of-origin. The Guggenheim SoHo (now closed), representing a secondary New York site, was opened in 1992. The early 1990s also marked initiatives to pursue additional global sites. Thus, at the end of Krens's reign, the Guggenheim Foundation had ownership of two museums – flagship site in New York designed by Frank Lloyd Wright and the Peggy Guggenheim Collection in Venice – and provided curatorial direction and management services to two museums, Guggenheim Museum Bilbao and Deutsche Guggenheim in Berlin. Furthermore, an ambitious project in Abu Dhabi had been announced in 2006 (with completion in 2012). Many other proposed projects such as the West Kowloon Cultural District in Hong Kong failed to materialize. In addition, sites had opened and closed: the Guggenheim SoHo (1992–99), which was criticized for requiring entry to the galleries via the museum's store (*NYT*, 6 February 1999), and the Guggenheim Hermitage Museum in Las Vegas (2001–8).

'The Guggenheim Foundation realizes its mission through exceptional exhibitions, education programs, research initiatives, and publications, and strives to engage and educate an increasingly diverse international audience through its unique network of museums and cultural partnerships'. The Guggenheim's mission statement is unremarkable until near the end: 'its unique network of museums and cultural partnerships' reflects the mindset of a cultural institution with expansionist tendencies. During what might be viewed – with the benefit of hindsight – as the height of his reign at the Guggenheim, Krens (2006) elaborated on the mission:

> The whole idea here is about a free exchange of commentary and ideas. It's a discourse on an international scale. In a contemporary society for contemporary art, with everything becoming ever more interconnected, I think it's an essential aspect of how museums have to confront the world.

That New York is to remain the Guggenheim Foundation's hub for its satellites throughout the world has been reemphasized as part of a post-Krens mandate. At the same time, the exposure of the Guggenheim brand has been about attracting global audiences. Attendance figures are measured globally, and each exhibition is measured in terms of its global impact rather than its local impact. For example, the

Guggenheim's online project is billed as a virtual museum, a natural extension of the satellite sites, with an objective to enhance the value of the Guggenheim as a cultural asset. A mid-1990s slogan on the global ambitions of the Guggenheim (with the Bilbao project in mind) – competing for the mind of Europe – now seems much too modest. Indeed, according to art historian David Carrier (2006: 217), Krens should be 'praised for understanding that only when high art is as popular as mass culture can it compete'.

Under the directorship of Krens, the Guggenheim recognized that opportunities exist to change the ways in which art museums compete. By museum standards, the Guggenheim is noted for aggressive brand leveraging: it has been the first museum brand to establish global credentials under its then banner – when Las Vegas was still active – of 'one museum, five locations' banner. Establishing a reputation based on one location – as with the Metropolitan, the British Museum, and the Prado, for example – is difficult to replicate for second-movers (with the Getty Museum being a well-endowed exception). Celebrity endorsers came in the form of respected architects designing signature buildings, a dominant feature of the Guggenheim brand from the start. National and global scale offered presence. As such the Guggenheim's relationship with visitors has been likened to pilgrimages: historically, one thinks about the Piero della Francesca trail. Krens (2008) has referred to Chartres Cathedral when discussing what he wanted Gehry to design at Bilbao:

> In the Middle Ages, when someone came to the city from a village, they had never seen buildings with more than one story before and then they stood in front of this massive cathedral. That's the effect I wanted to achieve. It's technology, cosmology, science and religion, all thrown together. Breathtaking.

Of course, to critics, an amusement park analogy, with reference to Disney's multiple sites, offers a better role model for the Guggenheim.

Many find it difficult to accept at face value the Guggenheim's response to critics that a motivation for multiple sites to make its collection accessible to a broader audience. The current director of MoMA, Glenn Lowry (in Cuno 2004: 138), has been unimpressed with the Guggenheim's conduct:

> What distinguishes the Guggenheim is that rather than keeping a fine balance between the museum as school and theater, a place of learning and a place of enjoyment, it has focused its energies on becoming an entertainment center and appears to be no longer interested in or committed to the ideas and the art that gave rise to the museum at its founding.

Lowry was referring to Guggenheim exhibitions from the early 2000s, like 'Giorgio Armani', 'Art of the Motorcycle' (sponsored by BMW), and 'Star Wars', which were criticized as unrelated to the museum's collection, and mounted to cater to corporate sponsors. Earlier critics such as Rosiland Krauss (1990) noted that the Guggenheim's permanent collection was being treated as trading capital, that its assets were being deployed (or leveraged) to expand the institution's presence and to enhance its financial stability. Her analysis was informed by changes that have taken place as a result of the free-market spirit of the 1980s: 'The notion of the museum as a guardian of the public patrimony has given way to the notion of the museum as a corporate entity with a highly marketable inventory and the desire for growth' (Philip Weiss cited in Krauss 1990: 5).

What can be suggested by the Guggenheim's first new site of the twenty-first century: Las Vegas? Central to the Guggenheim project was 'The Venetian Resort-Hotel-Casino' complex. On the former site of the Sands Hotel, home of Rat Pack performers like Frank Sinatra and Dean Martin, Sheldon Adelson, chairman of the Venetian, sought to establish the world's largest resort and convention centre under one roof. Both the Guggenheim Las Vegas (focusing on travelling exhibitions) and the Guggenheim Hermitage Museum (in partnership with the State Hermitage Museum in Russia) were attached to the Venetian; access was through the Venetian *only*. Rem Koolhaas was selected by the Guggenheim to create a museum building that would not be overlooked alongside the aggressive visual congestion of The Strip, the city's main artery. Las Vegas continues to upgrade its image as represented by the rhetorical shift from *gambling* (associated with vice and crime) to *gaming* (which is part of the leisure industry); this transformation into a so-called world class destination resort relies on competitive rivalry among the city's elite casino owners.

In the late 1990s, Steven Wynn, chairman of the Mirage Resorts, used works of art from his personal collection (including works by Renoir, Van Gogh, and Picasso) as another selling point to entice so-called high limit gamblers (an elite consumer segment). It was a clear example of using conventional fine art and antiques, as noted by John Berger (1972: 135) in *Ways of Seeing*, to enhance a casino's brand reputation:

> Any work of art 'quoted' by publicity serves two purposes. Art is a sign of affluence; it belongs to the good life; it is part of the furnishing which the word gives to the rich and beautiful.
>
> But a work of art also suggests a cultural authority, a form of dignity, even of wisdom, which is superior to any vulgar material interest; an oil painting belongs to a cultural heritage; it is a reminder of what it means to be a cultivated European.

The Venetian experiment was grander and more ambitious than that accomplished by Wynn. It was the first significant collaboration between an art museum and a casino-hotel in the USA. Assumed European connotations of good taste and distinction were explicit: as suggested by its name, the resort-hotel-casino complex positioned itself as Las Venice by reproducing the most recognized cultural features (e.g. Campanile di San Marco and the Rialto Bridge over the Grand Canal, including gondola rides) found in the Italian city-state. According to a spokesman for the Venetian (Kurt Ochida in the *Reno Gazette-Journal*, 14 July 2000):

> Culture is here to stay. People are finding that Las Vegas reinvents itself – in dining and in shopping and retail – it's now gaining a worldwide reputation as a place where you can actually seek culture, away from the typical stereotypes that have plagued Las Vegas for a long time.

Yet the treatment of art and culture envisioned by the Guggenheim–Venetian collaboration raised concerns, even by Gehry (cited in *Ion Vegas*, 20 October 2000): 'I'm worried about this kind of context. There may be a way to do it, but the fear is that it would all just become another theme, whether you like it or not'.

With an eye to replicating the success of Bilbao, the Guggenheim responded to a call by the West Kowloon Cultural District (WKCD) in Hong Kong, in 2005. The Guggenheim (2005) established a partnership with the Centre Pompidou and property developer Dynamic Sun International. The WKCD was part of a 40-hectacre waterfront site being developed by the Government of Hong Kong to create 'an integrated arts, cultural, and entertainment district' that offered 'an exciting possibility for cultural exchange, sharing, and dialogue'. Krens (2006) described the WKCD proposal in terms of size: 'Now this is a colossal scale. This is probably four or five times the scale of Bilbao'. Partnering with the Pompidou was used to justify the Guggenheim's globalization strategy: 'And more and more, you see the French museums adopting this direction as a matter of national policy' (Krens 2006).

Without making explicit reference to the Guggenheim's Hong Kong proposal, the AAMD (March 2006) proffered a more rigorous approach to the long-term consequences for art museums from revenue-generating partnerships with commercial organizations. In a 2006 interview with Charlie Ross, Krens accepted the criticisms of MoMA's Lowry as part of the competitive rivalry that exists in New York 'among the various institutions for audience and identity'. MoMA is the world's leading museum of modern art, according to Krens (2006), so the Guggenheim needs to develop methods to compete against it and the other leading art museums of modern art such as Tate Modern, the Pompidou, and Amsterdam's Stedelijk. At the time, with five museum venues, the Guggenheim sought to promote a total attendance figure – one visible measure of success – in excess of 2.5 million.

Krens has objected to critics who perceive the Guggenheim exporting a commodity that is somehow the same wherever the Guggenheim is situated. The notion of franchising, with its fast-food connotations, is not a word used by Krens. Rather he has talked about mutual exchange and the 'free exchange of commentary and ideas'. 'Pioneering' is how Krens (2006) has categorized the various partnerships with other institutions: 'The fact that these institutions would choose to work with us and enter into a long-term agreement to share collections, to share staff, to share programming, in effect, to regard ourselves as a kind of – how would you say – *free trade zone* or *strategic alliance* of some kind I think is significant' (my emphasis). Moreover, Krens (2008), in a post-director interview, noted the risks of being considered a 'pioneer': 'They're the people in a group who walk at the very front, who are the first to fall face down in the mud and the first to be shot in the back with an arrow'.

Almost immediately following the cancellation of the WKCD project, in 2006, the Guggenheim announced a joint project in Abu Dhabi to establish a museum as part of a much bigger cultural project. 'What I have planned in Abu Dhabi is so much bigger than what I've done so far. It'll be the kind of thing we've never seen before. The only expression I can think of to describe it is pharaonic', according to Krens (2008), drawing reference to Egyptian pyramids.

The Tourism Development and Investment Company (TDIC), with Sheikh Sultan Bin Tahnoon Al Nahyan as chairman and sole equity stakeholder of the Abu Dhabi Tourism Authority (tdic.ae), is master developer behind the transformation of

Saadiyat Island (saadiyat.ae). Saadiyat Island, located off the coast of Abu Dhabi (and linked by highway bridges), is proposed as a 'multi-faceted island offering a great variety of attractions to many different people' organized into seven districts (cultural, beach, retreat, reserve, marina, promenade, and lagoon):

> A buzzing business hub for international commerce; a relaxed waterfront home for residents; a cultural magnet for arts aficionados; the home of dazzling architectural icons; a pristine beachfront tourism destination and a focal point for compelling sporting experiences, such as the Gulf's only tidal and ocean golf courses. It will also be the only place in the world to house architecture designed by five individual Pritzker prize winners. Saadiyat Island will be an irresistible magnet attracting the world to Abu Dhabi – and taking Abu Dhabi to the world.
>
> This unique place will offer an entirely unique invitation to the discerning traveller. The island is infused with a richness that serves its visitors and residents cultural, social, emotional and environmental rewards. Indeed Saadiyat is positioned to become, an international destination of desire, a flagship for Abu Dhabi, a treasure for the world.

Central to Saadiyat, with a reported initial budget of $27 billion, is the cultural district's five projects, each associated with a Pritzker-winning architect. The Gehry-designed Guggenheim Abu Dhabi is massive at 450,000 square feet making it the largest and most complex Guggenheim project to date; it takes precedence over the smaller museum building Jean Nouvel has been commissioned to design as the Louvre Abu Dhabi. In addition to these two lead projects, which draw on museum partnerships, a performing arts centre is being designed by Zaha Hadid, and Tadao Ando has a commission for a maritime museum. Finally, Norman Foster's Foster + Partners is designing the Zayed National Museum, dedicated to Sheik Zayed bin Sultan al-Nahayan, founder and long-time ruler of the UAE,who died in 2004.

'One of the primary aims of Saadiyat Cultural District is to foster greater understanding and appreciation of the arts, as part of this strategy a programme of innovative artistic and cultural events has been developed to engage and inform a local and regional audience'. However, Negar Azimi, writing in the 'Art and Its Market' issue of *Artforum* (April 2008), notes the peculiar emergence of auction houses, contemporary art dealers, and museum projects in the UAE:

> An art world is undeniably materializing in the UAE but, oddly, in the reverse of the traditional trajectory, and perhaps even at the expense of a full-fledged art scene. The elements that typically preceded market activity – schools, critics, and curators – are all but absent.[13]

This has raised somewhat predictable claims in the West of oil-rich rulers buying culture by plundering the best art museums in the USA and Europe.

Concern was first mooted by a significant patron and board member, Peter Lewis, that too much attention was devoted to the Guggenheim's spokes (or satellites) with insufficient attention to the hub in New York. As such, Guggenheim Abu Dhabi may be a pyrrhic victory for Krens: no longer director of the Guggenheim Foundation, he remains as the senior advisor for international affairs developing and overseeing all aspects of the Abu Dhabi project. Tate has been cited by Krens (2006) as an example of doing nationally – with two museum sites in London and ones in both Liverpool and St. Ives – what the Guggenheim was doing on a global scale: 'it is an opportunity to use its collection and to reach a wider audience, and that's essentially what is driving us'. The WKCD partnership bid with the Pompidou was also noted as interest by French cultural institutions to work with the Guggenheim in advancing global initiatives. The Louvre Abu Dhabi has been more contentious. The Louvre agreement – essentially €400 million to lease the Louvre name for 30 years and another €900 million for curatorial and technical expertise – provoked the ire of many art professionals in France and abroad. A key petition criticizing the Louvre Abu Dhabi was initiated on Didier Rykner's website, La Tribune de l'Art (latribunedelart.com): in short, the project is not based on research or increasing the understanding of works of art; rather it is an example of two nefarious pressures, namely mercenary commercialization of selling national heritage to generate private funds and expansionist polices of foreign affairs associated with oil and military defence contracts. Yet the Louvre Abu Dhabi represents a beginning in France. An international agency for museums – including the Louvre and the Pompidou, along with others such as the Musée d'Orsay, the Château de Versailles, the Musée Rodin, and the Musée du Quai Branly, which are government-owned cultural institutions – has been established, with seeking new international partners as part of the agency's remit. However, there is merit in how Azimi concluded her *Artforum* (April 2008) article on the new Middle East market for art:

> But at its best, it stands to pioneer a new sort of cosmopolitanism, linking the cultural capitals of Cairo and Beirut – to each other and to the rest of the world – and to reinvigorate a region that has been subject to one too many narratives of failure.

This self-referential perspective, of seeing the Middle East not as Other but as opening out to the world, has many benefits. Certainly there is a potential to present Islamic art.

■ ■ ■

The fashion for Impressionist and Post-Impressionist paintings during the 1980s, fuelled by Japanese corporations, gave way to the rise of contemporary art, during the last 15 years, a glamorous world of finance, property, luxury brands, and celebrity. *Artforum* (April 2008), in a stroke of great timing before the credit crisis, used Damien Hirst's *For the Love of God* (2007) – a life-size cast of a human skull made of platinum, diamonds (weighing a total of 1,106.18 carats), and human teeth, with a reported price tag of £50 million[14] – as the cover for a feature issue on 'Art and Its Markets'. Artists like Hirst, Jeff Koons, and Takashi Murakami were key examples of auction house darlings, with prices in excess of $1 million. Yet, as Robert Storr (*The Art Newspaper*, 8 February 2007), director of the 2007 Venice Biennale and dean of the Yale School of Art, reminds us this can distort perceptions:

Reducing art's commercial value to zero means other values can emerge, other transactions can occur in the currencies of the imagination and intellect . . . market values frequently have little or nothing to do with enduring aesthetic or art-historical values. They are barometers of taste which is nearly always conservative compared to the lasting pleasures and challenges art has to offer.

Storr was drawing reference to the traditional role of the museum in taking works out of the marketplace once and for all.

NOTES

1 Introduction to Arts Management

1 In 1994, the ACGB was split into three arts councils: the Arts Council of England (now Arts Council England), the Scottish Arts Council, and the Arts Council of Wales. The Arts Council of Northern Ireland was also created as a distribution body for government and National Lottery funding.

2 For example, in the USA, the National Endowment for the Arts was 'established by Congress in 1965 as an independent agency of the federal government'; it is 'dedicated to supporting excellence in the arts, both new and established; bringing the arts to all Americans; and providing leadership in arts education' and 'is the nation's largest annual funder of the arts, bringing great art to all 50 states, including rural areas, inner cities, and military bases' (nea.gov/about). In its obituary, the *New York Times* (5 July 2008) noted that USA Senator Jesse Helms 'turned his hard-edged conservatism against civil rights, gay rights, foreign aid and modern art'. Helms 'liked his art uncomplicated' and was a pivotal character in the cultural wars of the 1980s: Helms 'took on the National Endowment for the Arts for subsidizing art that he found offensive, chiefly that of the gay photographer Robert Mapplethorpe and of the artist Andres Serrano over his depiction of a crucifix submerged in urine. He later led an ill-fated attempt to take over CBS, exhorting conservatives to buy up stock in order to stop what he saw as a liberal bias in its news reporting'. One unanticipated outcome has been the increased aesthetic interest – and market value – in the work of Robert Mapplethorpe.

3 The Vilar Institute for Arts Management at the Kennedy Center no longer exists. Alberto Vilar, an investor and arts philanthropist (as a prominent patron of opera including the Royal Opera House, the Metropolitan Opera, and the Salzburg Music Festival), was convicted of securities fraud in November 2008. The case of Bernard Madoff, a fund manager and philanthropist associated with Jewish charities, which was revealed in December 2008, is similar.

4 For the sake of simplicity, the two terms not-for-profit and non-profit (also spelled as nonprofit) will be used interchangeably to distinguish from commercial or for-profit organizations. Not-for-profit (or voluntary) is a more correct term than non-profit: the former is explicit in stating that the organization's purpose is not to make a profit – even if it does so by indicating an absence – whereas the latter could infer an organization that was unsuccessful in not earning a profit. Indeed three sectors of the economy can be distinguished. The commercial or for-profit sector is distinguished by a direct exchange relationship between the seller and buyer. The public sector is based on the collection of

taxes by the state and redistribution for so-called public services. The third sector (also called not-for-profit or voluntary sector), which fills a gap between the first two, has been described as a form of humanistic service.

5 As a more recent example of autobiographical management text, management consultant turned arts manager Michael Kaiser (2008) examines his turnaround experiences at five performing arts: Kansas City Ballet, Alvin Ailey Dance Theater Foundation, American Ballet Theater, the Royal Opera House, and the John F. Kennedy Center for the Performing Arts, where he was president at the time.

6 This definition was established by the Department of Culture, Media and Sport (DCMS) in 1998, that is to say at the outset of the New Labour mandate.

7 See Florida's website at creativeclasses.com, which is billed as 'the source on how we live, work and play'. Accessed 13 May 2009.

8 A case against film as art boils down to one or more of four complaints: movies are commercial; they are collaborations, more committee work than the responsibility of a single artist; they are technological products; and they mix genres, according to Garry Wills (in Silvers 2001: 72).

9 Tomkins's essay was included in the catalogue to accompany the exhibition 'A Tribute to Leo Castelli' (16 April to 17 May 1985 at London's Mayor Gallery).

10 For a more favourable view of the relationship between commerce and culture, see Bayley (1989), based on an exhibition at the Design Museum.

11 See, for example, the 'Shopping: a century of art and consumer culture' exhibition at Tate Liverpool (20 December 2002 to 23 March 2003), which is archived at tate.org.uk/ liverpool/exhibitions/shopping.

12 In considering exhibition collaborations between American art museums and for-profit enterprises, three similar areas are broached by the AAMD (March 2006): mission (does this collaboration further or distract from the museum's mission? Will the collaboration enhance public access to important works of art? Do the motives of the for-profit affect the non-profit institution's critical judgment?); financial (will the partnership change philanthropic support for the museum? Does the partnership address the museum's costs?); and trust (could the collaboration affect the good name or reputation of the museum? Is the lending of works of art appropriate – and will the works be well protected?).

13 The others on the *Gramophone* list include the YouTube Symphony Orchestra, the Simón Bolivar Youth Orchestra (Venezuela), the China Philharmonic Orchestra, and the Soweto-based Buskaid Ensemble.

14 'The mission of the United Nations "Principles for Responsible Management Education" (PRME) initiative is to inspire and champion responsible management education, research and thought leadership globally. The PRME are inspired by internationally accepted values such as the principles of the United Nations Global Compact [see unglobalcompact.org]. They seek to establish a process of continuous improvement among institutions of management education in order to develop a new generation of business leaders capable of managing the complex challenges faced by business and society in the 21st century' (unprme.org). As such PRME is 'a timely global call for business schools and universities worldwide to gradually adapt their curricula, research, teaching methodologies and institutional strategies to the new business challenges and opportunities'

2 Arts and the State

1   In the USA, preeminent research institutions on arts and cultural policy include the Princeton (University) Center for Arts and Cultural Policy Studies, the Curb Center for Art, Enterprise, and Public Policy (Vanderbilt University), and the Tisch School of the Arts (New York University).

2   State-sanctioned lotteries with some of the proceeds used to support the arts (e.g. the UK's National Lottery has the arts as one of the five good causes) have been criticized as a regressive form of taxation. Citizens from low income groups have a higher relative consumption of lottery tickets – not least of all so-called scratch cards as a factor of total income relative to high income groups – yet low income groups have a relatively low arts participation rate.

3   Note that the National Gallery of Art, based in Washington, DC, was not established until 1936 through the private generosity of Andrew Mellon. High entry barriers to establish a world class art museum – important works of art for a permanent collection are expensive and scarce (i.e. many are already in public collections hence not offered for resale) – mean that the Getty Museum of Art is an exceptional case, with the Malibu villa completed in 1974 and a bequest of stock valued at $700 million, in 1976, following the death of J. Paul Getty.

4   A recent poll of music critics in the USA, Europe, and Asia by *Gramophone* (21 November 2008) listed seven USA orchestras in the top 20. The Chicago Symphony Orchestra led the USA at No. 5, with Amsterdam's Royal Concertgebouw Orchestra in the top spot, followed by the Berlin Philharmonic, the Vienna Philharmonic, and the London Symphony Orchestra. The appearance of the Los Angeles Philharmonic and San Francisco Symphony on the list is one indicator of the wealth bases along the Pacific Coast of the USA generated from the more recent industries of entertainment and information technology.

5   See the backgrounder on SWFs by Lee Hudson Teslik, dated 18 January 2008, for the Council on Foreign Relations (cfr.org/publication/15251).

6   There is a view that attacks on banking secrecy in Switzerland by the USA and EU during the global financial crisis are an attempt to loosen the economic spoils that have accrued to Swiss banks.

7   The American Statistical Association (ASA) is right to identify some issues which shape the administration and communication of surveys: 'People are accustomed to seeing results of surveys reported in the daily press, incorporated in advertising claims, and mentioned on numerous occasions by political analysts, social critics, and economic forecasters. Much less frequent, however, is any discussion of the reliability of these surveys or what is involved in carrying them out. The wealth of reported information may easily lull the user into assuming that surveys are easy to undertake, and to overlook the many steps involved in a properly-conducted survey. If technical issues are recognized, there is a frequent tendency to assume that they should be safely left to the survey expert. In fact, many of the surveys that appear in the daily press are conducted under great time pressure and with insufficient allowance for the many different aspects of the process that need to be controlled. Yet, unless the reader of these survey results is aware of what is involved in a survey, and what quality controls are needed, s(he) is unable to form any opinion of the confidence to be placed in the results, and usually is not even in a position to know what questions to ask about such surveys' (Ferber *et al.* 1980: preface); see Scheuren (2004) for an update on surveys from the ASA.

8   In 2006 White Cube returned to the West End (Mason's Yard, which is near Duke

Street, with 12,500 square feet of exhibition space), and now operates two galleries in London.

3 Business and the Arts

1   In *Frames of Mind*, Gardner (1983) offered seven intelligences. Valued in schools are *linguistic intelligence* (i.e. involves sensitivity to spoken and written language, the ability to learn languages, and the capacity to use language to accomplish certain goals) and *logical-mathematical intelligence* (i.e. consists of the capacity to analyse problems logically, carry out mathematical operations, and investigate issues scientifically). Associated with the arts are *musical intelligence* (i.e. involves skill in the performance, composition, and appreciation of musical patterns), *bodily-kinesthetic intelligence* (e.g. entails the potential of using one's whole body or parts of the body to solve problems), and *spatial intelligence* (i.e. involves the potential to recognize and use the patterns of wide space and more confined areas). Personal intelligences are valued by business: *interpersonal intelligence* is concerned with the capacity to understand the intentions, motivations, and desires of other people, which allows people to work effectively with others; and *intrapersonal intelligence* entails the capacity to understand oneself, to appreciate one's feelings, fears, and motivations, which involves having an effective working model of ourselves, and to be able to use such information to regulate our lives.

2   Of course, there is a level of faddishness based on advancing Gardner's work. The emotional intelligence (EI) contribution of Daniel Goleman, in the mid to late 1990s, may be viewed as a case in point. Goleman (1996) is credited with coining the term EI, an emotional dimension that extends beyond interpersonal skills. He proffered EI a determining factor in the effectiveness of leaders. As one progresses to more senior levels, EI rather than rational intelligence (i.e. raw intelligence as measured by IQ and technical expertise) marks out the successful leader. What still needs to be asked, though, is why 'softer' skills like sensitivity, self-awareness, and integrity are deemed to be wanting in corporate managers. The underlying belief that business is too cold remains to be addressed. From a more critical perspective, the coercive aspects of emotional intelligence have come under scrutiny (Fineman 1993). Does EI represent another disciplinary mechanism, one that focuses on the social engineering of emotions?

3   A similar plea is made by Peter Drucker (1990: x), who proffers 'a changed human-being' as the product of a not-for-profit organization.

4   'Liberal humanism has dwindled to the impotent consciousness of bourgeois society, gentle, sensitive and ineffectual', according to Terry Eagleton (1983: 199). As a Marxist literary theorist, Eagleton was taking aim at Northrop Frye (1967), then still alive, and F. R. Leavis. In particular, Eagleton was questioning two related points: the transformative powers attributed to art; and what it means to be a 'better person' as the result of art. Can a similar charge be made against Charles Handy who, like Frye, seeks to nurture spiritual wholeness in a hostile world? Yes, according to Gibson Burrell (1997: 27): 'Handy pocket theory with all its superficiality, ease of travel, liberal humanistic stance, technobabble language and fundamentally conservative political leaning . . . [and] all that consultancy-speak'.

5   See Czarniaska-Joerges and Guillet de Monthoux (1994) and Brawer (1998) as examples of novels and plays being introduced as part of management education.

6   There is an assumption that the arts are oppositional to sports and science. The arts represent a feminine response, in contrast to other – namely masculine – activities used by

management to enhance productivity, including outward bound weekends, and elite athletes on leadership, motivation, stress management, and team dynamics. Whereas the arts are viewed as soft and easy, science is viewed as serious, challenging, and difficult – but not creative. Of course, this represents a fundamental misunderstanding of the artistic process, and minimizes the creativity associated with scientific work.

7 Unilever wanted to create global platforms.

4 Ownership and Management of Arts Organizations

1 See Sotheby's 'Form 10-K Annual Report' (particularly Part 1, which is extremely instructive in outlining Sotheby's business model) and its 'Investor Briefing' presentation; available at sothebys.com under 'Investor Relations'.

2 The British Private Equity and Venture Capital Association (bvca.co.uk) has instructive documents for non-specialists including 'A Guide to Private Equity' and 'Reporting Guidelines'.

3 See Terra Firma's 'Annual Review 2007' – its first – which outlines the principles of its portfolio business; available at terrafirma.com.

4 The balance sheet is a snapshot of the company's assets at a point in time; it represents the mass of assets used to generate a profit. The income (or profit/loss) statement shows the gains and losses of the company between a period of time bounded by two balance sheets. It measures total income and deducts total costs.

    A statement of cash flow, which links the income statement and two balance sheets, is of increasing importance – even before the current credit crisis.

    Short-term solvency highlights that liquidity is necessary for survival, which is to say that insufficient liquidity can lead to bankruptcy. Long-term solvency measures an ability to meet obligations to pay interest and principal on long-term debt. Debt is senior to equity in liquidation (thus interest before dividends). Profitability measures are based on sales (such as profit margin, which is an indication of the effectiveness of management and efficiency of operations) and returns on both assets (RoA) and equity (RoE).

5 EPS = Net Income ÷ Number of Common Shares. The P/E ratio = Stock Price ÷ EPS.

6 Gordon Gekko's 'greed is good' speech, at the annual general meeting of Teldar Paper, in *Wall Street* (1987) is couched in the rhetoric of Adam Smith.

7 A critique of the capitalist system that emerged by the start of the twenty-first century is offered in Joel Bakan's *The Corporation: the pathological pursuit of profit and power* (2004); see accompanying website thecorporation.com.

8 The owner wishing to sell their work of art has four principal options: sale or consignment to, or private sale by, an art dealer; consignment to, or private sale by, an auction house; private sale to a collector or museum without the use of an intermediary; or for certain categories of property (in particular, collectibles) consignment to, or private sale through, an internet-based service (such as eBay). The more valuable the property, the more likely it is that the owner will consider more than one option and will solicit proposals from more than one potential purchaser or agent, particularly if the seller is a fiduciary representing an estate or trust (Sotheby's 'Form 10-K' 2008: 3).

9 A complex array of factors may influence the seller's decision: the level and breadth of expertise of the dealer or auction house with respect to the property; the extent of the prior relationship, if any, between the dealer or auction house and its staff and the seller; the reputation and historic level of achievement by the dealer or auction house in attaining high sale prices in the property's specialized category; the desire for privacy on the part of

clients; the amount of cash offered by a dealer, auction house, or other purchaser to purchase the property outright, which is greatly influenced by the amount and cost of capital resources available to such parties; the level of auction guarantees or the terms of other financial options offered by auction houses; the level of pre-sale estimates offered by auction houses; the desirability of a public auction in order to achieve the maximum possible price (a particular concern for fiduciary sellers, such as trustees and executors); the amount of commission charged by dealers or auction houses to sell a work on consignment; the cost, style, and extent of presale marketing and promotion to be undertaken by a dealer or auction house; recommendations by third parties consulted by the seller; and the availability and extent of related services, such as tax or insurance appraisals and short-term financing (Sotheby's 'Form 10-K' 2008: 3).

10 The consignor's commission rate is on a sliding scale, which can range from 0 to 20 per cent; it is based on combined annual sales of property and the bargaining power of the consignor. In addition to the commission, the consignor tends to be charged expenses for illustration and insurance costs. The buyer of the property purchased pays a buyer's premium in addition to the hammer price. The rate of the premium – approximately 25–10 per cent on a sliding scale, from high to low – is disclosed in the auction catalogue. Thus the purchase price is the hammer price plus the buyer's premium; the buyer is also subject to sales or value added taxes on the premium.

11 Private treaty sales can offer privacy not associated with a public auction and represents an auctioneer acting like a dealer. For consignors, a leading auctioneer can tap into a global network of collectors (both individuals and institutions).

12 Christie's purchased Haunch of Venison, a leading dealer of contemporary art.

13 See the Antitrust Division of the USA Department of Justice (usdoj.gov/atr/public/press releases) to track the Sotheby's/Christie's case, one of classic cartel behaviour in price fixing, which received high media attention. It represented a conspiracy lasting more than six years, from April 1993 to December 1999, to suppress and eliminate competition by fixing prices in violation of the Sherman Act. Sotheby's and Christie's, as co-conspirators, also agreed to limit or eliminate other inducements to sellers, such as interest-free loans and charitable donations. In 2000, Sotheby's 'agreed to plead guilty and pay a $45 million criminal fine for fixing the price of commission rates charged to sellers of art, antiques, and other collectibles at auctions'; and 'the company's former president and chief executive officer, Diana D. Brooks, has also agreed to plead guilty to price fixing charges, and will cooperate with the Department's ongoing antitrust investigation' (5 October 2000). A year later, the former chairmen of Sotheby's and Christie's were indicted in an international price fixing conspiracy (2 May 2001). Taubman, former chairman of Sotheby's, was convicted of price fixing due, in part, to testimony from Christie's former chief executive officer, Christopher Davidge, who received amnesty. At the time of Taubman's conviction – jailed for one year and fined $7.5 million – he was the controlling shareholder of Sotheby's. Sir Anthony Tennant, Christie's former chairman, refused to travel to the USA, and there were no means for the Department of Justice to seek his extradition. To settle civil litigation of $512 million, Sotheby's and Christie's spilt the penalty; Taubman paid $156 million of Sotheby's share via Sotheby's shares. In May 2003, as part of civil litigation, Sotheby's issued vendor's commission discount certificates with a face value of $62.5 million.

14 On its website (tate.org.uk), Tate provides information on its governance structure as part of FAQs): 'Tate is a Non-Departmental Public Body (NDPB), whose prime sponsor is the Department for Culture, Media and Sport (DCMS). A NDPB is a body which has a role in the process of national government but is not a government department or part of one, and

operates at arm's length from Ministers'. 'Whilst we are not directly regulated by the Charity Commission, exempt charities like Tate can ask the Charity Commission to use some of the powers the Commission has over all charities. For example, in a case of potential trustee benefit (where a trustee may benefit directly or indirectly from Tate), we consult the Charity Commission to ensure the matter is handled appropriately. In certain cases, the Commission may provide us with an "Order" which grants us specific legal powers'.

15 The following is edited from the British Museum: The BM was created due to the generosity of Sir Hans Sloane (1660–1753), who offered his collection of books, manuscripts, and natural history specimens to King George II (reigned 1727–60) for the sum of £20,000, so that they would belong to the nation. However, the trustees had to appeal directly to the British Parliament. Many MPs saw an opportunity to establish a national museum. The British Museum Act was passed on 7 June 1753 (and remained in force until the British Museum Act of 1963). It created the BM in order to house the Sloane, Cotton and Harleian Collections, and set up a governing board of trustees.

16 The case of Elizabeth Esteve-Coll, who left the Victoria & Albert Museum (V&A) in 1995 during her second term as director to become one of the few women university vice-chancellors in the UK, addresses gender imbalances; it also highlights an individual with a non-traditional background who became director of a major art museum. Esteve-Coll was educated at Darlington Girls High School and completed her BA at Birkbeck College (i.e. the University of London college catering to mature or continuing education students) in 1976. Her primary career experience before moving to the V&A, in 1985, as keeper of the National Art Library was in higher education (head of learning resources at Kingston Polytechnic and then university librarian at the University of Surrey). In 1988, Esteve-Coll was appointed director of the V&A; the first woman to head a 'national museum and gallery' in the UK. Media attention by those hostile to her appointment became even more barbed and aggressive following the proposed 1989 restructuring, which focused on her background as a librarian without significant art history and curatorial experience. A femme-to-femme comparison, made by Sir John Pope-Hennessey (former director of the BM and the V&A), was a classic case of vitriol: 'There is an excellent precedent for appointing a woman as director: one of the most efficient and successful is Anne d'Harnoncourt, the director of the Philadelphia Museum of Art. I do not know Mrs. Esteve-Coll personally, but she is clearly in an altogether different and inferior class. . . . It would be generally conceded that there is a point beneath which no museum should debase itself. But not Mrs. Esteve-Coll, who with a crude publicity campaign and exhibitions like that of the collection of Elton John, has added a new meaning to the phrase, "She stoops to conquer" ' (*NYRB*, 27 April 1989: 13).

5 Arts Consumption and Consumers

1 It is instructive to distinguish between visitor/audience surveys and arts participation studies (see the National Endowment for the Arts-supported document by AMS Planning and Research 1995). Each has different purposes and methodologies. Audience surveys concentrate on known attenders, and are often limited to a sole arts organization; as such, attention is paid to a marketing agenda (e.g. to assess audience satisfaction levels or alternative subscription packages), or to measure the expenditure made by audience members as part of an economic impact study. The tradition of audience surveys among arts museums is more entrenched than for any other type of arts institutions, according to Schuster (1991). Pioneering work in arts research by the French sociologist Pierre Bourdieu,

for example, focused on the art museum. In many respects, the art museum serves as a proxy for arts organizations in the conventional sense. The art museum is rightly viewed as among the most complex, powerful, and successful of modern socio-political institutions. Art museums help to shape public perceptions concerning the meaning and role of art, and have been characterized as one of the most broadly resonant metaphors of our time. On the other hand, arts participation studies focus on the general population; both users and non-users of all types of arts programmes are included in the sample; and the research is often to aid policy development. The most well-known example is the Survey of Public Participation in the Arts (SPPA), a nationwide survey in the USA conducted by the National Endowment for the Arts, to gauge participation rates for arts and non-arts activities; time series data is available (surveys have been conducted in 1982, 1985, 1992, 1999, and 2002).

2 The London Consortium includes 'Cultures of Collecting' as a course unit on its masters and doctoral programme in humanities and culture studies; see londonconsortium.com/courses/culturesofcollecting.

6 Managing for Excellence and Artistic Integrity

1 Education and social origins, the dominant factors to predict visiting art museums, were also important in identifying art museum directors. DiMaggio (1988: 12) noted that art museum directors were 'predominantly upper middle class'; there was a highly select list of universities based on highly-rated art history departments (including the important role of Williams College). Fields with only one portal tend to recruit individuals with similar backgrounds, socialization, and values into important positions, which ensures that the such individuals fit easily into the roles available to them, according to DiMaggio (1988: 16–17), thus art museum directors entered the art museum field following completion of studies (43 per cent) or came from university teaching (25 per cent).

2 In a similar manner, Billy Bragg (London *Guardian*, 11 April 2009) wrote: 'While others chose to respond to Thatcherism with escapist songs and consumerist imagery, I was unable to escape the reality she had created. Try as I might to resist her, she provided the backdrop for all the songs I wrote in that turbulent period'.

3 Of course, there were earlier art movements outside of New York such as Neo-Expressionism (Germany) and the Transavantegarde (Italy) of the late 1970s and early 1980s.

7 Financial Investing in the Arts

1 Dover Books had the good sense of market timing to reissue these three books following the bursting of the dotcom bubble at the end of the 1990s.

2 An auction guarantee to consignors is a minimum price in connection with the sale of an object at auction; in the event that the object sells for less than the minimum price (auction guarantee), the auctioneer must fund the difference between the sale price at auction and the amount of the auction guarantee. If the object does not sell, the amount of the guarantee must be paid, but the auctioneer has the right to recover such amount through the future sale of the object. The auctioneer is obligated under the terms of certain auction guarantees to advance a portion of the guaranteed amount prior to the auction. This suggests that consignors benefit from a guarantee as the auctioneer assumes risk. However, most guarantees include a profit-sharing incentive for the auctioneer: for example, if the hammer price exceeds the auction guarantee, the auctioneer is generally entitled to a share of negotiated proceeds.

3 The reserve is the minimum price a consignor will accept for the lot to be sold at auction that has been negotiated in advance the auctioneer. The amount is not formally disclosed. The reserve cannot exceed the low estimate and is usually within 20 per cent of the low estimate. A lot that does not reach its reserve is bought in.

4 Mei and Moses created a consultancy, Beautiful Asset Advisors (artasanasset.com), with the Mei Moses Fine Art Index as a product.

5 Since then a second art fund, TFAFII, a Chinese Fine Art Fund, an Indian Fine Art Fund, and a Middle Eastern Fine Art Fund have been launched. See thefineartfund.com.

6 MAP press release, dated 21 February 2008, on launch of the new emerging markets art fund and meridianartpartners.com.

7 See v22london.com and v22plc.com.

8 PLUS markets, formerly known as Ofex, is a Recognised Investment Exchange (RIE) in the UK for small cap shares; its closest competitor is AIM. The market capitalization of V22 in April 2009 was £390,000 with mid-trading at 2.0 pence.

9 SOLT (solt.co.uk) was previously known as the Society of West End Theatres (SWET) until the name change in 1994.

10 A copy of the agreement between the producer and the author (the *licence*) is available for inspection at solicitors by appointment.

11 The Gabriel Fund in the UK, which represented a relatively modest way to enter the world of theatre angels, had a short lifespan in the 1990s.

8 Globalization and the Art World

1 For its supporters, globalization means spreading liberal democracy with political freedom linked to consumer choice. Critics of globalization (such as Naomi Klein, Joel Bakan, George Monbiot, and Adbusters) focus on the disembowelling public power. Though a brand is described as a distinguishing name or symbol (often in tandem) intended to identify the products of one firm and to differentiate the firm's offering from that of competitors, the tyranny of brands suggests that brands focus on 'meaning' not product attributes, and global brands restrict genuine choice by eliminating indigenous competitors. An emphasis on consumption devalues production by emphasizing the developing world's so-called free trade zones. Finally, branding is a balloon economy: it inflates with astonishing rapidity, but it is full of hot air.

2 Other passion investments include luxury collectibles (e.g. automobiles, boats, and jets) and sports investments (e.g. sports teams, sailing, and racehorses).

3 More recent writers include artist and critic Martha Rosler (1997), art market reporter Louisa Buck (2004), economic sociologist Olav Velthuis (2005), collector Adam Lindemann (2006), marketer Don Thompson (2008), and sociologist Sarah Thornton (2008).

4 Some primary market public dealers, particularly ones based in Europe, prefer the term gallerist, which has a less explicit reference to market transactions.

5 Private dealers do not operate a retail gallery space open to the general public. Private dealing tends to take place at the outset of a career in art dealing, when the costs of retail space may be too high, and near the end of a successful career as a gallerist (primary market public dealer).

6 The first day of the sale coincided with the collapse of the investment bank Lehman Brothers. Hirst's share from the sale was £95.7 million.

7 In the case of dead artists, reputations may have been established, though market taste can move the market value of individual artists up or down for time.

8　See McCarthy *et al.* (2005) for verification based on the current experience in the USA.

9　Prominent representation at leading contemporary art fairs – Art Basel, Art Basel Miami Beach, and the Frieze Art Fair – is instructive. Interviews with contemporary art dealers (de Coppet and Jones 1984; Lindemann 2006), *Art Review*'s Power 100, current advertising space in *Artforum*, the ranking of artists by Artfacts, lists of artists and dealer representation from Artnet, and consultation with colleagues at Sotheby's Institute of Art were also used. Establishing a working list of 25 contemporary art dealers would represent approximately 10 per cent of the dealers represented at Frieze (150+), Art Basel Miami Beach (250+), and Art Basel (300+) – that is to say the elite from an already highly select group. Art Basel and Art Basel Miami Beach also includes dealers (e.g. Acquavella, Daniel Blau, Richard Gray, Hopkins-Custot, Annely Juda, Marlborough, Moeller, Odematt-Vedovi, Sperone Westwater, Waddington, and Michael Werner) who are more focused on secondary dealing.

10　The Royal Academy of Arts has served as a focal point for London's traditional art trade, bounded by Christie's to the south and Sotheby's to the north.

11　In 2006, Gagosian opened a second London gallery, in the West End.

12　See the post-Pompidou analysis by Davis (1990), which appeared before the Guggenheim Bilbao, to trace the developments in museum and non-specialist audiences through architecture.

13　Azimi cites the Sharjah Biennial, established in 1993, under the directorship of Sheikha Hoor Al Qasimi, daughter of the ruling sheikh, as an exception. With respect to auction houses, Christie's and Bonhams operate in Dubai, which is also the site for Art Dubai, the leading art fair in the Middle East; Sotheby's has selected Doha, capital of Qatar, which is home to the Museum of Islamic Art.

14　The work was the centrepiece at White Cube (Mason's Yard) for Hirst's solo exhibition, 'Beyond Belief' (2007).

BIBLIOGRAPHY

The following is a working bibliography. Note that references to newspapers and journals – *IHT* (*International Herald Tribune*), *FT* (*Financial Times*), *IHT* (*International Herald Tribune*), *NYRB* (*New York Review of Books*), *WSJ* (*Wall Street Journal*), and *WSJE* (*Wall Street Journal Europe*) – and other like sources are cited as part of the main text. References to annual reports and other financial documents associated with individuals firms are noted in the main text. Institutional websites are also identified as part of the main text, or as part of discursive endnotes.

AAMD [Association of Art Museum Directors]. (2001) 'Revenue generation: an investment in the public service of art museums' (October).

———. (2006) 'Exhibition collaborations between American art museums and for-profit enterprises' (March).

———. (2006) 'Good governance and non-profit integrity' (June).

———. (2007) 'Art museums, private collectors, and the public benefit' (January).

———. (2007) 'Managing the relationship between art museums and corporate sponsors' (May).

ADAA [Art Dealers Association of America]. (2000) *Collector's Guide to Working With Artists*, New York: AADA.

Aaker, D. (1991) *Managing Brand Equity: capitalizing on the value of a brand name*, New York: Free Press.

———. (1995) *Building Strong Brands*, New York: Free Press.

Aaker, D. and Joachimsthaler, E. (2000) *Brand Leadership: building assets in an information economy*, New York: Free Press.

Abbing, H. (2002) *Why Are Artists Poor?: the exceptional economy of the arts*, Amsterdam: Amsterdam University Press.

Adizes, I. (ed.) (1972) 'Administering for the Arts' [special section], *California Management Review* (Winter): 99+.

Adorno, T. (1973; original German 1949) *The Philosophy of Modern Music*, trans. A. Mitchell and W. Blomster, New York: Seabury.

———. (1978; original German 1960) 'Culture and administration', trans. W. Blomster, reprinted in *Telos* (Fall): 93–111.

———. (1991) *The Culture Industry: selected essays on mass culture*, ed. and intro. J. M. Bernstein, London: Routledge.

Alessi, A. (1998) *The Dream Factory: Alessi since 1921*, Cologne: Konemann.

Alpers, S. (1995) *The Making of Rubens*, New Haven and London: Yale University Press.

Alsop, J. (1982) *The Rare Tradition: the history of art collecting and its linked phenomena*, [Princeton University Press] Bollinger Series 25, New York: Harper and Row.

Altshuler, B. (1994) *The Avant-Garde in Exhibition: new art in the twentieth century*, Berkeley and Los Angeles: University of California Press.

Alvesson, M. and Willmott, H. (eds) (1992) *Critical Management Studies*, London: Sage.

Amabile, T. (1998) 'How to kill creativity', *Harvard Business Review* (September/October): 76–87.

Amabile, T., Hadley, C., and Kramer, S. (2002) 'Creativity under the gun', *Harvard Business Review* (August): 52–61.

Amabile, T. and Khaire, M. (2008) 'Creativity and the role of the leader', *Harvard Business Review* (October): 100–109.

Andreasen, A. (1982) 'Non-profits: check your attention to customers', *Harvard Business Review* (May/June): 105–10.

Ansoff, H. I. (1965) *Corporate Strategy: an analytical approach to business policy for growth and expansion*, New York: McGraw Hill.

Appignanesi, L. (ed.) (1984) *Culture and the State*, London: Institute of Contemporary Arts.

Arnold, B. (2009) 'Caslon Analytics art funds note', http://www.caslon.com.au/artfundsnote. htm. Accessed 13 May 2009.

Arnold, M. (1932; original 1869) *Culture and Anarchy*, Cambridge: Cambridge University Press.

BHB [British Horseracing Board]. (2005) *Guide to Co-Ownership of Racehorses*, London: BHB.

——. (2006) *The Thrill of Ownership: a practical guide to owning a racehorse*, London: BHB.

BVCA [British Private Equity and Venture Capital Association]. (2004) *A Guide to Private Equity*, London: BVCA.

Bagozzi, R. (1975) 'Marketing as exchange', *Journal of Marketing* (October). 32–39.

Bailey, G. (1989) 'Amateurs imitate, professionals steal', *Journal of Aesthetics and Art Criticism* (Summer): 221–27.

Bakan, J. (2004) *The Corporation: the pathological pursuit of profit and power*, Toronto: Viking Canada.

Bales, C. and Pinnavaia, S. (2001) 'Art for more than art's sake', *McKinsey Quarterly* (no. 1): 59–67.

Baltzell, E.D. (1964) *The Protestant Establishment*, New York: Vintage Books.

Barasch, M. (1985) *Theories of Art: from Plato to Winckelmann*, New York and London: New York University Press.

Barenboim, D. and Said, E. (2004) *Parallels and Paradox: explorations in music and society*, London: Bloomsbury.

Barnouw, E. (1978) *The Sponsor: notes on a modern potentate*, New York: Oxford University Press.

Barragán, P. (2008) *The Art Fair Age*, Milan: Charta.

Bartels, R. (1968) 'The general theory of marketing', *Journal of Marketing* (January): 29–33.

Bataille, G. (1986; original French 1930) 'Museums', trans. A. Michelson, reprinted in *October* 36 (Spring): 25.

Battcock, G. (ed.) (1973) *The New Art*, New York: E. P. Dutton.

Baudrillard, J. (1994; original French 1968) 'The system of collecting', trans by R. Cardinal in Elsner and Cardinal (ed.) (1994): 7–24.

Baumol, W. (1986) 'Unnatural value: or art investment as floating crap game', *American Economic Review* 76 (May): 10–14.

Baumol, W. and Bowen, W. (1965) 'On the performing arts: the anatomy of their economic problems', *American Economic Review* (May): 495–502.

——. (1966) *The Performing Arts, the economic dilemma: a study of problems common to theater, opera, music, and dance*, Twentieth Century Fund Report, Cambridge, MA: Cambridge University Press.

Bayley, S. (ed.) (1989) *Commerce and Culture*, London: Fourth Estate in association with the Design Museum.

Bazin, G. (1967) *The Museum Age*, trans. J. van Nuis Cahill, New York: Universe Books.

Becker, H. (1982) *Art Worlds*, Berkeley: University of California Press.

Belk, R. (1995) *Collecting in a Consumer Society*, New York: Routledge.

Belk, R., Wallendorf, M, Sherry, J., Holbrook, M, and Roberts, S. (1988) 'Collectors and collecting', *Advances in Consumer Research* (vol. 15): 548–53.

Benjamin, W. (1969) *Illuminations*, trans. H. Zohn, ed. and intro. H. Arendt, New York: Schocken Books.

Bennett, O. (ed.) (1995) *Cultural Policy and Management in the United Kingdom: proceedings of an international symposium*, Coventry: Centre for the Study of Cultural Policy, University of Warwick.

Berger, J. (1972) *Ways of Seeing*, London: BBC and Harmondsworth: Penguin Books.

Besharov, G. (2005) 'The outbreak of the cost disease: Baumol and Bowen's founding of cultural economics', *History of Political Economy* 37(3): 413–30.

Berle, A. and Means, C. (1968: original 1932) *The Modern Corporation and Private Property*, second edn, New York: Harcourt, Brace.

Beswick, T., Creamer, A., and Pinard, M. (2004) *(Re)Educating for Leadership: how the arts improve business*, London: A&B.

Bianchi, F. (ed.) (1993) *Cultural Policy and Urban Regeneration: the west European experience*, Manchester: Manchester University Press.

Blau, J. (1991) 'The disjunctive history of U.S. museums: 1869–1980', *Social Forces* (September): 87–105.

Blaug, M. (ed.) (1976) *The Economics of the Arts*, London: Martin Robertson.

Blom, P. (2002) *To Have and to Hold: an intimate history of collectors and collecting*, London: Allen Lane.

Bois, Y.-A., Crimp, D. and Krauss, R. (1984) 'A conversation with Hans Haacke', *October* 30 (Fall): 23–48.

Boulding, K. (1972) 'Toward the development of a cultural economics', *Social Science Quarterly* (September): 267–84.

Bourdieu, P. (1984; original French 1979) *Distinction: a social critique of the judgement of taste*, trans. R. Nice, London: Routledge & Kegan Paul.

Bourdieu, P. and Darbel, A. (1991; original French 1969) *For the Love of Art*, trans. N. Merriman and C. Beattie, London: Polity Press.

Bourdieu, P. and Haacke, H. (1995) *Free Exchange*, trans. R. Johnson, Cambridge: Polity.

Bower, J., Bartlett, C., Uyterhoeven, H., and Walton, R. (1995) *Business Policy: managing strategic processes*, eighth edn, Homewood, IL: Irwin.

Bradshaw, A. and Holbrook, M (2007), 'Remembering Chet: Theorising the mythology of the self-destructive bohemian artist as self-producer and self-consumer in the market for romanticism', *Marketing Theory* 7(2): 115–36.

Brawer, R. (1998) *Fictions of Business: insights on management from great literature*, New York: John Wiley.

Brighton, A. (ed.) (2002) 'The rise and rise of management discourse', special issues of *Critical Quarterly* 44(3–4).

Brooke, J. (1989) *Discerning Tastes: Montreal collectors 1880–1920*, Montreal: Montreal Museum of Fine Arts.

Brown, S. (1995) *Postmodern Marketing*, London and New York: Routledge.

Brown, S. and Patterson, A. (eds) (2000) *Imagining Marketing: arts, aesthetics, and the avant-garde*, London and New York: Routledge.

Buck, L. (2004) *Market Matters: the dynamics of the contemporary art world*, London: Arts Council England.

Bullock, A. and Trombley, S. (eds) (1999) *The New Fontana Dictionary of Modern Thought*, third edn, London: HarperCollins.

Burnham, J. (1971) 'Hans Haacke's cancelled show at the Guggenheim', *Artforum* (June): 67–71.

Burrell, G. (1989) 'The absent center: the neglect of philosophy in Anglo–American management theory', *Human Systems Management* 8: 307–12.

——. (1992) 'The organization of pleasure', in Alvesson and Willmott (eds) (1992): 66–89.

——. (1997) *Pandemonium: towards a retro-organization theory*, London: Sage.

Byrnes, W. (2008) *Management and the Arts*, fourth edn, Boston and London: Focal Press.

Capgemini and Merrill Lynch. (2008) *World Wealth Report*. Merrill Lynch and Capgemini.

Carret, P. (2004; original 1930) *The Art of Speculation*, Mineola, NY: Dover Publications.

Carrier, D. (2006) *Museum Skepticism: a history of the display of art in public galleries*, Durham, NC and London: Duke University Press.

Catry, B. (2003) 'The great pretenders: the magic of luxury goods', *Business Strategy Review* (September): 10–17.

Caves, R. (2000) *Creative Industries: controversies between art and commerce*, Cambridge, MA and London: Harvard University Press.

Celant, G. (1985) *The European Iceberg: creativity in Germany and Italy today*, Toronto: Art Gallery of Ontario and Milan: Mazzotta.

Chadwick, W. (ed.) (1995) *Confessions of the Guerrilla Girls*, New York: HarperCollins.

Chagy, G. (ed.) (1970) *Business in the Arts*, New York: Paul S. Erikson.

Chandler, A. (1962) *Strategy and Structure: chapters in the history of the industrial enterprise*, Cambridge, MA: MIT Press.

——. (1977) *The Visible Hand: the managerial revolution in American business*, Cambridge, MA: Harvard University Press.

——. (1990) *Scale and Scope: dynamics of industrial capitalism*, Cambridge, MA: Harvard University Press.

Chong, D. (1997) 'Hans Haacke on museum management', *Museum Management and Curatorship* (16/3): 273–85.

——. (1998) 'A new name for the V&A?: in response to Alan Borg', *Museum Management and Curatorship* (17/4): 419–28.

——. (1999) 'A "family of galleries": repositioning the Tate Gallery', *Museum Management and Curatorship* (18/2): 145–57.

——. (2000) 'Why critical writers on the arts and management matter', *Studies in Cultures, Organizations and Societies* (6): 225–41.

——. (2003) 'Revisiting business and the arts', *Journal of Nonprofit and Public Sector Marketing* (11/1): 151–65.

Chong, D and Trappey, R. (2001) 'Privately held and managing well: the English Chamber Orchestra at 40', *International Journal of Arts Management* 3(2): 16–26.

Clark, K. (1969) *Civilisation: a personal view*, London: BBC and John Murray.

Colbert, F. (1994) *Marketing Culture and the Arts*, Montreal and Paris: Morin.

Conger, J. (1998) 'The necessary art of persuasion', *Harvard Business Review* (May/June): 84–95.

Coombs, D. (ed.) (1986) 'What price arts sponsorship?' Unpublished transcript.

Court, D., Freeling, A., Leiter, M., and Parsons, A. (1997) 'If Nike can "just do it" why can't we', *McKinsey Quarterly* (no. 3): 24–34.

Court, D., Leiter, M., and Loch, D. (1999) 'Brand leverage', *McKinsey Quarterly* (no. 2): 100–116.

Coutu, D. (2001) 'A conversation with literary critic Harold Bloom', *Harvard Business Review* (May/June): 63–68.

Cowen, T. (1998) *In Praise of Commercial Culture*, Cambridge, MA and London: Harvard University Press.

——. (2004) *How the United States Funds the Arts*, Washington, DC: National Endowment for the Arts.

——. (2006) *Good and Plenty: the creative successes of American arts funding*, Princeton, NJ: Princeton University Press.

Crimp, D. (1993) *On the Museum's Ruins*, Cambridge, MA and London: MIT Press.

Cuno, J. (ed.) (2004) *Whose Muse? art museums and the public trust*, Princeton, NJ: Princeton University Press.

Currid, E. (2007) *The Warhol Economy: how fashion, art, and music drive New York City*, Princeton, NJ: Princeton University Press.

Czarniawska, B. (1999) *Writing Management: organization theory as a literary genre*, Oxford: Oxford University Press.

Czarniawska-Joerges, B. and Guillet de Monthoux, P. (eds) (1994) *Good Novels, Better Management: reading organizational realities in fiction*, Chur, Switzerland: Harwood Academic.

DCMS/V&A [Department of Culture, Media and Sport / Victoria & Albert Museum] (2003) 'Three year funding agreement (2003–6) between the Department of Culture, Media and Sport and Victoria & Albert Museum'.

Damisch, H. (1989) 'The museum device: notes on institutional change', *Lotus International* 35: 4–11.

Danto, A. (1964) 'The artworld', *Journal of Philosophy* 61 (October): 571–84.

Darcy, E. (2007) 'because i'm inane' (20 October), newburydiaries.blogspot.com.

Davies, S. (1994) *By Popular Demand*, London: Museums and Galleries Commission.

Davis, D. (1990) *The Museum Transformed: design and culture in the post-Pompidou age*, New York: Abbeville Press.

De Coppet, L. and Jones, A. (eds) (1984) *The Art Dealers: the powers behind the scene talk about the business of art*, New York: Clarkson N. Potter.

Di Cicco, P.G. (2007) *Municipal Mind: manifesto for the creative city*, Toronto: Mansfield Press.

Diggle, K. (1984) *Guide to Arts Marketing*, London: Rhinegold.

DiMaggio, P. (1988) *Managers of the Arts*, Research Division Report 2, Washington, DC: National Endowment for the Arts.

DiMaggio, P. (ed.) (1986) *Nonprofit Enterprise in the Arts: studies in mission and constraint*, Oxford: Oxford University Press.

——. (ed.) (2001) *The Twenty-First Century Firm: changing economic organization in international perspective*, Princeton and Oxford: Princeton University Press.

DiMaggio, P. and Anheier, H. (1990) 'The sociology of nonprofit organizations and sectors', *Annual Review of Sociology* (vol. 16): 137–59.

DiMaggio, P. and Powell, W. (1983) 'The iron cage revisited: institutional isomorphism and collective rationality in organizational fields', *American Sociological Review* (vol. 48): 147–60.

DiMaggio, P. and Useem, M. (1978a) *Audience Studies of the Performing Arts and Museums:*

critical review, Research Division Report 9, Washington, DC: National Endowment for the Arts.

——. (1978b) 'Social class and arts consumption: the origins and consequences of class differences in exposure to the arts in America', *Theory and Society* (March): 141–61.

——. (1980) 'The arts in education and cultural participation: the social role of aesthetic education and the arts', *Journal of Aesthetic Education* (October): 55–72.

Dorian, F. (1964) *Commitment to Culture: art patronage in Europe; its significance for America*, Pittsburgh, PA: University of Pittsburgh Press.

Douglas, M. (1979) *The World of Goods: towards an anthropology of consumption*, New York: Basic Books.

Doyle, P. (1998) *Marketing Management and Strategy*, second edn, London: Prentice Hall.

Drucker, H. (2000) 'Wanted: UK venture philanthropists', http://www.philanthropyuk.org/Resources/Venturephilanthropy/Relatedpublications. Accessed 13 May 2009.

Drucker, P. (1954) *The Practice of Management*, New York: Harper and Row.

——. (1989) 'What business can learn from nonprofits', *Harvard Business Review* (July/August): 88–93.

——. (1990) *Managing the Not-Profit Organization*, Oxford: Butterworth Heinemann.

Duncan, C. (1989) 'The MoMA's hot mamas', *Art Journal* (Summer): 171–78.

——. (1995) *Civilizing Rituals: inside public art museums*, London and New York: Routledge.

Duncan, C. and Wallach, A. (1978) 'The Museum of Modern Art as late capitalist ritual', *Marxist Perspectives* (Winter): 28–51.

——. (1980) 'The universal survey museum', *Art History* (December): 448–69.

Eagleton, T. (1983) *Literary Theory: an introduction*, Minneapolis: University of Minnesota Press.

Eells, R. (1967) *The Corporation and the Arts*, New York: Macmillan.

Ehrenreich, B. and Ehrenreich, J. (1979) 'The professional-managerial class', in P. Walker (ed.) *Between Labour and Capital*, Hassocks: Harvester Press: 5–45.

Elsen, A. (1989) 'Museum blockbusters: assessing the pros and cons', *Art in America* (June): 24–27.

Elsner, J. and Cardinal. R. (eds) (1994) *The Cultures of Collecting*, London: Reaktion Books.

English Chamber Orchestra [ECO]. (1983) *ECO: into the eighties*, London: Spencedata.

Enis, B., Cox, K. and Mokwa, M. (eds) (1991) *Marketing Classics: a selection of influential articles*, eighth edn, Upper Saddle River, NJ: Prentice Hall.

Ewen, S. (1988) *All Consuming Images: the politics of style in contemporary culture*, New York: Basic Books.

Eyre, R. (1998) *The Future of Lyric Theatre in London*, London: HMSO.

Falk, J. (1998) 'Visitors: who does, who doesn't, and why', *Museum News* (March/April): 38–43.

Feingold, M. (1987) 'Philanthropy, pomp, and patronage: historical reflections upon the endowment of culture', *Daedalus* (Winter): 157–78.

Feldstein, M. (ed.) (1991) *The Economics of Art Museums*, Chicago and London: University of Chicago Press.

Ferber, R., Sheatsley, P., Turner, A., and Waksberg, J. (1980) *What is a Survey?*, Washington, DC: American Statistical Association.

Fillis, I. and Rentschler, R. (2006) *Creative Marketing: an extended metaphor for marketing in a new age*, London: Palgrave Macmillan.

Fineman, S. (1993) *Emotions in Organizations*, London: Sage.

Finn, D. (1984) 'Is there a legitimate role for public relations in the arts?', *Annals of the American Academy of Political and Social Science* (January): 57–66.

Fisher, M. and Worpole, K. (eds) (1988) *City Centres, City Cultures: the role of the arts in the revitalization of towns and cities*, Manchester: Centre for Local Economic Strategies.

Fitzgibbon, M. and Kelly, A. (eds) (1997) *From Maestro to Manager: critical issues in arts and cultural management*, Dublin: Oak Tree Press.

Flores, F. and Gray, J. (2000) *Entrepreneurship and the Wired Life: work in the wake of careers*, London: Demos.

Florida, R. (2002) *The Rise of the creative Class: and how it is transforming work, leisure, community and everyday life*, New York: Basic Books.

——. (2005) *The Flight of the Creative Class: the new global competition for talent*, New York: HaperBusiness.

——. (2008) *Who's Your City: how the creative economy is making where you live the most important decision of your life*, New York: Basic Books.

Flynn, N. (1993) *Public Sector Management*, second edn, London: Harvester Wheatsheaf.

Fox, C. (2007) *No Strings Attached! why arts funding should say no to instrumentalism*, London: A&B.

Fraser, A. (1991) 'Museum highlights: a gallery talk', *October* 57 (Summer): 103–22.

Frey, B. (1998) 'Superstar museums: an economic analysis', *Journal of Cultural Economics* 22: 113–25.

Friedman, M. (1962) *Capitalism and Freedom*, Chicago: University of Chicago Press.

Frye, N. (1967) *The Educational Imagination*, Toronto: Canadian Broadcasting Corporation.

Gailbraith, J. K. (1987) *A View from the Stands*, London: Hamish Hamilton.

Galenson, D. (2005) 'Anticipating artistic success (or, how to beat the art market): lessons from history', NBER Working Paper No. 11152.

Gardner, H. (1983) *Frames of Mind*, London: Heinemann.

Garnham, N. and Williams, R. (1980) 'Pierre Bourdieu and the sociology of culture', *Media, Culture and Society* (July): 209–23.

Gingrich. A. (1969) *Business and the Arts: an answer for tomorrow*, New York: Paul S. Erikson.

Ginsburgh, V. and Menger, P. M. (eds) (1996) *Economics of the Arts*, Amsterdam: Elsevier Science.

Goleman, D. (1996) *Emotional Intelligence*, London: Bloomsbury.

Goodwin, J. (ed) (2008) *International Art Markets: the essential guide to collectors and investors*, London: Kogan Page.

Grampp, W. (1989) *Pricing the Priceless: art, artists and economics*, New York: Basic Books.

Granovetter, M. (1973) 'The strength of weak ties', *American Journal of Sociology* (78/6): 1360–80.

——. (1985) 'Economic action and social structure: the problem of embeddedness', *American Journal of Sociology* (91/3): 481–510.

Grant, S. (ed.) (2003) *Art Nation: celebrating 100 years of the National Art Collections Fund*, London: Cultureshock Media in association with the National Art Collections Fund.

Gray, S. (2004) *The Old Masters*, London: Faber and Faber.

Greenberg, C. (1939) 'Avant-garde and kitsch', in Greenberg, *Art and Culture* (1961), Boston: Beacon Press: 3–21.

Greenberg, R. (1987) 'The acoustic eye', *Parachute* 46 (March/May): 106–8.

Greenberg, R., Ferguson, B. and Nairne, S. (eds) (1996) *Rethinking About Exhibitions*, London and New York: Routledge.

Grout, D. J. and Palisca, C. (1998) *A History of Music*, fourth edn, New York and London: W. W. Norton.

Grunenberg, C. and Hollein, M. (eds) (2002) *Shopping: a century of art and consumer culture*, Amsterdam: Hatje Cantz.

Guback, T. (1970) 'Review essay of Gringrich, *Business and the Arts*', *Journal of Aesthetic Education* (July): 131–37.

Guggenheim Foundation. (2005) 'Centre Pompidou and the Solomon R. Guggenheim Foundation announce partnership for Hong Kong proposal', press release (28 October).

——. (2006) 'Abu Dhabi to build Gehry-designed Guggenheim Museum', press release (8 July).

——. (2008) 'Thomas Krens to step down as director of Guggenheim Foundation', press release (2 February).

Guilbaut, S. (1983) *How New York Stole the Idea of Modern Art: Abstract Expressionism, freedom, and the cold war*, Chicago and London: University of Chicago Press.

Guthey, E., Clark, T., and Jackson, B. (2009) *Demystifying Business Celebrity*, New York: Routledge.

Haacke, H. (1981) 'Working conditions', *Artforum* (September): 56–61.

Hadfield, C. (2000) *A Creative Education: how creativity and the arts enhance MBA and executive development programmes*, report commissioned by Arts & Business, London.

Hague, D. (1993) *Transforming Dinosaurs: how organizations learn*, London: Demos.

Hall, P. (1998) *Cities in Civilisation: culture, innovation and urban order*, London: Weidenfeld and Nicholson.

Hamel, G. and Prahalad, C. K. (1994) *Competing for the Future*, Boston: Harvard Business School Press.

Handy, C. (1996) *The Search for Meaning*, London: Crane and Lemos.

——. (1997) *The Hungry Spirit: beyond capitalism*, London: Hutchinson.

——. (1999) *The New Alchemists: how visionary people make something out of nothing*, London: Hutchinson.

Hansmann, H. (1980) 'The role of nonprofit enterprises', *Yale Law Journal* (April): 835–901.

Harris, J. (2010, forthcoming) *Globalization and Contemporary Art*, London: Blackwell.

Harris, N. (1990) 'Polling for opinions', *Museum News* (September/October): 46–53.

Harris, P. and Flowers, J. (2001) *Art Collecting: the benefits for your business*, London: A&B.

Hartley, J. (2005) *Creative Industries*, Oxford: Blackwell.

Harvard Business School [HBS] (2003) 'Researchers contribute globalization of markets papers', HBS Working Knowledge series (16 June), hbswk.hbs.edu/item/3542.

Hatton, R. and Walker, J. (2000) *Supercollector: a critique of Charles Saatchi*, London: Ellipsis.

Heilbrun, J. and Gray, C. (1993) *The Economics of Art and Culture*, Cambridge: Cambridge University Press.

Hendeles, Y. (2004) 'Making history' (March), transcribed by T. Comeau, goodreads.ca.

Herzberg, F. (1968) 'One more time: how to motivate employees?', *Harvard Business Review* (January/February): 53–62.

Hill, E., O'Sullivan, C., and O'Sullivan, T. (2003) *Creative Arts Marketing*, second edn, Oxford: Butterworth-Heinemann.

Hillings, V. (1999) 'Komar and Melamid's dialogue with art history', *Art Journal* (Winter): 48–61.

Hobsbawn, E. (1994) *Age of Extremes: a short history of the twentieth century*, London: Michael Joseph.

Hobsbawn, E. and Ranger, T. (eds) (1983) *The Invention of Tradition*, Cambridge: Cambridge University Press.

Hoggart, R. (1957) *The Uses of Literacy: aspects of working-class life with special reference to publications and entertainments*, London: Chatto and Windus.

Holt, D. (1998) 'Does cultural capital structure American consumption', *Journal of Consumer Research* (June): 1–25.

——. (2003) 'What becomes an icon most?', *Harvard Business Review* (March): 43–49.

Hood, M. (1983) 'Staying away: why people choose not to visit museums', *Museum News* (April): 50–57.

Holbrook, M. (2005), 'Art versus commerce as a macromarketing theme in three films from the young-man-with-a-horn genre', *Journal of Macromarketing* 25(1): 22–31.

Horkheimer, M. and Adorno, T. (1973; original German 1947) *Dialectic of Enlightenment*, trans. J. Cumming, London: Allen Lane.

Hoving, T. (1992) *Making the Museums Dance: inside the Metropolitan Museum of Art*, New York: Simon and Schuster.

Hyde, L. (1979) *The Gift: imagination and the erotic life of property*, New York: Random House.

Impey, O. and MacGregor, A. (1985) *The Origins of Museums: the cabinet of curiosities in sixteenth- and seventeenth-century Europe*, Oxford: Clarendon Press.

Independent Task Force on the Future of the Art Gallery of Ontario. (1992) 'Final Report', Submitted to Ministry of Culture and Communications, Government of Ontario and the Board of Trustees, Art Gallery of Ontario. Toronto.

IndieVest (2009) 'IndieVest FAQs', http://www.indievest.com/faqs/members-producers.html. Accessed 13 May 2009.

Jenkins, R. (1992) *Pierre Bourdieu*, London and New York: Routledge.

Kaiser, M. (2008) *The Art of the Turnaround: creating and maintaining healthy arts organizations*, Lebanon, NH: Brandeis University Press.

Kaplan, R. and Norton, D. (1992) 'The balanced scorecard: measures that drive performance', *Harvard Business Review* (January/February): 71–79.

Karp, I. and Lavine, S. (eds) (1991) *Exhibiting Cultures: the poetics and politics of museum display*, Washington, DC: Smithsonian Institution.

Karp, I., Kreamer, C. M. and Lavine, S. (eds) (1992) *Museums and Communities: the politics of public culture*, Washington, DC: Smithsonian Institution.

Kay, J. (1993) *Foundations of Corporate Success: how business strategies add value*, Oxford: Oxford University Press.

Kellaway, L. (2000) *Sense and Nonsense in the Office*, London: Financial Times.

Keller, K., Sternthal, B., and Tybout, A. (2002) 'Three questions you need to ask about your brand', *Harvard Business Review* (September): 80–86.

Kelly, F. (2003; original 1930) *Why You Win or Lose: the psychology of speculation*, Mineola, NY: Dover Publications.

Kerrigan, F., Fraser, P., and Özbilgin, M. (2004) *Arts Marketing*, Oxford: Elsevier Butterworth-Heinemann.

Kirchberg, V. (1998) 'Entrance fees as a subjective barrier to visiting museums', *Journal of Cultural Economics* (February): 1–13.

Kirchberg, V. and Zembylas, T. (2009) 'RS12 (Arts Management: Sociological Inquiries)' at the 9th ESA Conference; see eupoeansociology.org.

Klein, N. (1999) *No Logo: taking aim at the brand bullies*, New York: Picador.

Klintsov, V. and von Lohneysen, E. (2001) 'Shall we dance?', *McKinsey Quarterly* (no. 4): 6–8.

Kolb, B. (2000) *Marketing Cultural Organizations: new strategies for attracting audiences to classical music, dance, museums, theatre and opera*, Dublin: Oak Tree Press.

Kotler, N. and Kotler, P. (1998) *Museum Strategy and Marketing: designing missions, building audiences, generating revenues and resources*, San Francisco: Jossey-Bass.

Kotler, P. (1972) 'The generic concept of marketing', *Journal of Marketing* (April): 46–54.

——. (1979) 'Strategies for introducing marketing into nonprofit organizations', *Journal of Marketing* (January): 10–15.

——. (1988) *Marketing for Nonprofit Organizations*, Englewood Cliffs, NJ: Prentice Hall.

——. (1999) *Kotler on Marketing*, New York: Free Press.

Kotler, P. and Andreasen, A. (1975) *Strategic Marketing for Nonprofit Organizations*, Englewood Cliffs: Prentice Hall.

Kotler, P. and Levy, S. (1969) 'Broadening the concept of marketing', *Journal of Marketing* (January): 10–15.

Kotler, P. and Roberto, E. (1989) *Social Marketing: strategies for changing public behaviour*, New York: Free Press and London: Collier Macmillan.

Kotler, P. and Scheff, J. (1997) *Standing Room Only: strategies for marketing the performing arts*, Boston: Harvard Business School Press.

Kotter, J. (1990) 'What leaders really do', *Harvard Business Review* (May/June): 103–11.

KPMG for the Department of National Heritage (DNH). (1994) *National Museums and Galleries Performance Indicators Steering Group Report*, London.

Krauss, R. (1990) 'The cultural logic of the late capitalist museum', *October* 54 (Fall): 3–17.

Krens, T. (2006) 'Thomas Krens, director of the Solomon R. Guggenheim Foundation, talks about the role of museums and the mission of the Guggenheim Museum', *Charlie Rose Show* (3 January).

——. (2008) 'Krens' museum for global contemporary art (interview)', Spiegel Online International (27 March), spiegel.de/international.

Landry, C. and Bianchini, F. (1995) *The Creative City*, London: Demos in association with Comedia.

Larson, G. (1983) *The Reluctant Patron: the United States government and the arts, 1943–1965*, Philadelphia: University of Pennsylvania Press.

——. (1997) *American Canvas: an arts legacy for our communities*, Washington, DC: National Endowment for the Arts.

Leadbetter, C. (1997) *The Rise of the Social Entrepreneur*, London: Demos.

——. (2001) *Surfing the Long Wave: knowledge entrepreneurship in Britain*, London: Demos.

Leadbetter, C. and Oakley, K. (1999) *The Independents. Britain's new cultural entrepreneurs*, London: Demos.

Ledbury Research. (2007) *Creative Liaisons: the luxury industry and the arts*, London: A&B.

Lee, M. O. (1999) *Wagner: the terrible man and his truthful art*, Toronto: University of Toronto Press.

Lee, S. (ed.) (1975) *Understanding Art Museums*, New York: American Assembly.

Leonard, M. (1997) *Britain: renewing our identity*, London: Demos.

Letts, C., Ryan, W., and Grossman, A. (1997) 'Virtuous capital: what foundations can learn from venture capitalists', *Harvard Business Review* (March/April): 36–44.

Levitt, T. (1960) 'Marketing myopia', *Harvard Business Review* (July/August): 45–60.

——. 'Marketing myopia: a retrospective commentary', *Harvard Business Review* (September/October): 177–81.

——. (1983) 'The globalization of markets', *Harvard Business Review* (May/June): 92–102.

Lindemann, A. (2006) *Collecting Contemporary*, Cologne: Taschen.

Lowell, S., Silverman, L., and Taliento, L. (2001) 'Not-for-profit management', *McKinsey Quarterly* (no. 1): 147–55.

Lowry, W.M. (ed.) (1984) *The Arts and Public Policy in the United States*, Englewood, NJ: Prentice Hall.

Lumley, R. (ed.) (1988) *The Museum Time Machine: putting culture on display*, London and New York: Comedia/Routledge.

Mackay, C. (2003; original 1841) *Extraordinary Delusions*, Mineola, NY: Dover Publications.

McCarthy, K. and Jinnett, K. (2001) *A New Framework for Building Arts Participation*, Washington, DC: RAND Corp.

McCarthy, K., Ondaatje, E., Brooks, A., and Szántó, A. (2005) *A Portrait of the Visual Arts: meeting the challenges of a new era*, Santa Monica, CA: RAND Corporation.

McCarthy, K., Ondaatje, E., and Zakaras, L. (2001) *Guide to the Literature on Participation in the Arts*, Washington, DC: RAND Corp.

McCarthy, K., Ondaatje, E., Zakaras, L., and Brooks, A. (2004) *Gifts of the Muse: reframing the debate about the benefits of the arts*, Washington, DC: RAND Corp.

McEwen, J. (1990) ' "Past-Present-Future" at the Tate', *Art in America* (June): 61–65.

McGee, S. (2006) 'High impact philanthropy', *Financial Planning* (March): 60–65.

McLean, F. C. (1997) *Marketing the Museum*, London: Routledge.

McShine, K. (1999) *Museum as Muse: artists reflect*, New York: Museum of Modern Art.

Man, J. (2009) *The Leadership Secrets of Genghis Khan*, New York: Bantam Press.

Markus, T. (1993) *Buildings and Power: freedom and control in the origin of the modern building type*, London and New York: Routledge.

Matthews, M. (2006) 'What is arts management', http://ltc.uww.edu/private/matthewm/html-test/module1/reading.html. Accessed 31 January 2007.

Mei, J. and Moses, M. (2002) 'Art as an investment and the underperformance of master-pieces', *American Economic Review* 92 (December): 1956–68.

——. (2005) 'Vested interest and biased price estimates: evidence from an auction market', *The Journal of Finance* 60 (October): 2409–36.

Meindl, J., Ehrlich, S., and Dukerich, J. (1985) 'The romance of leadership', *Administrative Science Quarterly* 30: 78–102.

Merriman, N. (1991) *Beyond the Looking Glass: the past, heritage, and the public in Britain*, Leicester: Leicester University Press.

Mescon, T. and Tilson, D. (1987) 'Corporate philanthropy: a strategic approach to the bottom-line', *California Management Review* (Winter): 49–61.

Meyer, P. *et al.* (1994) [Interview with Alex Melamid] 'Painting by numbers: the search for a people's art', *The Nation* (14 March): 134–48, 326, 328–29.

Micklethwait, J. and Wooldridge, A. (1996) *The Witch Doctors: what management gurus are saying, why it matters and how to make sense of it*, Oxford: Heinemann.

Minihan, J. (1977) *The Nationalization of Culture: the development of state subsidies to the arts in Great Britain*, London: Hamish Hamilton.

Mintzberg, H. (1973) *The Nature of Managerial Work*, New York: Harper and Row.

——. (1979) *The Structuring of Organizations*, Englewood Cliffs, NJ: Prentice Hall.

——. (1984) 'Who should control the corporation', *California Management Review* (Fall): 90–115.

——. (1989) *Mintzberg on Management*, New York and London: Free Press.

——. (1994) *The Rise and Fall of Strategic Planning*, Oxford: Oxford University Press.

——. (2004) *Managers Not MBAs: a hard look at the soft practice of managing and management development*, London: Pearson Education.

Mirza, M. (ed.) (2006) *Culture Vultures: is UK arts policy damaging the arts?*, London: Policy Exchange.

Mitchell, C. (2002) 'Selling the brand inside', *Harvard Business Review* (January): 99–105.

Mokwa, M., Dawson, W., and Prieve, A. (eds) (1980) *Marketing the Arts*, New York: Praeger.

Morgan, G. (1986) *Images of Organizations*, Newbury Park, CA: Sage.

——. (1993) *Imaginization: the art of creative management*, Newbury Park, CA: Sage.

Morris Hargreaves MacIntyre. (2004) *Taste Buds: how to cultivate the art market*, London: Arts Council England.

Moulin, R. (1987; original French 1967) *The French Art Market: a sociological perspective*, trans. A Goldhammer, Rutgers, NJ: Rutgers University Press.

Mulcahy, K. (1986) 'The arts and their economic impact: the values of utility', *Journal of Arts Management, Law and Society* (Fall): 33–48.

Murdoch, J. (1993) 'Attribution and the claim to objectivity', *International Journal of Cultural Property* (September): 319–34.

Muschamp, H. (1987) 'Chez muse: the American museum scene', *Lotus International* 53: 11–16.

Museum of Modern Art, New York [MoMA]. (1954) *Bulletin* 22/1–2.

Mysercough, J., Carley, M., Manton, K, and Feist, A. (1988) *The Economic Importance of the Arts in Britain*, London: Policy Studies Institute.

NEA [National Endowment for the Arts] (2004) *2002 Survey of Public Participation in the Arts*, Research Division Report 45, Washington, DC: National Endowment for the Arts.

Netzer, D. (1978) *The Subsidized Muse*, Twentieth Century Fund Report, Cambridge: Cambridge University Press.

Newhouse, V. (2005) *Art and the Power of Placement*, New York: Monacelli Press.

Newman, D. (1977) *Subscribe Now!*, New York: Theater Communications Group.

Nunes, P. and Johnson, B. (2004) *Mass Affluence: 7 new rules of marketing to today's consumer*, Boston: Harvard Business School.

O'Doherty, B. (1986) *Inside the White Cube: the ideology of the gallery space*, San Francisco: Lapis Press.

O'Hagan, J. (1998) *The State and the Arts: an analysis of key economic policy issues in Europe and the United States*, Cheltenham: Edward Elgar.

O'Hagan, J. and Harvey, D. (2000) 'Why do companies sponsor arts events', *Journal of Cultural Economics* (August): 205–24.

O'Reilly, D. and Kerrigan, F. (2010; forthcoming) *Arts Marketing: a fresh approach*, London: Routledge.

Ogilvy, D. (1983) *Ogilvy on Advertising*, Toronto: Pan Books.

Olins, W. (1989) *Corporate Identity: making business strategy through design*, London: Thames and Hudson.

Oliva, A. B. (1988) *Superart*, trans. H. Martin and A. Asher, Milan: Giancarlo Publications Editore.

Organization for Economic Cooperation and Development [OECD]. (1997) *OECD Economic Surveys: United States 1997*, Paris: OECD.

Ostrower, S. (2002) *Trustees of Culture: power, wealth, and status on elite arts boards*, Chicago: University of Chicago Press.

Pankrantz, D. and Morris, V. (eds) (1990) *The Future of the Arts: public policy and arts research*, New York: Praeger.

Papadakis, A. (ed.) (1991) *New Museology*, London: Art & Design.

Parker, M. (2002) *Against Management*, Cambridge: Polity.

Pavitt, J. (ed.) (2000) *Brand New*, London: V&A Publications.

Peacock, A. (1969) 'Welfare economics and public subsidies to the arts', *Manchester School of Economics and Social Sciences* (December): 323–35.

——. (1998) 'Review of Ruth Towse (ed.) *Baumol's Cost Disease*', *Journal of Cultural Economics* (November): 292–93.

Pearce, S. (ed.) (1991) *Museum Economics and Community*, London: Athlone

Perrow, C. (1986) *Complex Organizations: a critical essay*, third edn, New York: McGraw-Hill.

Peters, T. and Waterman, R. (1982) *In Search of Excellence*, New York: HarperCollins.

Pick, J. (1980) *Arts Administration*, London and New York: E&FN Spon.

——. (1986) *Managing the Arts: the British experience*, London: Rhinegold.

Pick, J. and Anderton, M. (1999) *Building Jerusalem: art, industry and the British millennium*, Amsterdam: Harwood.

Pine, J. and Gilmore, J. (1998) 'Welcome to the experience economy', *Harvard Business Review* (July/August): 97–105.

Pointon, M. (ed.) (1994) *Art Apart: art institutions and ideology across England and North America*, Manchester and New York: Manchester University Press.

Porter, M. (1980) *Competitive Strategy: techniques for analyzing industries and competitors*, New York: Free Press.

——. (1985) *Competitive Advantage: creating and sustaining superior performance*, New York: Free Press.

——. (1987) 'Corporate strategy: the state of strategic thinking', *Economist* (23 May): 17–22.

——. (1996) 'What is strategy', *Harvard Business Review* (November/December): 61–78.

——. (1998) 'Clusters and the new economics of competition', *Harvard Business Review* (November/December): 77–90.

——. (2006) 'Strategy for museums' (28 April), presentation for the American Association of Museums in Boston.

Porter, M. and Kramer, M. (2002) 'The competitive advantage of corporate philanthropy', *Harvard Business Review* (December): 57–68.

——. (2006) 'Strategy and society: the link between competitive advantage and corporate social responsibility', *Harvard Business Review* (December): 78–92.

Powell, W. and DiMaggio, P. (eds) (1991) *The New Institutionalism in Organizational Analysis*, Chicago and London: University of Chicago Press.

Power, M. (1994) *The Audit Explosion*, London: Demos.

Prieve, A. (1993) *Guide to Arts Administration Training*, New York: American Council for the Arts.

Prince, D. (1990) 'Factors influencing museum visits: an empirical evaluation of audience selection', *Museum Management and Curatorship* (June): 149–68.

Projansky, B. and Siegelaub, S. (1971) 'The artist's reserved rights transfer and sale agreement', three-page agreement, manuscript format, New York.

Raymond, T. and Greyser, S. (1978) 'The business of managing the arts', *Harvard Business Review* (July/August): 123–32.

Raymond, T., Greyser, S. and Schwalbe, D. (eds) (1973) *Cultural Policy and Arts Administration*, Cambridge, MA: Harvard Summer School Institute in Arts Administration.

——. (1975) *Cases in Arts Administration*, Cambridge, MA: Harvard Summer School Institute in Arts Administration.

Rectanus, M. (2002) *Culture Incorporated: museums, artists and corporate sponsorship*, Minneapolis: University of Minnesota Press.

Reiss, A. (1979) *The Arts Management Reader*, New York and Basel: Audience Arts.

——. (1986) *Cash In!: funding and promoting the arts, a compendium of imaginative concepts, tested ideas and case histories of programs and promotions that make money*, New York: Theater Communications Group.

Rentschler, R. and Hede, A.-M. (eds) (2007) *Global Museum Marketing: competing in a global marketplace*, Amsterdam: Elsevier Heinemann-Butterworth.

Reza, Y. (1996) *Art*, trans. C. Hampton, London: Faber and Faber.

Ridley, F. F. (1983) 'Cultural economics and the culture of economists', *Journal of Cultural Economics* (June): 1–26.

Ries, A. and Trout, J. (1981) *Positioning: a battle for your mind*, New York and London: McGraw-Hill.

Ripley, D. (1969) *The Sacred Grove: essays on museums*, New York: Simon and Schuster.

Robertson, I. (ed.) (2005) *Understanding International Art Markets and Management*, London and New York: Routledge.

Robertson, I. and Chong, D. (eds) (2008) *The Art Business*, London and New York: Routledge.

Rockefeller Panel Report. (1965) *The Performing Arts: problems and prospects*, New York: McGraw Hill.

Rogers, R. (1997) *Cities for a Small Planet*, London: Faber and Faber.

Rosen, S. (1981) 'The economics of superstars', *American Economic Review* 71 (December): 845–58.

Rosler, M. (1997) 'Money, power and contemporary art', *Art Bulletin* (March): 20–24.

Ross, A. (1995) 'Pollstars: Komar and Melamid's "The People's Choice" ', *Artforum* (January): 72–77, 109.

Said, E. (1992) *Musical Elaborations*, London: Vintage.

Sandle, S. (2004) *Creativity in Business: the development of the market in creative training*, London: A&B.

Sanjek, R. and Sanjek, D. (1991) *American Popular Music Business in the 20th Century*, New York and Oxford: Oxford University Press.

Saul, J.R. (2008) *A Fair Country: telling truths about Canada*, Toronto: Penguin.

Sawill, J. and Williamson, D. (2001) 'Measuring what matters in nonprofits', *McKinsey Quarterly* (no. 2): 98–107.

Schafer, D. P. (1992) *Canada's Contribution to the International Practice of Arts Management*, Waterloo, ON: Centre for Cultural Management, University of Waterloo.

Schein, E. (2001) 'The role of art and the artist', *Reflections* 2(4): 81–83.

Scheuren, F. (2004) *What is a survey?*, Washington, DC: American Statistical Association.

Schiller, H. (1989) *Culture Inc.: the corporate takeover of public expression*, New York and Oxford: Oxford University Press.

——. (1991) 'Corporate sponsorship: institutionalized censorship of the cultural realm', *Art Journal* (Fall): 56–59.

Schroeder, J. (2002), *Visual Consumption*, London: Routledge.

——. (2005) 'The artist and the brand', *European Journal of Marketing* 39(11): 1291–1305.

Schuster, J. M. D. (1987) 'Making compromises to make comparisons in cross-national arts policy research', *Journal of Cultural Economics* (December): 1–36.

——. (1991) *The Audience for American Art Museums*, Research Division Report 23, Washington, DC: National Endowment for the Arts.

Schwartz, B. (2004) *The Paradox of Choice: why more is less*, New York: HarperCollins.

Scruton, R. (1982) *Dictionary of Political Thought*, London: Macmillan.

Seltzer, K. and Bentley, T. (1999) *The Creative Age: knowledge and skills for the new economy*, London: Demos.

Serota, N. (1996) *Experience or Interpretation: the dilemma of museums of modern art*, London: Thames and Hudson.

Shafritz, J. (ed.) (1998) *Encyclopedia of Public Policy and Administration*, four volumes, Boulder, CO: Westview Press.

Shapiro, B. (1973) 'Marketing for nonprofit organizations', *Harvard Business Review* (September/October): 123–32.

——. (1988) 'What the hell is marketing-oriented?', *Harvard Business Review* (November/December): 119–25.

Sheard, W. S. and Paoletti, J. (eds) (1978) *Collaborations in Italian Renaissance Art*, New Haven and London: Yale University Press.

Shell, M. (1994) *Art and Money*, Chicago: University of Chicago Press.

Sheffield, M. (1976) 'Hans Haacke', *Studio International* (March/April): 117–23.

Sherman, D. and Rogoff, I. (eds) (1994) *Museum Culture: histories-discourses-spectacles*, Minneapolis: University of Minnesota Press.

Shore, H. (1987) *Arts Administration and Management: a guide for arts administrators and their staffs*, New York and London: Quorum Books.

Silvers, R. (ed.) (2001) *Doing It: five performing arts*, New York: New York Review of Books.

Silverstein, M. and Fiske, N. (2004) *Trading Up: the new American luxury*, Boston: Boston Consulting Group.

SMART Company. (2005) *Understanding Corporate Social Responsibility: a guide for arts organizations*, London: A&B.

Smith, A. (1776) *An Inquiry into the Nature and Causes of the Wealth of Nations*, fifth edn (1904), http://www.econlib.org/library/Smith/smWNCover.html. Accessed 13 May 2009.

Smith, W. (1956) 'Product differentiation and market segmentation as alternative strategies', *Journal of Marketing* (July): 3–8.

Staniszewski, M. A. (1998) *The Power of Display: a history of exhibition installation at the Museum of Modern Art*, Cambridge, MA: MIT Press.

Stigler, G. and Becker, G. (1977) 'De gustibus non est disputandum', *American Economic Review* (March): 76–90.

Stockil, T. (2008) *Artful Development: how different art forms can address business issues*, London: A&B.

Strum, D. (1985) 'Corporate culture and the common good: the need for thick description and critical thought', *Thought* (June): 141–60.

Taylor, F. (1945) *Babel's Tower: the dilemma of the modern museum*, New York: University of Columbia Press.

Taylor, P. (ed.) (1988) *Impresario: Malcolm McLaren and the British New Wave*, New York: New Museum of Contemporary Art and Cambridge, MA: MIT Press.

Thaler, R. (1985) 'Mental accounting and consumer choice', *Marketing Science* (Summer): 199–214.

——. (1999) 'Mental accounting matters', *Journal of Behavioral Decision Making* 12(3): 183–206.

Thomas, D. (2007) *Deluxe: how luxury lost its luster*, New York: Penguin.

Thompson, D. (2008) *The $12 Million Stuffed Shark: the curious economics of contemporary art*, London: Aurum Press.

Thornton, S. (2008) *Seven Days in the Art World*, London: Granta Books.

Throsby, D. (1994) 'The production and consumption of the arts: a view of cultural economics', *Journal of Economic Literature* (March): 1–29.

Toffler, A. (1967) 'The art of measuring the arts', *Annals of the American Academy of Political Science and Social Science* (September): 141–55.

Towse, R. (ed.) (1997) *Baumol Cost Disease: the arts and other victims*, Cheltenham and Northampton, MA: Edward Elgar.

——. (ed.) (2003) *A Handbook of Cultural Economics*, Cheltenham and Northampton, MA: Edward Elgar.

Turner, J. (ed.) (2000) *From Rembrandt to Vermeer: 17th-century Dutch artists*, London: Macmillan Reference.

Tusa, J. (1997) 'For art's sake', *Prospect* (January): 36–40.

——. (1999) *Art Matters*, London: Methuen.

Twitchell, J. (2004) *Branded Nation: the marketing of Megachurch, College, Inc., and Museum-World*, New York: Simon and Schuster.

Velthuis, O. (2005) *Talking Prices: symbolic meanings of prices on the market for contemporary art*, Princeton, NJ: Princeton University Press.

Vergo, P. (ed.) (1989) *New Museology*, London: Reaktion Books.

Vine, R. (1994) 'Number's racket', *Art in America* (October): 116–19.

Vogel, H. (2001) *Entertainment Industry Economics: a guide for financial analysis*, fifth edn, Cambridge and New York: Cambridge University Press.

Von Berswordt-Wallrabe, K. (1995) *Marcel Duchamp: Respirateur*, Schwerin: Staatliches Museum Schwerin and Ostfildern: Hatje Cantz Verlag.

Wallis, B. (ed.) (1986) *Hans Haacke: unfinished business*, New York: New Museum of Contemporary Art and Cambridge, MA: MIT Press.

Walliser-Schwarzbart, E. (ed.) (2003) *Art Market Switzerland*, Passages: the cultural magazine of Pro Helvetia (no. 35), Zurich: Arts Council of Switzerland Pro Helvetia.

Ward, F. (1995) 'The haunted museum: institutional critique and publicity', *October* 73 (Summer): 71–89.

Waterford, G. (1991) *Palaces of Art: art galleries in Britain, 1790–1990*, London: Lund Humphries.

Weil, S. (1994) 'Performance indicators for museums: progress report from Wintergreen', *Journal of Arts Management, Law and Society* (Winter): 341–51.

Wetlaufer, S. (2000) 'Common sense and conflict: an interview with Disney's Michael Eisner', *Harvard Business Review* (January/February): 114 24.

——. (2001) 'The perfect paradox of star brand: an interview with Bernard Arnault of LVMH', *Harvard Business Review* (October): 116–23.

Williams, R. (1980) *Problems in Materialism and Culture*, London: Verso.

——. (1983) *Keywords: a vocabulary of culture and society*, revised and expanded edn, London: Fontana.

Wilson, S. (1990) *Tate Gallery*, London: Tate Gallery Publications.

Wolff, J. (1981) *The Social Production of Art*, London: Macmillan.

Wood, J. (2000) *The Broken Estate: essays on literature and belief*, London: Pimlico.

Worpole, K. (2000) *Here Comes the Sun: architecture and public space in twentieth century Europe*, London: Reaktion.

Worpole, K. and Greenhalgh, L. (1996) *The Freedom of the City*, London: Demos.

Wu, C.-t. (2002) *Privatizing Culture: corporate art intervention since the 1980s*, London: Verso.

Young, C. (2003) 'Notes From the Inside', artist's statement produced for the exhibition catalogue for 'Beck's Futures' at the ICA, London, http://www.careyyoung.com/artiststexts/inside.html. Accessed 13 May 2009.

——. (2008) 'On Cildo Meireles', *Tate* magazine (issue 14), http://www.careyyoung.com/artiststexts/meireles.html. Accessed 13 May 2009.

Zolberg, V. (1994) 'Art museums and cultural policies', Journal of Arts Management, Law and Society (Winter): 277–90.

Zucker, P. (ed.) (1944) *New Architecture in City Planning*, New York: Philosophical Library.

Zukin, S. (1987) 'Gentrification: culture and capital in the urban core', *Annual Review of Sociology* (vol. 13): 129–47.

Index